Shakespeare Performed
Globe to Global

Founding editor: J. R. MULRYNE
General editors:
JAMES C. BULMAN, CAROL CHILLINGTON RUTTER

The Merchant of Venice

Second edition

Manchester University Press

To buy or to find out more about the books currently available in this series, please go to: https://manchesteruniversitypress.co.uk/series/shakespeare-in-performance/

Shakespeare Performed
Globe to Global

The Merchant of Venice

Boika Sokolova and Kirilka Stavreva,
with James C. Bulman

Second edition

MANCHESTER UNIVERSITY PRESS

Copyright © Boika Sokolova and Kirilka Stavreva
with J. C. Bulman 1991, 2023

The right of Boika Sokolova, Kirilka Stavreva, and
J. C. Bulman to be identified as the authors of this work
has been asserted by them in accordance with the Copyright,
Designs and Patents Act 1988.

First edition published 1991 by Manchester University Press
This edition published 2023 by Manchester University Press
Oxford Road, Manchester M13 9PL

www.manchesteruniversitypress.co.uk

British Library Cataloguing-in-Publication Data
A catalogue record for this book is available from the British
Library

ISBN 978 1 5261 5009 7 hardback
ISBN 978 1 5261 9540 1 paperback

This edition first published 2023
Paperback published 2026

The publisher has no responsibility for the persistence or
accuracy of URLs for any external or third-party internet
websites referred to in this book, and does not guarantee
that any content on such websites is, or will remain, accurate
or appropriate.

EU authorised representative for GPSR:
Easy Access System Europe – Mustamäe tee 50,
10621 Tallinn, Estonia
gpsr.requests@easproject.com

Typeset by Newgen Publishing UK

For Elliot Leader and Douglas Baynton

Contents

List of illustrations ix
Series editors' preface xiii
Prefatory note xv
Prefatory note to second edition xvii

Part I

I   An Elizabethan *Merchant*: performance and context 3
II Henry Irving and the great tradition 32
III Wayward genius in the high temple of bardolatry: Theodore Komisarjevsky 59
IV Aesthetes in a rugger club: Jonathan Miller and Laurence Olivier 83
V   The BBC *Merchant*: diminishing returns 111
VI Cultural stereotyping and audience response: Bill Alexander and Antony Sher 129
VII Shylock and the pressures of history 157

Part II

Segue: *The Merchant of Venice*: pressures of war, ideology, and the crises of late capitalism 171
I   Magical spectacles and nightmarish times: Max Reinhardt's productions of *The Merchant of Venice* 195
II Peter Zadek's challenges to the post-war German legacy of *The Merchant of Venice* 211
III A post-Holocaust balancing act: *The Merchant of Venice* directed by Trevor Nunn at the National Theatre, London (1999) 229

IV Desperate outsiders in a money-drunk world: *The Merchant of Venice* directed by Daniel Sullivan (2010) and Rupert Goold (2011) — 243

V Crises of the new millennium: *The Merchant of Venice* directed by Robert Sturua (2000) and Edward Hall (2009) — 263

VI *The Merchant of Venice* on film — 285

VII The search for justice: *The Merchant of Venice* in Mandatory Palestine (1936) and the Venetian Ghetto (2016) — 306

Appendices — 322

   A. Some significant twentieth- and twenty-first-century productions of *The Merchant of Venice* — 322

   B. Major actors and creative staff for productions discussed — 324

Bibliography — 333

Index — 348

List of illustrations

1 Henry Irving as Shylock at the Lyceum Theatre, 1879. [Courtesy of The Mansell Collection Ltd.]   34
2 Setting by William Telbin for Act II of Charles Kean's production, 1858. [Courtesy of the Shakespeare Centre Library, Stratford-upon-Avon.]   42
3 The Venetian set for Theodore Komisarjevsky's production of 1932, designed by Komisarjevsky and Lesley Blanch. [Courtesy of the Shakespeare Centre Library, Stratford-upon-Avon.]   63
4 Joan Plowright as Portia and Laurence Olivier as Shylock in the trial scene of the National Theatre production directed by Jonathan Miller, 1970. [Courtesy of The Kobal Collection.]   103
5 Bassanio (John Nettles) makes his choice: Oliver Bayldon's set for Belmot in the BBC production directed by Jack Gold, 1980. [Courtesy of BBC Enterprises Ltd.]   122
6 Gemma Jones as Portia and Warren Mitchell as Shylock in the trial scene of the BBC production, 1980. [Courtesy of BBC Enterprises Ltd.]   126
7 Antonio (John Carlisle) bullying Shylock (Antony Sher) in I.iii of the RSC production directed by Bill Alexander, 1987. [Courtesy of Joe Cocks Studio.]   135
8 'What demi-god / Hath come so near creation?' Bassanio (Nicholas Farrell) to Portia (Deborah Findlay) in the RSC production of 1987. [Courtesy of Joe Cocks Studio.]   155

x   *List of illustrations*

9   Seth Rue as Bassanio, Maren Bush as Portia, and Celeste Jones as Nessa in *District Merchants* by Aaron Posner, directed by Michael John Garcés, Folger Theatre, 2016. [Photograph by Teresa Wood. Courtesy of © Teresa Wood, Folger Shakespeare Library.]   186
10 The 'Resolution' of the trial in *The Merchant of Venice*, directed by Nicolas Stemann, Munich Kammerspiele, 2015. [Photograph by David Balzer. Courtesy of © david baltzer / bildbuehne.de.]   193
11 Campo San Trovaso before its transformation for Max Reinhardt's 1934 production of *The Merchant of Venice* for the first Theatre Biennale of Venice, with the bridge over the Rio degli Ognissanti in the middle, and the back entrance to the *squero* (boat-building shed) on the left. [Courtesy of © Archivio Storico della Biennale di Venezia, ASAC.]   201
12 Scenic design by Duilio Torres for Max Reinhardt's production for the 1934 Theatre Biennale of Venice. [Courtesy of © Archivio Storico della Biennale di Venezia, ASAC.]   201
13 The court scene in Max Reinhardt's production for the 1934 Theatre Biennale of Venice. [Courtesy of © Archivio Storico della Biennale di Venezia, ASAC.]   203
14 Gert Voss as Shylock in Peter Zadek's production for the Vienna Burgtheater, 1988. [© Gisela Scheidler, Roswitha Hecke and Reinhard Werner, courtesy of Archiv Burgtheater, Vienna.]   224
15 Gert Voss as Shylock and Pavel Landovský as Tubal in Peter Zadek's production for the Vienna Burgtheater, 1988. [© Gisela Scheidler, Roswitha Hecke and Reinhard Werner, courtesy of Archiv Burgtheater, Vienna.]   226
16 Derbhle Crotty as Portia and Alexander Hanson as Bassanio in Trevor Nunn's production for the National Theatre, London, 1999. [Courtesy of © Donald Cooper / Photostage.]   234
17 Tom Scutt's casino set with Rebecca Brewer as Stephanie (front left), Susannah Fielding as Portia (rear left), Emily Plumtree as Nerissa (rear right),

and Merry Holden as Conscience (front right) in
Rupert Goold's revival of *The Merchant of Venice*
at the Almeida Theatre, London, 2014. [Courtesy
of © Donald Cooper / Photostage.] 255

18 The 'Destiny' TV show hosted by Portia (Susannah
Fielding) and Nerissa (Emily Plumtree) in Rupert
Goold's production for the Royal Shakespeare
Company, Stratford-upon-Avon, 2011. [Courtesy
of © Donald Cooper / Photostage.] 257

19 Alexander Kalyagin as Shylock in Robert Sturua's
production for the Et Cetera Theatre, Moscow,
2000. Frame capture from the play's trailer.
[www.youtube.com/watch?v=vmJNFiLBa0s] 273

20 Kelsey Brookfield as Portia in the production of
Propeller and Watermill Theatre Newbury directed
by Edward Hall. Liverpool Playhouse, Liverpool,
2009. [Courtesy of © Donald Cooper / Photostage.] 278

21 Waihoroi Shortland as Hairoka (Shylock) next
to a painting of the owl Kaitaki by Selwyn Muru,
in Don Selwyn's film, *Te Tangata Whai Rawa O
Weniti*, or *The Maori Merchant of Venice* (2001).
Frame capture. 294

22 Al Pacino as Shylock and Jeremy Irons as Antonio
at the loan celebration banquet in Michael
Radford's film, *William Shakespeare's The
Merchant of Venice* (2004). Frame capture. 302

23 Studio portrait of Aharon Meskin as Shylock
in Leopold Jessner's production for the Habima
Theatre, Tel Aviv, 1936. [Courtesy of the Israeli
Center for the Documentation of the Performing
Arts, Tel Aviv University.] 311

24 Studio portrait of Shimon Finkel as Shylock in
Leopold Jessner's production for the Habima Theatre,
Tel Aviv, 1936. [Courtesy of the Israeli Center for
the Documentation of the Performing Arts,
Tel Aviv University.] 312

25 The trial scene in Leopold Jessner's production for
the Habima Theatre, Tel Aviv, 1936. [Courtesy
of the Israeli Center for the Documentation of the
Performing Arts, Tel Aviv University.] 313

26 The five Shylocks lament Jessica's flight in the Compagnia de' Colombari's production of *The Merchant in Venice*, directed by Karin Coonrod, 2016. Left to right: Ned Eisenberg, Andrea Brugnera, Adriano Iurissevich, Sorab Wadia, Jenni Lea-Jones. Frame capture from the production trailer for the performance. [www.youtube.com/watch?v=3rdl31DoPJE] 316

Series editors' preface

Since this pioneering Series was first launched in 1984, the study of Shakespeare's plays as scripts for performance has grown to rival the reading of Shakespeare's plays as literature among university, college, and secondary school teachers and students. The aim of the Series remains today what it was then: to assist this study by exploring how Shakespeare's texts have been realised in performance, in a multitude of different ways by actors, directors, and designers, and in the various media for which the plays have been adapted.

The idea of what constitutes performance has itself changed considerably in the past few decades, promoted by cultural anthropologists who have defined performance as a more inclusive set of social practices than theatre historians ever envisioned, a continuum of human actions ranging from ritual, sports, popular entertainments, and the performing arts to the enactment of social, gender, race, and class roles in everyday life. Advances in digital technology, too, have led to an expansion of what forms Shakespearean performance can take in various media – in theatres and less conventional playing spaces, in the cinema, and on the computer screen. They have also led to a fundamental questioning of what 'live' performance means – liveness being a basic tenet of performance studies – and to a better understanding of how viewers can become players in interactive performances. The rapid growth of media and digital technology, furthermore, has created a global market for Shakespeare that has not only encouraged intercultural exchanges by theatre companies, but also created new audiences for 'local' adaptations of the plays in parts of the world that once would have had scant familiarity with Shakespeare.

Each contributor to the Series has selected a number of productions of a given play and analysed them comparatively. Drawn from different periods, countries, and media, these productions were chosen not only because they are culturally significant in their own right but because they illustrate how the convergence of material conditions can shape a performance and its reception: the medium for which the text is adapted; the language in which Shakespeare's text is spoken; the performance style and aesthetic decisions made by directors and whether they embrace or flout tradition; the production's set, lighting, music, and costume design; the bodies, genders, and abilities of actors working individually but also in an ensemble; and the historical, political, and social contexts which condition audience responses to the performance.

We hope that audiences, by reading these accounts of Shakespeare in performance, may enlarge their understanding of what a playtext is and begin, too, to appreciate the complex ways in which any performance is a deeply collaborative effort. Any study of a Shakespeare text will, of course, reveal only a small proportion of the play's potential meanings; but by engaging issues of how a performance essentially translates a text into a work with cultural resonances and meanings beyond anything Shakespeare as author could have anticipated, our series encourages a kind of reading that is receptive to the contingencies that make performances of Shakespeare an art unto themselves.

James C. Bulman and Carol Chillington Rutter,
Founding Editors

Prefatory note

The theatre is a wonderful teacher. The many productions of *The Merchant of Venice* I have seen during the past twenty years have taught me more about the play than countless readings, and some of what I learned from them I hope to share with readers in the following pages. My responses to those productions, however, have not gone untested: they have been challenged, sharpened, and enriched by friends who have read the manuscript in whole or in part. I am especially grateful to my colleagues Doug Lanier, Jim Ogden, and Brian Rosenberg, three of the most generous readers one could hope to find; to my meticulous editors, Ronnie Mulryne and Margaret Shewring; to Miriam Gilbert and Bob King, who shared their production notes with me; and to Werner Habicht, whose knowledge of Shakespearean production in Germany helped me to flesh out Chapter VII (Part I).

I am grateful, too, to the librarians at the Shakespeare Centre in Stratford-upon-Avon – Marian Pringle, Sylvia Morris, and Mary White – whose patience and good humour are legendary; to Andrew Kirk at the British Theatre Museum and Bob Taylor at the Museum of the City of New York for their kind co-operation; to Liz Page in the Script Department of the National Theatre for allowing me to use Jonathan Miller's prompt book and other production materials; and to the staffs of the Lincoln Center Library, the Folger Shakespeare Library, the Senate House Library at the University of London, the British Library, and the Pelletier Library.

I am deeply indebted to Dan Sullivan, Andy Ford, and the Faculty Development Committee of Allegheny College for their unstinting support of this project; to the National Endowment for the Humanities for a fellowship which allowed me to undertake the research for it; and to the University College of Wales for providing me with an office – and the comforts of home – while I wrote the final draft. To all, my thanks.

J. C. B.
March 1990

All references in part I, unless otherwise noted, are to the New Cambridge edition of *The Merchant of Venice*, ed. M. M. Mahood (Cambridge, 1987).

Prefatory note to second edition

In writing this book we have incurred many debts. First and foremost we owe a debt of gratitude to Carol Rutter for entrusting us with the project, and to James Bulman for his generously shared knowledge, support, and meticulous reading of the final draft.

This analysis of the multicultural and multilingual European reception of *The Merchant of Venice* has only been possible thanks to the research and friendship of colleagues from ESRA, the European Shakespeare Research Association. Thank you all for years of generosity and support.

We would like to thank Shaul Bassi for warm hospitality and for enabling our research in Venice, Sabine Schülting for providing us with films of German productions and for her inspiring scholarship, Douglas Lanier for giving us access to a manuscript before its publication, Shelly Zer-Zion for her timely assistance with access to materials from the Israeli Center for the Documentation of the Performing Arts and the Habima Theater Archive, the late Mariangela Tempera for sharing copies of *Merchant* films, and the late Michael Hattaway for opening doors in New Zealand.

We extend our sincere appreciation to Miriam Gilbert and Jay Halio, colleagues who have dedicated years of their professional lives to the study of *The Merchant of Venice* and have been cherished personal friends.

Our institutions, Cornell College (Iowa, USA) and the University of Notre Dame (Indiana, USA) in England, have provided indispensable funding and research time. We are also grateful for the generous support of the Fulbright Commission and the Shakespeare In and Beyond the Ghetto Project.

The Folger Shakespeare Library has been a privilege and pleasure to work in, as have the 'Sts. Cyril and Methodius' National Library in Sofia, Archivio Storico della Biennale di Venezia, the libraries of the Shakespeare Institute and the Shakespeare Birthplace in Stratford-upon-Avon, the National Theatre Archive in London, and the New York Public Library for the Performing Arts.

Deep down the line of debts stands the Department of English at the University of Sofia, where our paths as scholars began, and where our professors, Marco Mincoff and Alexander Shurbanov, kindled our love of Shakespeare and taught us about research discipline and ethics.

Last but not least, our families, *semper eidem, semper fideles*, have endured endless hours of discussions, debates, and absences. Without their patience, humour, and sheer tenacity, we would not have succeeded. Anna Baynton's precision and writerly insights saved us from various infelicities; those that remain are our own.

B. S. & K. S.
March 2023

Part I

I

An Elizabethan *Merchant:* performance and context

If history is any judge, the crucial problem in staging *The Merchant of Venice* is how to balance its two distinct and seemingly unrelated plots. Although both ultimately derive from folk tales, Shakespeare dramatised them in such disparate styles that they seem to compete with rather than to complement one another. The casket plot, involving the winning of Portia by a lottery, is romantic, even at times Lyly-like: the scenes of wooing are witty; their pace, leisurely; their ethos, courtly. Above all, they are dominated by the comic resourcefulness of an aristocratic woman. The sordid bond plot, on the other hand, betrays its origins in darker legend. Dominated by men of business, the Venetian scenes have an urgency at odds with the leisure of Belmont: their prosaic idiom contrasts with the poetic formality of the wooing scenes, and their mercantile ethos calls into question the aristocratic assumptions of comic romance. By working such a tonal division between the two plots, Shakespeare made it difficult to bring them into an effective theatrical balance with one another. Venice and Belmont seem to belong to different plays.

To compound this difficulty, Shakespeare allowed the bond plot, to which he actually allots less stage time, to keep subverting the romance plot. The juxtaposition of the play's twin climaxes illustrates this subversion. Bassanio's winning of the lottery and Portia in III.ii, a scene full of romantic hyperbole, is immediately preceded by the passionately colloquial scene in which Shylock vows to take revenge on Antonio. Our knowledge of this sober turn of events invariably colours our response to Bassanio's victory, just as the power of Shylock's idiolect, with its unconventional rhythms and biblical repetitions – 'no ill luck stirring but what lights o'my shoulders, no sighs but o'my breathing, no tears but o'my shedding'

(III.i.74–6) – sets in arch relief the artifice of the verse spoken by Portia and Bassanio. When, therefore, a letter from Antonio interrupts the festivities in III.ii, it recalls us to Venice and to the bond plot. The nuptials are effectively broken, or at least postponed, by the obligation Bassanio feels to assist his friend; and in the eyes of many, a latent rivalry between Antonio and Portia for Bassanio's love here becomes overt (Kahn, pp. 104–12). In this scene, the bond plot intrudes on and threatens to overwhelm the comic romance.

Harley Granville-Barker, a pioneer in twentieth-century Shakespeare production, identified the rivalry between these plots as symptomatic of a problem in the play's design:

> How to blend two such disparate themes into a dramatically organic whole; that was [Shakespeare's] real problem. The stories, linked in the first scene, will, of themselves, soon part company. Shakespeare has them run neck and neck till he is ready to join them again in the scene of the trial. But the difficulty is less that they will not match each other by the clock than that their whole gait so differs, their very nature.
>
> (p. 71)

At the time Granville-Barker made this observation, *The Merchant* had virtually become Shylock's play, a vehicle for star actors. Belmont, as a result, had been butchered, and on occasion performances even concluded with Shylock's exit from the court, leaving the lovers' plot unresolved – and, one assumes, of little consequence. Given this history, it is no wonder Granville-Barker thought that the problem was inherent in the text: 'How', he asked, 'is the flimsy theme of the caskets to be kept in countenance beside its grimly powerful rival?'

It is a question any director of the play must ask. Most have found a true balance impossible to achieve. For reasons I shall discuss later, a growing fascination with Shylock as a symbol of oppression, representative of all Jews, has lent a cultural resonance to the bond plot that has made the lottery seem insubstantial, if not frivolous, in comparison. Those directors who *have* achieved a balance usually have done so by denying that resonance, insisting that both plots be taken on their own terms as folk tales, unencumbered by social and political history. After all, a Jew bargaining for a pound of Christian flesh is no more real than an heiress winning a husband by lottery or a condemned man being saved by a cross-dressing lawyer; all such absurdities require a willing suspension of disbelief. In such productions, *The Merchant* becomes a fairy tale wherein characters are types, action is allegorical, and Belmont proves as theatrically credible as Venice.

Certainly this was true of Terry Hands's production for the Royal Shakespeare Company in 1971, which, more than any other in recent memory, attempted to honour both plots as playful fictions. His intention was clear in the opening scene, where fantastically dressed merchants rolled giant dice and pushed 'enchanting toy galleons' (*Daily Telegraph*, 31 March 1971), replicas of Antonio's argosies, across a stage floor that was a mosaic of azure oceans and golden continents. Here, in miniature, was a model of life: the serious business of trade was encoded as a game of Ludo. Hands thus introduced a metaphor for all the 'games, gambles, wagers, bonds' that were to follow in both Venice and Belmont (*Birmingham Post*, 31 March 1971). Understood in this way, Bassanio's hazarding for Portia became just as significant as Antonio's gambling with his ships: its magnitude was signified by the giant caskets of gold, silver, and lead from which he had to choose, the last of which contained a life-size effigy of Portia herself. Such romantic fictions, of course, work against any notion of bourgeois realism in this most money-oriented play; and Hands tried to solve the problem, as one critic observed, by 'siting the play in no place at all – or perhaps I should simply say in a theatre' (*Financial Times*, 31 March 1971). Such self-reflexive theatricality was reinforced by groups of spectators who from time to time stood at the rear of the stage looking on, as an audience at a play.

Shylock, too, was appropriately fantasticated. An extravagantly theatrical villain who spoke with a Yiddish accent tinged with the native Welsh of actor Emrys James, he bared his teeth at his enemies, bayed like a dog for Christian blood, and even barked at Antonio on the line, 'But since I am a dog, beware my fangs!' (Prompt book III.iii.7). As several critics noted, James conceived of Shylock as an actor and stole shamelessly from the bag of tricks of Shylocks past – 'a stage villain,' according to John Barber, 'barefoot, robed in old curtains, with a mouthful of spittle and plenty of "oi-yoi-yoi"' (*Daily Telegraph*, 31 March 1971). An exotic among other exotics, he was not so much an outcast of any recognisable Western society as the ogre of a fairy tale. One could readily believe that he wanted his pound of flesh because, in fairy tales, ogres eat people.

Within the assumptions of such implausible fictions, Shylock's villainy at the trial was strikingly credible. He flourished his props – knife and scales in either hand – like an allegorical figure of Justice untempered by Mercy (Slater, p. 177). As his moral opposite, the Portia of Judi Dench proved equally credible: charmingly boyish, confident, authoritative. When her pleas for mercy met deaf ears, however, she became visibly uneasy. Then, in the nick of time, just as Shylock moved behind the flinching Antonio and placed the dagger on his bare chest (see cover photograph), Portia screamed 'Tarry a little' (IV.i.301), surprising even herself with the sudden inspiration to save the day with a legal quibble. Hands's staging of the trial, by critical consensus, thrillingly dramatised the allegorical oppositions inherent in the play: the victory of Mercy over Justice, of the New Law over the Old, of Charity over Greed, of Belmont over Venice.

There are consequences for staging *The Merchant* in this way, however, for fantastication suppresses the individuality and psychological subtlety with which Shakespeare invested his characters. As B. A. Young observed, Hands so deliberately under-emphasised the personalities of the characters that their performances were 'externalised', every point made by some simple visible means (*Financial Times*, 31 March 1971); and Jonathan Raban concurred that characters were 'dehumanised ... stereotypes' serving what he took to be Hands's moral theme (*New Statesman*, 9 April 1971). Romantic comedy, however, despite the implausibility of its plots, is deeply concerned with the plausibility of human behaviour; and in the modern theatre, its success depends on the ability of actors to get an audience to respond to them as real people. This may not have been entirely true of the Elizabethan theatre, in which actors submerged the individual in the type: they strove not to create particular 'identities' or 'inner selves' for their characters as actors do in naturalist theatre, but rather to imitate behaviour that would be understood as appropriately and recognisably general (Hattaway, pp. 72–9). Today, however, to make their performances convincing, actors must seek humanly explicable motives for the things they say and do. It is not sufficient for them simply to think of their characters as moral abstractions. Characters in *The Merchant*, however fanciful, may be seen to act in ways so complex and ambiguous as to cast doubt on any simple allegorical assumptions.

Antonio, for example, the most enigmatic character in the play, is willing to sacrifice himself for his friend. Some critics posit that he embodies the ideals of platonic friendship or Christian *caritas*. But this does not explain *why* he acts as he does, nor why audiences sense in him a languor and a self-deprecation – 'I am the tainted wether of the flock, / Meetest for death' (IV.i.114–15) – that lead him to want to martyr himself and, by doing so, to bind Bassanio to him for life. 'Commend me to your honourable wife,' he tells Bassanio:

> Tell her the process of Antonio's end,
> Say how I loved you, speak me fair in death,
> And when the tale is told, bid her judge
> Whether Bassanio had not once a love.
>
> (269–73)

Actors would have difficulty understanding an abstract motivation for such lines: can *caritas* explain the emotional burden Antonio now places on his friend? Rather, these sentiments have suggested to actors that Antonio may feel an unfulfilled, possibly homosexual longing for Bassanio: even the comic matter of the rings wherein Portia tests Bassanio's fidelity to her often becomes, at Antonio's insistence, a test of Bassanio's love for *him* instead (Tennenhouse, p. 62). Psychoanalytic explanations are usually more useful to actors than allegory.

Nor are Portia's motives free from question. Allegorically, she may be the embodiment of mercy, functioning like the Virgin Mary of medieval miracle plays who, as Molly Mahood reminds us (p. 9), interceded with divine grace on behalf of the hero. By saving Antonio's life, furthermore, she frees her husband from a guilt that might forever burden him, and thus spares their marriage into the bargain. More realistically, however, Portia, as a woman in a patriarchal society, may betray a desire to usurp male prerogatives. She has no power herself: her fate has been dictated by her father's will, and all she inherits is won in an instant by Bassanio. Is she sensible of this disempowerment? And if so, does she go to Venice in male disguise more to test her mettle in a man's world than to administer divine mercy? Such questions lead one to examine the nature of her 'inspiration' in saving Antonio. Has the quibble occurred to her on the spot, or does her knowledge of the law – gained perhaps from consulting Doctor Bellario, and demonstrated when she lists the penalties for an alien's seeking the life of a citizen – suggest that she has plotted her strategy well in advance? We may reasonably conclude that she arrives at court with her trump up her sleeve: 'no jot of blood' (302). But if this is true, why does she wait so long to play it? Does she want to allow Shylock sufficient opportunity to show mercy, knowing that the law will come down on him hard if he does not? Or, less charitably, does she simply allow him rope enough to hang himself? Furthermore, does she realise that by saving her trump to the last possible moment, she brings extraordinary anguish to Antonio and to her husband? Or might that be – as psychoanalytic studies have suggested – precisely her intention?

This potential for dramatising relationships in *The Merchant* as shifting and unpredictable defies the neat schematisation towards which allegory tends. *How* audiences view the play thus depends on how directors adjust the balance between psychological realism and the play's deep allegorical structure. Directors usually find that the play resists any attempt to strait-jacket it with one particular concept. Hands certainly found this to be true. Despite his uses of enchantment, the actors' search for credible motivation kept disrupting the fantasy, with Portia so sensitive to her rivalry with Antonio that she became, in the words of the actress who played her, a most unpleasantly 'neurotic' heroine (Biggs, pp. 153–9). Conversely, directors who privilege the play's realism often do so at the expense of the allegorical constructs that give the play its moral grounding. They tend to foreground the plight of Shylock, who in many ways is the least conventional, most believably idiosyncratic of all the characters, and relegate the romantic artifices of Belmont to a subordinate role. This happened in Jonathan Miller's famous 'Victorian' *Merchant* for the National Theatre in 1970. His Venice was so authentically detailed, so rich in social nuance, that Belmont simply could not provide a credible alternative to it: thus Miller satirised the casket plot as a patently insincere fiction by which the bourgeoisie disguised their avarice. Such choices suggest that we, in our century, conceive of drama more categorically than Shakespeare could have anticipated. One reason for this may be that the nature of theatre itself has changed. *The Merchant* is a play whose potential to be various things at once – allegory and folk tale, romantic comedy and problem play – may have been realisable only on the Elizabethan stage (Figure 1).

Shakespeare's theatre was unlike our own. Audiences stood or sat very close to a bare, thrust stage, and such intimacy fostered a participatory pact between actors and audience in which actors relied on the audience to piece out a performance's imperfections with their thoughts. The participation of the audience was necessary to foster any illusion of reality because the bare stage itself did not. Props were few; costuming, most of it Elizabethan, was eclectic; and plays were performed during the afternoon, in broad daylight. Such conditions, far from a liability, were in fact liberating: they attested to the Elizabethan audience's capacity for multi-consciousness, for adjusting imaginatively to a complex mixture of formal and realistic elements, and for losing themselves in the play while remaining aware of its artifice (Styan, *Shakespeare Revolution*, pp. 164–5).

On such a stage, actors could move in and out of their roles more easily than actors do today. They could speak in character yet at the same time signal to the audience their conventionality, thereby preserving their fictive credibility while acknowledging their status as players. As Michael Hattaway has argued, the conception of acting as 'personation' paradoxically involved not only a quest for authenticity of character, but also an element of feigning or self-conscious role-play – as the etymology (from the Latin *persona*, mask) suggests – at odds with the modern notion of personality (pp. 78–9). Actors would use mimicry and stand 'apart' from the characters they played to achieve the desired response from the audience. Such flexibility may best be seen among those low comedians who played the clowns, such as Lancelot Gobbo, whose debate with his conscience over whether to leave Shylock's service owes a debt to the psychomachia of Morality plays. Drawing on a primitive theatrical tradition, Lancelot's comic monologue often proves a stumbling block in modern productions: it is not comfortably contained within the frame of naturalistic theatre. Its effect on the Elizabethan stage, however, would have been different, the actor performing much as a stand-up comedian would perform today, addressing the audience directly, at once in and out of character, and, by eliciting their response, making the scene a participatory experience. By all accounts clowns like Will Kempe, who probably played Lancelot Gobbo, exploited this potential for give-and-take, altering material at each performance, extemporising, milking an audience for laughs. As Peter Thomson suggests, Hamlet's complaint about clowns – 'Let those that play your clowns speak no more than is set down for them ...' (*Hamlet*, III.ii.43–51) – may have been Shakespeare's *ad hominem* attack on Kempe (p. 35). The idea of adlibbing, of course, may offend our notion of the sacredness of Shakespeare's text; but in fact, as recent scholarship has shown, texts of his plays were unstable (see Honigmann; also Goldberg). As part of a rapidly changing repertory, they were modified to suit theatrical exigencies – what actors were available, and how many – and no doubt were unwittingly altered by actors who, pressed by the demands of a gruelling schedule and little rehearsal time, had to depend on their ability to extemporise simply to get through a performance. Clowns like Kempe, therefore, only did by design (and perhaps to excess) what was common practice among actors.

Direct address to the audience may have characterised the acting of Shylock as well. We cannot know whether the actor who first essayed the role exploited its comic potential (doubtful tradition has it that young Richard Burbage played Shylock in a red wig), but certain devices suggest that he may have bid for audience response in a way comic villains since the days of the Vice had done. In his first scene, for example, Shylock acknowledges his intention to catch Antonio on the hip in an aside that is disarmingly direct: 'I hate him for he is a Christian' (I.iii.34). Later, the scene affords the actor an opportunity for mimicry in the comic vein of Lancelot Gobbo, as when Shylock feigns the role of humble supplicant before Antonio:

> Shall I bend low, and in a bondman's key,
> With bated breath and whisp'ring humbleness,
> Say this:
> 'Fair sir, you spat on me on Wednesday last,
> You spurned me such a day, another time
> You called me dog ...'
>
> (115–20)

This is very much an actor's turn, a flamboyant appeal to the audience. And when, after he has been ridiculed for crying in the streets over the loss of his ducats and his daughter, he delivers his vehement self-defence as a Jew, he again may speak both in and out of character. On the one hand, he attempts in the speech to justify an odious revenge against Antonio, something he has already confessed to the audience he hungers for. Yet the series of rhetorical questions he asks – 'Hath not a Jew eyes? Hath not a Jew hands, organs, dimensions, senses, affections, passions?' (III.i.46–7) – extends beyond the immediate context of the play to become an overarching plea for toleration; and it is quite possible that the actor delivered this speech directly to the audience, as a soliloquy, rather than to Solanio and Salarino.

The same may have been true of Portia's eloquent plea for mercy. Certainly this rhetorically sophisticated speech would seem a bit out of character for the mere youth she pretends to be: it stands as a set piece, an expression of Christian values at once *of* the play and beyond it. Its original delivery would have been complicated by another convention of Elizabethan theatre, that of male disguise. Shakespeare's audience accepted disguise as an artifice far less alien to reality than we regard it today. It suggested a conception of character more ludic than our demands for naturalism will allow. Further, the trying-on of roles signified the potential for one character to have a multiplicity of selves: it revealed that Portia, like other disguised Shakespearean heroines, understood how to think and act like a man. Her anticipation of cross-dressing prompts a satiric evaluation of the masculine behaviour she will imitate:

> [I will] speak of 'frays
> Like a fine bragging youth; and tell quaint lies
> How honourable ladies sought my love,
> Which I denying, they fell sick and died –
>
> (III.iv.68–71)

Yet in court, Portia's 'worthy doctor' outwits men at a more serious game. Her knowledge of the law, a male preserve, is greater than theirs, her eloquence more persuasive, her authority surer. And by maintaining her authority throughout the charade with the rings in Act V, Portia differs from other heroines such as Rosalind who relinquish control when they shed their male disguises.

The Elizabethan practice of boy actors playing women's roles complicated matters further. No doubt boys did a creditable job of impersonating women, and audiences readily accepted them as such. Such acceptance, however, does not imply the same thing as our contemporary notion of suspended disbelief, for, as we have seen, certain signals reminded the Elizabethan audience of theatre's essential artifice: the audience would have accepted a boy as Portia and yet remained fully cognisant that Portia was a boy. This multi-consciousness made particularly playful the scenes of cross-dressing in which onstage 'women' assumed male 'disguises', which paradoxically allowed the boy actors to resume their male identity – to drop their dresses, put on pants, and speak and act *as* boys. In *The Merchant* Shakespeare provides three cross-dressings, Jessica's, Nerissa's, and Portia's, the compound effect of which is to insist on the artificiality of the convention (Shapiro, *Boy Heroines*, p. 110). Jessica's disguise would have been most familiar to Elizabethan audiences, because it drew on Italian comedy for the resourceful, headstrong daughter determined to deceive her father by escaping his house in male attire. This conventional use of disguise, however, barely anticipated the more intricate effect of Portia's cross-dressing at the trial.

It has been argued that on the Elizabethan stage, Shakespeare submerged Portia's gender identity so completely in the fusion of Balthasar with the boy actor that the audience would have perceived her *only* as male (Geary, p. 58). Indeed, unlike other disguised heroines who keep us aware of their gender through periodic asides and soliloquies, Portia never breaks her cross-gender concealment. Yet in subtler ways, as Michael Shapiro points out in his study of *Boy Heroines in Male Disguise* (pp. 117–20), Shakespeare insists on the presence of 'Portia' throughout the trial and thereby keeps the dynamic of sexual transformation before the audience. When Bassanio, for example, generously offers Shylock twice, even ten times the money owed him – Portia's money – it is 'Balthasar' who disallows the offer. In the theatre, this confrontation often brings Bassanio face to face with Portia, a situation which, by hinting at the risk she runs of being discovered, comically heightens our awareness of her identity. Later, when Antonio's 'Commend me to your honourable wife' (IV.i.269) prompts Bassanio to profess that he would sacrifice that wife to free his friend, he is not aware, as we are, that his wife is within earshot. Portia's reply – 'Your wife would give you little thanks for that / If she were by to hear you make the offer' (284–5) – may be delivered directly to him by

'Balthasar', or as an aside to the audience; in either case, Portia's voice is heard. Gratiano's similar offer meets a like response from Nerissa, an echo which compounds the effect of the comedy. And when, at last, Portia asks for Bassanio's wedding ring as tribute, the layering of sexual identities yields a humorous irony. 'Balthasar' challenges Bassanio to break an oath to his wife by accusing him of ungenerosity, yet the audience simultaneously sees Portia playing mercilessly on her husband's divided loyalties. Her wry admonition, 'I pray you know me when we meet again' (415), is directed as much to the audience as to him; for who is the 'me' the audience is to know? The boy actor has been playing games with them as well as with the court. As Balthasar, he has played both a heroine in disguise and, no doubt more convincingly, himself. When he is next seen at Belmont, he will have resumed his 'real' identity as Portia, yet the audience would recognise that identity as no more than conventional transvestism. Such ironies are lost in the modern theatre, where actresses have difficulty establishing their credibility as young men and thus make of the trial a more absurd fiction than it ever would have been for the Elizabethans.

Other Elizabethan staging practices would have enhanced the audience's appreciation of the play's design. The minimal use of props in a neutral space, for example, allowed Shakespeare to establish a rhythm of scenic juxtapositions that both confirmed and challenged the oppositions between Venice and Belmont. Allegorically, of course, the casket plot and the bond plot represent antithetical values: Belmont and Venice are poles apart. Yet on a bare stage, every place is here, every moment is now. Belmont and Venice are the same place because they are undifferentiated by representational sets: the neutral playing space ensures fluid transitions from scene to scene and makes correspondences readily apparent. The first two scenes of the play, for instance – one in Venice, the other in Belmont – are strikingly similar in design. Portia's opening line, 'By my troth, Nerissa, my little body is aweary of this great world' (I.ii.1–2), echoes Antonio's opening line, 'In sooth I know not why I am so sad' (I.i.1). Both characters, in a sense, surfeit with too much. Antonio's friends proffer reasons for his sadness, all of which he dismisses, just as Nerissa lists the suitors who account for Portia's weariness, all of whom she dismisses. The parallel structure is clear; and though differences are obvious – the merchants are concerned with money, the women with marriage – the parallelism indicates that the women of Belmont are as much *like* the men of Venice as *unlike* them. Furthermore, Shakespeare works a remarkably fluid transition between these scenes. At the end of the first scene, Bassanio launches into a lyric paean to Portia which anticipates her arrival on stage; and by mentioning the Jasons who come in quest of her, he introduces the subject of Portia's conversation with Nerissa. He in effect summons them up: a Venetian can create the Lady of Belmont through words alone, and no sooner do we imagine her than she appears. Bassanio thus serves as a link between the casket plot and the bond plot: loved by both Antonio and Portia, he becomes the agency for bringing them together.

The mirroring of scenes in a neutral space was Shakespeare's favourite device for establishing a rhythm of correspondences. Perhaps the overriding correspondence in *The Merchant* is between those who sue for money and those who sue for love. Like Portia's suitors, Bassanio and Antonio are suitors to Shylock – and for money, which is a tacit goal of Portia's suitors as well. The succession of suits early in the play demonstrates how effectively Elizabethan stagecraft could create a network of relationships among scenes (Overton, pp. 29–30). The line in which Portia caps her disparagement of her suitors, for example – 'Whiles we shut the gate upon one wooer, another knocks at the door' (I.ii.110–11) – provides an apt transition to the next scene, which opens on Shylock's rehearsal of Bassanio's request for 3,000 ducats; for as Shylock notes, Bassanio is a wooer too: 'Monies is your suit' (I.iii.111). This successful suit is followed immediately by the entrance of Morocco who, to sue for Portia's hand, must agree to the hard condition never to marry if he chooses wrong. The rhythm hereby established culminates in Bassanio's hazarding for Portia, a scene in which she metamorphoses the mercantile vocabulary by which Venetians 'sue' into something of transcendent value:

>   for you
> I would be trebled twenty times myself,
> A thousand times more fair, ten thousand times
> More rich, that only to stand high in your account
> I might in virtues, beauties, livings, friends,
> Exceed account.
>
>   (III.ii.152–7)

The speech is no sooner spoken, however, than word arrives that Antonio must pay a mortal price for having incurred a debt to Shylock. Such fluid dramatic configurations as these preserve a fine balance between the two plots, a balance forfeited when staging becomes too representational.

The bare stage would also have lent more dramatic weight to Act V, which in 'realistic' productions is sometimes scanted as an embarrassing excrescence, a contrived return to the artifices of Belmont to ensure a happy ending. Granted, the trial is a hard act to follow; but the contrivance of Act V might have had more point on the Elizabethan stage than it has today. In it, Shakespeare cleverly recapitulates the bond plot that has threatened to upset the comedy in Act IV. Using Bassanio's and Gratiano's loss of their rings as a ploy, Portia vows to break off the nuptials (just as they were broken before) until Antonio stakes his life upon the loyalty of his friend (much as he has done before). Now, however, we perceive no risk in Antonio's doing so, for we know that Portia will pull strings – or rings – to get these men off the hook, just as she has done at the trial. An Elizabethan audience would have been aware of yet another level of meaning; for throughout the scene, Shakespeare kept them alert to the fact that Portia and Nerissa were really males who now, paradoxically, had resumed their female disguises. The audience's awareness of the boy actors inside the dresses, as Shapiro observes (*Boy Heroines*, pp. 125–6), is repeatedly piqued by references to male identity –

Nerissa	The clerk will ne'er wear hair on's face that had it [the ring].
Gratiano	He will, and if he live to be a man.
Nerissa	Ay, if a woman live to be a man.
Gratiano	Now by this hand, I gave it to a youth, A kind of boy, a little scrubbed boy No higher than thyself ...

(V.i.158–63)

Portia, furthermore, uses legal jargon one last time, probably with a wry smile, to remind us of her appearance in the courtroom as Balthasar (Mahood, p. 166 n.):

> Let us go in,
> And charge us there upon inter'gatories,
> And we will answer all things faithfully.

(297–9)

This final evocation of the trial would have had particular point on the Elizabethan stage, where locations were undifferentiated; for here, in this very space and only minutes earlier, Antonio came within a hair's breadth of being killed, Bassanio nearly lost a friend, and Portia, quite possibly, a happy marriage. The bare stage thus would have reinforced the correspondences between Acts IV and V by serving simultaneously as Belmont and, through imaginative recall, as the court of Venice. The comic artifices by which Act V recreates and resolves the tensions of the trial attest to the suggestive neutrality of Elizabethan staging and to the capacity of Elizabethan audiences to perceive a play on different levels.

One cannot, of course, be certain how *The Merchant* was staged in Shakespeare's theatre, and it would be presumptuous to speculate how an Elizabethan audience might have responded to it. At most, using social history to provide a context, one may hazard a guess. Apparently *The Merchant* was a popular play. The Lord Chamberlain's Men acted it *'diuers times'*, according to the Quarto text of 1600; and as the King's Men, they performed it twice at court in 1605. The popularity of any play, of course, is determined in part by how successfully it captures the mood of its audience: their attitudes, their *mores*. Few plays were so successful in doing this as *The Merchant*. By dramatising the tensions inherent in a nascent capitalist society – the acquisition of wealth weighed against the perils of trade, class antagonisms, the changing role of women, prejudice against minorities – it held a mirror up to London of the 1590s. That Shakespeare grafted such contemporary concerns on to the material of folk tale may seem surprising; but folk tales themselves enshrine the myths of the cultures from which they emerge, and Shakespeare's play does much the same thing. Like the society for which it was written, it has money at its heart.

The Merchant spoke to its first audience in complex ways. English trade had grown enormously during the final decades of the sixteenth century: a burgeoning merchant class had accumulated considerable wealth and, inevitably, wished to share power with those aristocrats who had traditionally held it. Class tensions thus arose between city entrepreneurs who, having made their fortunes, were in a position to buy what they could not take, and the landed gentry who, having inherited theirs, sought to maintain a hierarchy of privilege. Venice appealed to the Elizabethan imagination as a place where mercantile interests and social privilege were not mutually exclusive. An opulent centre of world trade and banking, founded in liberty and famous for toleration, Venice represented a vigorous fusion of cultures where those on the margins of society – Jews especially – did business daily with those at the centre (Grubb, pp. 43–4). In the eyes of Shakespeare's audience, therefore, Antonio and his companions were engaged in typically Venetian activities.

Their class attitudes, however, were decidedly English. One hears in their opening conversation a distinction between the noble 'signor' or 'rich burgher', Antonio (I.i.10), whose argosies are the envy of Venice, and those lesser men of trade – Solanio, Salarino[1] – whose business calls on them. Although Venice had been in decline as a maritime commercial power since the mid-sixteenth century and few shipping magnates had the social standing of Antonio (Pullen, pp. 379–408; Mahood, p. 13), Shakespeare chose to perpetuate the Myth of Venice because it served his purpose: English merchants were aggressively acquiring the wealth, confidence, and social privilege that their Venetian counterparts were fearful of losing. In 1596, one might have found more Antonios in London than in Venice.

Elizabethans might have heard in this scene, too, some class tension between the lesser merchants and Antonio's 'worthier friends' (61) – Bassanio, Gratiano, Lorenzo – fashionable young men who apparently have the leisure (or idleness) not to work at all. 'We'll make our leisures to attend on yours,' Salarino pointedly tells them on departing (68). Bassanio, we learn, has taken the usual course for the son of an aristocratic house: 'a scholar and a soldier', he has served 'in the company of the Marquis of Montferrat' (I.ii.93–4), returned home, and gambled away his father's estate. He thus depends on a rich friend, as impecunious aristocrats often did, to supply his wants. In an emergent capitalist economy like England's, there was plenty of room for opportunists, and it is feasible that the audience would have recognised Bassanio as one. His explanation of how he plans to pay back his debts by further speculation is suspect: clearly he intends to exploit his friendship with Antonio and, if possible, exploit the heiress of Belmont as well. 'In Belmont is a lady richly left' (I.i.160).

The view of Belmont as a green world, a society based on inherited wealth and removed from the anxieties of commerce, is not necessarily at odds with this Venetian concern with capital.

For the 'imaginative space' of Belmont, as J. R. Mulryne rightly suggests (p. 7), 'is that of the great house' which increasingly, in England as in Venice, was purchased and sustained with the profits of commercial enterprise. Shakespeare may have found an analogue for Belmont in the lavish estates on the Veneto, where the Venetian patriciate, having turned away from trade, were enjoying the fruits of their success: 'the journey to Belmont represents for the former merchants of Venice ... the acceptance of an aristocratic life-style that without abandoning Venetian wealth contrasts in a marked way with the style of their former existence' (Mulryne, p. 8). Even if one defines Belmont in more traditionally English terms as an estate of the landed gentry, the same would hold true; for the maintenance of aristocratic values paradoxically eschewed, yet was predicated on, abundant capital.

Such values inform the casket lottery, wherein any suitor worthy of Portia should by nature recognise the difference between outward show – gold and silver, the media of commercial exchange – and inner merit. Winning the lottery presupposes that the victor have *sprezzatura*, which Castiglione defines in *The Courtier* as the means by which aristocrats recognise in one another an inherent worth that upstarts cannot buy. Bassanio shares this aristocratic assumption with Portia. His eloquent speech bears witness to it –

So may the outward shows be least themselves:
The world is still deceived with ornament.

(III.ii.73–4)

– and proves thereby that however tainted he may be with Venetian opportunism, he nevertheless is to the manor born. Alone among the suitors, he recognises the value of meagre lead; as a reward, he earns Portia and, with her, her father's place in the hierarchy. Having lost his own estate, he comes to govern hers.

This is a capitalist fairy tale indeed. In it, Shakespeare bridges the worlds of commerce and inherited wealth by allowing Belmont to incorporate Venice, to subsume new-gotten gain under a conservative vision of aristocratic privilege. This adds a powerful social dimension to the romantic affirmations of Act V that would not have been lost on Shakespeare's audience; for once Portia has intervened at the trial to ensure victory by her innately superior values, the victors are free to move with her to Belmont, a green world *sustained* by money but not consumed with the *getting* of it. Some, however, are excluded from this world. Among them are Portia's erstwhile suitors who, despite their noble breeding, do not fit into her particular version of aristocratic privilege. The list includes worthies from Naples, France, Germany, Scotland, and England, all of whom she summarily dismisses with xenophobic barbs about their national characters. More pointedly dismissed are the two suitors who venture to choose: the black Prince of Morocco, whose bravado recalls the Marlovian excesses of Tamburlaine, and the Prince of Arragon, whose elegant self-absorption glances at those Spaniards who were the butt of English jokes. Nowadays, the suitors are commonly played for laughs, but such playing invalidates the dramatic premise of the lottery by making them too clearly unworthy of Portia. Although Arragon is more comically stereotypical than Morocco, neither suitor is necessarily ridiculous: each in his own way is eligible, articulate, and worthy of marrying a woman of Portia's class. The reason she rejects them is that she harbours prejudices which a majority of Elizabethans would have shared: Morocco is the wrong race, and Arragon the wrong nationality. Therefore, when she tartly bids them farewell, calling Arragon a 'deliberate fool' (II.ix.79) and saying of Morroco, 'Let all of his complexion choose me so' (II.vii.79), her xenophobia would not have been reprehensible to the audience. Indeed, it might have won her their approval.

Most notably excluded from Portia's community, and most victimised by its prejudices, is Shylock. In him, Shakespeare created a character who conformed in many ways to the anti-Semitic stereotype prevalent in Elizabethan England. On numerous occasions characters attest to his villainy: Solanio and Salarino mock him as a miser who cares more for his ducats than his daughter; Antonio damns him as a figure from a Mystery play –

> The devil can cite Scripture for his purpose.
> An evil soul producing holy witness
> Is like a villain with a smiling cheek ...
>
> (I.iii.90–2)

Lancelot Gobbo, who famishes in his service, proclaims the Jew 'the very devil incarnation' (II.ii.20–1); and even his daughter Jessica calls his house a 'hell' (II.iii.2) and plots to escape it. Shylock's behaviour, furthermore, would seem to justify these bad opinions. He openly admits to the audience,

> I hate [Antonio] for he is a Christian;
> But more, for that in low simplicity
> He lends out money gratis, and brings down
> The rate of usance here with us in Venice.
>
> (I.iii.34–7)

Significantly, his two reasons for hating Antonio are not causally connected: the one invokes an age-old antipathy which Jews, as Christ-killers, supposedly felt towards Christians; the other invokes the stereotype of Jewish greed. Shylock's barbarism is confirmed by Jessica when she confides to her Christian hosts that she has 'heard him swear / ... That he would rather have Antonio's flesh / Than twenty times the value' of the bond (III.ii.283–6). Shylock uses ironic humour to lure Antonio into agreeing to this bond as 'a merry sport' (I.iii.138); but once it appears the argosies are lost, he turns deadly earnest:

> Go, Tubal, fee me an officer ... I will have the heart of him if he forfeit, for were he out of Venice I can make what merchandise I will.
>
> (III.i.99–102)

That Shylock's revenge is apparently sanctioned by Venetian law does not make it any less barbaric: in fact, his insistence on law without mercy represents a Pauline distortion of Judaism that went largely unchallenged in the Renaissance (J. Cooper, pp. 117–24; Glassman, pp. 14–83). Little wonder, then, that Shylock's forced conversion to Christianity, often so repugnant to modern audiences, was welcomed as a just retribution by Elizabethans, who commonly regarded the soul of a Jew 'as already forfeit in so far as he, like his forebears, refused to acknowledge the Christian Messiah. Baptism alone, it was believed, could put a Jew in the way of salvation' (Mahood, p. 19).

Some knowledge of the history of anti-Semitism in England is critical to an understanding of the stereotype with which Shakespeare appealed to his audience's prejudices. Jews first came to England after the Norman Conquest. Operating out of a special Exchequer of Jews, they financed the needs of court, aristocracy, and clergy during a period of national expansion: in effect, they were tolerated only to the degree they were willing to be extorted. During the Crusades, however, persecution of Jews erupted on a large scale throughout Europe, and England was not exempt; riots, pillage, and killing grew more and more frequent. The arrival of mendicant Dominican friars may have contributed to the expulsion of the Jews in 1290, yet the primary reason was economic. For by the thirteenth century, taxes were exceeding Jewish resources, the Jews' money-lending monopoly had been broken by the Lombards, and Edward I could safely expel them without incurring financial hardship. Jews were not officially readmitted until 1655, under Cromwell, though a few hundred real or pretended converts to Christianity did remain. Some of them were attached to the court; others were prosperous merchants; none conformed to the anti-Semitic stereotype (Sanders, pp. 339–51; Sinsheimer, *passim*).

When *The Merchant* was first performed in late 1596 or 1597, therefore, Jews had not lived in England for over three hundred years, and anti-Semitic myths had been able to grow and prosper unimpeded by the presence of Jews to refute them. Most widespread was the myth of child murder: Jews were said to steal Christian children, crucify them, and use the blood in the Passover ritual. One hundred and fifty such cases were reported, the most notorious being the death of young Hugh of Lincoln, recounted in the tale told by Chaucer's Prioress. Jews' daughters, furthermore, always beautiful, were believed to act as decoys for these children. Another popular myth was that Jews caused the black death by poisoning wells and such like. The fact that many Jews were doctors perpetuated the myth, and it contributed even as late as 1594 to the frenzy surrounding the case of Ruy Lopez, a Portuguese Jew who, as physician to the Queen, was accused of attempting to poison her.

The early English stage reinforced the stereotype by dressing villains of the Corpus Christi plays in Jewish cloaks and horned hats, often completing the identification with a circle of yellow cloth on the arm, which since 1215 had been the badge of European Jewry (Fisch, pp. 13–18). Judas in particular was said to have looked very much like the devil with his red wig, hook nose, and usurer's bag. This tradition may have carried over to the Elizabethan stage as well, if one believes the following description of Shylock's appearance in a ballad written by an actor in the 1630s (and published in *The Royal Arbor of Loyal Poesie*, 1664):

> His beard was red; his face was made
>   Not much unlike a witches.
> His habit was a Jewish gown
>   That would defend all weather;
> His chin turn'd up, his nose hung down,
>   And both ends met together.
>
> (Thomas Jordan, 'The Forfeiture')

The most immediate source for Shakespeare, Marlowe's *The Jew of Malta*, first performed c.1590, revived in 1594 to capitalise on the Lopez affair and again in 1596, just prior to *The Merchant*, provided a contemporary dramatic inspiration for Shylock. A wealthy Maltese Jew, Barabas is a miser – in love with his ducats more than his daughter – who conspires to undermine the ostensibly 'Christian' government that has levelled taxes on him and his fellow Jews to finance its wars. Through him, Marlowe attacks Christian hypocrisy much as Shakespeare may be said to do through Shylock (Dessen, 'Stage Jew', pp. 231–45). Yet the differences between Shylock and Barabas are significant. Barabas without remorse poisons his daughter along with the nuns with whom she has sought refuge; Shylock's anger over Jessica's defection is altogether more familial. Barabas plots treachery on the authority of Machiavelli; Shylock seeks revenge through the course of law. Ultimately, they are products of different societies. Barabas is like those Jews who, in medieval England, were expected to finance – through taxation and extortion – the activities of a government that barely tolerated them. Shylock, on the other hand, does business in the more tolerant climate of the Venetian Republic. He is a usurer; and it is in this capacity that he raises some of the play's most vexing questions about the relationship of the outsider to those in power.

In the view of many Elizabethans, usury and Judaism were virtually synonymous. The advent of a money economy, the decay of the old aristocratic houses, chronic borrowing, and thrift sapped by the availability of easy credit all produced tensions within Elizabethan society. The money-lender, according to Wilbur Sanders, 'though merely the economic instrument of new desires, had all the resultant tensions and crises laid to his door; and the money-lender was, by an ineradicable popular association, the Jew' (pp. 345–6). Historical circumstances explain this association. Jews had been allowed to lend money at interest because Christians were forbidden to do so: the Gospels taught that it was wrong to lend for gain, and people still assented to Aristotle's belief that it was unnatural for money to breed more money. This belief underlies Antonio's attack on Shylock for taking 'a breed of barren metal' (I.iii.126). 'Is your gold and silver ewes and rams?' he asks, implicitly pointing out the disparity between natural and unnatural increase, to which Shylock wryly replies, 'I cannot tell, I make it breed as fast' (87–8).

Like Antonio, Elizabethans commonly condemned usurers as wolves, devils, and heretics: they were 'greedie cormoraunte wolfes in deede, that rauyn vp both beaste and man' according to *A Discourse upon Usury* (1572); their 'houses were called the devils houses, his fields the devils croppe', according to *The Death of Usury, or, The Disgrace of Usurers* (1594). Behind such virulence lay the fear that capitalism itself might be ungodly. Were the old religion and the new mercantilism fully compatible? Was the 'thrifty' pursuit of trade distinguishable from the 'prodigal' indulgence of greed? (Moisan, p. 189). As an emergent economic power, England of course placed a great value on her merchants, and usury was necessary to ensure that their ventures could thrive. Furthermore, not only merchants, but Parliament and the Queen herself sought the resources of usurers – virtually none of whom in fact were Jews (Draper, pp. 39–45); and the Queen, by putting a ceiling of 10 per cent on lending rates, officially condoned the practice. Usury and trade thus existed in an embarrassing symbiotic relationship that no tract against usury could suppress.

The Merchant reflects this anxiety over how best to accommodate the new mercantile ethic. Although the play formally reconciles the monied classes under the dominant aristocratic ideology at Belmont (W. Cohen, p. 772), performance history reveals that it resists such easy closure; for Shylock, whose usury is necessary to effect this reconciliation, is not so casually dismissed by the audience as he is by the ducal court. Economic necessity may turn him into the kind of wolf or devil condemned in anti-usury tracts, but he also may be seen to serve as a scapegoat for the Christians, bearing the burden of their guilt, mythologising an evil – greed – from which they would like to dissociate themselves (Girard, pp. 100–19).

Shakespeare seems to acknowledge as much when he has Shylock plead his own humanity – 'I am a Jew' – at the very moment he is being most savagely mocked. This speech has so powerfully bid audiences to understand him as a victim of Christian bigotry that it has taken on a life of its own outside the play.

Shakespeare offers audiences other reasons to sympathise with Shylock as well. His first exchange with Antonio establishes that his malice is not without cause: he accuses Antonio of berating him on the Rialto, calling him misbeliever and cut-throat dog, spitting on his Jewish gaberdine, and kicking him across his threshold like a stranger cur – provocation enough, one would think, for anyone to rebel. Yet Antonio is unrepentant:

> I am as like to call thee so again,
> To spit on thee, to spurn thee too.
> If thou wilt lend this money, lend it not
> As to thy friends ...
>
> (122–5)

Shakespeare's audience may have thought that Antonio was in the right: if one condemns usury as a diabolical practice, as Elizabethans were told to do, then of course one would not expect him hypocritically to flatter Shylock, even if he was suing for a loan. But, alternatively, they might have found his speech surprisingly angry, for as many of them no doubt realised, usury was a necessary evil; and on the stage, no matter what Shylock may allegorically signify, it is difficult *not* to see him as a human being victimised by a smug community of merchants who tolerate him only when, as now, he proves useful to them.

The Christianity of the Venetian community is thus very much at issue. At the trial, Portia's plea for Shylock to have mercy is counterpoised with Gratiano's vindictive – and familiarly anti-Semitic – attacks on his character: 'O be thou damned, inexecrable dog' (IV.i.128); 'Thy currish spirit / Governed a wolf' (133–4); 'thy desires / Are wolfish, bloody, starved, and ravenous' (137–8). And when the law turns against Shylock to protect the interests of those in power, the Christians administer mercy most strangely: they strip him of his money and his religion, the very things for which, as a Jew, he lives. 'You take my life / When you do take the means whereby I live,' he cries (372–3); and historically he is right, for usury was one of the only ways in which Jews were allowed to earn a living. Twice before Christians have contributed to his financial undoing: Antonio by forfeiting the bond, and Lorenzo by stealing his ducat-laden daughter. Here, his undoing is completed. If one regards Shylock as evil, then of course this turn of events must seem good: the devil is exorcised, the Jew turns Christian. Yet Shakespeare endows Shylock with enough integrity to complicate our response to his defeat. This interplay between the individual and the type is interestingly reflected, as Bill Overton observes (pp. 28–9), in variations of speech prefixes in the Quarto, where *Jew* precedes those speeches that tend to characterise Shylock as a traditional villain – his nasty aside in I.iii, his harassment of Antonio and the Jailer, and that portion of the trial where he exults in his apparent victory – and *Shylock* precedes those in which he deviates from the type: his domestic conversation with Jessica and Lancelot, his explosions of grief and anger in III.i, and all his speeches at the trial after Portia has defeated him. If these variations originated in Shakespeare's manuscript (and a scribe, compositor, or theatre official is unlikely to have introduced them), they afford us a glimpse of how consciously Shakespeare sought to revise the stage Jew as a credibly complex human being. His success in doing so is proven by four hundred years of stage history.

That seventeenth-century audiences may have found Shylock the play's most absorbing character is evidenced by George Granville's adaptation of 1701. Called *The Jew of Venice*, thereby awarding Shylock a titular prominence that may reveal how he had come to be regarded (and which, in fact, the Stationers' Register records as the play's alternate title on 22 July 1598), Granville's adaptation responded to the demands of a 'refined' age to make Shakespeare conform to the dictates of generic decorum, as if the products of his untutored genius needed to be purged of those anarchic pressures which our own age regards as their chief glory. In brazen testimony to the arrogance of the age, Bevill Higgons provided a Prologue in which Shakespeare's ghost praises Granville's improvements:

> These Scenes in their rough Native Dress were mine;
> But now improv'd with nobler Lustre shine;
> The first rude Sketches Shakespear's Pencil drew,
> But all the shining Master-strokes are new.

(35–8)

By briefly examining what Granville excised and revised in order to accommodate the play to the requirements of his stage and audience, we may learn what features of the original were deemed indecorous, or at least problematic, for performance in the early eighteenth century.

To exploit the new theatre technology, with its painted flats and more representational scenery, Granville drastically reduced the number of scenes from twenty to nine. This reduction of course retarded the quick transitions and juxtapositions characteristic of Elizabethan staging. Granville also eliminated many secondary characters as either superfluous to the action or too lowly comic to be appropriate for it. The Gobbos were first to go; they were followed by Solanio and Salarino, by Tubal, and even by Portia's unsuccessful suitors. Thus began an exodus that would be imitated in later, more spectacular productions, the effect of which was to throw a greater emphasis on the 'big' scenes – Bassanio's choice of the lead casket, Antonio's trial – and to jeopardise the network of correspondences that had made Shakespeare's original so compelling.

In his Advertisement for the play, Granville promises that the reader 'will observe so many Manly and Moral Graces in the Characters and Sentiments, that he may excuse the Story' (Spencer, p. 347). Such graces particularly inform the friendship between Antonio and Bassanio, the latter played by Thomas Betterton, for whose heroic acting style the play served as a vehicle. Granville filled their scenes with chivalric protestations of love, honour, fame, and self-sacrifice, such as these with which Antonio concludes the first act:

> There is not the least Danger, nor can be,
> Or if there were, what is a Pound of Flesh,
> What my whole Body, every Drop of Blood,
> To purchase my Friend's Quiet! Heav'n still is good
> To those who seek the Good of others. Come, *Bassanio*,
> Be chearful, for 'tis lucky Gold we borrow:
> Of all the Joys that generous Minds receive,
> The noblest is, the God-like Power to give.
>
> (I.iii.163–70)

There is no mercantile talk in Granville's Venice: the text is purged of the capital concerns that made Shakespeare's Venice seem authentic. Instead, its manners and speeches are modelled on the ideals of a precapitalist age which English Augustans were attempting, through art, to appropriate as their own.

Like other dramatists of the period, Granville sacrificed psychological credibility to the 'interests of moral clarity' (Spencer, p. 12), so that his characters were generalised and their motivation easily understood. Bassanio is a case in point: what motivates his quest for Portia is not a desire for her wealth, but love alone. Thus, when Portia dedicates herself to him after he has chosen right, her speech is shorn of the ambiguous mercantile vocabulary that made it so allusive in Shakespeare's play; and Bassanio's response to her emphasises love's magnanimity – a concept from heroic drama – instead of love's 'worth'. Such magnanimity ennobles the trial as well, which Granville was careful to purge of its potential rivalry between Antonio and Portia for Bassanio's love. In place of Bassanio's vow that he would sacrifice his wife to deliver Antonio – a remark that carries moral, if not sexual, ambiguity – Granville inserted conventional testimonials to the value of friendship. Intent on idealising the Venetians as courtiers, he suppressed the questionable motives that made them recognisably human.

The most notable suppressions occurred in the role of Shylock. Thomas Doggett, an actor noted for low comedy, played him as a caricature miser who, according to the Prologue, is punished as a *'Stock-jobbing Jew'* (29), possibly modelled on disreputable sharpers of the London Exchange. In keeping with the aristocratic prejudices of Granville (later Lord Lansdowne) and his audience, Shylock lost the individuality with which Shakespeare had imbued him. His richly colloquial speeches to Antonio are conflated and vulgarised:

> Be this
> The Forfeiture.
> Let me see, What think you of your Nose,
> Or of an Eye – or of – a Pound of Flesh
> To be cut off, and taken from what Part
> Of your Body – I shall think fit to name.
> Thou art too portly, Christian!
>
> (I.iii.124–30)

At the supper to which he is bid forth – a scene Shakespeare chose not to write – Shylock follows the Christians' toasts to Love and

Friendship with a toast of his own to his Mistress Money. And robbed of the opportunity to defend himself against the goading of Solanio and Salarino and to express anguish over his losses to Tubal, he becomes simply an abstracted figure of revenge, as clear in his villainy as his antagonists are in their virtue (Zimbardo, p. 224). Shylock's behaviour at the trial is thus predictably diabolical. Refusing Bassanio's generous offer to die in place of his friend, he reveals a motive more sinister than any Shakespeare ascribed to him; for, he gloats,

> When [Antonio] has paid the Forfeit of his Bond,
> Thou canst not chuse but hang thy self for being
> The Cause: And so my ends are serv'd on both.
>
> (206–8)

Given such transparent allegory, it is odd that Granville omitted Shylock's forced conversion to Christianity – evidence, perhaps, that this harsh condition had proven distasteful even to early audiences. Its omission would have been consistent with Granville's aim of suppressing the problematic nature of Shakespeare's text and offering in its place the decorous comedy Shakespeare *should* have written.

Yet there were objections to his adaptation. Nicholas Rowe in 1709 protested the reduction of Shylock to a comic turn: 'tho' we have seen the Play Receiv'd and Acted as a Comedy, and the Part of the *Jew* perform'd by an excellent Comedian, yet I cannot but think that it was design'd Tragically by the Author' ('Life', p. 9). Rowe here argues for the potential of Shylock to turn the play from comedy to its opposite. Indeed, the focus returned to a more fully fleshed Shylock when, in 1741, Charles Macklin persuaded the management of Drury Lane to restore Shakespeare's play in a text that included Portia's suitors, both Gobbos, and Tubal. Macklin was renowned as a comedian, famous for roles such as Osric, Touchstone, and Trinculo, so that, according to John Russell Brown, 'his Shylock cannot have been "tragic", but all witnesses affirm that he gave full vent to the Jew's contrasted passions' (p. xxxiii). Macklin's interpretation would have satisfied Rowe's call for 'a savage Fierceness and Fellness' of purpose: he apparently terrified audiences by his ferocity in III.i and his portentous silences at the trial. In its menacing power, Macklin's portrayal drew attention away from the Venetians and even from the Portia of Kitty Clive who, as Balthasar, comically aped the mannerisms of well-known lawyers of the day. His Shylock held the stage to the end of the century, for a total of 316 performances; and despite its anti-Semitic appeal, his portrayal so altered audiences' perception of the play that one commentator imagined a future adaptation, written by a Jew, in which Shylock would become the wronged hero, his opponents overwhelmed by remorse (Hole, p. 566).

Clearly the potential of Shylock to disrupt the comedy had seized the popular imagination. Before long Belmont began to be trivialised: the suitors were (once again) eliminated, songs and dances were added, and although such notable actresses as Sarah Siddons and Peg Woffington played Portia, 'there is every indication that *The Merchant* had become Shylock's play' (Brown, *Merchant*, p. xxxiii). This was even more the case in the nineteenth century, when, in a line beginning with Edmund Kean, productions in England, America, and Germany transformed the play into the history of a tormented Jew who, when injured, would fight his oppressors with a terrible, contemptuous scorn. Donning a black wig, Kean broke with the traditional red-bearded, hook-nosed Shylock by infusing 'credibly human qualities into ... a mythical figure' (see Lelyveld, pp. 39–60). Passionate and sober by turn, he played Shylock, in the words of Coleridge, 'by flashes of lightning', and III.i became for Kean, as it had been for Macklin, the lightning rod that grounded his performance. In that scene, one spectator wrote, Kean's 'voice swells and deepens at the mention of his sacred tribe and ancient law' (*Examiner*, 16 March 1828). In his exchange with Tubal, he riveted audiences with instantaneous shifts of grief and rage; and by delivering asides as if they were soliloquies, he bid for sympathy. His bid was most successful, apparently, when, wishing his daughter dead at his foot with the jewels in her ear, Kean recoiled in revulsion at his own unnaturalness and, with his face buried in his hands, murmured 'No, no, no.'

William Hazlitt, who was in the audience on the opening night in 1814, wrote that Kean's 'Jew is more than half a Christian. Certainly, our sympathies are much oftener with him than with his enemies. He is honest in his vices; they are hypocrites in their virtues' (*The Chronicle*, 6 March 1816). Shylock's claim to moral superiority over the Christians turned the trial into a painful ordeal rather than a celebration. In the words of one recent editor, 'the collapse of this intelligent and vulnerable man was horrible to watch; the reaction of the spectator who, in Heine's hearing, exclaimed "the poor man is wronged" was only a little more extreme than that of the audience as a whole' (Mahood, p. 44). Shylock's exit from the court thus came to be regarded as a fitting conclusion to the play, and Act V was often omitted.

These changes were in keeping with the sensibility of the early nineteenth century. Just as Granville had revised *The Merchant* to accommodate the expectations of his decorous age, so Kean and his followers found that the play spoke, through Shylock, to a Romantic age whose fascination with passionate individuality and exotic difference made Shakespeare's tragedies more popular than his comedies. Tellingly, measured by the number of performances, *The Merchant* was second only to *Hamlet* in popularity during the century. It was embraced by such great tragic actors as William Macready in England and Edwin Booth in America, whose performances are copiously documented by Toby Lelyveld in *Shylock on the Stage*. Furthermore, *The Merchant* grew grander as stage technology advanced. Throughout the Victorian period an increasing emphasis on spectacle, on the splendour of painted and then architecturally representational scenery, tended to focus audiences' attention on the play's most picturesque character, Shylock, in his authentic Venetian context. Charles Kean's production in 1858 was celebrated for recreating the Rialto with remarkable fidelity, and the Bancrofts took pains to reproduce such specific locales as the Sala della Bussola for their production in 1875 (Shewring, pp. 89–94). Depictions of Belmont were far less evocative; the fantastic goings-on at Portia's palace evidently inspired the Victorians less than the more credible events occurring at the Doge's. Their preference for Venice over Belmont revealed an even deeper preference for psychological and historical realism over the comic artifice with which Shakespeare had carefully balanced his two plots. This tradition reached its apogee in Henry Irving's production at the Lyceum Theatre in 1879, which firmly established *The Merchant* as one of Shakespeare's great tragedies.

Not long ago, an American critic argued that *The Merchant* 'dramatises not the triumph of one set of values over another, but the transformation of conflicts into harmonies that incorporate what at the same time they transcend' (W. Cohen, p. 766, on Danson). The history of performance would suggest otherwise. The anarchic pressures of the text have usually resisted such harmony: it has been difficult, if not impossible, for directors to balance the dramatic, ideological, and aesthetic alternatives Shakespeare offers. As a result, *The Merchant* has invited more tampering and revision than any other of his plays. What follows are accounts of how, in the past hundred years, *The Merchant* has been adapted not only to the prevailing theatrical technology and taste, but to ever-changing social and political contexts as well. Something in the mythology of the play has appealed so fundamentally to an audience's sense of cultural identity that each age has used *The Merchant* as a mirror to reflect its own face. That the play is capable of revealing so many faces may help to explain its enduring fascination.

Note

1 For an explanation of why the three Venetians named in Q1 – Salanio, Salarino, and Salerio – are usually, and probably mistakenly, reduced to two – Solanio, Salerio – in editions and in performance, see Mahood, pp. 179–83.

II

Henry Irving and the great tradition

If the test of a good production is that it brings new insight into a play and prompts audiences to return to the text, then Henry Irving's *Merchant* was triumphant. Opening in 1879 to almost universal acclaim, it 'naturalised' the emotionally volatile, theatrically vengeful Shylocks popularised by Macklin and Kean while at the same time, in its quest for historical verisimilitude, epitomising Victorian values in staging. It became the most influential *Merchant* ever produced, running for 250 performances during its first season alone and, over the course of twenty-five years, a total of a thousand performances both in England and on tour – eight times – in America (L. Irving, p. 708). It helped to make Irving a legend and cast the mould for *Merchants* well into the twentieth century.

Irving was the foremost actor-manager of the nineteenth century. This implies a number of things about the organisation of his theatre that were instrumental in his production of *The Merchant*. The actor-manager system revolved around a single authority figure who planned the repertory, cast, and directed each play, and usually starred in it. Primary focus, therefore, was on the talents of one individual, not on an entire company as in Shakespeare's theatre: there were no 'sharers' at Irving's Lyceum. The artistic hegemony inherent in this system reflected the patriarchal structure of Victorian culture in general – the submission of all members of a family to the will of the father. At best, such authoritarianism resulted in a stylistic coherence and ensemble playing that achieved a marvellous unity of effect; and it is for such effects that Irving is best known. At worst, the divided duties of actor and director clashed, and the actor-manager's desire to perform a role distorted the design of the whole by subordinating all facets of production to his overbearing ego.

Both the strengths and the weaknesses of the system may be observed in Irving's *Merchant*. His company was still in its formative stages: he had taken control of the Lyceum from the Batemans only a year earlier, in 1878, inaugurating his management with a production of *Hamlet*, and had begun slowly to replace the Batemans' mediocre actors with better ones, most notably Ellen Terry. *The Merchant* thus became a test case for his managerial discipline. He selected the play to showcase his own talents, and reasonably so, since audiences would come to see him act, and as a manager he had to be concerned with box-office revenue. Irving was noted for idiosyncratic portrayals. He had a towering stage presence – an ungainly carriage and a stride that caricaturists loved. According to his contemporary William Winter, his 'stilted and angular' way of moving resulted from a 'nervous excitement' that made him compelling to watch; his range of facial expressions was 'weird, eccentric, saturnine, mystical'; and his voice, 'neither copious nor resonant', was alternately tender, piercing, and vibrant – 'the flute and not the trumpet' (or in the words of those less charitable, forced and nasal). Although these characteristics rendered him capable of 'erratic and dazzling excursions into the domain of grim or grotesque ... humour', he nevertheless demonstrated through them 'a soul and mind rich in the capacity to feel and to translate the tragic aspects of humanity' (pp. 8–10). Irving had won instant fame when he used these mannerisms to magnetic effect as Mathias in *The Bells*, and it is likely that he was attracted to the role of Shylock because it offered him similar opportunities to display eccentric pathos.

Irving's account of how he came to do *The Merchant* is instructive. He had accepted an invitation from the Baroness Burdett-Coutts to accompany her and her friends on a cruise to the Mediterranean in the summer of 1879, with perhaps nothing more in mind than collecting a few prints in Venice to inspire designs for a revival of *Othello* or *Venice Preserved* (Brereton, vol. 1, p. 295). He could not have anticipated that, in Tunis, his imagination would be sparked by the picturesque figure of a Levantine Jew 'whose romantic appearance and patriarchal dignity against the background of his native landscape was so much at variance with the popular conception of his race which was held by Western Europeans' (L. Irving, p. 333). Irving returned home determined to recreate that dignity in *The Merchant*, telling his acting manager Bram Stoker, 'I never contemplated doing the piece which did not appeal very much to me until we were down in Morocco and the Levant. You know the *Walrus* ... put into all sorts of places. When I saw the Jew in what seemed his own land and in his own dress, Shylock became a very different creature. I began to understand him; and now I want to play the part – as soon as I can' (Stoker, vol. 1, p. 84).

This narrative reveals two things: first, the Victorians' fascination with historical accuracy in their stage productions, and second, their attempt to bring a realistic awareness of cultural difference to the portrayal of 'the other'. The nineteenth century had firmly ensconced Shakespeare behind the proscenium arch, inhibiting the fluidity of action for which his plays were known: thus removed from their audiences, productions depended more and more heavily on spectacle – on lavishly representational illusions of 'reality' – to please the public, and often the sets earned the loudest applause,' just as they do on the stages of London and New York today. The elaborate realisations of specific locales, so alien to the neutral space of the Elizabethan theatre, may have been an inevitable cultural by-product of British imperialism, resonant of the material wealth which conquest had brought; certainly, as Richard Foulkes

Figure 1 Henry Irving as Shylock at the Lyceum Theatre, 1879. Courtesy of The Mansell Collection Ltd.

suggests, they were reinforced by the Victorian appetite for historical exhibitions of all kinds (*Victorian Stage*, pp. 5–6). Irving, I should note, for the most part used only painted canvas in his sets for *The Merchant*; and though his decision to do so may have been dictated by the constraints of time, he claimed thereby to 'have endeavoured to avoid hampering the natural action of the piece with any unnecessary embellishment' (preface to his acting edition of *The Merchant of Venice*). His sets, executed by designer Hawes Craven, nonetheless were praised for their rich and sombre colours and for their archaeological detail in depicting Renaissance Venice (Moore, pp. 205–6). His sumptuous costumes, too, were clearly patterned on those of Renaissance painters. As one spectator observed, 'The pictures of Moroni and Titian had been studied for the dove-coloured cloaks and jerkins, the violet merchant's gown of Antonio, the short hats ... and the frills. The general tone was that of one of Paolo Veronese's pictures' (Fitzgerald, p. 103). Irving's trip to Venice, therefore, powerfully inspired his imagination with images of an earlier, vastly wealthy commercial empire whose culture the Victorians had in many ways tried to emulate.

More importantly, the narrative reveals Irving's fascination with the Jew. He was inspired to play a role, not to mount a historical pageant, and everything would be subordinated to his playing of that role (Foulkes, 'Trial Scene', p. 313). His attraction to the Levantine Jew sprang in part from a Victorian interest in what we now call the Third World, those peoples whom the English had subjugated to their imperial will and whom they now were refashioning in their own image. The English prided themselves on their toleration: after centuries of blatant anti-Semitism, Jews, albeit few, were becoming assimilated into the highest ranks of society and were gaining access to political power; a Rothschild was elected to Parliament in 1847, and Benjamin Disraeli, who according to one observer resembled Irving in manner and speech, was Prime Minister when Irving first staged *The Merchant* (Fraser, pp. 313–14; also Craig, p. 191). Irving thus focused attention on questions of social morality raised by Shylock – the rights accorded to aliens, the prejudices of those in power – which he regarded as central to Shakespeare's art. For him, Shakespeare was an eminent Victorian and the stage a forum to advance the moral agenda of a nation, as these remarks made in 1881 suggest: 'If you uphold the theatre honestly, liberally, frankly, and with discrimination, the stage will uphold in the future, as it has in the past, the literature, the manners, the morals, the fame, and the genius of our country' (Irving, *The Drama*, p. 31).

These are the words of a man confident of his own national values; and indeed, everything about his conception of Shylock reflected this cultural imperialism. What struck Irving most about the Levantine Jew was not his exotic difference so much as his inherent dignity and patriarchal nobility. Years later he recalled his impression of that Jew: 'I saw a Jew once, in Tunis, tear his hair and raiment, fling himself in the sand, and writhe in a rage, about a question of money – beside himself with passion.' This much would seem to conform to the anti-Semitic caricature of the previous age; but Irving insisted that the Jew quickly regained his composure: 'he was old, but erect, even stately, and full of resource. As he walked behind his team of mules he carried himself with the lofty air of a king' (Hatton, p. 269). By conceiving Shylock in this regal image, Irving transformed him from a seething, malevolent Semite into a natural aristocrat, 'almost the only gentleman in the play'. If he rejected the demeaning stereotype of Shylock as 'a mere Houndsditch usurer', he replaced it with another, nobler stereotype which betrayed an impulse to universalise Shylock as strong as that of actors who had once sought to reduce him to comic villainy: 'Shakespeare's Jew', Irving claimed, 'was ... not a mere individual ... [but] a type of the great, grand race ... a man famous on the Rialto; probably a foremost man in his synagogue – proud of his descent – conscious of his moral superiority to many of the Christians who scoffed at him, and fanatic enough, as a religionist, to believe that his vengeance had in it the element of godlike justice' (Hatton, p. 269).

It is one thing to argue this in theory, quite another to put it in practice. Irving of course realised that Shylock *was* an individual and had to be played as such, and that his decision to play Shylock as a gentleman therefore demanded more specific justification. Interviewed while on tour in America in 1884, he provided such justification in terms that sound like special pleading. Shylock, he argued, 'is a merchant, who trades in the Rialto, and Bassanio and Antonio are not ashamed to borrow money of him, nor to carry off his daughter. The position of the daughter is, more or less, a key to his own. She is the friend of Portia' (Hatton, p. 265). This is a wilful misreading of the text: there is no evidence Shylock was himself a merchant, Bassanio and Antonio do indeed have qualms about borrowing from Shylock, and the suggestion that Jessica's 'friendship' with Portia (when they have never met before) attests to her father's gentility borders on the absurd. Nevertheless, Victorians were prepared to accept this as a perfectly reasonable defence of Shylock and, with it, to dismiss the conception of him as a usurer:

> Shylock was well-to-do – a Bible-read man, as his readiness at quotations shows; and there is nothing in his language, at any time, that indicates the snuffling *usurer* which some persons regard him, and certainly nothing to justify the use the early actors made of the part for the low comedian. He was a religious Jew; learned, for he conducted his case with masterly skilfulness, and his speech is always lofty and full of dignity. Is there a finer language in Shakespeare than Shylock's defence of his race?
>
> (Hatton, p. 266)

Shylock's sentiments, of course, are not always lofty; some do indeed expose him as a snuffling usurer (though Irving purged the most blatant of them to preserve his decorous image); and to argue that Shylock's quotation of the Bible identifies him as a learned man falls little short of perverse, for 'The devil can cite Scripture for his purpose' (I.iii.90). Most revealing of all, however, is Irving's celebration of Shylock's 'I am a Jew' as a defence of his race. This speech, as we have seen, builds inexorably towards Shylock's justification of revenge – a loathsome end, no matter what the provocation – and in the past it had been delivered as such. But Irving passed over its immediate dramatic function to universalise it as a plea for racial tolerance. Perhaps nothing better indicates the Victorians' willingness to redeem the Jew in light of their own cultural values.

Irving's Shylock, therefore, was very much the product of his age, a man marked by an intense pathos and a keen sense of injury that bespoke the refined sensibilities of his race, a businessman whose dignity and intelligence, to the outrage of some, rivalled those of a Rothschild (L. Irving, p. 355). However distorted, this interpretation of Shylock came as a revelation to audiences. Yet it smacked of a cultural solipsism masquerading as moral enlightenment, for in fact Irving seemed unable to imagine refinement and dignity in anyone whose manners did not ape those of the Victorians themselves. A review of his performance in the *Chicago Tribune* cited in *Mr. Henry Irving and Miss Ellen Terry in America* confirms this suspicion with its myopic self-righteousness: 'It is a nineteenth century Shylock ... a creation only possible to our age, which has pronounced its verdict against medieval cruelty and medieval blindness.'

Irving's sense of historical verisimilitude, therefore, both in the design of his production and in his portrayal of Shylock, was more anachronistic, idealised, and even operatic than his audiences realised. Always compellingly believable, his *Merchant* tended to romanticise Shakespeare's play by heightening its pathos and striving for grand theatrical effects. Yet these effects, seldom simple, demonstrated the subtle psychological nuances of which Irving's naturalistic acting (as it was then conceived) was capable. They were in evidence the very first time Shylock appeared. The set, 'A Public Place in Venice', occupied the full depth of the stage (Hughes, 'Shylock', p. 252). Behind the wall of a quay, which spanned the entire upstage area, ran a canal in which a small ship was moored: it was outlined against a backcloth depicting the imposing colonnade of the Doge's Palace in the distance. Steps at stage centre led from a rostrum down to the quay, littered with bales left there by coolies in scene i, and it was down these steps that Irving made his memorable entrance.

Given the priorities of the Victorian theatre and the relative immaturity of Irving's company, it is not surprising that reviewers described Irving's entrance in detail while virtually ignoring how others in the cast essayed their roles. Salanio and Salarino were dismissed as 'skipping, featherbrained fops' (*Blackwood's Edinburgh Magazine*, December 1879, p. 650); the middle-aged Antonio of Henry Forrester impressed critics as dull and weak (*The Times*, 3 November 1879); and Bassanio, played by the company's juvenile lead, proved so innocuous that he was soon replaced by another. None of them could match the richly textured performance of Irving's Shylock. The tapping of his walking stick could be heard before he appeared; it hinted that he was old and infirm enough to need the support of a cane. A glimpse of Shylock proved this to be so: he was a man near 60, a bit stooped, with an iron-grey wisp of beard (*The Spectator*, 8 November 1879). He was dressed soberly, not unlike the other men doing business on the Rialto: his fur-trimmed brown gaberdine, faced with black, and a short robe underneath it were relieved by a multi-coloured sash; and on his head he wore a cap with a yellow stripe, an historical emblem of Jewish oppression (see Figure 1). In the opinion of Percy Fitzgerald, he was 'not the conventional Hebrew usurer with patriarchal beard and flowing robe, dirty and hook-nosed, but a picturesque and refined Italianised Jew, genteelly dressed, a dealer in money in the country of Lorenzo de' Medici' (p. 131).

An anonymous account of Irving's performance in the British Theatre Museum titled *Critical Notes on Shylock as Played by Sir Henry Irving*, handwritten by a contemporary who must have seen the play on numerous occasions, provides a wealth of detail. Shylock descended the steps to the quay slowly, looking suspiciously at Bassanio as he muttered 'Three thousand ducats, well' (I.iii.1), drawing figures on the floor with his walking stick as if debating the sum, and pausing after each line to let Bassanio linger in uncertainty. Irving used pauses and hesitations as a strategy to suggest that he was revolving the advantages of the bargain in his mind; but on 'I will be assured I may' (24) he became suddenly defiant. Thereafter his acting grew compulsively unpredictable. The 'deadly rancour' with which he 'hissed out' his scorn of Antonio – 'I hate him for he is a Christian' (34) – dramatically contrasted with the 'affected courtesy' with which he greeted him. He delivered his account of Jacob with patriarchal reverence, but that reverence soon yielded to bitterness as he upbraided his old enemy for past injustices – 'Signor Antonio, many a time and oft ...' (98) – bending low in mock humility to recite 'Fair sir, you spat on me on Wednesday last' (118) and delivering with particular fervour 'Hath a dog money?' (113), a line which, according to the anonymous account, 'revealed a whole chapter in the history of the Jews, as Shylock, the individual was, for the nonce, Shylock the representative of the whole tribe of Israel'. The alacrity with which reviewers saw in Shylock's performance a whole 'history of the Jews' indicates how snugly Irving had fitted his interpretation to prevailing cultural biases.

This speech became the psychological cornerstone of Irving's portrayal. Throughout it he stood apart, a strange and gaunt figure, varying his gestures, first rigid with scorn, then low with studied humility. Its passion carried over to his next speech as well – 'Why look you how you storm!' (130) – which a note in Irving's acting edition suggests made Shylock aware that he, not Antonio, had lost control. Suddenly conscious of his error, he craftily drew himself in, adopting a propitiating manner on 'I would be friends with you' (131) and assuming an injured innocence in order to further his plot. Half cringing, half mocking, with his arms outspread, shoulders raised and head bowed, he sought to soothe Antonio. On 'This kindness will I show' (136), a stage direction in Irving's prompt book indicates that he 'Places his hand upon him, at which Antonio draws back resentfully. At this Shylock draws a foot apart, showing (aside) his enmity, although he assumes friendship' (Mellish prompt book, p. 39). Several reviewers commented on this moment, noting that Shylock's contempt was finely etched when 'he touched the Christian merchant, and, seeing the action resented, bowed deprecatingly with an affectation of deep humility' (*Saturday Review*, 8 November 1879).

Antonio's shrinking from Shylock spoke worlds about the social ostracism the Jew had suffered and elicited great sympathy for him, even to the point of justifying (for some) his nomination of a pound of flesh in the bond. Irving later spoke about his playing of the scene:

> One of the interesting things for an actor to do is to try to show when Shylock is inspired with the idea of this bargain, and to work out by impersonation the Jew's thought in his actions. My view is, that from the moment Antonio turns upon him, declaring he is 'like to spit upon him again,' and invites him scornfully to lend the money, not as to a friend, but rather to his enemy ... from that moment I imagine Shylock resolving to propose his pound of flesh, perhaps without any hope of getting it. Then he puts on that hypocritical show of pleasantry which so far deceives them as to elicit from Antonio the remark that 'The Hebrew will turn Christian; he grows kind.'
>
> (Hatton, p. 267)

According to the anonymous account, the intensity of Shylock's hatred reached a climax when, after Bassanio and Antonio had exited laughing, he walked slowly to the steps, ascended two, paused, then turned to the audience 'as shaking with rage he raised his stick above his head and uttered an inarticulate curse in his throat three times'.

Such potent stage images help to explain how Irving transformed Shylock into his finest tragic role, a vengeful victim of racial intolerance. Yet performances do not remain static during the run of a play; they change according to audience response, or the actor's mood, or circumstance, and Irving was not immune to such things. His Shylock perceptibly coarsened over the years, growing more adamant in his lust for Antonio's flesh (Lelyveld, pp. 91–5). A stage direction in a prompt book used for an American tour in 1895 and copied by Fuller Mellish, who played Lorenzo, calls for 'a cry of fiendish and cruel exultation' from Shylock at the end of I.iii. as his hand reaches out in a grasping manner, like a tiger to seize his prey (pp. 26–7). The scene with Tubal in particular afforded Irving an opportunity for big emotional effects. Although his playing of the scene originally was restrained, reviewers within a few years began to comment on the ferocity he displayed on hearing news of Antonio's losses. A critic in the *Manchester Guardian* noted in 1881 that, in contrast to his performance two years earlier, Irving 'kindles very rapidly into flame ... there is, indeed, something animal in the Jew's entire loss of self-control, and Mr. Irving spares us no detail of the wild eyes, wolfish teeth, and foaming mouth – but it is consummately played' (Brereton, vol. 1, p. 346). Audiences apparently liked such unrestraint, and Irving offered them more of it. He delivered his lament beginning 'Why there, there, there, there!' (III.i.66) with a strange 'mixture of rapacity, pathetic despair and stunned abstraction', according to the anonymous account, cutting references to his ducats in order to focus attention on the loss of his daughter (Moore, p. 202). And to compound the agony of 'loss upon loss', he opened his robe and repeatedly smote himself on the breast, slowly and heavily, perhaps in the manner of the Jew he had once seen in Tunis (Winter, pp. 139, 190). Such histrionics might have alienated audiences from a lesser actor, but Irving never lost their sympathy. Indeed, for all one knows, he might have deliberately coarsened his performance with an actor's sense of daring to see whether he could snatch tragic pathos from the jaws of excess.

However histrionic, these effects at least were validated by the text. But Irving occasionally embellished his tragic portrayal with stage business that went beyond the text. In II.iii, for example, a conflation of Shakespeare's II.v and II.vi, he staged a spectacle contrasting Shylock's sobriety with the festive abduction of Jessica that, for effect, rivalled grand opera. The set, designated 'Shylock's house by a bridge', was extravagant – one hundred stage hands were required to set it up – for against the Venetian backdrop Irving had constructed a practicable bridge over the canal (Hughes, 'Shylock', pp. 254–5). This idea was not new: Charles Kean had included such a bridge in his production of 1858, but it had not been put to such dramatic use as Irving was to put it (see Figure 2). Over that bridge Shylock left to dine with the Christians. No longer drab, he was now attired in a robe of rich design with a bright scarf to cover his head, 'flaunt[ing] his wealth in the Christian dogs' faces', in the opinion of Ellen Terry (*Memoirs*, p. 147). After a silent leave-taking of Jessica, he slowly wound his way up the steps of the bridge, leaning heavily on his stick, lantern in hand, and murmuring to himself, 'Fast bind, fast find' (II.v.52). Pausing at the top, he glanced once more at the home he was loath to leave; then, keeping his eyes fixed on his daughter, he slowly ambled off.

What followed was an interlude of Irving's own invention that grew increasingly elaborate over the years, as a comparison of prompt books shows. In the original production, which used

Figure 2 Setting by William Telbin for Act II of Charles Kean's production, 1858. Courtesy of the Shakespeare Centre Library, Stratford-upon-Avon.

a prompt book now located in the British Theatre Museum, a gondola carrying a lady and a zither-playing noble passed along the canal while masquers – three ladies, two gentlemen – entered laughing and climbed the steps in order to catch a glimpse of the gondola. Gratiano, Solanio, and Salarino, wearing masks and dominoes, passed them as they entered and conversed for thirteen lines, decorously omitting Gratiano's references to 'the strumpet wind', at which point another gondola, festooned with lanterns and full of revellers, moved on slowly and stopped before Jessica's window, where she was serenaded with a barcarolle (p. 34). Lorenzo entered; he and Jessica played their brief scene together with much humour as Lorenzo pretended to lose the box of ducats she had thrown to him, and they eloped amid a whirl of masquers with tabors and pipes. Antonio was written out of the scene. Mellish, in his prompt book of some years later, described a more lavish conclusion to the scene. The Belmont-bound party, while making their escape, was met on the bridge by masquers who engaged them in playful mime: Gratiano and Salarino doffed their hats and kissed the ladies, whose escorts feigned to draw swords. Four pierrots then bounded over the bridge and formed a ring on the stage; they were soon joined by more masquers who, preceded by boys and girls strewing flowers, formed a larger ring around them; and together they danced a whirligig of time, pierrots whirling one way, masquers the other (pp. 46–53). When their dance was done, reported *Harper's New Monthly Magazine*, the 'masked revellers, merrily singing, passed in the cold moonlight across the bridge over the canal, while a lighted gondola, with throbbing guitars and blended voices, glided below' (cited in *Mr. Henry Irving and Miss Ellen Terry in America*).

The stage emptied; ripples of laughter died away; one heard the tapping of Shylock's walking stick. Then, in an interpolated scene illustrative of Irving's genius, Shylock entered carrying his lantern, slowly wending his way home from dinner. He crossed the bridge, descended the steps, and crossed stage left to his house. He knocked at the door three times, slowly. There was no answer. He paused: the silence disturbed him. With greater deliberation he knocked again, three times. Then, 'raising his lantern to search the darkened upper windows, across his features came a look of dumb and complete despair' (anonymous account). The curtain fell on this picture of 'unrelieved simplicity' (Lelyveld, pp. 85–6), 'the image of the father convulsed with grief (Winter, p. 182).

Nothing in the production elicited sympathy for Shylock so much as this scene. It provided a moment of calm after the chaos of carnival, of restraint after youthful abandon. Furthermore, by so poignantly portraying a man betrayed by his own flesh and blood, Irving appealed to the sacred Victorian belief in the obedience of children, a belief here violated by a rebellious daughter who, in the opinion of *The Spectator*, 'amply justifies his plain distrust of her, an odious, immodest, dishonest creature, than whom Shakespeare drew no more unpleasant character' (8 November 1879). No one objected that this scene was not Shakespeare's or that it cheapened with sentiment Shakespeare's more rigorous conception of Shylock. And few, if any, recognised its source in the scene where Rigoletto entered his house to discover, with horror, that his daughter had been abducted by masked men who had duped him into holding the ladder for them, his cries of 'Gilda, Gilda!' echoing throughout the opera houses of Europe (Moore, p. 202). This was a time when great composers and librettists, by extracting vivid emotional effects from Shakespeare's plays, were managing to transform them into grand opera. Irving simply reversed the process by importing an effect from Verdi; and in so doing, he made Shylock into a figure whose anguish over his daughter and whose tragic pathos as a freak tricked by his social superiors rivalled those of his great operatic progenitor, the hunchback jester of Mantua.

Irving's penchant for archaeological realism, for creating detailed illusions of place, had inevitable consequences for the shape of the play. As had been the case with other nineteenth-century productions of *The Merchant*, his elaborate staging forced him to compress and rearrange scenes to minimise the number of set changes required: by alternating 'big' scenes with smaller 'front' scenes played before a painted cloth, and by conflating scenes that might reasonably be played together such as II.v and II.vi discussed above, he reduced the number of set changes from nineteen to twelve (Hughes, 'Shylock', p. 251) and, more significantly, reduced the number of alternations between Venice and Belmont by four (Moore, p. 203). For the first two acts the Venetian scenes were played in sequence, broken only by I.ii, which was staged as a front scene; similarly, the wooing scenes at Belmont were conflated and postponed until Act III, where they were played together with only one interruption (a conflation of II.viii and III.i, also staged as a front scene). As a result of such changes, the quick alternation of scenes which Elizabethan staging had facilitated, with the attendant juxtaposition of ideas and values, was replaced by a simpler and structurally damaging isolation of the Venetian (here, tragic) scenes from the Belmont (comic) scenes. This drastically upset the balance that Shakespeare had striven to create and led, eventually, to Granville-Barker's observation that the play's two distinct plots may be irreconcilable.

By giving pride of place to the tragedy of Shylock, Irving in effect suppressed the plot of the three caskets and relegated Belmont to a position inferior to Venice. His displacement of the women's sphere of action further indicated the hegemony of the actor-manager system and, indeed, of the Victorian patriarchy; for although Irving was praised by his contemporaries for restoring a relatively complete text of *The Merchant*, he in fact used less of the text than his two most scenically lavish predecessors, Charles Kean and the Bancrofts, and was particularly brutal in cutting the Belmont scenes (Moore, p. 203). As might be expected, he omitted passages that disparaged Shylock: Solanio and Salarino's derogatory remarks about him – 'his stones, his daughter, and his ducats' – in II.viii and their mockery of him – 'Out upon it, old carrion' – in III.i; the whole of Lancelot Gobbo's spirited exchange with Jessica about her father's tyranny in II.iii; and their similar banter in III.v. Such omissions helped to preserve Shylock's decorum as a tragic figure by denying his affinity with earlier comic stage Jews. Deeper cuts, however, were made in the casket plot: the Prince of Arragon disappeared altogether (thus, presumably, leaving the audience in the dark as to which was the casket when Bassanio made his choice), and Morocco's two scenes were compressed into one, II.i serving as an introduction to his selection of the gold casket in II.vii. As a result, the thematic significance of hazarding all one has – a pursuit Portia's suitors have in common with the venture capitalists in Venice – was markedly weakened, for the audience could not readily weigh events in Belmont against those in Venice.

Other cuts were made to avoid offending Victorian sensibilities. Shylock, for instance, was not allowed to speak of urine, nor Gratiano of cuckoldry. Portia's wit was the chief victim of Irving's scalpel; as Alan Hughes notes (p. 252), she 'has a bawdy streak in her character which was mercilessly eradicated'. Irving did not allow her to be so bold as to suggest that a hot temper may leap o'er a cold decree (I.ii.17–20) nor so worldly as to speculate that the Neapolitan prince's mother might have played false with a smith (41–3). She was too decorous to insult the English and the Scots (54–79), too prudent to risk saying that she would do anything rather than marry a sponge (94–5), too obedient to entertain the idea of circumventing her father's will (99–104). The impulse to transform Portia into a Victorian lady determined cuts in her later scenes as well: she was not allowed to mention hell (III.ii.18–21, III.iv.11–21), nor to take delight in a male disguise that might suggest she is 'accomplished with that [she] lacks' (III.iv.60–1), nor to taunt Bassanio that she would deny neither her body nor her bed to the learned doctor (V.i.227–33). Irving may not have realised that by trying to make Portia conform to the manners of his own sexually repressed society, he was robbing her of a wit and earthiness that had once made her a credible antagonist for Shylock.

Or perhaps he did; for some cuts blatantly demonstrate Irving's will to suppress the romance of the casket plot in favour of the bond plot. He was most ruthless in III.ii, from which he pruned nearly seventy lines, eviscerating Bassanio's role and reducing Portia's considerably as well. Gone is Portia's apostrophe to 'these naughty times' that 'puts bars between the owners and their rights' (18–19); gone, the charming lines in which she banters with Bassanio about being 'upon the rack' (25–7). Gone is the lyrical effusion in which she compares him first to a new-crowned monarch, then to Alcides – 'He may win, and what is music then?' (47–62); gone, too, his Petrarchan praise of her eyes, the most ornately romantic passage in the play (115–29). Gone, his comparison of himself to an athlete who still stands in doubt of the prize (141–6); gone, his confession of a wild feeling of joy when he is no longer in doubt (177–83). The effect of these cuts is to streamline the scene, to eliminate lyrical expressions of passion in order to get right to the heart of the matter: Bassanio's choice of the lead casket, his claiming Portia as his prize, and her dedication of herself and her wealth to him. The fundamentals of the plot remain, but much of what invests them with romantic beauty is lost. Clearly Irving wished to stage the scene with dispatch in order to get on with the trial, and Shylock's apotheosis.

Paradoxically, however, this scenic arrangement allowed Act III – which, in Irving's script, included all the Belmont scenes from Morocco's entrance to Bassanio's departure for Venice – to unfold at its own pace and to find its own rhythm. Belmont, as a consequence, emerged as a world morally and aesthetically at odds with Venice, resistant to the correspondences one might have discovered on the Elizabethan stage. Here, Ellen Terry was free to indulge herself by playing the wooing scenes as drawing-room comedy. In her, Irving had found a master-mistress of comic art. She had played Portia before, opposite Coughlin in the Bancrofts' unsuccessful production a few years earlier; Irving's production thus afforded her an opportunity to draw on her earlier conception of the role and, over the next twenty years, to refine it. An emotional actress whose 'tears follow[ed] quickly upon her laughter' (Winter, p. 69), she captivated critics with her natural grace, her charm, her gaiety, her intelligence. The *Chicago Daily News* found 'her comedy exquisite, her pathos touching, and her elocution round as a middle-age madrigal in the mouths of cathedral chorister boys' (cited in *Mr. Henry Irving and Miss Ellen Terry in America*). William Winter concurred: 'Her voice is perfect music. Her clear, bell-like execution is more than a refreshment – it is a luxury ... Her simple manner, always large and adequate, with nothing puny or mincing about it, is a great beauty of the art which it so deftly conceals' (p. 36). Perhaps this was the key to Terry's popularity: she had a generosity that concealed art.

Her playing of the scene with Bassanio amply displayed that generosity. The curtain rose to reveal a formal drawing room graced with elegant furniture and potted palms – more Victorian than it was Venetian. Portia and Nerissa were discovered on a settee; a page stood behind them, three women attendants upstage. Portia was 'radiantly beautiful in her Venetian robes of gold-coloured brocaded satin, with the look of a picture by Giorgione' (Brereton, vol. 1, p. 306); her hair, too, was gold. In fact, Michael Booth suggests that Terry appealed to audiences as a work of art who, by combining the images of both maiden and temptress, became a cultural icon for Victorian womanhood: she was an enchantress of gold mixed with virginal beauty – a twinning not unfamiliar to the Pre-Raphaelites (p. 83). Such aesthetic appeal was reinforced by the charm of her acting, at once chaste and coy. When Bassanio entered – handsomely attired in rose-coloured silken hose, a golden doublet, and a long rose cloak slung over one shoulder – she greeted him eagerly, unafraid to show her love but a bit coquettish. She caressed his hand rather forwardly while urging him to tarry (*Blackwood's*, December 1879, p. 653), but on 'Beshrew your eyes!' (III.ii.14) she turned blushingly away, holding a fan between their faces as if to hide her embarrassment. When he moved to the caskets, *The Times* reported that she seemed sorely tempted to break her vow; anxiety could be 'seen in her face, in her eyes, in her twitching fingers' (3 November 1879); and while he made his choice, she engaged in romantic byplay with him that many reviewers commented on: her 'surging love ... ever and anon would vent itself in ejaculations more eloquent than words' (*The Referee*, 2 November 1879). Nevertheless, when Bassanio touched the casket of lead, 'she did not fly to him, she let him open the casket, find the picture, read the legend, and sat there looking at him, smiling and quoting the legend ahead of his reading' (*San Francisco Chronicle*, 6 September 1893). Her restraint fled, however, when he knelt before her to claim the prize: she gave him her hand, he rose to embrace her; as she spoke to him of 'the full sum of me' (157) she allowed him to place her hands on his breast; and at the conclusion of her speech 'she submissively and tenderly hid her face upon his breast' as well (Mellish, pp. 72–3).

Such behaviour may seem tame enough to a modern audience, but for a few Victorian critics it proved unacceptably demonstrative. An anonymous review in *Blackwood's* not only found her too forward to preserve the essential modesty of Portia, but found that forwardness the more offensive for being *public*. The reviewer complained that 'too much of what Rosalind calls "a coming-on disposition" in Miss Terry's bearing towards her love ... might tempt her to break her father's will' (p. 653); and here, as in the matter of Jessica's elopement, we tread on the sacred Victorian ground of family obligation, especially that of the child to her father. Terry, the reviewer observed, 'fails especially to suggest the Portia that, as Shakespeare most carefully makes us aware, would have sacrificed even her love for Bassanio, deep as it is, had he failed to win her by the process appointed by her father'. In reviews of this production, as in Irving's own remarks, Shakespeare keeps resurfacing as an eminent Victorian.

It was an open secret that this critic was none other than Theodore Martin, husband of Helen Faucit, who had been the great Portia of the preceding generation. Faucit's Portia had epitomised traditional Victorian womanhood – mature, not at all girlish, 'a woman of strong character and high intellectual culture' according to Martin's biography of his wife (p. 324; also Foulkes, 'Helen Faucit', pp. 27–37). Her portrayal had emphasised such values as self-sacrifice in love, obedience to the father's will, and righteousness in pleading the Christian cause – such emphases as made her acting in the trial scene more convincing than in the wooing scenes. That some professional jealousy may have crept into her husband's appraisal of Terry's more spirited performance should not surprise us; but he was not alone in his criticism. John Ruskin, in a famous letter, censured Terry for failing to achieve the 'majestic humility' he thought was owed Portia (L. Irving, p. 346); Henry James likewise objected that she was 'too free and familiar, too osculatory in her relations with Bassanio' (James, p. 143); and in his introduction to the play in *The Henry Irving Shakespeare*, F. A. Marshall concurred, though less censoriously, that 'one cannot help thinking that, if her father's absurd legacy of the caskets had resulted in the choice of an uncongenial husband, Portia would not have found it difficult to set aside the parental injunction in spirit if not in letter' (p. 252).

Such carping was perhaps an inevitable response to a Portia who was an original – a young, impulsive, blithe spirit, as original in her way as Irving's Shylock was in his. Terry herself admitted that her Portia was more wilful and independent than audiences were accustomed to: where Helen Faucit had invoked the bonds of family loyalty to defend submission to her father's will, Terry struck a liberationist stance as the 'new woman' who used her wits to get her way and thereby challenged traditional Victorian expectations of female behaviour. In a lecture titled 'The Triumphant Women', she noted that she had found the commentary of Danish critic Georg Brandes useful to her conception of Portia as 'independent, almost masculine in her attitude towards life'. 'This orphan heiress', she explained, 'has been in a position of authority from childhood. She is used to acting on her own authority ... She is the spoiled child of fortune, or would be if she were not so generous' (*Four Lectures*, p. 117). How, then, does Terry justify Portia's surrendering all she has to Bassanio? 'It is clear that Portia's gracious surrender is a "beau geste", and little more. The proof is that she retains her independence of thought and action' (p. 118). Here is a new reading of the text indeed. As further proof that she regarded Portia as self-determined, Terry commented in her *Memoirs* that she had been persuaded by an Italian essay to believe that Portia chose the song 'Tell me where is fancy bred' deliberately to tip off Bassanio as to which casket contained her picture. 'And why shouldn't Portia sing the song herself?', she asked. 'She could make the four rhymes, "bred, head, nourished, fed" set the word "lead" ringing in Bassanio's ears. A woman of Portia's sort couldn't possibly remain passive in such a crisis in her life' (p. 152).

What Terry thought in 1908, of course, may not be what she thought in 1879. She grew in her roles and, as the years passed, grew also in her feminist convictions. Martin was the only critic of her original performance who had accused her of actually violating the spirit of her father's will; others had noted only her *potential* for doing so. Her Portia was unconventional but not, finally, subversive. As Terry put it, Portia was 'the fruit of the Renaissance, the child of the period of beautiful clothes, beautiful cities, beautiful houses, beautiful ideas' (*Four Lectures*, p. 116). Although Terry attributed these things to the Renaissance, her conception of the role was clearly anachronistic; for what she portrayed was a young woman of Victorian London whose manners might grace a drawing room in Mayfair (Boston *Evening Transcript*, 13 December 1883). As such, her Portia happily sacrificed dignity – even modesty – for the new spirit of the age. After all, one critic asked, how much dignity could there be in a Portia who 'lounges idly on the sofa as Nerissa describes her lovers?' (Scott, p. 169).

Ironically, Faucit's Portia might have been tonally more consistent with Irving's Shylock than Terry's was: her high seriousness, maturity, and sense of decorum would have made her a more appropriate antagonist for him at the trial and truer to the moral dimension he tried to bring to the play. Yet paradoxically, by allowing the casket and bond plots to develop almost independently of one another, each in its own style, Irving's production realised the play's potential to be both moral tragedy *and* romantic comedy – two plays in one; and in doing so, it honoured the text's competing generic claims more fully than Irving may have recognised, or wished.

In the trial scene the two styles clashed – and the male hegemony of the actor-manager system asserted itself – most royally. This was to be the climax of Irving's tragic performance, and Ellen Terry was expected to accommodate her style of acting to his. The evocation of the ducal palace itself seemed to favour the heightened realism at which Irving was so skilled. According to Percy Fitzgerald, the set, 'with its ceiling painted in the Verrio style, its portraits of Doges, the crimson walls with gilt carvings, and the admirable arrangements of the throne, etc., surely for taste, contrivance, and effect has never been matched' (p. 130; also Foulkes, 'Trial Scene', pp. 313–16). But his description does not do justice to the operatic spectacle to which the audience was treated. The stage was crowded with spectators – nobles, guards, and clerks. With a flourish of trumpets, eight Magnificoes in black velvet caps and gowns, followed by the Doge 'habited in a rich crimson cap and robe' with pages holding his train, entered and marched to their places on the dais (Boston *Herald*, 13 December 1879). This much was similar to Charles Kean's staging. But among the spectators in the rear, Irving included Tubal and a small gathering of Jews (*Athenaeum*, 8 November 1879, p. 605); and the use to which he put them attested to the universality of racism and once again distinguished his production from its predecessors.

The prompt book transcribed by Mellish details how the scene began. Part of the crowd of spectators

> point and jeer as two Jews enter. One of the Jews brushes against Gratiano who angrily resents it. Solanio and Salarino interpose and the Jew retires upstage right, joining the other Jew. While this has been going on, some of the crowd at the back – all of whom have been watching the foregoing – take the opportunity to jeer at three Jews who are amongst them; the guards interpose across the barrier, and with their halberds, gently force the three Jews into a corner by themselves right. The rest of the crowd now keep apart from them.
>
> (p. 89)

By opening the scene in this way, Irving conditioned his audience to sympathise with these Jews before a line of dialogue was spoken. When he entered, looking gaunt and older in the short gown for which he had exchanged his gaberdine, he scanned the crowd for a friendly face, spotted one of the Jews upstage right, went to him, then gently and fervently pressed his hand (Mellish, p. 90): Irving clearly wanted Shylock to be regarded not as a solitary victim, but as belonging to a whole persecuted race.

Furthermore, he used these Jews as a silent chorus to direct the audience's responses to Shylock. They provided a kind of cheering section, 'laughing at his mordant jests' and cueing the audience to laugh as well (Odell, vol. 2, p. 423). Those jests were made with an irony that suggested the theatrical control of which this Shylock was capable: the 'grotesque touch of humour' when he suddenly produced the scales from the folds of his garment, for example, 'never failed to cause amusement'; nor did his mock surprise at Portia's request that he have a surgeon ready: 'Without a word Shylock came to her side, peered over her shoulder with short sighted eyes at the document in her hands, and pointing at the various items with his knife as if to find it there inscribed, his face all the while expressing a bland simplicity mingled with cunning, said "Is it so nominated in the bond?"' (Fitzgerald, p. 107). He maintained control of the scene in other ways as well, tempering his malice with tones of subdued scorn, refusing to raise his voice, remaining calmly indifferent to Portia's pleas, Gratiano's gibes, and Bassanio's offers of gold. Here was none of the melodramatic exultation or 'fiendish eagerness' that had characterised the performances of Macklin and Kean at the trial: the fixed purpose of Irving's more naturalistic Shylock was better communicated through the controlled emphasis with which he spoke four key lines, underscored and rewritten in the interleafings of one of his prompt books, now at the Folger Shakespeare Library (Lelyveld, p. 88): *I would have my bond, I stand for judgement, I stand here for law,* and *I stay here on my bond* (IV.i.87, 103, 142, 238).

Nor did Shylock lose control in defeat. When the judgement came, it appeared to strike him 'like lightning' (*Saturday Review*, 8 November 1879); crushed, he dropped his knife and his scales and stood as though mesmerised, his lips murmuring incoherent words (Scott, p. 70). The provision that he become a Christian hit him particularly hard, and its force was registered in the shock of the Jews who looked on, 'among whom the sentence condemning Shylock to deny his religion falls like a thunderbolt' (*The Theatre*, November 1879, p. 274). Yet this was but a prelude to the heroic performance that followed when, like the Tunisian Jew who had once so impressed Irving, Shylock regained his composure and 'left the court with a dignity that seemed the true expression of his belief in his nation and himself' (*Saturday Review*, 8 November 1879). This exit, for which Irving used the whole width of the stage, has been most fully described by Irving's grandson, who gleaned details from many contemporary accounts:

> When Shylock grasped the severity of his sentence, his eyelids became heavy as though he was hardly able to lift them and his eyes became lustreless and vacant. The words 'I am not well' ...' were the plea of a doomed man to be allowed to leave the court and to die in utter loneliness. But Gratiano's ill-timed jibe governed Shylock's exit. He turned. [Bram Stoker recalls that Irving 'dropped his shoulder and shrank from the touch of Gratiano', vol. 2, p. 296.] Slowly and steadily the Jew scanned his tormentor from head to foot, his eyes resting on the Italian's face with concentrated scorn. The proud rejection of insult and injustice lit up his face for a moment, enough for the audience to feel a strange relief in knowing that, in that glance, Shylock had triumphed ... As he reached the door and put out his hand towards it, he was seized with a crumpling convulsion. It was but a momentary weakness indicated with great subtlety. Then, drawing himself up to his full height once more, Shylock bent his gaze defiantly upon the court and stalked out.
>
> (L. Irving, pp. 343–4)

At the last, Irving's Shylock was intensely human. As Lelyveld concludes, 'overshadowing his threefold role of usurer, outraged father and vengeful creditor, is the haunting figure of a retreating, broken old man' (pp. 90–1). Ellen Terry's engaging young doctor of laws could not compete with such tragic pathos. She was a figure from a different play, and though reviewers praised her refined delivery of 'The quality of mercy', no one regarded her as an opponent worthy of Shylock. In a scene where Portia's victory traditionally had been thought to represent the triumph of mercy over mean-spirited legalism, Irving muted the allegory and made Portia the agent of Shylock's tragic downfall instead. Terry recognised that she and Irving were working at artistic cross-purposes. 'I found that H I's Shylock necessitated an entire revision of my conception of Portia,' she complained in her *Memoirs*, 'especially in the trial scene, but here there was no point of honour involved. I had considered, and still am of the same mind, that

Portia in the trial scene ought to be very *quiet*. I saw an extraordinary effect in this quietness. But as Henry's Shylock was quiet, I had to give it up. His heroic saint was splendid, but it wasn't good for Portia' (p. 128).

Here, apparently, was yet another instance of the actor-manager imposing his will on a text and expecting others in his company to gauge their performances accordingly. But Terry was as strong-willed as Irving; and if she couldn't play Portia as she wished in this scene, she nevertheless resisted playing the role *his* way. Instead of the naturalism he strove for, which would have required her to make her male disguise as credible as possible, she acted 'Balthasar' in a charmingly romantic style appropriate for light Victorian comedy and consistent with her playing of the wooing scenes. In other words, she played Portia still, and *Blackwood's* understandably found her too 'little in earnest' to convince either the audience of her masculinity or the court of her serious purpose (December 1879, p. 653). *The Spectator*, which elsewhere praised Terry's performance, complained of 'the absence of all pretence at incognito' and 'the absurdity of a quantity of curling hair under the beretta of a lawyer in a piece costumed with such elaborate accuracy in other respects' (8 November 1879). In fact, she used her black silk lawyer's gown (later replaced by an ornate gown of crimson) more to flaunt her femininity than to hide it, and she fooled no one when she archly pretended to shield her face from her husband (*The Theatre*, 1 January 1880). Indeed, observed the aptly named *Truth*, 'she has disguised herself so badly that her husband and anyone else must, unless they were blind, have seen in a moment who she is' (6 November 1879); yet the lines that might best have justified a suspension of her male disguise – 'Your wife would give you little thanks for that ...' (284–5) – were cut (Foulkes, 'Helen Faucit', p. 32). Years later, in response to such criticism, Terry herself maintained that 'the impenetrableness of a disguise is a dramatic convention' that wins instant acceptance in the theatre (*Four Lectures*, p. 119); and however wrong she may have been in this case – however miscalculated the effect of her feminine 'Balthasar' on audiences – her remark nevertheless points to a crucial difference between her conception of how Elizabethan comedy should be played and Irving's. Terry would not for a minute have *expected* to be taken for a male. Her understanding of conventional disguise assumed a ludic element – a sense of play shared with the audience – that by its very nature eschewed naturalism. This, of course, is a defensible way to interpret Portia's role at the trial, but it contradicted and, as the critical comments above suggest, was ultimately swallowed up by the detailed authenticity of Irving's performance.

Irving's bid for tragic pathos also made it difficult for Terry to keep the moral allegiance of the audience, especially at the crucial moment when she stopped him cold with 'no jot of blood' (302). One spectator confessed to being 'distinctly disappointed when, by means of a miserable legal quibble, Shylock was cheated of his pound of Antonio's flesh' (Hiatt, p. 172). This response, of course, suggests how powerfully the emotional appeal of Irving's performance inhibited the ethical appeal of Portia's; and others objected to the staging of the trial precisely because it led to such distortion. Graham Robertson, for instance, argued that Irving's 'heroic martyr upset the balance of the play and ruined Portia's trial scene'. His allocation of the trial scene to Portia reveals a bias grounded in ethos rather than pathos.

> How small and mean sounded her quibbling tricky speeches when addressed to a being who united the soul of Savonarola and the bearing of Charles I with just a touch of Lord Beaconsfield that made for mystery. After her best effect, we momentarily expected the Doge to rise, exclaiming: 'My dear sir, pray accept the apology of the Court for any annoyance that this young person has caused you. By all means take as much of Antonio as you think proper, and if we may throw in a prime cut of Bassanio, and the whole of Gratiano, we shall regard your acceptance of the same as a favour.'
>
> (pp. 54–6)

As if in defiance of the naturalism that led to such distortion, Terry insisted that Portia's behaviour, even at the trial, was motivated not by logic, but by romantic inspiration. Unlike Helen Faucit, who maintained that Portia must have plotted legal strategy with Dr Bellario beforehand and left nothing to chance, not even the quibble, Terry argued that the quibble had sprung spontaneously from Portia's female intuition and had nothing at all to do with Bellario. Taking a liberal stand for the power of woman's intellect, she speculated that Bellario had probably told Portia that the law had no remedy in such cases: 'He advised her to try an appeal to Shylock's mercy, and if that failed, to try another to his cupidity. If *that* failed, well then I fancy the learned Bellario may have suggested trying a threat.' One hears in these remarks some disparagement of male reason, provoked perhaps by Terry's frustration over Irving's refusal to accommodate her style of play.

> To my mind, and I have always tried to *show* this in the trial scene, Portia is acting on a preconcerted plan up to the moment of pronouncing sentence: then she has an inspiration, and acts on that. Hence her 'Tarry a little: there is something else.' There has flashed through her brain suddenly the thought that a pound of flesh is not quite the same as a pound of flesh and blood ... I am convinced that this bit of casuistry was not conceived by Shakespeare as being carefully planned. It strikes me as a lightning-like inspiration – just such an inspiration as a woman might have when she is at her wit's end, and is willing to try anything to avoid defeat.
> (*Four Lectures*, pp. 120–1)

Though to a late twentieth-century ear her analysis may sound like sexual stereotyping, attributing to women an intuition at odds with male rationality, her argument by Victorian standards was decidedly feminist; for by drawing the distinction in favour of women and by speaking of Portia's inspiration in laudatory terms (it is, after all, what saved the men from themselves at the trial), she revealed a strong commitment to what was then regarded as manifestations of the feminine – to intuitive reason, to comic artifice, to romance – in the face of a masculine logic that was always ready to dismiss such things as irrelevant.

To his credit, Irving restored Act V – an act traditionally dropped by actor-managers intent on ending the play with Shylock's downfall. Although he cut all the bawdy from it and, a worse offence, cut some of the loveliest verse in the play, such as Portia and Nerissa's exchange about moonlight and music (92–110), the act nevertheless revived the feminine artifices that had been sacrificed to the cause of naturalism in Act IV and rounded out the play as romantic comedy. The set itself depicted a scene of 'summer luxury' far airier than the heavy interior of the court (Winter, p. 74) – a terraced garden bathed in moonlight against a backdrop of Portia's Palladian villa. Irving achieved the effect of moonlight through new gaslight techniques he had developed, and reviewers were quick to appreciate it: 'The moon rose from the lagune, through the level bars of vapor, over the lighted palace of Belmont', rhapsodised *Harper's*, while 'in the garden, on a seat of marble, Jessica and Lorenzo told their love' (cited in *Mr. Henry Irving and Miss Ellen Terry in America*). Portia entered dressed in 'a train of deep tint of purple silk, bordered with gold embroidery, worn over a petticoat of dull gold' (Indianapolis *Daily Journal*, 9 February 1884) – a costume in which, as the Victorians' golden girl, she could fittingly resume her sparkling style of play. She was, again, charmingly in her element, good humouredly chiding Bassanio for the loss of his ring and magnanimously welcoming all her visitors to the nuptial festivities. A stage direction in Mellish's prompt book illustrates her generosity of spirit: after the couples move to enter her house and Portia has spoken the final line of the play, promising to 'answer all things faithfully' (299) – Gratiano's bawdy last speech has of course been cut – she 'suddenly remembers Antonio, and conveys in pantomime how selfish it was of them to have forgotten him. She turns round, graciously smiles, extends her hand' (p. 125). This resumption of comic values after the tragic sobriety of the trial scene struck a few reviewers as 'an ironic post mortem in which the villains of the Erinyes dance upon the hero's grave' (Hughes, 'Shylock', p. 263), but most were untroubled by the tonal disjunctions caused by the return to Belmont.

Nevertheless, in late May of 1880 the production again fell victim to Irving's agenda as actor-manager. He decided to drop Act V and replace it with Wills's *Iolanthe*, a light vehicle well suited, he thought, to the talents of Ellen Terry. True, its omission was not his last word: he did reinstate the act from time to time. But clearly he had come to regard the play as a vehicle for himself, 'and from this time on he was able to do with or without the fifth act, as mood or policy prompted him' (Lelyveld, pp. 92–3). Certain assumptions were implicit in his decision: first, that it was legitimate to think of Shakespeare's plays, as Victorians were wont to do, as character studies more than total works of art; second, that *The Merchant* belonged to Shylock, not to Portia; third, that as a consequence, the play was tragic rather than comic, and the tone of moral gravity in Shylock's defeat ought not to be jeopardised by a return to comic harmony in the fifth act; fourth, and most condescendingly, that

Ellen Terry's more 'artificial' acting style could be better employed in Victorian comedy than in Shakespeare.

These assumptions, largely unchallenged by his contemporaries, suggest how successfully Irving's *Merchant* captured the spirit of the age. It held the stage until 1905 – a quarter of a century- and spawned a host of imitators. In fact, most productions of the play for the next fifty years paid homage to Irving, directly or indirectly, and his celebrated stage effects were often carried to absurd lengths, as when the Shylock of Beerbohm Tree, having returned home from dining with the Christians, first knocked at the door of his house, then, in a rage, entered, ran to all the windows calling frantically for Jessica, and finally rushed back through the door, flung himself on the ground, tore his garments, and sprinkled ashes on his head (Lelyveld, p. 100). The best clones of Irving's production were more temperate, featuring tastefully representational sets and restrained, dignified Shylocks; but none dimmed the memory of Irving's incomparable achievement. Scant attention was paid to William Poel's attempts in 1898 and 1907 to return to Elizabethan staging practices and to play Shylock as the comic, red-wigged, hook-nosed villain he assumed Shakespeare had intended. Even in the decades between the world wars, audiences persisted in regarding *The Merchant* with Victorian high seriousness and expected their Shylocks to be tragically sympathetic. Winthrop Ames's production of 1928, for which the Mellish prompt book was used, epitomised how Irving's conception had evolved: in it, George Arliss played the most patrician of all Shylocks, a suave, rich, well-tailored broker who made no concessions to comedy, responded stoically to the loss of his daughter and his ducats, and plotted with the poise and intellectual cunning of a Disraeli. Shylock by this time had become 'merely a dignified British gentleman who happened to be playing Shylock' (Lelyveld, p. 110), the logical extension of Irving's attempt to transform the Tunisian Jew into his own countryman. This conception was not effectively challenged until 1932 when, in Stratford-upon-Avon – that bastion of bardolatry – a Russian *émigré* named Komisarjevsky overturned Victorian stage traditions like a bear in an English china shop (Figure 3).

III

Wayward genius in the high temple of bardolatry: Theodore Komisarjevsky

> Frank Benson returned for the last time to Stratford at a Whit Monday matinée of *The Merchant of Venice* acted by the Old Bensonians in the old manner, the Venetian scenes in sequence followed by the Belmont scenes. Lilian Braithwaite travelled down to play Portia; Cedrick Hardwicke, Tubal; Robert Donat, Lorenzo; Nigel Playfair, Arragon. It was an afternoon of pardonable emotion, and the curtain fell when Benson's Shylock left the strict court of Venice; anything else would have been anti-climax. Presently, to the sustained roar of cheering, Bridges-Adams placed a laurel chaplet at Benson's feet.
>
> (Trewin, p. 137)

Frank Benson's last performance at Stratford, on 16 May 1932, had symbolic as well as emotional significance. Benson had served his apprenticeship with Irving at the Lyceum; not surprisingly, then, as manager of the Shakespeare Festival until 1919, he perpetuated Victorian stage practices, and his *Merchant*, as Trewin's account indicates, clearly was cut from Irving's mould, reaching a tragic climax at Shylock's departure from the trial. Unknown to all but perhaps managing director W. Bridges-Adams, however, was that at this matinée, Victorian *Merchants* gasped their last; for Bridges-Adams, in a calculated move to catapult the Festival into the twentieth century, had invited Russian-born Theodore Komisarjevsky to stage *The Merchant* as the first guest director at the new Shakespeare Memorial Theatre. Komisarjevsky had begun his career at his sister's theatre in St Petersburg (she was the noted actress Vera Komisarjevskaya) as assistant to her *regisseur* – a word he preferred to director – Meyerhold. Later he became the director of first the Imperial Theatre and then the State Theatre in Moscow, where he gained fame as an interpreter of Chekhov; and two years after the Revolution he left for the Continent and England, where his involvement in expressionist and other avant-garde theatre movements, along with his erudite treatises on the evolution of theatrical styles and, particularly in England, his successful stagings of Chekhov, brought him to the attention of Bridges-Adams (Beauman, pp. 125–6; Mennen, pp. 386–7). For the hidebound Stratford Festival, he was a radical choice; and the play he chose to direct could not have been more deeply encrusted in stage tradition or, as the account of the Benson matinée suggests, riper for his revolutionary pluck. As Ivor Brown remarked in the *Week End Review* (30 July 1932) after seeing Komisarjevsky's *Merchant*, Stratford would no longer be 'just a repository for the dry bones of the Bensonian convention', for the Russian iconoclast had gone there 'with the clown's poker and the costumier's largesse, wherewith he has given the solemn tradition a ludicrous trouncing. What is both remarkable and admirable is that the governors of the theatre invited this wayward genius into the high temple of Bardolatry, and gave him full freedom to use his talented, capricious hand.'

Komisarjevsky deliberately set out to overturn the pictorial realism, the attention to historical detail, the naturalistic acting, and the moral sententiousness that had characterised *Merchants* for more than fifty years. He used a complete text (all but fourteen lines), restoring scenes to their correct sequence and reinstating characters (Arragon, the Gobbos) often cut; he emphasised all the elements of farce and festive comedy that Irving and his disciples had so studiously suppressed; and above all, he eschewed the tragic conception of Shylock, which he identified with nineteenth-century actor-managers for whom, he believed, star turns and the profit motive were more important than artistic integrity. With a Marxist view of how theatre had evolved, he argued that economics were the decisive factor in the rise of the actor-manager system: 'those actors who were enterprising and dexterous enough to make money by their performances enforced their leadership upon theatrical companies. Their management served neither social ideas (a lot they cared about them!) nor theatrical art, but the interests of their own self-exhibitionism and their pockets.' The megalomania inherent in this system, he protested, gave actor-managers 'a monstrous idea of their own artistic worth' and promoted 'anarchistic-individualistic' ideas inimical to the 'basic elements of theatrical art – dramatic action expressed by the synthesis of an ensemble of players and of different arts' (*Civilisation*, pp. 10–11, 75–6). By championing such a synthesis, of course, Komisarjevsky appealed – with a political difference – for a return to the organisation of the Elizabethan theatre as a collective enterprise.

A star Shylock in a mercantile Venice became, for him, a metaphor for the greed of a bourgeois theatre he abhorred. Although Irving – 'an aristocrat of Merchants' as he was of actor-managers (p.102) – was not exempt from his lash, Komisarjevsky inveighed most heavily against a German Jewish actor named Bogumil Dawison, who, he complained,

> transformed Shakespeare's comedy ... into a tragedy and acted Shylock as a leading character, in the same manner as many English and Continental actors did after him. Dawison transformed the twisting, comic devil outplayed by Portia into a deceived, noble and emotional Jew, thereby upsetting the whole balance of the comedy and introducing a false social motive, quite alien to Shakespeare's gay, fairy-tale world, represented half mockingly, half lyrically, in *The Merchant of Venice*.
>
> (p. 84)

The phrase 'false social motive' is the key to Komisarjevsky's dismissal of the Victorian conception of the play as a study in racial prejudice. In his eyes, the ennoblement of a 'twisting, comic devil' was clearly wrong: it pandered to a false sense of social morality and cheapened the play with sentiment. For all its engagement with issues of race and class, he argued, *The Merchant* remained fundamentally a fantastic comedy; and as such, it did not comfortably lend itself to the 'realism' of nineteenth-century bourgeois theatrical practices in which its spirit too often had been entombed. The English penchant for archaeological productions and naturalistic acting in particular, as 'practised by H. Beerbohm Tree and Henry Irving, [is] considered in this country, even to the present day, to belong to what is called the legitimate and sound Shakespearean tradition'. But Komisarjevsky objected that these practices had 'nothing to do with Shakespeare' and criticised the alacrity with which the reactionary English 'delighted in a repetition of those nineteenth-century liberties, which, obscuring the real sense of Shakespeare's plays, in no way serve their interpretation' (pp. 100–1).

In his production of *The Merchant*, therefore, which opened just two months after Benson's valedictory performance, Komisarjevsky set out to restore the 'real sense' – by which he meant the theatrical or ludic sense – of Shakespeare to English audiences. His agenda was strongly influenced by the writings of German anti-naturalist Georg Fuchs who, averse to the '"monkey-like" imitations of everyday life', championed the essential *irrationality* of the theatre and argued that sets, costumes, and acting alike should imaginatively express the emotional and rhythmic movement of the play (*Civilisation*, pp. 130–3; also Mennen, pp. 388–9). Komisarjevsky thus drew on a potpourri of styles and periods, considering (like Fuchs) the ideas and emotions of a play to be a synthesis of a diverse history of human thought, not representative of one specific time or culture (*Costume*, p. 159). Meyerhold had experimented with similar expressionist techniques in his work for the Moscow Art Theatre, so it was perhaps not surprising that his protégé Komisarjevsky should evolve a production style for *The Merchant* that was playfully and wildly eclectic, its elements unified only by the 'creative work of [his] irrational self' (*Civilisation*, pp. 23–4).

His sets for Venice and Belmont reflected his training in Russia and on the Continent. In an essay called *Settings and Costumes in Europe*, he assessed the influence of cubism and expressionism on theatrical design and singled out for particular praise Picasso's set designs for Diaghilev and his own for productions in Moscow, which, he said, were inspired by the principles of Kokoschka (pp. 12–13; also *Costume*, pp. 160–2). In *The Merchant*, his set for Venice combined cubism with the colouration of the Fauves: a topsy-turvy array of brightly coloured buildings and bridges at odd angles, staircases that defied perspective, dizzying towers, barber poles, and a Bridge of Sighs that split right in two before the eyes of the audience (see Figure 3); and it was all bathed alternately in a crimson or pea-green glow, colours such as 'one has never been so lucky to see ... on this earth' (*Birmingham Post*, 26 July 1932). The Venetian painted cloth, used for front scenes, was equally expressive, depicting a canal with sails, a cock-eyed column holding up a vaulted ceiling, crooked houses and bridges in the distance, and, atop it all, a crescent moon. Spectators at the opening night were astonished – a few were appalled – by Komisarjevsky's ingenuity. He has provided 'the Venice of popular dreams', exclaimed the

Figure 3 The Venetian set for Theodore Komisarjevsky's production of 1932, designed by Komisarjevsky and Lesley Blanch. Courtesy of the Shakespeare Centre Library, Stratford-upon-Avon.

Birmingham Gazette (26 July 1932), 'a mass of broken Bridges of Sighs set at the eccentric angles a man might view them from late at night'. The *Daily Express* was more hostile: 'The set was riotously out of perspective ... The pillar of St. Mark's leaned drunkenly against a nightmare Venetian tower surrounded by a confusion of flying bridges' (26 July 1932). Commenting on Komisarjevsky's fantastic use of stage machinery, the *Birmingham Post* observed that 'Venice split in two and the Lion of St. Mark went one way while the Bridge of Sighs went the other', and *The Times*, seeking a rational explanation for such nonsense, suggested that Komisarjevsky must have intended to 'set before us the histrionic Venice of the untravelled Elizabethan' (26 July 1932).

Most reviewers welcomed both his designs and his ingenious use of the machinery of the new stage as an invigorating slap in the face of tired tradition, but there were dissenters. The *Birmingham Mail*, only partially grasping Komisarjevsky's purpose, complained that the crooked architecture of Venice and 'generous elasticity as to period' contributed to 'the artificiality of the whole thing' and protested that his 'method of scene changing becomes ... wholly destructive of illusion' (26 July 1932). *The Times*, finding such artifice 'reckless and affected', asked whether or not there was 'something to be said ... for beginning with strict realism the telling of stories as incredible as the stories of the pound of flesh and the caskets' (26 July 1932). And the *Daily Express* displayed an almost humorously philistine contempt (if not incomprehension) of the production's anti-naturalist bias: 'In a sentence,' the reviewer concluded, 'Komisarjevsky tried to practise his flair for expressionism and burlesque on the finest drama of a Jew that has even been written – and failed in miserable confusion' (26 July 1932).

Such 'confusion' – or, less pejoratively, eclecticism – governed the design of costumes as well. Komisarjevsky was an authority on costume design, having written a history of *Costume of the Theatre* in 1931, just prior to his production of *The Merchant*. The expressive quality he had brought to the sets he also recommended for costumes, which, he thought, should reveal facets of character through symbolic or surreal association, not historical accuracy. He announced in advance that his costumes for *The Merchant* would 'represent a mixture of Veronese and English of the period of James I' (*Birmingham Mail*, 26 July 1932). Yet even this is misleading, for the costumes, though they had 'an air of Renaissance sumptuousness', in fact were fantasticated, drawing inspiration from various *theatrical* traditions rather than from one or two cultures or periods. As Ivor Brown wrote in the *Observer*, assuming the voice of Komisarjevsky, 'We do not ask your rational attention. But it is a gorgeous fairy-story and we shall fancy-dress it for your delight' (31 July 1932). And fancy-dress it he did. The Venetians were outlandishly flamboyant in huge ruffs, vividly coloured doublets and hose; and Antonio was most flamboyant of all. This sad merchant, customarily attired in sombre colours to reflect his disposition, here sported a pair of flame-coloured tights that 'gave the lie immediately ... to the traditional view' of his character. In addition, he wore a grotesquely exaggerated ruff which, according to the *Birmingham Post*, made 'his face like the head of John the Baptist on a charger' (26 July 1932); and throughout the trial he 'preened himself in the little mirror that hung from a ribbon round his neck, emphasising the impression given in the first scene', during which he fondled a rose, that the reason for his melancholy was that he was indeed in love – with himself (*Stratford-upon-Avon Herald*, 29 July 1932). Komisarjevsky thus transformed Antonio, whose motivation is always something of a problem for directors, into a 'depraved exquisite' (*Daily Telegraph*, 26 July 1932), a near relation to Malvolio, 'a Venetian dilettante in a poetic languor' who, one feels, 'would not much mind the cutting off of his flesh so long as it did not disfigure his aesthetic magnificence' (*The Stage*, 28 July 1932).

Komisarjevsky's irreverent wit expressed itself in other costuming as well. Gratiano, with humorous topicality, was coiffured to look like Rudolph Valentino (*Evesham Journal*, 30 July 1932); and Portia's suitors, traditionally played for their exotic appeal, here appeared as buffoons. The Prince of Arragon, a foppish grotesque who bowed to Portia with swaggering affectation, was accompanied by a 'fat little attendant' (*Coventry Herald*, 30 July 1932) who reminded one reviewer of a creature out of *opéra bouffe* (*Sheffield Telegraph*, 1 August 1932). The Prince of Morocco was even more outlandish. Usually played as 'a dusky paladin with a good deal of sex appeal', he was reduced to 'an out-and-out blackamoor, so like Al Jolson that one expects him to drown his disappointment with a stave of "Sonny Boy"' (*Birmingham Mail*, 26 July 1932). In the words of another, he was 'made up as a nigger minstrel with a Mexican sombrero on his head' (*Birmingham Gazette*, 26 July 1932); and still another saw him as 'a black-faced embodiment of the Captain' who shows his 'derivation from the Commedia dell'Arte' (*Birmingham Post*, 26 July 1932).

Morocco's derivation from El Capitano suggests how indebted Komisarjevsky was to the *Commedia* tradition, a style whose extravagant use of colour and comic exaggeration he found wonderfully expressive. He had devoted a long section of his book on costume to the *Commedia*; his description of El Capitano therein as a braggart soldier in stripes with tight breeches, a wooden sword, and a small tabarro with long feathers clearly illustrates Morocco's lineage (*Costume*, p. 117). The *Commedia* style inspired costume designs for other characters as well. Portia, for example, was dressed as a Columbine, the sweet associations of pastoral simplicity made ironic by the worldliness with which Fabia Drake played the role. Even more explicitly, the Gobbos, father and son, were attired like a piebald Scapino and Pantalone – the young man in patches and ruffs, the old man in yellow slippers, red breeches and stockings, a tight jacket, red bonnet, and a half mask with a long nose. Such costumes suggest how far Komisarjevsky wished his *Merchant* to be regarded as play – as the product of an eclectic theatrical imagination – rather than as a representation of any recognisable society.

'Perhaps the Lancelot Gobbo of Bruno Barnabe comes nearer to his heart than any of the players,' speculated the *Birmingham Weekly Post* (30 July 1932), and the speculation was surely right. For Barnabe had trained in mime under Komisarjevsky at the Royal Academy of Dramatic Art and had researched clowns of the *Commedia*, so that his role as the production's presiding genius of comedy was inevitably informed by that tradition. Komisarjevsky set the play during carnival, a time of music and dance when Venice 'has no period but that of eternal masquerade' (*Observer*, 31 July 1932). To create that festive mood, the production opened with a masque of pierrots led by Barnabe, who assumed the role of Harlequin. Fantastically dressed in a striped suit and a yard-high hat, Harlequin strutted on to the stage and beckoned to his mummers. They, all dressed in black and white dominoes and wearing masks with long noses, appeared from every corner of the set, pirouetting over the bridges of Venice and dancing acrobatically to a version of Bach's Toccata and Fugue in D Minor played by a concealed orchestra (*Midland Daily Telegraph*, 26 July 1932). Then, on a cue from Harlequin, they scampered off to make way for the first actors in a comedy – *The Merchant of Venice* – that was to be performed, presumably, as a part of the carnival celebrations: Antonio and his friends suddenly appeared behind Harlequin, as if he had summoned them. Two or three reviewers took the performance of *The Merchant* that followed to be a 'revels' play; but as Barnabe soon reappeared in the habit of Lancelot Gobbo – his double role readily apparent to the audience – one could, alternatively, interpret this opening sequence as Lancelot's dream, establishing a more profoundly irrational world in which the role-play and absurdities of carnival take on, for the dreamer, a reality of their own. In either case, the festive licence of the opening scene made the fantastic premises of *The Merchant* – the terms of Shylock's bond, the lottery by which Portia must be won, the cross-dressing of all the play's women: such things as prove problematic in realistic productions – explicable.

'One found the old and too familiar material joyously rewrought into a dazzling pattern of fantasy,' wrote one reviewer (*Sheffield Telegraph*, 1 August 1932). Komisarjevsky has created a world, concurred another, 'where everything ... becomes excusable, and nothing outrageous' (*Birmingham Mail*, 26 July 1932).

The Gobbos, in fact, set the tone for the revelry in the play-within-the-play. The lengths to which Komisarjevsky went to emphasise their clowning are revealed by elaborate stage directions in his prompt book. At their first meeting, for example, not only does Lancelot attempt to disorient his father by spinning him around, he also pushes Old Gobbo right into Bassanio on 'To him, father' (II.ii.97), pushes him again – so hard that the old man falls down – on 'as my father shall specify' (102), then picks him up and *carries* him to Bassanio. This horseplay continues throughout the scene. In subsequent scenes, furthermore, Old Gobbo toddles dutifully behind his son – even though the text does not specify his presence – so that the two of them can perform running gags together, like the *lazzi* of *Commedia* tradition (Mennen, p. 395). In II.iii, when Lancelot bids a tearful farewell to Jessica, Old Gobbo is there to wipe his son's eyes with a giant handkerchief. In II.v, he adds a funny double echo every time Lancelot echoes Shylock's 'Why, Jessica!' And when Shylock advances on them – 'Who bids thee call?' (7) – Lancelot falls backwards over his father, the two of them winding up in a heap on the floor. Lancelot himself is also introduced into scenes where Shakespeare did not intend him to be. In Belmont, he is on stage – and given comic business – throughout Bassanio's wooing of Portia in III.ii; he is there again in III.iv, when Portia puts Lorenzo in charge of her house; and his clowning with Jessica and Lorenzo dominates III.v, right up to his entrance at the end to announce, in mime, that dinner is ready.

The roles of Lancelot and Harlequin merge again in Act V. Lancelot's presence there, of course, is justified: he enters at i.39 with news of Bassanio's impending arrival, and there is no indication that he departs thereafter. But where other directors had usually found a way to usher him off as a figure too low to intrude on the play's romantic conclusion, Komisarjevsky wished to round out his fantasy with the clown. Barnabe at first sat unobtrusively by the proscenium to observe; but the director then found comic business for him to do. Where the text indicates *A tucket sounds*

(121), Lancelot mimicked the blowing of a horn, making a joke of Lorenzo's subsequent line to Portia, 'Your husband is at hand, I hear his trumpet' (122). The joking continued when, as Bassanio spoke his aside 'I were best to cut my left hand off / And swear I lost the ring defending it' (177–8), Lancelot, happy to be of service, offered him a knife – a humorous allusion to the trial scene just past. And when all the couples had departed (even Antonio entered into the spirit of their festivity) Lancelot was left alone. He summoned the pierrots, just as he had once done as Harlequin: they entered as before, pirouetted around him, then bounded off as quickly as they had come, leaving him to yawn and stretch. This brought the revels full circle: clearly the audience was to think of the two hours' traffic as the fruit of a clown's imagination, if not his dream, no more substantial than *The Taming of the Shrew* may become when it is preceded by the induction with Christopher Sly.

It is instructive to recall that Irving, too, had incorporated dancing pierrots in his production of *The Merchant*; but there, they were participants in the masques Shylock commanded Jessica to ignore, a momentary diversion – naturalistic enough, in context – from the sobriety of the bond plot and a frivolous contrast to the tragedy of the Jew. In Komisarjevsky's *Merchant*, the pierrots required no such justification. They represented the spirit of carnival and, like so much else in the production, defied naturalistic explanation. Even the entrances and exits of characters playfully violated the illusionistic 'world' defined by the proscenium arch. Aware that audiences were disappointed that performances continued to be confined by that arch in the new Shakespeare Memorial Theatre, Komisarjevsky took the liberty of breaking through it. Barnabe, as Lancelot, led the way by effecting his first entrance hand over hand down a rope hung from a gallery over the apron of the stage (*Daily Telegraph*, 26 July 1932); and later on he performed his scenes with Jessica on a tower located outside the proscenium. Venetians climbed on to the stage from the orchestra pit 'as if landing from gondolas' (*Sheffield Telegraph*, 1 August 1932); and Portia and her suitors arose as if from nowhere on an elevator which, as we shall see, occasionally took them to heights well above the stage. Perhaps the *Birmingham Gazette* described the situation best: 'Nobody came on the stage from the wings – they all came on as if conjured by magic from nowhere, either from behind masked figures, from out of the orchestra well, from beneath the stage by trap doors, or else they were let down from the flies above' (26 July 1932). Such effects were comically disorienting. By keeping the audience uncertain where characters had come from or where they were going, they enhanced the surreal quality of the production and made spectators themselves participants in the dream.

New theatrical technology allowed for a fluidity of play unknown on the Victorian stage; and if Komisarjevsky used that technology to excess, at least he did so in order to thwart the expectations of representationalism to which audiences had grown accustomed. Set changes between Venice and Belmont flamboyantly called attention to their own theatricality: at the conclusion of the very first scene, when Bassanio spoke to Antonio of a lady in Belmont richly left, 'the audience was permitted a full view of the rolling stage in action. The Venetian street scene ... divided in the centre, half sliding off on each side'; and as the cyclorama changed from apple green to deep pink, 'a lift carrying Belmont rose to stage level with Portia and Nerissa poised like Dresden china figures – a theatrical reinforcement of Bassanio's description of Portia's virtues' (*Midland Daily Telegraph*, 26 July 1932). The Belmont set, more classically formal in style, contrasted with the riotous disproportions of Venice: it consisted of a cluster of steps, geometrically designed to look like sculpture, and a large, free-standing wall panel in the shape of a scroll on which were painted musical instruments in the style of Picasso. The overlapping of scenes achieved while the set change was in progress established both a rhythmic and a visual counterpoint between Venice and Belmont that, as Richard Mennen suggests, reinforced the stylistic differences between those two worlds inherent in the text (p. 390); and these differences became even more apparent when, in subsequent scenes, the Belmont set moved to even greater heights.

In contrast to the scenes in Venice, which opened with a flurry of activity, each of the wooing scenes began as a *tableau vivant*, with Portia and Nerissa statuesquely rising from the depths as the lift took them to a level eight feet above the stage, the suitors rising only to the level of the stage below, where they were to make their choices from caskets located beneath the platform – literal-minded critics persisted in calling it a 'roof garden' – on which Portia was standing. 'The purpose of this device', wrote the critic of *The Times*, 'is to show us the shining, desirable Portia poised on high, while her unwelcome suitors blunderingly woo her on a lower level, and to let her descend later to Bassanio's level' (26 July 1932). But Komisarjevsky had more in mind, for this arrangement also commented wryly on the representational way in which the casket scenes had been staged in the past. Three decorated panels covered the 'pavilion' beneath the upper platform (*Birmingham Mail*, 26 July 1932), on the middle of which the three caskets were fancifully *painted* – an urn with a smiling face for gold, a purse for silver, and a plain bucket for lead. None of them was in any sense real. The reviewer for the *Daily Telegraph* protested that 'the casket scenes happened in a horrible little curtain grotto beneath Portia's garden' and thus failed to convey the romantic opulence he expected (26 July 1932); but the literalism of his response was countered by others who recognised that those caskets 'were painted ... very much after the manner of a Victorian pantomime' (*Birmingham Post*, 26 July 1932) and in their comic presentationalism served not only to satirise the absurdity of the lottery, but to burlesque the tradition of theatrical representationalism as well.

Komisarjevsky applied irreverent brush strokes not only to the design but to the direction of the wooing scenes. If the suitors' costumes were drawn from various comic traditions, so too was their behaviour. In one inspired moment noted by most reviewers, 'the Prince of Morocco, black-faced and with thick, red lips, [rose] out of the ground under a red umbrella' held by his black servant (*Birmingham Gazette*, 26 July 1932; also *Evesham Journal*, 30 July 1932). Portia viewed him from above with disdain, and indeed he seemed to deserve little else; for his manner was as theatrical as that of a black minstrel, and when he found the death's head inside the gold casket, he rolled his eyeballs and delivered 'Oh hell! What have we here?' (II.vii.62) not as a prince, but 'just as a motorist would who has burst a tyre' (*Stratford-upon-Avon Herald*, 29 July 1932). The swaggering Arragon, too, proved more fool than prince: he was constantly upstaged by his fat little attendant who nodded in agreement at comically inappropriate places, such as when Arragon, seeing the fool's head he had chosen, asked, 'Are my deserts no better?' (II.ix.59). Neither suitor could possibly have proved worthy of Portia, and so – as the set impishly implied – she kept her distance.

When Bassanio arrived, however, she 'descended' – as *The Times* put it – 'to his level'. She was not a traditionally romantic Portia: Komisarjevsky's conception of the play would not have allowed that. In fact, as Fabia Drake reported in a BBC broadcast in 1959, he had told her that she must play the scene with Bassanio 'not sentimental – physical' (Mennen, p. 393). Those three words, she said, liberated her from the stumbling block of tradition and charged her with what she called 'a new vibrancy' – and what reviewers called a youthful zest for love. She 'clearly sustains some human warmth beneath the porcelain poses', reported the *Week End Review* (30 July 1932); and where once Ellen Terry was criticised for being too forward with Bassanio, Drake clung to him and at one point impulsively threw her arms around his neck without fear of censure. Sexual desire, apparently, would prompt her to do anything – even flout her father's will. When Bassanio asked to be left to his fortunes and the caskets, the lift rose to the upper level, but Portia remained below with him – 'leaning, languorously, against the edge of the proscenium' (Mennen, p. 393) – ready to be of assistance. And assistance he needed, for his values were no more pristine than hers: money, apparently, weighed as heavily as love in his desire to win the lottery. Not surprisingly, then, when it appeared that Bassanio was about to plump for the golden casket, Nerissa – obviously at Portia's prompting – put him 'on the right track' by 'shamelessly stress[ing] the syllables in the "Fancy" lyric which rhyme with "lead" – until he could not possibly go wrong' (*Birmingham Mail*, 26 July 1932).

Ellen Terry, writing in 1908, defended Portia's right as an independent woman to circumvent her father's will in this way, though she had never stooped to such subversion in performance. But 1932 was a more liberated age, and Fabia Drake's Portia was unabashedly determined to marry the man of her own choosing. Male reviewers, however, objected to her strategy for doing so. The *Daily Telegraph* called it 'an uncommonly dirty trick' which undermined the idealism that should have made Bassanio the *inevitable* winner of the lottery. The *Christian World* concurred that Portia's trick undercut the play's romantic fictions with a baser reality, reducing the hero and heroine to mere poseurs so that 'Bassanio's lengthy discourse on the relative values of gold and silver and lead is turned into a piece of hypocritical attitudinising' (4 August 1932). But perhaps such criticism took the production too seriously; for in the world of carnival, the release of inhibition means everything and morality counts for naught – or, as the *Birmingham Gazette* put it, 'the arraignment of morality is incidental ... the comic interlude all important' (26 July 1932). This is not to suggest that the comedy was devoid of moral observation; indeed, Komisarjevsky used the licence of carnival to make pointed social criticism about the values of the bourgeoisie. 'All those young men,' he announced in advance, 'Bassanio, Lorenzo, Gratiano, Salarino, and the rest – will be put in their place. They will be shown as the dissipated, fast, bright young people like the crowd we have in London today' (*Birmingham Mail*, 7 July 1932): Komisarjevsky alludes to the spoiled darlings of England's monied classes who seemed oblivious to the fact that the economic system which had kept them rich had also led to a terrible depression. In his production, then, comic romance gave way to topical satire, and moral sententiousness to a light-hearted indictment of contemporary social values.

That same topicality informed the trial scene, which Komisarjevsky staged as farce, overturning the tradition that had for so long made it the tragic capstone of the play. His satirical intentions were made clear in an interview: 'The court scene', he said,

> will present some new aspects. If such a law could exist as that by which the Jew could take his pound of flesh, then most certainly it would be allowed to shed the victim's blood and the claimant could not be expected to cut the flesh to the exact pound. The thing would be absurd. That scene represents the crash of justice in the face of prejudice.
>
> (*Birmingham Mail*, 7 July 1932)

The key word here is *absurd*, for Komisarjevsky believed that the power of the fable lay in its illogic, in its irrational theatricality. 'Justice is brought to nought by a girl', he continued, citing Portia's 'sweet unreasonableness' as the principle governing the scene.

Komisarjevsky thus designed the trial to bring to a climax the irrationality, and amorality, of a dream. Appropriately played on the Belmont set rather than in Venice – the levels had been rearranged, with the geometrical steps now forming a dais for the Duke – the scene reflected the surrealist style of Portia's world and the priority of her (questionable) values. The costuming, too, reflected Komisarjevsky's satirical intent. 'I shall try to bring out the power of that scene', he said,

> by having all the senators of the Doge's Court sitting around in a uniform dress, their faces covered by uniform masks. Not a human face will be visible but Portia's, and in the background there will be painted a shadowy ensemble of the court crowd – the sort of people who gloat over sensations in our present-day courts.
>
> (*Birmingham Mail*, 7 July 1932)

In the event, the crowd painted on the scroll-shaped wall had the faces of sheep; the magnificoes, costumed in scarlet robes and ruffs, had faces made up in white rather than masked; and, during the proceedings, the entire court followed Portia and Shylock like spectators at a tennis match, looking mindlessly now this way, now that (Mennen, p. 395).

The action at the trial was rife with a comic invention that illustrated the patent injustices of the judicial process. The old Duke, who kept nodding off during the trial and waking up with a start 'like his prototype in "Alice"', could in no way dispense justice (*The Stage*, 28 July 1932): he even fell asleep while his doddering clerk read the letter from Bellario (Shakespeare assigns those lines to the Duke himself) – its opening line, 'Your grace shall understand, that at the receipt of your letter I am very sick' (IV.i.150–1), delivered so as to suggest that the Duke's letter had caused Bellario's illness (Mennen, pp. 395–6). The jury, according to one reviewer, 'brought to mind the Ku-Klux-Klan', an association Komisarjevsky would have welcomed (*Coventry Herald*, 30 July 1932); but as I have already noted, the defendant on whose life they were to pass judgement, Antonio, preened in the mirror that hung about his neck as if the only thing he feared about death was the disfigurement of his face. Was such a man – vain product of a comically decadent bourgeoisie – worth saving?

If such absurdities blunted the point of Komisarjevsky's satire, so too did Portia's appearance from the orchestra pit as a contemporary young barrister sporting 'a Henry Lyttonish wig and bicycle wheel spectacles' (*The Stage*, 28 July 1932) – a disguise reminiscent of that worn by Kitty Clive who, in Macklin's *Merchant*, aped the mannerisms of famous lawyers of *her* day. The wit of Fabia Drake's performance perfectly matched that of Komisarjevsky's conception: most reviewers found her Balthasar a refreshing departure from tradition, 'a credible ... young doctor of laws, and not merely a young woman who' – *pace* Ellen Terry – 'had previously played the part in a scarlet robe' (*Birmingham Post*, 26 July 1932). Drake took the scene more 'as a frisky adventure in male impersonation' (*Sheffield Telegraph*, 1 August 1932) than a serious attempt to instruct the court in Christian virtue; and when Komisarjevsky told her that the 'quality of mercy' speech should be delivered not as a declamation but simply as an answer to Shylock's question, 'On what compulsion must I?' (179), she was happy to oblige: 'Portia, leaning over her desk, snaps the poor old Jew's head off with the retort – the effect is electrical' (*Birmingham News*, 22 May 1933).

In the most blatant rejection of stage tradition, this trial scene tried to dramatise 'the crash of justice in the face of prejudice' *without* encouraging the audience to feel much pity for Shylock. True, stage directions in the prompt book indicate that Gratiano spat at Shylock and pushed him to his knees, but Komisarjevsky did not want such business to elicit sympathy for a man who, according to him, was little more than a caricature of malice. How, one wonders, can prejudice be regarded as ignominious if its object is so clearly deserving of it? 'The point of Shylock is revenge, and revenge can never be sympathetic,' he claimed. And although 'there is a hint of triumph about the Jew, even at that crucial point in the court when after everything has been taken away from him he admits that he is crushed with the plaint that he does not feel well' (*Birmingham Mail*, 7 July 1932), Komisarjevsky thought it wrong for that hint of triumph to be magnified into the tragic exit that had won Irving so much praise. *The Times*, discerning in this Shylock a 'vulpine and instinctive' nature at odds with the tragic dignity of Shylocks past, approved of the way in which Komisarjevsky handled his departure from the trial: 'Rightly, [Shylock] lets himself be dismissed from the Court without the least straining after heroic gesture, making an exit that well befits the crushed and sordid usurer who ... would now be only too content to take his three thousand ducats and let the Christian go' (26 July 1932). In this way, Komisarjevsky succeeded in offering an alternative to Irving's interpretation as no director had done for over half a century.

It is symptomatic of Komisarjevsky's success that reviewers focused not so much on individual performances as on the overall aesthetic of his production – its style, its tone, its design. This, I think, was the real breakthrough of his *Merchant:* that it diverted attention from the nineteenth-century notion that the play was 'about' character and drew attention instead to the directorial *concept*. The star actor was thus supplanted by the director, or, to use Komisarjevsky's term, the *regisseur*, who, more than any actor-manager would have found possible, was expected to synthesise all the elements of a production into an artistic whole. 'The *regisseur* is a spiritual leader, a kind of magician, psychologist and technical master,' he wrote, who must be flexible rather than tyrannical and adapt his concept to 'an individual actor's mode of expression', because he 'respects the creative individualities of his actors and knows that no more can be achieved by the methods of the drill sergeant than by committee meetings' (*Civilisation*, pp. 18–19). The acid test of Komisarjevsky's willingness as a *regisseur* to adapt his concept to the 'creative individualities of his actors' came in his debate with Randle Ayrton over how Shylock should be played.

Regarding Shylock as a role that had been inflated out of all proportion by actor-managers bent on displaying their own egos, Komisarjevsky was determined to shrink the Jew down to a size befitting the villain of a comedy who appears, after all, in only five scenes. Komisarjevsky, one may recall, abhorred the way in which bourgeois theatre had sentimentalised Shylock – in England, that sentiment had led to the mawkishness of Frank Benson's farewell matinée – and he therefore strove to desentimentalise him. In Ayrton, he apparently found an actor suitable for the task. Noted for roles as diverse as Lear and Malvolio, Ayrton was described by fellow-actor Sebastian Shaw as

> a short squat man, with grey hair, a broad expansive face, a large nose. He was ugly ... but you were never conscious of that, just of his tremendous power. He had a curious, almost ugly voice too, slightly nasal in quality, but with the most extraordinary range: it could move in a moment from lightness and delicacy to rawness and passion.
>
> (Beauman, p. 88)

From this description, one may easily envisage Ayrton's Shylock as a malevolent stage Jew or even, in his more comic scenes, as a pantaloon from the *Commedia*. Instead of the traditional Jewish gaberdine he wore a brightly coloured costume – the *Daily Mail* thought he looked like 'Mr. Willy Clarkson at an Albert Hall fancy dress ball' (26 July 1932) – and he played Shylock in a conversational tone 'with an amusing accent and a sense of humour which is quite unexpected' (*Birmingham Post*, 26 July 1932). Critics generally agreed that he revived a conception of the role too long dormant in the theatre. According to the *Observer*, Shylock was played as he might have been on Shakespeare's stage, as 'a wicked old scamp to be detested of the audience, a scamp with drollery inherent, but meriting all the punishment that comes his way' (31 July 1932). The reviewer clearly approved of Komisarjevsky's challenge to the sentimental tradition: 'Ayrton's performance is strong, clear, sardonic, and never sentimentalised or expanded with irrelevant goings on.' The critic of the *Daily Herald*, showing an anti-Semitic stripe to which the production obviously appealed, agreed that Komisarjevsky 'had the courage to show Shylock what I always thought him to be – a terrible old scoundrel. He made him as he was before Irving, in order to placate Jewish patrons of the theatre, pretended that a moneylender who wanted to cut a pound of flesh from a living man was really a noble-hearted gentleman' (29 July 1932).

Despite Komisarjevsky's claim that he intended the trial to expose racial prejudice, therefore, few critics interpreted it that way; and it is difficult to see how they could, given his attempt to turn Shylock into a grotesque suitable for the carnival entertainment his *Merchant* had become. But Komisarjevsky ultimately met an obstacle in Ayrton, who, as a veteran actor of the old school, would not – or could not – fully comply with his approach. Having played Shylock at Stratford before, Ayrton was well aware of the role's complexity and potential for tragic pathos; according to Fabia Drake, he was at first 'completely appalled by Komisarjevsky's interpretation' and apparently, for a time, resisted the invitation to see Shylock as in any way a caricature of revenge (Mennen, p. 394). The situation was a difficult one for the director: as Mennen reports, Bridges-Adams had chosen the company at the beginning of the season, as was Stratford's policy, and had allotted each production only five or six rehearsals. 'In other words, Komisarjevsky had not cast Ayrton, had no contractual leverage over him, and certainly had no time to cajole him into an interpretation he opposed and which may have been beyond his abilities' (p. 394). Yet lest we credit Ayrton with too much opposition, we should recall that the text itself resists the reduction of Shylock to comic villainy; and as an actor, Ayrton may simply have been responding more to the lines he was given to speak than to a director's concept. A few reviewers recognised in the power of Ayrton's performance something that transcended stereotype, and the terms in which they describe him are remarkably like those used to describe Macklin's performance two centuries earlier. Shylock 'is not quite all the monster that Mr. Komisarjevsky, reverting to the old tradition, would make him', asserted the *Manchester Guardian* (26 July 1932); and the *Daily Express* remarked that his 'refreshing, cynical humour' in the first scene yielded later to 'a cold fury that was degrees above the tattered passions of more conventional Shylocks' (26 July 1932). Such fury reached its peak in III.i, when a storm of wind and thunder brewed during his confrontation with Solanio and Salarino – a loud clap punctuated 'She is damned for it' (26) – and gathered force as, Lear-like, he vented his passions with Tubal under an 'ominous coppery green' sky (*Western Sunday Independent*, 31 July 1932). The effect of the scene may have been melodramatic, but in the opinion of one critic, it revealed the futility of trying 'to treat Shylock as a rascally and belaboured pantaloon' (*Sheffield Telegraph*, 1 August 1932).

The differences between Ayrton's and Komisarjevsky's conceptions of Shylock reflected the divergent potentials of the role as written. In his attempt to scale Shylock down to a size appropriate for a *Merchant* indebted to the traditions of mime, dance, *Commedia*, and farce, Komisarjevsky risked reducing him to a comic stage Jew; and to some degree Ayrton must have been willing to oblige, for a number of critics saw him as that – 'a nasty old card who gets uncommonly rough justice for behaving like an uncommon ruffian' (*Week End Review*, 30 July 1932). But the pressures of the text and Ayrton's own proclivity to play a more human role resisted that reduction, so that Shylock ultimately did not appear to most critics to be simply two-dimensional. The struggle between the comic type – which is a part of Shylock's heritage – and what *The Times* called Shakespeare's 'divination that the Jew is also a human being' may ironically have benefited the production by making it more accurately reflect the tensions within the text itself. The *Sheffield Telegraph* eloquently spoke of how those tensions were manifested in performance. Ayrton,

> the finest Shylock we have seen since Irving, played the game for his producer for all he was worth by stressing the grasping squalid side of the Jew's nature. But he was bound in honour to play the game for Shakespeare too, and from the glorious humanity [note here the vestige of Victorian assumptions about the play] ... of Shakespeare's treatment of Shylock there is no escape. Mr. Komisarjevsky has succeeded in making us forget Shylock when he is not there: but when he moves upon the stage, and until he quits it in pitiful disaster, the feast of fancy and artifice is ruled, in the old way, by the skeleton.
>
> (1 August 1932)

The skeleton of which the reviewer speaks, of course, is that of Irving; and in strange ways, I would suggest, it dances in the shadows of Komisarjevsky's production as surely as it rattles through the prose of this review. Komisarjevsky went to great lengths to refute Irving's legacy: by dressing Ayrton in fantastical garb, giving him an exotic accent, and asking him to play the role for all its malicious humour, he tried to recapture the 'twisting, comic devil' that he thought the Elizabethan Shylock had been (*Civilisation*, p. 84) and thereby to put to rest the tragically heroic figure Shylock had become in the nineteenth century. Yet Victorian tradition permeated his thinking about the play so much that he was even prepared to borrow its most celebrated effect – the interpolated scene in which Shylock returns to an empty house – in a form altered to suit his more political purpose. Komisarjevsky's recollection of that effect in an interview for the *Birmingham Mail* suggests how deeply he felt the anxiety of influence.

> I have always felt that ... the traditional last scene is wrong. Shylock should not be allowed to knock at his own door to discover that Jessica has flown with a Christian. I shall arrange it so that after the lovers have gone off together, the young men of the fast dissipated Christian set will remain in the Venetian setting talking over the case. Shylock will cross the stage towards his house and find it seized, with two Venetian guards at the door. Then will be seen the reaction of those who convicted him unjustly.
>
> (7 July 1932)

Rejecting what he saw as the false pathos of Shylock's traditional return, Komisarjevsky nevertheless decided to appropriate that tradition to make a statement about social injustice. Without ever questioning whether the scene was in fact Shakespeare's, he vowed to use it to indict the strong-arm tactics of a 'dissipated' ruling class that had convicted the Jew 'unjustly': Shylock was to be barred from entering his own house. In the event, however, Komisarjevsky did not alter tradition even that much. Stage directions in his prompt book indicate that when the masquers have departed, 'Shylock enters ... sees money lying on floor and open door'; he 'calls Jessica three times', and then, hearing no response, 'closes door slowly'.

However fantastic his *Merchant* was, therefore, and no matter how he decried the 'false social motive' imposed on the play by previous directors (*Civilisation*, p. 84), Komisarjevsky was not oblivious to the moral, social, and political implications of its performance. True, he eschewed the psychological subtlety, the naturalistic style of acting, and the pictorial realism that had characterised productions of the preceding fifty years; but his production was not frivolous for all that. His new aesthetic was part of a revolutionary agenda, and he was abundantly aware of the social and political context in which it would be interpreted. Komisarjevsky himself averred that 'it is absurd to assert, as some do, that the art of the theatre is a purely aesthetic function and has nothing to do with "propaganda", either moral, religious, or political' (*Civilisation*, p. 2). In fact, I would argue that his production – even in its rejection of the past – covertly addressed the social divisions and political upheavals that were rocking Europe in the 1920s and early 1930s.

Komisarjevsky was an outspoken proponent of socialist dictatorships. In a book called *The Theatre and a Changing Civilisation*, which he published in 1934, just two years after his production of *The Merchant*, he lamented that Europe had languished for so long under effete democratic governments. The capitalist values of European society, he argued, had had a dire impact on the theatre, which held an unflattering mirror up to the bourgeoisie (pp. 1–14, *passim*). Under the direction of visionary *regisseurs* such as himself, however, the theatre could help to guide social reform; and in his eyes, such *regisseurs* found their political counterparts in the likes of Lenin, Stalin, Hitler, and Mussolini – dictators born out of the failure of imagination in European democracies. Where 'the old democracies pandered to the spirit of conservatism and to old people, and bred mediocrities, conflicting and mercenary passions and anarchy', he wrote, the new leaders have 'genuine idealistic foundations' (p. x) – such idealism as should, in his view, bring about a revolution in the theatre as well. Of his own country, he believed that

> if the snobbish Russian aristocrats and the highbrow Russian intellectuals had possessed a power of vision and had collaborated with the Soviets upon their coming into power, and if the Jews and the Christians had not imagined that there were two separate Gods ... and if all of them together, including the cosmopolitan bankers ... had found a higher purpose in life than land and money-grubbing and organising the exploitation of man by man, then there would have been no revolutionary massacres in Russia nor any Jew-baiting in Germany.
>
> (p. x)

Good sentences and well pronounced. From them, one might deduce that he saw reflected in *The Merchant* these very concerns about a capitalist culture – here, Renaissance Venice – so perniciously rich, so full of money-grubbing and exploitation, that it bred the sort of persecution Shylock suffers. Considered in light of his political ideology, Komisarjevsky's *Merchant* may be seen to have had a socialist dimension; and while it may not have sentimentalised the play's morality as earlier productions had done, it satirically observed how bourgeois decadence could lead to racial prejudice. That, at least, was Komisarjevsky's avowed intention: he conceived of the Venetians as 'dissipated' young idlers and Shylock as a man who, however malevolent, suffers injustice at their hands. The kangaroo court in sheep's clothing makes just this point.

But this interpretation of the production may be too charitable. It is called into question by Komisarjevsky's argument, in the same text, that the purges of the Communist revolution in Russia, during which so many citizens were, 'as the expression goes, disposed of', and the denial of all rights of citizenship to Jews during the 'Nazi Upheaval' beginning in 1933 were, however regrettable, an understandable and even necessary consequence of 'any mass progressive movement'; for, he claimed, there has never been progress 'without bloodshed and injustice being inflicted on certain groups of people, and, however sentimental we may be, our feelings must not be allowed to blind us to the positive and progressive sides of the Fascist, Communist and Nazi movements' (*Civilisation*, pp. ix–x). For Komisarjevsky to claim, in an interview prior to his production, that Shylock was victimised by 'the crash of justice in the face of prejudice', then to speak as an apologist for the increasingly violent oppression of Jews in the name of progress smacks of hypocrisy, and suggests that his *Merchant* may have been informed by more extreme political views than he was willing to admit. We may recall how strenuously he objected to those actor-managers who sentimentalised Shylock as a bourgeois tragic hero; here, he objects to a 'sentimental' humanism – in other words, an abhorrence of atrocities – that would blind us to the achievements of socialist dictatorships. The objectivity with which he claimed to squelch such sentiment allowed him, in the name of art, to fashion Shylock as a figure most audiences could jeer at and dismiss as justly punished. The critic of *The Times*, covering his own response in the cloak of historical distance, spoke for many when he speculated that, if an Elizabethan 'retained his taste for a little Jewbaiting he might have laughed uproariously at the despairing rage of the crafty alien usurer hoist with his own petard. Moral sensibility does not lend itself to such laughter, but we may confess that the hardening process so skilfully applied by the actors to our hearts is good for the play' (26 July 1932).

One could argue, of course, that treating any play as an exercise in style will result in a reductive view of humanity and lead, inevitably, to totalitarian theatre: the moral contradictions of Komisarjevsky's *Merchant* may thus appear to have sprung from the tyranny of style rather than from a consideration of politics. Nevertheless, Komisarjevsky achieved more than an aesthetic revolution in his production. He overturned a tradition of playing Shylock that for more than half a century had embodied the moral enlightenment of Western culture and dramatised the tragic consequences of racial prejudice. By dispensing with the traditions of bourgeois theatre, he dispensed as well with a sentimental Shylock – the one was a product of the other; and in his place he offered audiences (so far as Ayrton would allow) a 'twisting, comic devil' more appropriate, he thought, for the naive 'fairy tale' world of *The Merchant* (*Civilisation*, p. 84). But there was nothing naive about Komisarjevsky's conception of that world: as his remarks indicate, he knew that one cannot, by artistic fiat, divorce a play from cultural values and moral questions that have accrued over centuries of production. In fact, his Shylock was nearly indistinguishable from the anti-Semitic stereotype promoted by Komisarjevsky's favourite dictator who, at that very time, was turning Jews into scapegoats for the ills of the capitalist system in Germany and was even using *The Merchant of Venice* and *The Jew of Malta* as comic propaganda to advance his racist agenda in the theatre. And did Komisarjevsky, by analogy, do any less? By dehumanising Shylock as a 'crafty alien usurer', didn't he, as *The Times* attests, encourage audiences to harden their hearts against him and to laugh at his punishment and expulsion? From the perspective of sixty years, is it possible *not* to hear an ominous warning in the reviewer's claim that this 'hardening process' was 'good for the play'? Komisarjevsky, I would submit, staged *The Merchant* as a carnival of denial and found a receptive audience for it: indeed, the production proved so popular it was revived the following year. It must have tapped into the anxieties of a people who, in the throes of economic crisis, sought escapist entertainment and found it in the fantasy of a fortunate heiress; a people who, in their readiness to hiss the wealthy Jew, averted their gaze from anti-Semitic activities abroad that would, in years to come, make the tragedy of Shylock dwindle into insignificance.

IV

Aesthetes in a rugger club: Jonathan Miller and Laurence Olivier

The spectre of Henry Irving hovered uncannily over the National Theatre's 1970 production of *The Merchant of Venice*. Even the circumstances of production resembled those at Irving's Lyceum: Laurence Olivier, who, as director of the National, was the modern equivalent of an actor-manager, had not had a major new role, nor his company a successful production of Shakespeare, in several years, when Kenneth Tynan persuaded him that *The Merchant* might offer such an opportunity; and what was good for Olivier would, of course, be good for the National (Cottrell, pp. 360–1). Like Irving, Olivier was best known for his tragic roles – Hamlet, Richard III, Othello. When he assayed Shylock, therefore, it was clear that his *Merchant* would serve as a vehicle for a famous tragedian. Yet there were other similarities as well: just as Irving's Lyceum came to be regarded as a shrine to what was noblest and best in Victorian culture, so Olivier believed that the National Theatre had a duty to nurture his country's most civilised traditions and values. For him, therefore, as for Irving, *The Merchant* should not pander to popular prejudices with comic stereotypes, but promote 'a feeling of dignity and austerity'; it should eschew romantic artifice in order to 'search for reality'. To achieve a 'reality' his audience would recognise, Olivier decided to update the play to 1880, 'that period when the Victorians had found their maturity' (*On Acting*, p. 119) and, incidentally, the very time when Irving was revolutionising the way audiences viewed *The Merchant*.

What did Olivier mean by maturity? Most probably, that by the late nineteenth century, those economic and social relations determined by capitalist expansion had become so firmly fixed that they were ossified. England was no longer, as in Shakespeare's day, riven by the residual values of feudalism, but was a sophisticated market economy, its ruling classes dedicated to the expansion and control of global supply and demand. It was a world, as Olivier said, of 'tall hats and frock coats', of 'clean and polished fingernails' (*On Acting*, p. 119); a world in which merchants did business in City offices or on the stock exchange, not on quays; a world in which antagonisms between the landed gentry and the new monied classes had grown more subtle, since those with money had for centuries been acquiring land and titles and thus, to the common eye, were all but indistinguishable from the old aristocracy. It was a world where usurers were now called bankers or financiers; a world where Jews such as Rothschild and Disraeli seemed (but only seemed) at last to have overcome the obstacles that for so long had denied them the rights of citizenship. By updating the play to 1880, therefore, Olivier appropriated Shakespeare's text to explore a society in which the economic and social tensions emergent in Elizabethan England had become more intricate and codified.

Indeed, every age has appropriated *The Merchant* for its own purposes. By the ingenious cutting and repositioning of scenes, Irving had transformed the play into a tragedy of social alienation. His strategy was to appeal to the pride Victorians took in their enlightened racial tolerance; that fact that, to do so, he had to fashion his sixteenth-century Shylock as very much an English gentleman did not strike audiences as at all unusual. Shakespeare too, they surmised, was an eminent Victorian who had the misfortune to be born three hundred years before his time, and only they, having achieved the apogee of civilisation, could rightly discern the true message of *The Merchant*. In young Jonathan Miller, Olivier found a director who was willing to appropriate both Shakespeare's text *and* Irving's conception of it to demonstrate how the presumably enlightened Victorians to whom Irving appealed were themselves philistines, their prejudices all the more insidious for being cloaked in shows of courtesy and good will. Miller, a theatrical iconoclast with an interest in social history far keener than Olivier's, located the roots of modern prejudice not in theology, but in economic theory and power relations. 'Modern anti-Semitism,' he argues, 'as Hannah Arendt (*The Origins of Totalitarianism*) has shown, has something to do with nineteenth-century capitalism and politics rather than with biblical theories about the death of Christ.' Jewish financiers often provided the capital with which industrialists made their fortunes, but such provision did not guarantee them access to power or social privilege. In fact, Jews came to be blamed for exploitation, unemployment, market fluctuations, and other economic woes for which capitalists had no ready solutions. Miller used Shakespeare's text to develop such themes: he set Shylock 'within the context of the Rothschilds Banking House, which found that great wealth and prestige never meant exemption from the hatred and anti-Semitism of European society – whose rapid economic and political expansion the Rothschilds were helping to finance' (Miller, *Plays and Players*, p. 53).

What particularly interested Miller was not overt differences between Christians and Jews, but the ways in which ethnic groups 'look for appearances which will substantiate their prejudices'. He therefore envisaged a Shylock not exotically different from the Gentiles, but socially and culturally assimilated.

> Allowing Shylock to appear as one among many businessmen, scarcely distinguishable from them ... made sense of his claim that, apart from his customs, a Jew is like everyone else ... I felt that there was no need in a nineteenth-century setting to distinguish him except by the customs and rituals that he follows discreetly in his home. This highlights and emphasises the absurdity of the racial prejudice.
>
> (Miller, *Subsequent Performances*, pp. 155–6)

Updating the play thus served Miller's agenda as readily as an anthropologically 'correct' production served Irving's; both directors sought thereby to discover the origins of their own culture's attitudes towards Jews, and both suppressed the play's comic potential in order to present the 'real' – that is, the tragically verisimilar – Shylock as a representative of his whole persecuted race.

Where Irving strove for verisimilitude by reconstructing a Venice inspired by the paintings of Bordone, Giorgione, and Veronese, Miller's Venice was inspired by photographs taken by the Count de Primoli at the end of the nineteenth century, photographs which depicted young men frequenting waterside cafés, the bustle of richly detailed piazzas, the faded splendour of *fin de siècle* society. Julia Trevelyan Oman attempted to capture the Venice of de Primoli's photographs behind the proscenium arch of the Old Vic, itself a nineteenth-century picture frame. Her set was a 'golden-ochre piazetta' of colonnades and graceful arches, flanked by flats of a church and a borsa (*Drama*, Summer 1970). Upstage were two Palladian loggias, mirror images of one another, which swung open to reveal the interiors of, respectively, Shylock's house – tastefully sober in its deep-grained woods, bookcases, and busts – and Portia's house, all golden draperies, overstuffed furniture, and Victorian bric-a-brac. By creating a richly pictorial set reminiscent of those on the Victorian stage, Oman confined the action to a novelistic world in which Miller's reading of the play would make sense. Such a set, however, as Peter Ansorge observed, did not 'easily absorb the violent, quickchanging rhythms of the Elizabethan drama – which were designed to portray human experience in an open context, as opposed to the closed, private world of the nineteenth-century novel' (*Plays and Players*, June 1970). At a time when the National's great rival, the Royal Shakespeare Company, was developing a self-consciously theatrical style modelled in part on the Berliner Ensemble – a presentational style which acknowledged the virtues of breaking through the proscenium arch to play directly to the audience – Miller's production was deliberately reactionary and illusionistic, evocative of 'the rather dull, Adriatic mercantile life that Italo Svevo recreates in his novels' (*Subsequent*, p. 107).

The first stage directions in the prompt book indicate how realistically Miller intended his Venetians to go about their business: 'Extras coming from church ... Extras in background carrying parcels with sacks over heads ...'. And amidst this mundane activity, the play opens on the interior of the elegant Café Florian: 'twelve café chairs, three round tables, two oblong tables; white table cloths, brass coffee pot, cups, saucers, liqueur glasses, bottle of Strega, silver tray'. The props define a world of privilege and help to convey Miller's view that the play is driven by class divisions and social injustice.

Here Antonio sits, reading a newspaper on a banquette, sipping coffee. A distinguished grey-haired man in a morning suit, looking like an 'elder Forsyte, with rolled umbrella and spats' (*Daily Telegraph*, 29 April 1970), he speaks with two younger men who clearly are concerned more with his business ventures – and their own coffee – than with his sadness. Their attire and umbrellas identify them as City men, lesser merchants than Antonio; and when Bassanio enters, Miller makes us very aware of their antagonism toward the leisured class. 'We leave you now with better company,' Solanio sneers (I.i.59); and his sarcasm is echoed by Salerio when he speaks of the 'worthier friends' (61) whose company Antonio will prefer to theirs: these merchants thus betray disapproval, perhaps envy, of those who have inherited wealth and never had to work for it. Such disapproval may be warranted, too, for Bassanio and his companions are played as aristocratic idlers who pointedly snub their social inferiors – Bassanio's acknowledgement of Salerio and Solanio, 'Good signors both, when shall we laugh?' (66) is patently insincere – and exploit the generosity of their friend: Gratiano intercepts the waiter to drink a glass of Strega intended for Antonio.

Predicated on class consciousness, the friendship of Antonio and Bassanio elicits a complex response. Jeremy Brett's Bassanio is no youth: a fortyish gigolo in a dashing check jacket who greets his patron 'with a gently teasing kiss on the upstage cheek' (*Punch*, 6 May 1970), he is worshipped by the dignified and understated merchant, a man who is just a bit too old to qualify as a friend and too intimate to be a father. With characteristic hyperbole, Miller suggests that 'the relationship between Bassanio and Antonio made me think of the relationship of Oscar Wilde and Bosie where a sad old queen regrets the opportunistic heterosexual love of a person whom he adored' (*Subsequent*, p. 107). However strained the analogy, Brett's Bassanio is clearly a cunning opportunist: sitting next to Antonio, he feigns ingenuousness as he discusses his debts, acts hesitant to say the word 'money', looks uncomfortable as Antonio presses him to get to the point; then, turning away and rising from his seat at the table, he describes Portia – 'In Belmont is a lady richly left' – to the accompaniment of a violin which strikes up on the word *richly*. The cloyingly romantic music (one critic called it 'Café Chopin') underscores the insincerity of the speech: Bassanio's delivery is arch, affected, calculating. Money motivates his quest for Portia as surely as it underlies his friendship with Antonio. Miller thus identifies Bassanio as a leech who will suck his friend dry: their parasitic relationship is quite at home in the Café Florian, where material success and moral impoverishment go hand in hand – where Bassanio, cheered to have prevailed so easily, slaps his gloves instead of a tip into the waiter's outstretched hand and saunters off, leaving Antonio to pay the bill.

It is to this world that Shylock would like to belong. Olivier seized the opportunity to give Shylock as much psychological depth as a tragic hero, paying careful attention to the subtle ways in which aliens learn to cope in a hostile environment, just as Irving had done a hundred years earlier. Yet unlike Irving, whose model was a Levantine patriarch, Olivier conceived of Shylock as a *Victorian* Jew, a banker striving for assimilation but not yet in command of the manners or *noblesse oblige* of a Rothschild. Driven by a first-generation desire for social respectability, he would paradoxically emulate those very Gentiles he abhors. He dresses like them, only better: wearing a black frock coat over black striped trousers, carrying a silver-topped walking stick and a newspaper from which he reads current market prices through a golden pince-nez – 'then let me see, the rate' (I.iii.96) – he is every inch the financier. Only the yarmulka hidden by his top hat identifies him as an outsider.

In creating so compellingly believable a Shylock, Olivier eschewed the stage tradition that had so often caricatured the Jew: 'Shylock owed more to Benjamin Disraeli than to Fagin, physically and mentally,' Olivier avers. 'There was to be no stropping of knives on the soles of shoes, no fingering the sharpness of the blade, no splitting hairs with the curved edge, no spitting oaths on to the courtroom floor, no rolling eyes to the deaf gods. I was determined to maintain dignity and not stoop physically and mentally to Victorian villainy' (*On Acting*, p. 119). His reference to Disraeli is not merely fortuitous, for he admits in *Confessions of an Actor* 'to having been so impressed by the interpretation of Disraeli by Mr. George Arliss in an exceptionally good talkie made in 1929 that, to be honest, I lifted it (pinched is such a common word) for my playing of Shylock'. Even here, Olivier communicates the bourgeois sense of decorum – 'pinched is such a common word' – with which he invested his Shylock. From Arliss he borrowed the Disraeli curl on his forehead and the Disraeli mouth: he had a special front row of teeth made, with its companion extra lower gum, and took particular pride in the authenticity they lent to his appearance. 'These two little friends', he admits, 'made my mouth area from just underneath my nose to the top of my chin protrude enough (one feature is sufficient) to lend a semitic look to my whole countenance without further sculptural addition' (p. 236).

This set of false teeth and gums helped him to affect an accent that spoke volumes about his social aspirations. As J. C. Trewin observes, Olivier's Shylock 'knows that he is an alien in Venice, but he seeks to ingratiate himself with the Christians, to imitate the affectations of their speech, to clip words like "meanin'" and "speakin'" ... [yet is] probably aware that his carefully nurtured accent can slip into plebeian vowel sounds, and that the game he plays is fruitless' (*Illustrated London News*, 9 May 1970). Irving Wardle, too, astutely concludes that, although in appearance Shylock is virtually indistinguishable from Antonio,

> within ... he has been incurably maimed by the process of assimilation. His delivery is a ghastly compound of speech tricks picked up from the Christian rich: posh vowels and the slipshod terminations of the hunting counties. 'I am debatin' of my present state,' he spits out, fingering a silver-topped cane; and then spoils the gesture by dissolving into paroxysms of silent, slack-jawed laughter.
>
> (*The Times*, 29 April 1970)

Shylock is thus at once a creation and a victim of his society. He apes the dress, the manners, and the speech of his social 'betters', and even surpasses them in word-play. His delight in puns, for example, is never more outrageous than when, dressed to dine with the Christians in a cream-coloured stole over black tails, he delivers lines rich in social resonance – 'Well, thou shalt see, thy eyes shall be thy judge / The difference of old Shylock and Bassanio' (II.v.1–2) – pronouncing the middle syllables of 'Base-aini-o' in such a way as to make a plural anus of his host (*Punch*, 6 May 1970). At times such as this, he seems supremely confident of his place in the community of Gentiles, superior to them in wit and style. Yet in so far as he exaggerates their affectations or does not quite get the accent right, he verges on the grotesque; and the hint of grotesqueness, of course, only reinforces the prejudices of those who all along have known that he was not one of them. Benedict Nightingale summarises the problematic social position of Olivier's Jew: 'He is a foreigner in a public school, an aesthete in a rugger club, a gargoyle in a gallery of classical faces, a profoundly emotional being in a world where emotions embarrass people, and one can readily imagine the history of snubs and mortification behind him' (*New Statesman*, 8 May 1970). Like many a nineteenth-century critic, Nightingale imagines a social and psychological history for Shylock. Olivier's performance invites him to do so.

In order to refashion the play as a realistic portrait of late Victorian society – a society in which Jews were nominally assimilated and prejudices more covert than they had been in Elizabethan England – Miller had to adjust Shakespeare's text. Such adjustments are evident as early as I.iii. When Antonio enters to enquire about the loan, Shylock tips his hat to him, and the courtesy is returned. These men will be civil to each other, for civility is the badge of all their tribe; only by dodging and circling one another do they betray their deeper antagonism. Miller cuts the entire aside (33–44) in which Shylock confides,

> I hate him for he is a Christian;
> But more, for that in low simplicity
> He lends out money gratis, and brings down
> The rate of usance here with us in Venice ...

– thereby effacing both the economic and the religious motives for Shylock's wanting to catch Antonio 'upon the hip'. Such sentiments clearly belong to an earlier age, just as the aside itself does (an Elizabethan device that has no place in illusionist theatre); and when we are denied the privilege of overhearing Shylock's thoughts, his motives for agreeing to the bond remain necessarily opaque (Sullivan, pp. 33–4). Like the Venetians, we must try to fathom his motives by closely observing his behaviour, and his behaviour gives us much to think about. It has great humour and mimetic vigour: his gentle greeting to Antonio, 'Your worship was the last man in our mouths' (52), is accompanied by masticatory jaw movements; and when he tells how Jacob 'peeled me certain wands' (76), he inserts his walking stick through his outstretched hand with corkscrew movements, which suggests not only the peeling process, but animal copulation as well (Billington, p. 84).

Yet Shylock drops his mask of bonhomie when Antonio insists on an answer. With controlled fury he turns on his old rival: 'Signor Antonio, many a time and oft / In the Rialto you have rated me / About my monies ...' (98–100), unearthing a buried pun in *rated*, the word he has just emphasised while checking his paper for the current rate of usance (96). He lispingly ridicules Antonio's aristocratic accent on 'you come to me, and you say / "Shylock, we would have monies"' (107–8), pointing his stick accusingly on '*you* say so, / *You* ...' (108–9), the explosive force of each *you* laying bare the humiliation to which the Christian community has subjected him. But he regains his composure to propose the 'merry' bond; and in this context, it is precisely that – a bond made in jest, a loan of three thousand ducats gratis, an uncharacteristic show of generosity from a Jew known for sharp business practices. Olivier delivers his lines with ingratiating humour: 'let the forfeit / Be nominated for ...' – and here he pauses, searches for an idea; and when it comes, he tosses it off with wry wit while touching Antonio's lapel – 'an equal pound / Of your fair flesh' (141–3). In the world of Victorian business, a bond which specified the forfeiture of a pound of flesh would have been simply incredible. Here, Shylock appears to use it as a throw-away, in self-mockery – proof, perhaps, of how mistaken the Christians have been in him. Pleased with Antonio's consent, he removes his glove to offer his hand; but Bassanio's objection to the condition leaves him again humiliated, his 'kind' offer spurned, his hand unshaken. Contemptuously, Olivier slings his stick over his shoulder and does a marvellous false exit – 'If he will take it, so; if not, adieu' (162) – spinning on his heels the moment Antonio relents. Having exposed the distrust with which Christians and Jews regard each other, the scene returns to feigned civility, doffed hats, and smiles.

Miller thus encourages his audience to discover in Shakespeare's Venice a precursor of modern society. The play was ripe for his revision. For a century, certainly since Irving, it had been widely recognised as a play whose comic form did not comfortably resolve the issues of racism and social class it broached, and the horrors of the Holocaust only served to sharpen our focus on them. By updating the play to the late nineteenth century, Miller forced audiences to confront those issues without the reassurance provided by the historical 'difference' of an Elizabethan staging. The society he created more closely resembled their own, the codes of conduct were familiar, the subtleties of prejudice readily recognisable. His interpretation often challenged what generations of playgoers had taken the play to mean, but in doing so it seldom worked against the text. Three instances stand out. First, Miller fashioned wooing scenes which subverted the romantic values traditionally ascribed to them. Second, he reshaped the drama of Shylock's revenge to make it more humanly credible. And third, he made discordant the ostensible harmonies of Act V. In these ways, he demystified a text encrusted with stage tradition and thereby inspired a generation of directors to review the play in light of contemporary cultural biases.

Where Irving's insistence on Shylock's essential humanity and Venice's realism clashed with Ellen Terry's romantic conception of Belmont, Miller's production was all of a piece, stylistically consistent throughout. In 'Miller's thoughtful deformation of Shakespeare', writes J. W. Lambert, assuming a standard reading of the play, Belmont is not 'the neoplatonic fancy of an ideal world of love, music and moonlight' (*Drama*, Summer 1970), but the fantasy world of the *nouveaux riches*, a tasteless tribute to consumerism. *This* is what men seek, the lucre for which they hazard all they have; and as such, it becomes the focus of the play's capitalist values, not an alternative to them. Belmont – just as it might have done in an Elizabethan production – serves as the feminine mirror into which Venetians look to see their own greed prettily reflected.

Portia's first scene with Nerissa alerts us to the equation of Belmont with Venice. The loggia opens to reveal Portia in her boudoir, every inch the chatelaine of Belmont: elegantly dressed in corset, bustles, and petticoats, she moves comfortably amid her Victorian stuff – shawls and cushions, oriental carpets and lace curtains, chairs and settee, vases filled with lilies, ferns, and peacock feathers – the queen of all she surveys. As Nerissa opens letters from would-be suitors and reads off their names, Portia squints at slides of them through an antique viewer: the device quickly establishes both the period – the dawn of the technological age – and Portia's fondness for toys. Furthermore, it distances her from her suitors: they become mere excuses for her to display her wit. And this Portia has wit aplenty. Joan Plowright plays her with the command of a woman of years. Searching for a Jamesian source, Miller compares her with Isabel Archer (*Plays and Players*, March 1970); Nightingale less charitably calls her a bossy suffragette with little moral conviction (*New Statesman*, 8 May 1970); and Peter Ansorge, 'a new rich snobby spinster [with] a determination to buy a husband' (*Plays and Players*, June 1970). No young maiden who will submit to the will of her father, this Portia knows what she is about, and it is *not* her father's business.

Audiences were either amused or outraged by the way in which Portia – and Miller – sent up her suitors. By 1970, it had become customary to play the suitors for laughs: Komisarjevsky's satirical treatment of them had proved so popular that subsequent directors readily followed suit. The farce of Morocco's wooing scene is very much in the vein of Komisarjevsky: in a conflation of II.i and II.vii (by now, a convention), Morocco is caricatured as 'a diplomatic Al Jolson minstrel just back from the colonies' (*Plays and Players*, June 1970). Not the 'tawny Moor all in white' with three or four followers indicated by the stage direction, he enters alone, dressed in Victorian military regalia like a colonial officer in whom the ideal of cultural assimilation is turned to folly. His blue uniform, complete with epaulettes on the shoulders and a banner around the chest, suggests that he is a proud product of British imperialism, someone with a public school education who may do very well when he returns to his own country but should not expect to mix races with Portia. In fact, Portia and Nerissa shriek when they see him, shocked that someone of his leer might actually *win* the lottery. But the scene gives him short shrift: in the tradition of Irving, much of his eloquent speech in praise of Portia is cut (including lines 38–59), thus sharpening his focus on the caskets alone, which he inspects formally, arm bent at the waist, white-gloved hand gesturing, and his speech comically arhythmic with the kind of foreign pronunciations ('deserb' for 'deserve') that will forever make him the butt of jokes among the ruling class. Pausing at the silver casket to ask, 'What if I strayed no farther, but chose here?' (35), he breaches all decorum by sliding an arm around Portia's waist; she recoils from his touch. Once he has chosen, however, the scene hastens to its conclusion. The naked disappointment of his 'O, hell! What have we here?' (62), like that of Komisarjevsky's Morocco, underscores the pomposity of his proud boasts, and all that remains of his scroll reading is four lines – 65–6, 69, and 73 – which quickly deflate his social presumption and lend more point to Portia's tart dismissal of him and all of his complexion.

Miller's ingenuity shows to even better advantage in the scene of Arragon's wooing. Usually played as an effete young nobleman, Arragon here is reduced to a palsied *senex amans*, the last gasp of the titled aristocracy who, 'tottering into the contest as if from a ducal old folks' home, has entirely lost control of his motor faculties' (*The Times*, 29 April 1970). The staging makes a mockery of his suitability as a contestant for Portia's hand. 'Armed with spectacles rather than a scimitar ... clad in tails and white tie, white hair wildly erect ... Arragon walks blindly past the caskets, submitting to the two women's pushes in finding his way' (Schlueter, p. 171). Portia exasperatedly interrupts him as he rehearses the injunctions of his oath, cutting all but the first line of his speech; and taking the article of agreement out of his hand, she offers him a cup of tea instead, into which he keeps putting sugar cubes until, with a comic arbitrariness, he returns the eighth cube to the bowl and absentmindedly drops the silver tongs into his coat pocket. Massive textual cuts bring him quickly to his choice, but only a deft manoeuvre by Nerissa prevents him from putting the key into the wrong – the lead – casket. The prize he wins, the 'portrait of a blinking idiot', elicits a senile cackle; and as he departs, he kisses Nerissa's hand (though Portia has extended hers) and gives Portia the portrait to keep, promising never to marry.

Such comedy makes mischief of the casket plot; for if Portia's suitors are patently unsuitable – if their merits are exploded by absurd pomposity or grotesque senility – and if, furthermore, their hazarding for her entails no element of risk, then one cannot take the romantic premises of the lottery seriously. As June Schlueter argues, 'in agreeing to the conditions of the test, [Arragon] has hazarded nothing, for the prospect of continuing his royal line through a legitimate – or any – heir is as laughable as it is unlikely'. The imposition of hard conditions seems intended to limit choosers to those who might be worthy of Portia – 'a strategy that has worked with the suitors from foreign lands who have earlier taken their leave'. That Morocco and Arragon accept those conditions would seem to argue in them a merit lacking in the others. 'But the reduction of Arragon to dotage' – and, I might add, the reduction of Morocco to a figure of imperial fun – 'makes a mockery of this purpose' and raises the possibility that Portia, the prize, 'may be bestowed unearned' (p. 171).

Her father's inspiration for protecting her from the undeserving may not, after all, be foolproof. Yet Miller offers something in compensation, for by rigging the casket plot, he justifies Portia's taking matters into her own hands. If she does not teach Bassanio how to choose right, she may be condemned to a miserable marriage. In order to spare herself from the likes of Morocco and Arragon, therefore, she must feel no compunction about flouting her father's will; she must (with a relish that would have seemed even more timely in 1970 than today) liberate herself from male tyranny and assert her right to self-determination. A woman of 40, after all, should know her own mind about finding a husband, and it is only Plowright's expertly comic playing that keeps us from wondering why she hasn't married earlier, or what in God's name her father was up to by keeping his grown daughter closeted for so many years.

Portia meets her perfect match in Bassanio, whose designs on her money are as calculating as her strategy to catch him. With a gambler's instinct for winning, he follows the rules of romantic courtship to the letter, performing the casket ritual with mock sincerity and counting on Portia's ingenuity to help him out. Olivier admits that he had waggishly suggested Bassanio should be Portia's *only* suitor, coming disguised first as Morocco, then as Arragon, one way or the other guaranteeing a victory. Though the suggestion mercifully was not taken up – it would too radically have debased the moral and mimetic credibility of Belmont – it nevertheless demonstrates that for this production, Bassanio all along was conceived to be a self-serving poseur, and the outcome of the lottery a foregone conclusion.

Miller's staging provides ample opportunity for such role-play. The lovers enter III.ii in riding habits (Belmont apparently is hunt country), wielding their crops suggestively and discussing the lottery without much emotional conviction. Portia adopts a teasing tone when she tells Bassanio, 'I could teach you / How to choose right,' then adds unconvincingly, 'but then I am forsworn. / So will I never be' (10–12); and she delivers her behest, 'If you do love me, you *will* find me out' (41, her emphasis) in such a way as to alert him to some chicanery to come. After such calculation, the mythic hyperbole of her paean to Bassanio rings false; indeed, much of it (53–60) is cut, denying him the status of young Alcides and her the unlikely role of virgin tribute. But enough remains so that her injunction 'Go, Hercules' prompts the audience to cynical laughter: there is simply too great a gap between the demigod she envisages and the charlatan we see to make the analogy credible.

We do not wait long to discover what her ploy is: she will use the song, 'Tell me where is fancy bred', to cue him which casket to choose. The possible subliminal message of the song, both in its focus on fancy's deceptions and in its implicit rhyme with 'lead', have long been noted; even Ellen Terry had entertained but dismissed the notion that Portia intends to subvert her father's will by such means. Miller, however, found the subversion irresistible. Bassanio is just about to address the caskets when two middle-aged sopranos, referred to in the prompt book as 'the Gemini', dressed in lead-coloured satin gowns with their hair pulled back into buns, bustle in and distract him. As they begin their *bel canto* duet, they advance on Bassanio, crowding the ornate pedestal on which the caskets rest and fixing their gaze unashamedly on the lead casket when they sing 'In the cradle where it lies' (69). When it is over, the performance of these leaden belles is rewarded with applause – ours and Bassanio's.

The ingenuity with which the Gemini give away Portia's secret is enormously amusing, but equally amusing is Gratiano's dimwitted response. Thinking he has got the clue, he points decisively to the silver casket. Bassanio, however, is more astute than his friend: having exchanged a knowing smile with Nerissa, he is prepared to play the part required of him. Brushing Gratiano aside, he addresses the caskets in the same declamatory style with which he described Portia to Antonio in the opening scene; and although the speech is drastically cut, he nonetheless says what he *needs* to say to appear a lover who will not be deceived with ornament. Pausing at the lead casket, 'here choose I' (107), he steals a glance at Portia, who puts her hands to her face in premeditated amazement. And when he unlocks it to discover – with all the surprise he can muster – her portrait, he launches into the most artificially Petrarchan of all his speeches, 'What demi-god / Hath come so near creation?' (115–16), gesturing extravagantly as he praises each feature of her painted face, checking over his shoulder to see the effect of his hyperbole, and, confident of success, reaching a breathless climax on 'But her eyes!' (123) as she, like an ageing *ingénue*, bats her lashes and wipes away a tear.

The two lovers thus get what they want with their eyes open, feigning compliance with the rituals of courtship demanded by her father and by society. Their charade is splendidly ironic. In one sense, the lyric speeches which fall so trippingly from their tongues preserve the romantic ethos of Belmont. But those speeches are not for a moment believable; they are *acted*. Miller's cynical depiction of Belmont, therefore, provides no ethical alternative to the world of Venice as more conventional interpretations argue it should: all passion here is unfelt; all talk of love, mere pretence. When Portia wishes herself 'A thousand times more fair, ten thousand times / More rich ... only to stand high in [his] account' (154–5), her sentiments do not redeem Bassanio's vocabulary of mercantile value, as they commonly are said to do, but instead reaffirm the very values that have brought him to her. Worth, in Belmont as in Venice, remains a commodity: 'the full sum of me / Is sum of something' (157–8), Portia puns, as Bassanio surveys the riches he may now take title to. Thus, through the ambiguous language of value, Miller's Belmont codifies the risks and rewards of venture capitalism and perpetuates the romantic fictions – love, honour, obedience – by which a mercantile society disguises its fundamental greed. In Miller's hands, however, that disguise is joyously penetrable.

The joy Miller takes in demystifying Belmont has inevitable consequences for the bond plot, for against such chicanery as the Christians practise, Shylock's passion stands out as something finer, nobler, and more sincere. To ensure that we recognise the distinction, Miller reshapes the text to Shylock's advantage, cutting such obviously prejudicial lines as 'I did dream of moneybags tonight' (II.v.18) or, more significantly, the entirety of II.viii and Shylock's aside against Antonio. The Victorian gentility for which Miller strove makes these adjustments not only permissible, but necessary: Shylock in this period would not admit to hating Antonio because he is Christian, or because he lends out money gratis, any more than Antonio would spit on Shylock in public or kick him over his threshold. The bond, as we have seen, becomes not a ruse to mask a deeper malice as it was for Irving, but a means by which Shylock strives to win the acceptance of the Gentiles by playing according to *their* rules. And Miller revises Shakespeare's text most startlingly when he suggests that Shylock's revenge is motivated not by an implacable hatred of Christians, but by the loss of Jessica, and by this alone.

Miller seeks to explain Shylock's revenge as the anguish of a bereaved father. He had informed Olivier that the marriage of a daughter to a Christian is 'the very most appalling disaster that can happen in an orthodox Jewish family', who 'in such circumstances hold a funeral service for the errant girl, whose name is struck from the family records, and from then on she is dead to them. When it happens to Shylock as a Christian "joke", he is stirred to the boiling point of fury and proceeds to his vengeance as is not only natural but in fact his expected duty' (*Confessions*, p. 235). To excuse Shylock's lust for a pound of Christian flesh as a 'natural' and 'expected' behaviour may seem to strain the text, yet Olivier found a brilliant strategy for communicating to the audience just that in III.i. As the scene begins, he lurks on the balcony above his loggia, observing Salerio and Solanio as they gossip about Antonio. When he descends to them, in his shirtsleeves, obviously distraught, his accusation has a deadly force: 'You knew, none so well, none so well as you, of my daughter's flight' (III.i.20–1). Their mockery goads him to further fury, as does their mentioning the losses of Antonio, who obviously now will not be able to repay his debt to Shylock. Their intention is spiteful, but it backfires; for by mentioning Antonio's losses, they prompt Shylock to think about the merchant as a scapegoat for his own loss of Jessica. He screams uncontrolled, 'There I have another bad match: a bankrupt, a prodigal, who dare scarce show his head on the Rialto' (35–6), and then proceeds to the downstage railing where he rests for support, his back to the audience, as if gazing into a canal. As a bell tolls, apparently a death knell, he suddenly turns around, raises his hand to his lower lip with a look of malicious inspiration, and mutters, 'Let him look to his bond' (37). Here it occurs to him *for the first time* that the bond may serve as a vehicle for retribution: an Antonio for a Jessica. Miller thus invites us to feel that Shylock's 'depth of love for Jessica has become twisted into bottomless hate for Antonio by a kind of psychological *lex talionis:* his beloved daughter, his heart, has been taken from him by a Christian, so his revenge will be to remove the heart of a Christian' (Perret, p. 147).

So inspired, Olivier speaks the rest of the speech rapid fire, the speed and tension of his delivery indicating that he at last has found an outlet for all the years of humiliation he has suffered. He bears down threateningly on Salerio and Solanio, who are mere reeds in the wind of his passion; their 'thou wilt not take his flesh' (40), spoken through nervous laughter, sounds as fearful as it is ineffectual. His series of rhetorical questions beginning with 'Hath not a Jew eyes?' (47) thus becomes not a plea for pity but a clarion call to revenge, 'senses, affections, passions' building to the kind of rolling-eyed emotion that characterised Olivier's Othello years earlier. He cuts the next four lines in order to arrive more quickly at the word 'revenge' (52), a word he insistently emphasises by slapping his right hand into the palm of his left and shooting the thumb of his left hand outwards like 'a butcher slapping a piece of meat on to a weighing machine' (Billington, p. 86). The speech reaches a climax when, as he arrives at the last question – 'what should his sufferance be by Christian example?' (55) – we await the expected answer, 'Why, revenge', but it doesn't come. He slaps his right hand into his left, extends his thumb, then, overcome with grief, pauses on 'Why' and, panting heavily, cannot utter the final two syllables. The effect is breathtaking: 'revenge' never echoes more clearly in our ears than here.

Shylock's emotional intensity contrasts sharply with the coolly detached playing of the Christians, and the contrast is sharpest when Shylock enters his house, leaving Salerio and Solanio, unmoved by his grief, to observe Tubal's approach with smug disdain: 'Here comes another of the tribe' (61). There is, to borrow Shylock's phrase, more difference between their blood and the Jews' than between red wine and Rhenish: where, typically, productions suggest some conspiracy between the Jews, with Tubal serving as Shylock's collection agent, Miller advances the idea that Tubal, another top-hatted banker all in black, has come to offer condolences to a grieving friend. A sense of mourning haunts the scene: Olivier enters with a dress draped over his arms – the very dress Jessica has shed onstage to take on a male disguise at the end of II.v – stroking it, as if it were his daughter's hair, and sighing 'Why, there, there, there, there' (66). The image resonates with Shakespearean associations of fathers lamenting the loss of children, just as the line itself anticipates Lear's cry that Cordelia will come again 'never, never, never, never'. Miller points out:

> In *King Lear*, as in *Merchant*, a daughter who betrays her father seems, in his eyes, to die when she denies him her love. Holding the empty dress, Olivier appeared to be carrying the corpse of the departed daughter, as Shylock wishes when he says 'I would my daughter were dead at my foot, and the jewels in her ear! Would she were hearsed at my foot, and the ducats in her coffin!'
>
> (*Subsequent*, p. 108)

With a debt to Freudian psychology, Shylock here sublimates his grief by fixating on the loss of his ducats; he is one of those people who, as Benedict Nightingale observes, 'under stress become obsessed with details, minutiae, rather than face trouble squarely' (*New Statesman*, 8 May 1970). Therefore, when he hurls the dress to the floor and, stooping over it with his arms extended backwards in an Othello-like paroxysm of grief, wishes his daughter dead at his foot, we understand his words to express his deeper wish to have her back.

Shylock's exchange with Tubal is sometimes played for laughs. The information Tubal metes out, alternating news of Jessica's expenditures and Antonio's losses, moves Shylock to such extremes of agony and ecstasy that his behaviour may seem ludicrous. In this production, however, Shylock's mood swings are psychologically credible, poignant rather than comic, and Tubal parcels out information sparingly to protect Shylock's feelings, not to toy with them. Reduced almost to incoherence as he babbles 'no ill luck stirring but what lights o' my shoulders' (74–5), Shylock pricks up his ears at the news of Antonio's ill luck. 'I thank God, I thank God!' (81) he cries in falsetto, beating Tubal on the breast with his fists and then, on 'Is it true, is it true?', breaking into a gleeful dance around the dress that calls his sanity into question. Much noted by critics, this skip-like dance was inspired by the little jig of triumph done by Adolf Hitler in a railway carriage at Compiègne when he heard that France had surrendered. Olivier, who remembered the newsreel, 'was delighted with the unpredictable peculiarity of this gesture' (*Subsequent*, p. 108). But joy quickly yields to sorrow. Returning to his senses and to Tubal, he asks (adding his own words to the text), 'Didst thou hear naught else in Genoa, hm?' (84); and learning that Jessica has sold the turquoise he had of Leah, he sinks to his haunches to protest that he would not have given it for a wilderness of monkeys. The prolonged wail that escapes his lips on the first syllable of *wilderness* leads to a fit of sobbing – and blowing his nose into a large handkerchief – during which Tubal's consolation goes unheeded (Foulkes, 'Shylock', p. 32). Then, regaining his composure, he draws himself up, walks to the table, removes a tallis from the drawer, folds it, touches it to his lips, and drapes it over his head as he bids Tubal to meet him at the synagogue. This image has a profound significance: for the first time in the production,

Miller reveals the importance of Jewish heritage to a man who has striven to deny it but who now, at a time of emotional dislocation, turns to it for solace. Going to the synagogue affirms, for Shylock, a world of values he has all but forsaken; it is a place to reclaim his birthright. Shylock's passion recalls him to his roots. And when he vows to have the heart of Antonio, his intention is less economically motivated than Shakespeare ever intended: the rest of his line, 'for were he out of Venice I can make what merchandise I will' (101–2), is tellingly omitted.

With the help of textual adjustments, therefore, Miller enables Shylock to become a tragic figure maimed by his struggle for assimilation. The authenticity of feeling in this scene surpasses anything of which the Gentiles are capable. Yet to communicate such feeling, Olivier resorts to a heroic acting style seemingly at odds with the naturalism towards which the production has striven. In III.i, Olivier forsakes restraint for the grand gestures he had once used in *Othello*, his pinched nasal tone giving way before the thundering crescendos of heroic passion. By breaking out of the restrained acting style in which he aped his Christian 'betters', Olivier draws a powerful dramatic contrast between himself and the 'civilised' society which has failed to assimilate him. He was attacked for this: one critic wrote that 'once Olivier crumbles the business man is forgotten ... and we watch another version of Othello falling back into dark, tribal blood rites. The Venetian setting dwindles into a cardboard background for an "heroic" performance ... Olivier's Shylock isn't a Jew, but an actor with a Jewish director up his sleeve' (*Plays and Players*, June 1970). Yet for all its wit, this criticism betrays a cultural bias, an expectation of stereotypical Jewish behaviour that at once belittles Miller's achievement and ignores the dramatic *function* of Olivier's shift in acting style. As Michael Billington observes, 'the terrifying and exhilarating spectacle of a full-scale piece of heroic acting' is strikingly incongruous 'in an orderly, mercantile late-nineteenth-century setting' and makes tragically significant 'the tension between period and style' (p. 83). The heroic style in which Olivier displays his grief effectively isolates him, both morally and aesthetically, from the society of his fellow actors.

This scene, not the trial, is the climax of the production; it is a bravura demonstration of how one who is ostracised from a genteel but closed community must break under the pressure of failed expectations. At the trial, Shylock tries to compose himself once again in the only way he can, by aping *their* manners and playing by *their* rules. Determined not to reveal the nature of his injury to those who have injured him, he refuses to give a reason for seeking Antonio's life other than the 'lodged hate' he bears him, allowing mildly offensive analogies (some men 'cannot contain their urine' (IV.i.50) when they hear a bagpipe) to work as defences against a world that has proven itself his enemy. The one thing he *can* rely on, he thinks, is the law, whose ostensible impartiality underpins the economic system and helps to maintain Venice's credibility as an arena for international trade. Shylock knows he is appealing to the self-interest of the ruling class when he warns, 'If you deny [the bond], let the danger light / Upon your charter and your city's freedom!' (38–9). He is aware that he has them in a bind: if they honour the spirit of the law and maintain its proper indifference to individuals, then Antonio will be murdered; if they violate it to save one of their own, then they will risk discrediting the legal foundation on which Venetian enterprise depends (Eagleton, pp. 35–8).

Miller's staging of the trial is appropriately muted, restrained, and bloodless. Such restraint was not to everyone's liking: Harold Hobson complained that 'in the long history of *The Merchant of Venice* the trial scene can never have generated so little excitement; it is as flat as a puncture' (*Sunday Times*, 3 May 1970). The exciting public spectacle Hobson might have preferred, however, would have been singularly out of place in a society whose members gather in small chambers to make gentlemen's agreements and to assert their corporate privilege (from the Latin for 'private law'). Miller's Victorian power-brokers set great store by form: soberly dressed in business suits, they shake hands upon entering and sit in red leather chairs around a large table. Shylock, briefcase in hand, makes up one of them, tapping his fingers impatiently as they try to strike a bargain, smugly reminding them that the law protects his rights as well as theirs. Like them, he preserves the veneer of civility. This court is no place for him to carry scales or sharpen a knife against the sole of his shoe – a servant sharpens the knife behind him, and he intimates that the scales are ready off stage – nor is it a place for Antonio, sitting opposite him, to betray his anxiety, trained as he is in the art of the stiff upper lip. All that distinguishes Shylock from

Figure 4 Joan Plowright as Portia and Laurence Olivier as Shylock in the trial scene of the National Theatre production directed by Jonathan Miller, 1970. Courtesy of The Kobal Collection.

Antonio, in fact, is the yarmulka he wears, and that is little enough to lend plausibility to Portia's question, 'Which is the merchant here and which the Jew?' (170; see Figure 4).

Portia herself, however, is implausible. Her disguise strains belief in the most fanciful of productions, and it becomes an absurd incongruity in Miller's, where the leap of faith required to accept her as a man seriously compromises the naturalism he seeks to impose on Shakespeare's text. Such incongruity is the inevitable result of an attempt to suppress the allegorical and folkloric origins of the play in favour of its more topical, realistic potential: the cross-dressed heroine appears to have strayed in from another play far more naive than this. Joan Plowright is clearly not comfortable playing Balthasar. Yet her costume (black juridical robe, black hat, white cravat), her resonant voice, and her assertive, businesslike demeanour make her convincingly masculine, if not convincingly male, and suggest that she might (if only women were allowed) survive as well as men in the corporate world of Venice. No young fairy-tale princess with a penchant for performing miracles, she, like Shylock, strives to establish her legitimacy through a knowledge of Venetian law.

The scales of justice, of course, are tipped against Shylock. The pretence to impartiality, the insistence on the disinterestedness of the law, only makes Portia's quibble seem the more underhand and Shylock's defeat the more prearranged. Miller conceives of the quibble much as Terry Eagleton does, as an absurd adherence to the *letter* of the law at the expense of its *spirit*, a reading of the law which, 'aberrant because too faithful,' skates 'perilously close to promoting "private law"', or class privilege. As a strategy, it is perfectly in keeping with Portia's manipulation of the lottery in Belmont: it bespeaks a morality far more 'interested' than she would admit to. Such a strategy, of course, 'threatens to bring the law into disrepute', just as Shylock warned it would. The 'ruthless precision' with which Portia interprets the text 'parallels Shylock's relentless insistence on having his bond'; and by forcing the Christians to outdo his own legalism, Shylock is, in a sense, vindicated (Eagleton, p. 37). Such vindication brings small comfort, however, when the Christians use the law not only to deny Shylock his pound of flesh, but to dispose of his life and living as well. Shylock's case may blow the sanctimonious cover of Venetian law and expose it as the handmaiden – or whore – of those in power, but this production does not allow us to forget that Shylock suffers nonetheless.

In defeat, Olivier returns one last time to the heroic tradition of Irving. When he hears the penalties against an alien, he turns around to utter a cry that will not come; then 'his quivering hand reaches out for the rail to steady himself. When Antonio demands that he presently turn Christian, Shylock crumples over the rail, just as Irving had done, where two Jews in attendance help him to his feet; and as he mutters 'I am content' (390), his back rigid and eyeballs bulging, he is apparently suffering a seizure or stroke. This prepares us for the most celebrated moment in the production, when, a few seconds after his long Irvingesque exit, he emits an otherworldly keening, 'sharp and intense at first and then barbarically extended – that reminds one of a wolf impaled on a spike and dying a slow death' (Billington, pp. 88–9). If Olivier 'wanted something to remain ringing in the ears long after [he] was in the dressing room, something that would stay with the audience through the sweetness and light of the final romantic comic scene' (*On Acting*, p. 130), he certainly succeeded. His wailing left the Christians momentarily speechless in the knowledge of what they had done: Bassanio in particular seemed troubled, raising a hand in protest, then turning his back to the others (Perret, p. 153). On the Victorian stage, such an effect might have required the omission of Act V as irrelevant to the tragedy that has just occurred.

Shylock's grand exit casts a pall over Act V, just as Olivier wished. The return to Belmont has little sweetness and light; and despite the lovely Victorian conservatory in which the lovers meet, their games do not affirm marital harmony so much as anticipate discord. Miller rejects the romantic resolution towards which the play's comic form would seem to point and insists instead on the text's resistance to closure (Howard, pp. 122–6). This resistance is immediately apparent in Lorenzo and Jessica's mythic celebration of the night. In most productions, their nocturne takes the form of playful banter: references to such doomed lovers as Troilus and Cressida, Dido and Aeneas, Pyramus and Thisbe are but comic provocations to a declaration of love. In Miller's version, however, these references portend disharmony in Belmont, for Lorenzo and Jessica speak at cross purposes, he attempting to humour her, and she, sadly disillusioned, accusing him of false promise: 'In such a night / Did young Lorenzo swear he loved her well, / Stealing her soul with many vows of faith, / And ne'er a true one' (V.i.17–20). On each line, Jessica moves further downstage away from Lorenzo, while he, oblivious to what she feels, follows her, intent only on teaching her all he knows about music. Looking priggish in his white summer suit, Lorenzo is 'a dogged, middle-class didactic Hampstead mini-intellectual' who punctuates his observations with stabs of his pipe and spreads out a handkerchief before sitting down to give Jessica 'a much-needed education, during which ... she falls asleep, like Miranda bored rigid by Prospero, but without the latter's textual sanction' (*Drama*, Summer 1970).

If Miller finds no textual sanction for this, neither does he expressly contradict the text: Jessica's interaction with the Christians is something Shakespeare sketched so lightly that a director of Miller's imagination could virtually invent her character. With a sensibility born of his own study of social anthropology,

Miller asks questions of Jessica most directors would not think to ask. How does she adjust to having betrayed her father? Does she regret having given up her home and her religion to marry a Christian – and, in particular, *this* Christian? How does she feel when, introduced at Belmont, her first task is to condemn her father before a group of people largely unknown to her? Does such disloyalty win her acceptance? How is she, a Jew, treated at Belmont? The answers Miller provides are far from reassuring. They transform Jessica's brief scenes into a tragedy to parallel – and extend – her father's.

Throughout the production, she has acted melancholy, not at all the giddy, venturesome girl one might expect. Wearing attire as subdued as Shylock's, she has led a life of puritanical sobriety; even her elopement is undertaken not in the spirit of carnival, but with apprehension. Her relationship with her father is formal. She gives him a kiss upon entering (II.v) and hands him his gloves, hat, and walking stick as he departs to dine with the Christians; and when he entrusts the keys of the house to her, he lays his hand gently on her head – a relatively demonstrative sign of affection in the repressed Victorian society Miller creates. This father and daughter share a strong familial bond, a bond based on love, duty, and obedience to patriarchal values. And when these values, however confining, are so sincerely expressed, one can only wonder why Jessica would wish to exchange them for those of the hypocritical Christians – unless she is motivated by the same hunger for assimilation her father is.

In Belmont, Jessica pays for her mistake. The Christians there are as patronising to her as members of an exclusive club might be to a Jew brought one evening as a guest. Portia manages to forget her name on two occasions, addressing Lorenzo as 'you and ... ah ... ah ... [with a prompt] Jessica!' (III.iv), and treats her with condescension both as a woman and a Jew. Coming from Shylock's sober household, Jessica cannot but be struck by the crass materialism and emotional chill of the group she has married into: she can no more be assimilated into their society than could her father. Her reluctance to embrace the Christians' values is strongly implied when she admits, 'I am never merry when I hear sweet music' (69); but Lorenzo, ever out of tune with her, provides an academic explanation for her melancholy full of analogies that only 'intellectualise her emotions' (*Queen*, June 1970) and reveal how little he understands her. The potential for such discord resides in the text, but it took Miller's sensitive ear to mark the music.

Even when the principals enter from their victory in Venice, Miller holds romantic harmony at bay. He uses the episode of the rings to bring all values into question. Traditionally, this episode has been seen to recapitulate within a comic frame the theme of hazarding all one has and ultimately to reaffirm the lovers' faith to one another. We know that Portia's and Nerissa's test of their husbands has been all in fun and that they themselves, even after lying with the doctor and his clerk, are as pure as driven snow. Yet the comic banter about infidelity sounds curiously tainted when spoken by characters we have been taught not to trust: with their cavalier disregard of the spirit of oath and law still fresh in our minds, we hesitate to credit the faith they swear to one another now. Miller explains,

> We are led to the conclusion ... that there are no unarguable moral axioms, and that the weight one gives to any principle can be redistributed from one occasion to the next. And that is really what the whole play reflects, as it raises questions about those to whom you owe debts of gratitude, of loyalty, whether filial, cultural, social, or that of friendship, and shows the contradictory tensions that arise from the different pulling threads.
> (*Subsequent*, p. 157)

By keeping those contradictions before us, Miller refuses us the comfortable closure that a traditional performance of Act V would bring. Even the manna Portia drops in the way of starving people to ensure a happy ending tastes bitter and leaves the starving unsatisfied. Manna comes in the form of two pieces of paper: one a letter that tells Antonio his argosies have suddenly come to harbour, the other a deed in which Shylock bequeaths his estate to Jessica and Lorenzo. In a less socially conscious production, these pieces of paper might bring great joy to the recipients by guaranteeing them a livelihood. Here, however, they remind us of the various ways in which the monied classes throughout the play have secured their fortunes by manipulating others with letters, bonds, deeds, wills – documents that unfailingly serve the interests of those who interpret them. Antonio's letter may be added to this list. Portia delivers it with a wry detachment that winks at the 'strange accident' (278) by which she chanced on it and thereby pokes fun at the romantic ethos that would have us credit such accidents. In real life, things like this do not happen. Lost argosies do not miraculously come to harbour any more than cross-dressed women save men's lives in court. Such fictions disguise the more ruthless means by which the rich stay rich.

Miller uses Shylock's deed of gift, however, to focus our attention on the cost to others of keeping the Antonios of this world rich. In the text, Jessica does not respond to the deed or speak at all; Shakespeare leaves her with a silence to be interpreted as the director wishes. Usually she plays the happy convert, apparently satisfied with the outcome of the trial and eager to take part in the nuptial festivities. Miller, however, fills her silence with unspoken remorse. Jessica does not regard the deed as any kind of gift: as she pores over it, she walks slowly away from the group, conscious of betraying both her father and her heritage, guilt and doubt darkening her face. As the lovers exit laughing, Lorenzo, puzzled by her sadness, leaves her to her thoughts and joins the others. Only Antonio remains with Jessica, each of them holding a piece of paper – he the letter, she the deed. But when he catches her eye and, instinct with sympathy, extends a hand to her, she turns away. Realising his own complicity in causing her grief, he crumples up the letter and reluctantly exits. As our focus narrows to Jessica alone, we hear an offstage voice plaintively intoning the Kaddish, 'the eternal wail and lamentation of Orthodox Jewish prayer' (*Daily Express*, 29 April 1970). It is a dirge for the father who is now dead to her; it is a dirge for the daughter who would retreat from a world to which she, like Shylock before her, has tragically committed herself. The moment is inspired: it unsettles rather than affirms, it counters comic reconciliation with tragic isolation, and it crystallises the process of alienation that Miller has used the play to explore.

I say 'used' the play because, in the eyes of most who saw the production, Miller appropriated Shakespeare's text to foreground themes that preoccupied Western societies in 1970 but may not have preoccupied Shakespeare in quite the same way: the moral bankruptcy of the bourgeoisie, the hypocrisy with which those in power stay in power, the subtle ways in which society marginalises its minorities, and, in particular, the insidious effects of prejudice on those minorities who strive to be assimilated. These concerns are implicit in the text; in the production, they are made explicit by Miller's understanding of social relations. He inscribes contemporary cultural concerns in an Elizabethan text and, according to Ronald Bryden,

> virtually rewrites the original to do so. Out goes much of the comedy, out Belmont's fairy-tale romance. Instead, there's the assumption that the central, unavoidable experience of the play is that explosion of frank, murdering tribal hatred at the core of it; that the task of any revival is not to skirt around this, but to create afresh a believable world from which it can spring.
>
> (*Observer*, 3 May 1970)

Perhaps, in 1970, it was inevitable that such hatred was seen as the core of the play: society was divided over the same questions about wars of imperialism and global hegemony that had divided Victorians a hundred years earlier, and that made Miller's decision to set the play in 1880 particularly apropos. To many in 1970, the world seemed to be run by a conservative elite. The American military was seeking to determine the future of South East Asia, famine and revolution were sweeping Africa, students were protesting throughout Europe and America, and blacks were demonstrating for civil rights. Establishment had become a dirty word, and those who opposed it grew increasingly incensed with the ways in which those in power imposed their values on other cultures and kept minorities oppressed.

This context may help to explain the impact Miller's *Merchant* had on its audiences. 'An angry black or an embattled student will very likely hear the voice of his own defiance in Olivier's Shylock, and should certainly recognise his quintessential enemies, complete with top hats, canes, Waspish accents and polite contempt,' wrote Benedict Nightingale (*New Statesman*, 8 May 1970). 'In a period like this, increasingly conscious of its insistent minorities, wary of its silent majorities, and nervous of bloody conflict between the two, it looks like the play Shakespeare ought to have written.' The *ought* raises the most fundamental question of all, for by accommodating the play to a social and political context in many ways different from Shakespeare's, Miller essentially fashioned a play of his own. He appropriated Shakespeare's text, and with it his cultural authority, to advance an ideological agenda peculiar to his own time. Was Miller's *Merchant* Shakespeare's?

This question, of course, can only be answered with another: whose Shakespeare? Miller did what any director of Shakespeare does: he tailored the play to suit his cast, his venue, and his audience. Invariably, in the process of staging a Shakespeare play, a director will adapt and revise the text in light of current cultural assumptions and values: such revision is sometimes conscious, sometimes not. Irving revised *The Merchant* as radically for his age as Miller did for his; and like Irving's, Miller's production, especially after it was televised worldwide in 1973/4, in effect *became* the play for a generation of audiences. By calling into question what the play traditionally was thought to be about, Miller discovered a new way of looking at *The Merchant* that made Shakespeare – at least for the moment – our contemporary.

V

The BBC *Merchant:* diminishing returns

Ten years after his production for the National Theatre, Jonathan Miller had the opportunity to produce *The Merchant of Venice* again, this time for the BBC as part of its ambitious plan to record all of Shakespeare's plays. In the interim, he had radically altered his view of the play, which he now saw as 'totally symmetrical in its prejudices', with Shylock as culpable as the Christians (PBS Interview, 23 February 1981). 'We did not want to make him into a pantomime devil or merely a noble, all-suffering victim,' Miller declared, modifying his approach of a decade earlier; nor, he said, should the play be made to redress the wrongs of recent history, for 'if the only point of view you have is the point of view of your own time, the past becomes foreshortened and very flat' (*New York Times*, 22 February 1982). In his attempt to honour the past by reflecting *its* ideological biases – not our own – in his new production of the play, Miller strove to be truer to what he understood Shakespeare's original intentions to have been than he was in his 'Victorian' *Merchant*.

Miller's new-found respect for tradition may in part have been a response to the BBC's brief that productions for the series be 'orthodox', by which was meant no tampering with the text and no updating of the period. This requirement apparently was dictated by American corporate sponsors who, fearful of directorial intervention, wanted school children to see their Shakespeare dressed in doublets and hose in the best Old Vic tradition. Such traditions are themselves, of course, the historically naive products of nineteenth-century theatrical practice; but Miller, undaunted, made a virtue of necessity. 'The requirement that I stick to something which is recognisably period happens to coincide with an interest of mine, which has been growing in the last year or two, in trying to return to the sixteenth century because it is interesting in its own right' (*Quarto*, pp. 9–12). Miller therefore redefined orthodoxy as an academic challenge. Citing the work of recent social historians, he set out to reconstruct the fundamental 'Elizabethanism' of the plays, creating for each one a sort of period verisimilitude that would demonstrate how Shakespeare engaged the social and political attitudes of his audience (Bulman, 'BBC Shakespeare', pp. 571–81).

It may seem odd that I credit Miller with responsibility for the BBC *Merchant* when in fact the production was directed not by him, but by Jack Gold. My reason for doing so is that Miller, as executive producer of the series during 1980–1, habitually exerted a strong influence over his directors. When not directing himself (which he often did: six productions in two years), he hired directors who had little or no experience with Shakespeare and who therefore might prove susceptible to the power of his suggestion (Wells, pp. 48–9). Gold, known primarily as a film director, was an apt pupil, and Henry Fenwick's account of the production makes clear that Miller was omnipresent during the taping and helped to shape Gold's interpretation of the play (pp. 17–25). I do not mean to imply that Gold was merely a puppet: his comments suggest that he brought considerable intelligence to the text and exercised decisive control over the televisual strategies of the production. Nevertheless, as a newcomer to Shakespeare, he proved remarkably receptive to Miller's concept of Elizabethan 'tradition', so much so that hereafter, when I speak of Gold, the reader should bear in mind that it is often impossible to distinguish his work on *The Merchant* from that of Miller.

The likeness of their vision is apparent in their rationale for having Warren Mitchell play Shylock as an ethnic Jew. In an interview with Fenwick they claimed that Shylock's 'Jewishness' was authentic because a triumvirate of Jews – Miller, Gold, and Mitchell – made it so. 'Watching non-Jews trying to be Jews is just awful,' declared Gold, with an oblique reference to Olivier and other Shylocks of the English school. 'I've seen two versions and it's like watching Englishmen trying to be American ... it's always phoney.' Mitchell's Shylock, on the other hand, was resolutely unassimilated, antagonistic to the proprieties of bourgeois Venetian behaviour: 'there was no way he could act that wasn't Jewish' (Fenwick, p. 23). His looks were emphatically Semitic: he was short, square, and balding, his curly grey hair wildly unkempt, his beard thick, his attire a black gaberdine and yarmulka. His gestures were of a piece with his looks: his nodding head and quick hands, far more expressive than those of the Gentiles, marked him as typically 'Jewish', and he spoke with a thick Middle European accent that most critics identified as Yiddish – an anachronism which immediately stamped him for modern audiences as the alien he would have been in sixteenth-century Venice (*Shakespeare on Film Newsletter* 5 (May 1981), 2). This squat, domestic, garrulous little man, this comic figure with a plaintive face, was the Shylock whom Gold and Miller called authentically Jewish.

Yet their claim for Mitchell's authenticity may be questioned, for in fact his portrayal bordered on caricature. His Shylock was laden with 'an incessant series of bromidic Jewish mannerisms' that seemed at times to reduce him to a stock figure from old comedies (*Christian Science Monitor*, 20 February 1981): always ready with a laugh or a genial shrug, he rolled his eyeballs on 'Yes, to smell pork' (I.iii.27) and frequently invaded the space of others, crowding them like a salesman too insistently pushing his wares. For one critic, he resembled 'a seedy pawnbroker' (*New York Times*, 23 February 1981); for another, 'a poor Jewish pedlar in some place like Pinsk' (*The Listener*, 18–25 December 1980). Such responses reveal how strongly Mitchell harked back not to the Elizabethan stage Jew – a tradition to which Miller might have appealed – but to the more recent stage 'Yid' of music-hall revues and vaudeville skits. This heritage made it hard to take Shylock's villainy seriously (Shapiro, *Shofar*, p. 7); and indeed, Mitchell shamelessly exploited the traditions of music-hall performance. Appropriating the comedian's direct address to his audience, he spoke his asides straight to the camera, breaking the illusion of naturalism with a theatrical device to ingratiate himself with the viewer. He used it first on 'How like a fawning publican he looks' (I.iii.33), a speech Miller excised from his earlier production so that Olivier could preserve his decorum as a Victorian gentleman. Mitchell delivered the speech *sotto voce*, winning the viewer's confidence with his easy familiarity and direct eye contact. He used the device even where the text did not warrant it, as when, leaving to dine with the Christians, he addressed 'But wherefore should I go? / I am not bid for love …' (II.v.12–15) not to Jessica, but to the camera – acknowledging the audience as blatantly as stage comedians do.

Laughter throughout characterises Shylock's relationship with the Christians: more than a mark of his garrulous disposition, it works in subtle ways to weave a complex web of deception and intimidation. At the outset, it seems primarily to be the means by which Shylock disguises his malicious intent with false *bonhomie*, most obvious when he laughs at the absurdity of the 'merry bond' and gets Antonio to laugh along with him. Yet later on it serves to disguise his pain, and the suggestion of its darker purpose complicates our response to Shylock. Uncomfortable laughter rings throughout the scene in which he is taunted by Solanio and Salerio. It begins when they engage him in a game of verbal wit. As Marion Perret observes (p. 156), Shylock's anger over his daughter's 'flight' (21) prompts them to refer to her as a bird, and his pun in response to Solanio's use of 'dam' (25) – 'She is damned for it' (26) – encourages them further to belittle his pain in word-play. But their game is also physical: when Shylock complains, 'My own flesh and blood to rebel!' (28), Solanio – taking the complaint as a comic reference to sexual desire – lunges for his genitals: 'Rebels it at these years?' (29). And in the exchange that follows, Salerio, played by a burly Welsh actor who towers over the diminutive Mitchell, locks his arm around the Jew's neck from behind, laughing genially as if to pass off the stranglehold as good humour. At this point Shylock in self-defence laughs too, trying to act as though he is enjoying their game; but his laughter as he catalogues Antonio's abuses – 'thwarted my bargains, cooled my friends, heated mine enemies' (45) – grows increasingly forced and creates a disquieting sense of his helplessness. Even his explanation for Antonio's behaviour – 'and what's his reason? I am a Jew' (46) – a line that introduces a speech customarily accorded the reverence of holy writ, here simply feeds the hilarity of his tormentors. 'Ah!' they exclaim in mock surprise, with comic gestures that mirror those of Didi and Gogo in *Waiting for Godot*; and to each of the rhetorical questions that follow they respond with mimicry until, inspired by 'If you tickle us, do we not laugh?' (51), they tickle Shylock mercilessly and reduce him to tears. The kinship between laughter and tears so feelingly dramatised here provokes Shylock's climactic question, 'And if you wrong us, shall we not revenge?' (52). The moment he utters the word revenge, all laughter stops: Shylock has put a stop to this physical abuse in the only way he could, by threatening to take measure for measure. The Christians have not taken him seriously up to this point; nor perhaps has the audience, who may have been lulled into a sense that he is no more than a stage Jew. Here, quietly swearing revenge, all passion spent, he gains a more human dimension.

Shylock warns his audience elsewhere, too, against too easy an acceptance of the anti-Semitic stereotype. The chief means by which he does so is to nod knowingly or look at the camera each time one of the Christians launches into a diatribe against Jews or usury, as if to say, with Ronald Reagan, 'There you go again'. When, for instance, Antonio asks Bassanio to mark how 'the devil can cite Scripture for his purpose' (I.iii.90), Shylock is seen standing behind them nodding his head, obviously having heard it all before. He makes us more conscious of the anti-Semitism that permeates his culture, and we are therefore inclined to nod with him when, later on, Antonio vents even more racial spleen in a speech that curses his 'Jewish heart' (IV.i.80). Gold uses this strategy most tellingly at the trial, when Shylock is shown smiling with feigned interest at Gratiano's furious invective – 'O be thou damned, inexecrable dog ... Thy currish spirit / Governed a wolf ... ' (IV.i.128–38) – while he whets his knife on his shoe and tests its sharpness on a hair pulled from his head. The camera's relentless focus on Shylock's murderous intent as we simultaneously hear the sort of anti-Semitic vituperation that has led him to seek revenge teases us to link the two as cause and effect, and perhaps, by so doing, to accept such abuse as sufficient provocation for murder. Gold's strategy at once preserves and subverts the stereotype of the villain Jew.

This tension between caricature and credible humanity also informs the two scenes in which Shylock comes closest to winning our compassion. In the first, during his exchange with the dignified, Hasidic Tubal, Gold alienates us from Shylock by demonstrating the selfishness of his cause. When Shylock laments, 'The curse never fell upon our nation till now' (III.i.67–8), Tubal opens his arms as if to query whether, in his private grief, Shylock has forgotten sixteen hundred years of Jewish history; as Michael Shapiro notes, the emphasis in Shylock's reply, '*I* never felt it till now', bespeaks an isolation from other Jews and an obliviousness to their suffering that likens him to Marlowe's Barabas (*Shofar*, p. 8). Tubal further underscores Shylock's inhumanity by stopping his mouth in horror when he wishes his daughter dead at his foot. Such apparent lack of paternal feeling, however, is contradicted by the anguish Shylock expresses when he hears that Leah's ring has been pawned for a monkey. A doleful cello accompanies the look of pain that crosses his face as he recalls his beloved wife; and the camera continues to play over his face when, bidding Tubal to meet him at the synagogue, he rends his cloak in a ritual gesture of mourning.

At the trial, too, Gold goes to some lengths to alienate us from Shylock. Little humanises him: implacable in his hate, he gloats over his bond, waves his knife in the faces of his adversaries, and, in close-up, uses the point of that knife to find just the right spot on Antonio's bare chest to make his incision. This inhuman behaviour, however, is balanced by the brutality with which the Christians dispense mercy to him in the form of conversion. Forced to his knees, Shylock suffers a cross to be hung around his neck and, in close-up, is made to kiss it. The camera here again, as at the conclusion of III.i, lingers over his expression of agony. Such moments permit us to pity the man who has endured the loss of his ducats, daughter, wife, and religion. They are effective precisely because they contrast with the prevailing theatricality of Mitchell's interpretation, investing with humanity a character who elsewhere flirts with caricature.

Gold and Miller further adjust our perspective on Shylock by making attractive those characters who have most cause to hate him, Lancelot Gobbo and Jessica. Such emphasis bears witness to how fundamentally Miller's view of the play had changed since 1970, when the comedy of Lancelot's servitude and Jessica's elopement intruded awkwardly on the social realism of Venice – or since 1973, when those scenes were cut altogether from the televised version of that production. In Miller's 1980 *Merchant*, the scenes are played in full. Lancelot's stage ancestry is as readily identifiable as Shylock's: appearing from beneath a bridge to deliver his monologue straight to the camera, he resembles Scapino from the *Commedia*, an appealing scamp whose ingenuity at getting a new livery we admire and whose casual cruelty to his father seems comically justified. His appeal is of a piece with Jessica's, for she too betrays her origins in Italian comedy of intrigue – the resourceful daughter who outwits her father in order to join her lover. Where in 1970 Miller disguised those origins by refashioning her as a melancholy Jew in whom her father's tragedy would be re-enacted, in 1980 he used her as an exuberant gauge of Shylock's unnaturalness. She is passionate, outspoken, and disdainful of his inhibitions; and in so far as we approve of her affair with Lorenzo, we censure the father who would obstruct it. Leslee Udwin's dark, deep-voiced Jessica knows how to assert herself in a man's world. Like Lancelot and Shylock, she addresses the camera directly to win our confidence: 'Alack, what heinous sin is it in me / To be ashamed to be my father's child!' (II.iii.15–16) she asks, and we do not doubt the sincerity of her question. She mocks Shylock behind his back, mouthing 'Fast bind, fast find: / A proverb never stale in thrifty mind' (II.v.52–3) even as he speaks it – a proverb she no doubt has heard too often. And the same mockery informs her determination to leave him by donning a male disguise: she spits 'I have a father, you a daughter, lost' (55) directly into the camera, confiding her plan to us while clutching the ring Lorenzo has sent her.

Sexual passion is the key to her relationship with Lorenzo. Although Gratiano insinuates that money must motivate his desire for her – 'Now, by my hood, a gentle and no Jew!' reveals only how impressed he is by the weight of the ducats she has thrown down (II.vi.52) – Lorenzo clearly is as much in love with her as she with him. In fact, they cannot keep their hands off each other. Their banter at the opening of Act V is sexually charged: Jessica, clad in a white nightgown that all but exposes her ample breasts, delivers 'In such a night as this ...' repeatedly in the most seductive tones, wrapping her arms around Lorenzo's neck, with her lips nearly touching his as the camera moves in for a close-up. When a messenger interrupts them with news that Portia will return before dawn, an embarrassed Lorenzo stops her from apparently reaching inside his shirt (her hand has moved below the range of the camera); but their love play continues when, reclining on a moonlit bank, he puts his hand inside her gown while ironically disparaging 'this muddy vesture of decay', the body (64). Such sexual subtext makes their romantic charges and counter charges sound suspiciously like foreplay, and that is exactly what Gold had in mind. Insisting on a naturalism ingrained in the medium, Gold argued that their scene together, while full of exquisitely romantic verse, is nevertheless *'not a poetry contest*. They happen to be two realistic characters, so I turned it into a sexual contest ... [They] have probably been making love to each other non-stop ever since [their arrival at Belmont] and can't wait to get each other back into bed' (Fenwick, p. 18). Such a conception liberates Jessica from her father as absolutely as guilt kept her bound to him in Miller's previous *Merchant*. In both productions a realistic subtext is allowed to transform the artifice of the verse, but the latter production at least keeps Petrarchanism in the service of love, not betrayal.

It should not surprise us to hear Gold or Miller speak of how to make Shakespeare seem more real or natural, because television has long been regarded as an intrinsically naturalistic medium. The main problem in adapting Shakespeare for television, according to Sheldon Zitner, is how to translate 'plays written for a highly stylised stage to a medium whose typical visual imagery is more realistic in detail and effect, and whose visual and emotional frames are much more restricted' (p. 35). Television's framed image, as Raymond Williams suggests, has a 'direct cultural continuity' with the room in which we sit to watch (p. 9): it creates little sense of depth, works best in medium distance and close-up, and tends to diminish large theatrical effects. The televised version of Miller's 1970 production played to these strengths. In its attempt to recreate the Venice of a hundred years ago, the stage production already had a strongly naturalistic bias: one may recall that Julia Trevelyan Oman's set was inspired by *photographs* taken by the Count de Primoli. The medium of television simply realised that bias more fully. The Venetian scenes occurred in richly detailed interiors where characters were framed in their 'natural' space: the ornate Café Florian, the understated ducal chamber, and Shylock's house which, decorated with classical busts, oriental rugs, and walnut bookcases, looked as elegant as any in Mayfair. Furthermore, the theatrical origins of the production were suppressed: all the frankly non-illusionist asides, the slapstick comedy of the Gobbos, and Jessica's stealing away in the habit of a boy were, as I have mentioned, omitted, and direct address to the camera would have been out of the question. Other striking stage moments were reconceived for television. Shylock, for instance, no longer entered carrying Jessica's dress in III.i, but instead was discovered holding her picture to his breast, stroking it as he might stroke her hair, to create a smaller, more intimate effect. Although the outdoor scenes in Venice (what few there were) betrayed their studio origins, those at Belmont were absolutely 'real': filmed on location at an English country house, they showed sweeping lawns, vast terraces, and Portia and Bassanio leading their horses back to the stables after a morning's ride. Television thus helped Miller to fulfil his ambition of fashioning *The Merchant* as a naturalistic nineteenth-century drama suitable for Masterpiece Theatre.

By 1980 he had come to understand the conventions of television differently. Where before he had avoided theatrical artifice by radically reshaping the text, now he was willing to exploit the theatricality of the television medium itself: Shakespearean realism, he acknowledged, was not necessarily the same thing as naturalism. Conscious that earlier productions in the BBC series had faltered in their attempts at naturalism – shooting *As You Like It* on location had only made its comic artifices look absurd: one cannot translate pastoral to a real countryside and expect it to be credible – he sought visual analogues for the television screen in Renaissance painting, choosing to allow the conventions of one medium to inform our perception of another. Where previous directors had looked to television itself for inspiration, Miller looked to the gallery – to Titian, Tintoretto, Veronese. As John Wilders, the series' literary consultant, commented, 'the television screen resembles the stage in that it depicts characters who move and speak, but its two-dimensional surface, rectangular shape and surrounding frame also make it look like a picture'. Visual quotation from paintings of the period, therefore, 'calls attention to the artifice of the plays and does justice to those tableaux which are as much a part of Shakespeare's dramatic language as is his dialogue' (*Times Higher Education Supplement*, 10 July 1981, p. 13).

Miller's use of such visual quotation in the productions he directed, beginning with *Antony and Cleopatra*, proved so controversial that it renewed critical interest in the series; not surprisingly, then, all the directors and designers who worked for him followed his lead. Oliver Bayldon, for instance, spoke almost as glibly as Miller of the artists who had inspired his design for the two 360-degree backcloths used in *The Merchant* – Venice's a mottled blend of ochre and sienna, Belmont's of blue and grey. On his list one finds Canaletto, Turner, 'some shades of Piper ... Monet crept in too, of course' (Fenwick, pp. 18–19). The costumes likewise were patterned on those in Renaissance paintings. According to their designer, Raymond Hughes, the palette used for costuming the Venetians was Titian's: blacks and oranges, burnt umbers and dull greens to capture 'the moody, gloomy sections of the play' (Fenwick, p. 20). These ornate costumes bespoke great wealth – furs, plumed hats, doublets and capes trimmed with gold – and did not distinguish social rank. All the Gentiles looked noble, and the Jews were costumed no less richly, though they wore more sombre colours, Jessica in a dress of brown, Shylock and Tubal in black. The costumes for Belmont were altogether more ethereal and softer in focus, their blues and greens drawn from Canaletto and (though Hughes does not acknowledge the source) Botticelli. Portia moved through her garden like a queen of pastoral in an olive-green dress, her golden tresses adorned with a coronet of laurel: the allusion to Botticelli's *Primavera* signifies the mythic dimension that this Portia was allowed to achieve.

Gold, however, was not so determined as Miller to replicate the details of a particular artist's vision; rather, he intended only to create the *impression* of a Renaissance canvas. Where Miller and his disciple Elijah Moshinsky (whose *All's Well* and *A Midsummer Night's Dream* alluded to works by Rembrandt and Vermeer) laboured to create static tableaux, Gold believed that the essence of television lay in movement. He did not want to be bound by the sets; thus he required them to be minimal and abstract in order to allow the camera to move. 'I used the sets with an enormous amount of freedom and usually on single cameras,' he recounted. 'I could do long tracking shots right across the studio if I wanted to; it really was like being on location in Venice, though there was no pretence that we were in a real place' (Fenwick, p. 20). The qualification – that there was no pretence of 'real place' – is instructive: it reveals that Gold, like Miller, understood that the reality of Shakespearean drama is inherently different from that of most television drama. He explained his concept of reality in spatial terms. 'If you imagine different planes, the thing closest to the camera was the reality of the actor in a real costume ... then beyond the actor is a semi-artificial column or piece of wall, and in the distance is the backcloth, which is impressionistic.'

The sets for *The Merchant*, therefore, do not disguise their studio origins, but capitalise on them. Venice is composed of three free-standing Doric columns, an archway (in which Shylock is first seen in a striking silhouette), walls of peeling plaster, and a small bridge in which one sees reflected water (obviously a lighting effect) from the canal below. It is a set with many angles – characters appear from around corners, or through arches, or from under bridges – and one delights in discovering the ingenuity that allows these structural units, most of them on casters for easy mobility, to keep reappearing in apparently different places. The Belmont set, on the other hand, has a greater feeling of space and does not attempt to trick us into believing that we are in different places. All the action occurs within one arena – a kind of formal garden with a studio floor – in which artifice is palpable. The isolated structural units forbid any sense of architectural illusion: a grand, free-standing staircase leads into the garden; beyond it stands a fanciful pavilion or gazebo modelled on an Edwardian folly, 'a curlicued Temple of Atalanta' with a filigree dome that allows light and shadow to play in it (Fenwick, p. 19). Flanking the gazebo are abstract, pyramid-shaped shrubs and, next to them, free-standing pillars resembling those in Venice only more delicate. Even the caskets are located in this space, directly across from the gazebo. A gauze curtain is swept aside to reveal the three pedestals, standing starkly against the mottled-blue backcloth as if themselves a part of the garden. In fact, indoors and outdoors are not differentiated here: by framing nearly all the elements in a single shot – pedestals with caskets, pillars, pyramidal shrubs, gazebo (see Figure 5) – the camera makes us keenly aware that Belmont is a studio and that the actors occupy an artificial space. Only their acting can convince us of the play's reality.

The television camera functions much as the director of a stage production, only its power is more absolute. It serves as the eyes of the audience, directing attention to one part of the studio and away from another, denying the spectator any choice of where to look. Furthermore, the camera not only restricts but also diminishes what the audience sees. Unlike Shakespeare's public theatre, it affords little sense of depth, and long shots tend to trivialise ceremonial scenes and reduce crowds of actors to so many ants. The medium, in short, is incapable of presenting the complex group dynamics on which Elizabethan drama so heavily depends. It handles best a group of two or three figures, commonly focused in close-up, whose

Figure 5 Bassanio (John Nettles) makes his choice: Oliver Bayldon's set for Belmot in the BBC production directed by Jack Gold, 1980. Courtesy of BBC Enterprises Ltd.

'talking heads' more easily fit a small frame. Using the techniques available – montage, cutting, camera movement and angle – the television director must therefore try to arrive at some compromise between the theatrical demands of the text and the requirements of his more intimate medium.

Gold sought such a compromise by occasionally breaking conventional televisual strategies – the kind of camera work that has become, in Graham Holderness's phrase, 'the familiar discourse of television' (p. 69) – with more overtly theatrical techniques. Such devices as characters' delivering their asides to the camera, for example, make us acutely aware of our role as spectators: they break the illusion on which television customarily depends and acknowledge the artifice of the medium. Gold used his camera most theatrically for the wooing scenes in Belmont. We view them from a distance as through a proscenium arch, the camera placed where an audience might sit. Blocking of the scenes is frontal, with Portia and the attendants grouped formally behind the suitors as though on a stage; and the camera remains for the most part stationary while each of the three suitors makes his choice. All of them address their speeches directly to the camera, dropping the more naturalistic device of thinking aloud (the cinematic solution for dramatic monologue) in favour of playing to the audience. The trouble is, the audience is absent; and without its immediate response, actors on television cannot successfully replicate the dynamics of live theatre. The result, as one critic complained, is that the wooing scenes have seldom been less funny or convincing (*Cahiers Elisabéthains*, 19 April 1981, p. 128).

Gold, however, was determined to convince us of the love Portia and Bassanio feel for one another, and so for their scene together he resorted to more traditional televisual techniques. Portia speaks her hyperbolic praise of Bassanio (III.ii.40–62) in close-up but not *to* the camera; we simply hear her reverie (she is thinking aloud) and see in her face a radiant sincerity. And once Bassanio has made his choice and turns to claim her with a loving kiss, the camera moves in to capture them at close range, peering over their shoulders as they speak to one another, catching them in profile as they embrace, *showing* us how heartfelt their love is. The camera, as it scrutinises their faces, speaks more than words. Gold's camera work is unobtrusive; it offers what television has conditioned us to regard as natural ways of seeing. Through it, he allows us to credit Bassanio and Portia as the hero and heroine of romance: he a noble knight and pure, seemingly unaffected by the mercantilism that might have motivated his quest for her golden fleece; she a dewy-eyed damsel who, in a telling slip, reverses the priorities of her wish to be, for his sake, 'A thousand times more fair, ten thousand times / More rich' (154–5). This Portia would be a thousand times more rich but ten thousand times more fair. Money, as John Kerrigan observes, seems to play little part in this affair of the heart: Gold systematically suppressed the play's cash nexus in favour of romantic sentiment (*Times Literary Supplement*, 19 December 1980). The problem for some critics was that he used the intimacy of the medium to engage us with that sentiment uncritically, so that instead of viewing romantic tradition through the lens of social history as a manifestation of aristocratic privilege, he may unwittingly have recreated the sort of fancy-dress, ideologically naive Shakespeare popular with audiences forty years before.

Gold's success in reducing Shakespeare's most expansively theatrical scenes to the intimate dimensions of television can perhaps be better judged by his treatment of the trial scene. Seven years earlier Miller, in adapting his National Theatre production for television, had chosen to minimise the trial's theatricality by dramatising it as a private hearing, confined to the Duke's chambers where the opposing parties could sit around a table and air their grievances with gentlemanly decorum. Miller had elected to sacrifice the public dimension of Shakespeare's traditionally climactic scene in order to achieve the naturalism he thought television required. Critics complained that the scene had never been less exciting; moreover, its naturalism made the disguises of Portia and Nerissa look jarringly out of place and the premises of the bond plot seem absurd. The theatrical fictions of the play worked against Miller's use of the medium.

Gold found a way to preserve the scene's theatricality while making the action acceptably 'real' in televisual terms. His strategy was to create a number of discrete smaller scenes within the larger scene Shakespeare wrote, juxtaposing a sequence of private moments with the public occasion of the trial. His use of the camera was so adroit that it never called attention to the artifice of his technique. He introduced the scene with a tracking shot, following the fur-trimmed Duke from above and behind as he strode into a hall crowded with bystanders and proceeded to his canopied dais. This shot clearly established the trial as a public spectacle in the grand tradition of the nineteenth-century stage: Irving would have been at home in it. But as soon as the Duke turned to speak with Antonio, the camera narrowed its focus to the two men, who thus were allowed to address one another with a familiarity that belied the formal context. In effect, Gold used the camera to establish private relationships within the public ceremony of the court proceedings. He returned to this strategy again and again: the Duke, commanding that room be made for Shylock (whose entrance had been picked up in a long shot), called him forward to reason with him quietly as the frame tightened to exclude all onlookers; but Shylock, unwilling to submit his grievance to private arbitration, turned back to the court on the line, 'If you deny it, let the danger light / Upon your charter and your city's freedom!' (IV.i.38–9), raising his voice as the camera widened its focus to include those onlookers whom the Duke had excluded. The reverse of this occurred when Shylock, called upon to justify his unwillingness to take money instead of flesh, chose to address the Duke alone, suggesting in conversational tones that there was a Venetian precedent for his bond: 'You have among you many a purchased slave ...' (90). For television audiences, their exchange had greater impact because the camera reduced it to a private confrontation.

Gold's strategy benefited most those moments that tend to lose force when they are played too histrionically. This was especially true for Antonio's farewell to Bassanio, which the medium allowed to culminate in a passionately whispered 'Say how I loved you' (271), and Bassanio's equally impassioned confession that he did not esteem his wife above Antonio's life. As the camera closed in on their embrace, this became the most intimate of scenes. The lines were not spoken for others in the court to hear, so they had to be overheard; as a result, those who responded to them could do so only in reaction shots, their responses revealing private pique rather than public wit. Portia spoke 'Your wife would give you little thanks for that' (284) as an aside to Nerissa, and Shylock delivered 'These be the Christian husbands!' (291) – a line often played for laughs – in *sotto voce* to the camera, as a prelude to his sad reflection on the fate of his daughter.

The dynamic interplay of public and private moments also offered a solution to the problem of how to make Portia's playing 'Balthasar' credible. The most theatrically naive of the play's conventions, the male disguises worn by Portia and Nerissa are particularly troublesome for television, whose insistent focus on faces makes their identity immediately clear to viewers and thus strains the credibility of the trial. Such disguises, as Miller's earlier production would attest, subvert all attempts at naturalism. Gold, however, used the camera to preserve a balance between the self-conscious theatrical artifice of their assumed roles and a televisual realism sufficient to compel belief. Portia's entry in a jurist's robe of vermilion and black is tactfully captured in a distance shot: it creates a sense of her role as public defender and spares us the embarrassment of wondering why those gathered at court do not spot her at once as a woman. Having established her public role, she proceeds to alternate formal address to the court with private appeals to Shylock, modulating her voice from the stentorian (male) to the more conversational (female). In a medium shot, she quotes the

Figure 6 Gemma Jones as Portia and Warren Mitchell as Shylock in the trial scene of the BBC production, 1980. Courtesy of BBC Enterprises Ltd.

terms of the bond to the men assembled around her, proclaiming in grave tones that the pound of flesh must be 'cut off / Nearest the merchant's heart' (228–9; see Figure 6). Suddenly, the camera moves in to a close-up as she urges Shylock in more intimate tones to 'Be merciful: / Take thrice thy money; bid me tear the bond' (229–30). Shylock replies to her in kind, offering an explanation for her ears only, until Antonio interrupts their *tête-à-tête* by calling for judgement. Portia then resumes her masculine voice – 'Why then, thus it is' (240) – and the camera once again backs away to make us aware of the public occasion.

Portia thus uses the intimacy of the medium to deliver as personal appeals lines which are usually spoken as public address, moving in and out of her roles as 'Portia' and 'Balthasar' with more frequency and greater nuance than is possible on the stage. This has the ultimate effect of making her male disguise more credible, because we can more easily see the woman struggling within it. Clearly, she offers Shylock every opportunity to save himself: knowing the hold the law has on him as an alien, she repeatedly pleads with him to show mercy, to understand her message aright. The subtleties of her facial expressions and modulations of voice suggest that she is as concerned to save Shylock as she is to save Antonio: television allows us a privileged glimpse into her motives that theatre audiences are denied. Only when Shylock proves intransigent, his knife poised over Antonio's flesh, does Portia submerge her identity fully within that of 'Balthasar' and proceed to judgement. The camera, in a long shot, frames the whole court as Portia, now acting as prosecutor, reads from a book of Venetian statutes what 'justice' may be offered Shylock. His humiliation is public; and in a high-angle shot, as from the dais on which the Duke sits, the camera shows Gratiano and Salerio pushing Shylock to his knees to beg for mercy.

Such techniques ensure that the play will not be received as Shylock's tragedy. In terms of both ethos and art, Portia has controlled the trial: the intricacies of her role-playing have made her, for once, more interesting than Shylock and have assured us of her benevolent purpose. With Miller whispering in his ear, however, Gold could not allow the problematic morality of the play to remain unexplored. The trial concludes, as Marion Perret observes (p. 160), not on a celebratory note, but on two close-ups that poignantly mirror one another: Shylock kissing the cross that Salerio presses to his lips, and Bassanio kissing Portia's ring before relinquishing it under pressure from Antonio. Both kisses signify a breaking of oaths – Shylock's to his faith, Bassanio's to his wife – that has the potential to muddy the waters of reconciliation with which Belmont would baptise all comers. Miller, as we have seen, allowed such unresolved problems to disrupt the comic closure of his production for the National Theatre. But Gold does not go so far: his Shylock has been too stereotypical for his defeat to dampen the festivities of Act V, his Bassanio too noble for the question of loyalty to Portia to be taken seriously. True, Gold pointedly alludes to Miller's earlier production by having Jessica pore over her father's deed of gift (accompanied by the cello that once underscored his grief). But as this hint that she may feel compunction for having treated her father badly is unsubstantiated by anything that has gone before, her last-minute remorse seems gratuitous; and in the event, she takes Lorenzo's hand and happily exits to join the others. Likewise, the concluding tableau of Antonio sitting alone and unpartnered, gazing in the direction of the happy couples, is insufficient to disturb our sense of comic closure. The implication that his abiding melancholy springs from unrequited love for Bassanio has by now become a theatrical commonplace and cannot by itself resist the play's romantic affirmations. In effect, Gold used such moments as *gestures*, as if he wished to acknowledge the play's potential for raising subtextual problems but was ultimately unwilling to sacrifice to them the comic resolution he had so carefully prepared for.

Critical response to the production was mixed. Some reviewers approved of Gold's restraint, praising his direction as 'simple and direct' (*Shakespeare on Film Newsletter* 5 (May 1981), 2) and carefully balanced so as not to offend, indebted to many traditions but slave to none. Others found Gold's lack of intervention objectionable, protesting his reluctance to foreground such issues as greed, racism, disloyalty, and sexual ambiguity as a wilful denial of the play's performance history. In fact, Gold may not have known that history. By his own admission inexperienced as a director of Shakespeare, he may have been more concerned with simply *telling* the story than with the cultural implications of that story. And where critics such as John Kerrigan might have wished for a more radical manipulation of the medium to heighten our awareness of the play's artificiality – 'to expose the artifice of the screened spectacle and reveal subtleties within it which a theatre audience, restricted to a single point of view, would miss' (*Times Literary Supplement*, 19 December 1980) – Gold's impulse was to fall back on the conventional techniques with which he was familiar, reducing stage artifices to the dimensions of the small screen to create a convincing 'reality' in televisual terms. His success in doing so may be measured by the number of critics who found his *Merchant* balanced, simple, direct, and inoffensive. In the theatre, these are not necessarily terms of praise. In television, they usually are.

VI

Cultural stereotyping and audience response: Bill Alexander and Antony Sher

Bill Alexander's production of *The Merchant* for the Royal Shakespeare Company in 1987, revived the following year in London, grappled with the play's offensive subject matter more daringly than any production in recent memory. Refusing either to rehabilitate Shylock as the play's moral standard-bearer (as Miller had done in 1970) or to treat him from a safe historical distance as a comic 'Elizabethan' Jew (as Miller had done in 1980), Alexander courted controversy, seeming almost to invite accusations of racism. The controversy sprang in part from his refusal to honour the distinctions between romance and realism, comedy and tragedy, sympathy for and aversion to Shylock, from which stage interpreters have traditionally felt they had to choose. By intensifying the problematic nature of the text, Alexander modulated the dynamics of audience response: he goaded audiences with stereotypes only to probe the nature of their own prejudices; he confronted them with alienation in different guises in order to reveal the motives for scapegoatism. His Shylock was grotesque – at once comic, repulsive, and vengeful. Yet he was made so in part by those Venetians who needed someone on whom to project their own alienation; Venetians who, in their anxiety over sexual, religious, and mercantile values, were crucial to the transaction Alexander worked out between Shakespeare's text and contemporary racial tensions.

Take, for example, Alexander's innovative staging of the trial scene, the acid test of a production's credibility. At a key moment, when Portia conceded that Shylock was entitled to his pound of flesh, the preparations for surgery were chillingly unconventional. The Duke, habited like a Catholic Monsignor with a large silver cross around his neck, fell to his knees to intone a *Salve Regina*;

Bassanio, dissolved in tears, threw himself prostrate before the disguised Portia; Antonio was taken forcibly upstage and bound to a pole as to a cross; and Shylock, who had been on his knees to sue for justice, suddenly rose in triumph, raised his clenched fists to heaven to demand 'A sentence!' (IV.i.300), and moved downstage to begin a ritual that played on age-old fears of Jewish bloodlust.

Such rituals, of course, have nothing to do with Judaism, though, as Derek Cohen argues, Shakespeare may have thought they did when he had Shylock immediately follow his vow to 'have the heart of [Antonio] if he forfeit' (III.i.100–1) with a request that Tubal meet him at the synagogue, as if a synagogue were 'a mysterious place where strange and terrible rituals were enacted' (p. 109). Alexander's production, however, forced that association on us. Shylock performed his ritual while chanting in Hebrew: in the absence of any appropriate prayer in Jewish liturgy, Rabbi Dr Allen Podet, adviser to the production, supplied a Seder night prayer which calls upon a vengeful God to 'Pour out Thy wrath upon the nations that know Thee not and upon the kingdoms that call not upon Thy name' (*London Theatre Record*, 23 April–6 May 1987). The cacophony created by these rival incantations – Shylock's Seder prayer and the Duke's *Salve* – signified a clash of ideologies which, as I shall argue later, had more to do with the dynamics of power than with religion; but Shylock's compulsive behaviour was fascinating to observe because it *appeared* to spring from some deep religious conviction, or 'messianic madness' (*Daily Mail*, 30 April 1987), or Abraham-like determination 'to visit the wrath of Jehovah upon the Gentiles' (*Independent*, 1 May 1987). As he chanted, he doffed his black gaberdine and donned a tallis, sprinkled a few drops of blood from a horn case with his hand on to a white cloth, then poured out the rest, lifted the cloth to heaven, and swept upstage to place it at Antonio's feet as if in preparation for a ritual slaughter. As the chants grew more cacophonous, Shylock made a wide arc, swinging his arms in rhythm; then, with startling violence, he ran at Antonio to tear his shirt off. Like one possessed, he circled behind Antonio, cupped one hand around his victim's neck, and in the other raised a dagger above his head. The crowd screamed.

Suddenly, as if by miracle, Portia cried 'Tarry a little!' (IV.i.301). Her voice full of anxiety, she had to shout to be heard; but as she explained the law, the crowd fell silent. Her quibble about 'no jot of blood' may have been a desperate remedy, but it stopped Shylock dead. In an interview for *Drama* Antony Sher, who played Shylock, noted with dismay that audiences spontaneously applauded this moment. 'The problem with this production, which seeks to point out racism, is that we may appeal in exactly the wrong way to any racists in the audience ... Often, in the trial scene, when the tables are turned on me, there's a roar of delighted applause. I feel hurt by that. It's like being at a Nazi rally' (p. 29). Sher may have found such a response disconcerting, but it clearly demonstrated the power of the production to persuade audiences to buy the absurd premise of the folklore plot – to believe that the Jew would actually *take* his pound of flesh. Alexander's staging stripped bare Shylock's motives, revealed the origins of the scene in primitive rituals of human sacrifice, and, in the name of humanity, begged audiences to condemn it. Jeremy Kingston's review for *The Times* (27 April 1988) made just this point: 'I do not know the nature of the earnest rituals that Sher performs with shawl and prayer before advancing on his victim, but it is the sort of scenic colour that in other epochs would have the mob baying for Jew blood.' Audiences were thus *invited* to cheer Portia's victory over Shylock. That cheer did not necessarily signify that they condoned anti-Semitism (though some perhaps did), nor that the production was morally unambiguous. It did signify, however, that emotionally, at that moment, they sided with the Christians against the Jew.

Sher deliberately made Shylock offensive – so offensive, in fact, that the production itself was attacked for promoting an anti-Semitic stereotype. Although such attacks unduly simplified the moral complexity of the production, Alexander nevertheless encouraged audiences on a visceral level to loathe Shylock and, consequently, to suspect that they were being coaxed into the very racial intolerance which, according to Sher, the production took pains to expose. In outward appearance, Sher's Shylock was exotically unassimilated – 'a lip-smacking, liquid-eyed Levantine bargain hunter', according to the *Jewish Chronicle* (8 May 1987). His 'bright robes and flashing eye' reminded one critic of 'Holman Hunt's biblical canvases at their most dreamingly hallucinatory' (*Financial Times*, 27 April 1988). and another of drawings by David Roberts (*London Daily News*, 30 April 1987). Squat, bear-like, and barefoot, dressed in bulky gaberdine with unkempt hair and a straggly beard, Shylock was played with the coarse physicality for which Sher is noted: he gestured 'with not just his hands but his entire body' (*The Listener*, 14 May 1987), and his gait was 'a sort of seafaring waddle interrupted with sudden ferocious descents to a crouching position' (*Financial Times*, 30 April 1987). Grimly determined, he moved through Venice with 'the thrusting quality of someone used to pushing his way ... through stone-throwing, catcalling mobs' (*Guardian*, 1 May 1987). This portrayal, then, in its dangerous unpredictability, recalled unassimilated Shylocks of earlier times, from Macklin to Kean.

Sher took this approach for good reason. In the interview for *Drama*, making a veiled allusion to Olivier's celebrated performance nearly two decades earlier, he stressed that he wanted to break with recent stage tradition and to portray Shylock as 'someone obviously apart. The modern trick is to put *The Merchant* into the eighteenth or nineteenth century and present Shylock as an assimilated, sophisticated Jew. We didn't want that' (p. 28). In defiant rejection of the patrician, Westernised Shylock who had held the stage for so long, Sher – a South African and a Jew by birth – portrayed an Eastern Jew closer to his own Semitic roots. Just as he had in his celebrated portrayal of Richard III, for which Olivier's performance had proved a similar obstacle, Sher sought to overturn the tradition of 'English' characterisation and to play Shylock afresh. He conceived of characters – English king and Levantine Jew alike – from an alien perspective, in light of cultural models different from those traditionally offered to British actors. Thus, where Olivier's Shylock was elderly, dignified, and patriarchal – a Rothschild or a Disraeli – Sher's was younger, earthier, and crass – a rug dealer at a bazaar. What Hugh Richmond writes of Sher's Richard was true of his Shylock as well: 'it needed only a hint that Olivier had used a bit of business for Sher to reject it outright, as if the truly Shakespearian idea of art as an accumulation of insights from successful precedents were intolerable' (p. 109).

In particular, Sher explicitly rejected the narrow focus on anti-Semitism common to post-Holocaust productions:

> We didn't want our production to be about anti-semitism only but about racism more generally. Curiously, although I was born Jewish, *The Merchant of Venice* has always said more to me as a South African. There's something about the way in which Shylock is moved to exact extreme penalties by the extent of the barbarism he endures

Cultural stereotyping and audience response

which seemed to me to have applications to South Africa and the Middle East today.

(p. 28)

Sher, therefore, drew his image of Shylock not from Jews who today, in Israel as elsewhere, are largely Westernised, but from other Semitic peoples far more threatening to the middle-class audiences who flock to Shakespeare in London and Stratford: Arabs, Palestinians, Iranians, peoples who are associated in the Western mind with frightening and unpredictable extremes of behaviour, with Islamic fundamentalism, death threats, and acts of political terrorism. Sher's Shylock invoked the image of such alien and often misunderstood peoples, ignorance of whose traditions and values all too readily has led to racial prejudice. His behaviour at the trial played on audiences' fears of religious fanaticism, the blood ritual recalling not Judaism, but the vengeful outbursts of Ayatollah Khomeini bent on destroying the Great Satan – and eventually, in his fatwa of 1989, settling for the heart of Salman Rushdie.

Sher calculated his performance to play on bourgeois audiences' intolerance of racial difference. When we first see him in I.iii, he is squatting cross-legged on a cushion under a black canopy, as if in a souk, an abacus and scales beside him, beads in hand – 'a gypsy Jew in a canopied lair' (*Financial Times*, 30 April 1987). He is wearing a striped kaftan over baggy trousers and a turban on his head, his gestures broad and Semitic, and his pinched, nasal delivery punctuated by a nervous, high-pitched laugh which irritates when it would most ingratiate. Sher uses his vocal limitations intelligently: to compensate for his thin and reedy tenor, he affects an accent full of awkwardly self-conscious pronunciations, such as 'Wenice' for Venice and 'suffeesent' for sufficient. By mispronouncing words in this way, he teasingly appeals to his listeners' linguistic snobbery – both the Venetians' and the audience's – and invites the ethnic ridicule that Third World pronunciations typically provoke. Worse, he laughs at his own jokes (the pun on 'pie-rats' evokes an uncouth snort), pretends at first not to see Antonio, then confides to the audience in an intimate sing-song, 'I hate him for he is a *Kleestiun*.'

Sher taunts the audience with his Middle Eastern stereotype. He plays on the insecurity of the privileged classes, on their fear of minorities who, having learned to be overtly solicitous, sneer behind their backs and try to wrest power from them. When Bassanio comes to beg money of Shylock, as Miriam Gilbert astutely observes in her production notes, he asserts his power simply by remaining on his cushion. Bassanio, standing uneasily in front of him, shifts from foot to foot; and when Shylock asks, 'May I speak with Antonio?' (I.iii.25), Bassanio does not spy the trap: pausing to consider, he awkwardly offers what he thinks is the dinner invitation Shylock is fishing for, only to have that invitation turned viciously against him: 'Yes, to smell pork" (27). Shylock's strategy changes when a more powerful antagonist, Antonio, appears on the scene. Turning with mock surprise to greet him, he grovels and fawns as the merchant steps forward – 'Your worship was the last man in our mouths' (52) – the rug dealer in spite of himself, eager to make a sale. Yet, in a gesture that smacks of cultural defiance, Shylock goads Antonio with vulgarity. When explaining to him how 'Yakov' got his ewes and rams to do the deed of kind, he vigorously slaps his fist against his open palm to imitate coital sounds – at one point doing so right in Antonio's face. Here is the alien rubbing his obscenity in the nose of Christian decorum. Even more crudely, to seal the bond Shylock spits in his hand before offering it to Antonio. Such behaviour is provocatively offensive. We do not blame Antonio for reviling Shylock. We would do the same. Sher dares us not to.

Audience response to Sher's Shylock is complicated, however, by his mistreatment at the hands of the Christians. Antonio, the chief offender, is played as a virulent anti-Semite, self-righteous enough to feel that he need not treat Shylock any better than a dog. Physical violence characterises even their first encounter. When he grows irritated by Shylock's rehearsal of the terms of the bond, Antonio grabs the abacus out of Shylock's hand, hurls it across the stage, then turns to him and asks, 'Well, Shylock, shall we be beholding to you?' (I.iii.97). An odd way to gain one's attention, such violence clearly asserts Antonio's cultural privilege: he knows he need fear no reprisal, and he flaunts that knowledge. As Shylock shrinks before him, Antonio continues to bully, brusquely raising him up with both hands on 'lend it not / As to thy friends' (124–5; see Figure 7) then, on 'lend it rather to thine enemy' (127), shoving him centre stage, where Shylock crumples into a ball and offers, in turn, 'kindness'.

Cultural stereotyping and audience response 135

Figure 7 Antonio (John Carlisle) bullying Shylock (Antony Sher) in I.iii of the RSC production directed by Bill Alexander, 1987. Courtesy of Joe Cocks Studio.

Physical intimidation is present in other scenes too, where Shylock is mercilessly ridiculed, jostled, and beaten. In II.viii, for example, Salerio observes that all the boys in Venice follow Shylock to mock him, 'Crying his stones, his daughter, and his ducats' (24): a group of street urchins actually materialises in Alexander's production, and they are worse than Salerio reports. They hound Shylock in early scenes, making noises before his door and drowning out his lines with cat-calls; later, when he enters lamenting the loss of his daughter, they mimic him with 'My ducats! My daughter!' and pelt him with stones. Blood streams down his forehead. Yet such violence, however malicious, is mere child's play compared with that of Salerio and Solanio. When Shylock accuses them of knowing of Jessica's flight, they taunt him both verbally and physically, gloating over his losses and tossing him between them like a beanbag. When he cries, 'She is damned for it' (III.i.26), they push him to the floor and prod him with sticks, as one would a steer, beating him as he rolls downstage towards the precipice. When he reaches it, they threaten with their sticks to push him off the edge and into the canal. This threat lends a mordant irony to the line with which Shylock stops their intimidation: when asked what Antonio's flesh would be good for, he replies, casting a glance at the water beneath, 'To bait fish withal' (42).

That line introduces Shylock's famous self-defence, and in it he turns the tables on his oppressors. On 'if you wrong us, shall we not revenge?' (52), he suddenly grabs the stick with which Salerio has beaten him and threatens them with it. Shylock now holds the position of power. Alexander thus underscores the production's governing idea: 'The villainy you teach me I will execute, and it shall go hard but I will better the instruction' (56–7). The point is made visually: Shylock has seized the weapon from his assailants and may, by their example, use it. Their violent abuse has driven him to seek a like revenge on Antonio – a point pounded home each time he beats his breast on the word 'revenge'. Shylock has become their monster, their Frankenstein, offering them a grotesque image of their own Christianity. Sher explains the idea with a contemporary analogy: 'the more violent is the segregation and racism, the more bloody will be the revenge so that brutality breeds brutality and you end up with people putting car tyres round their enemies' necks and igniting them' (p. 29).

Alexander makes this idea clearest in the motif of spitting – a motif so powerful that Peter Hall borrowed it (as he borrowed so much else from Alexander) for his production of *The Merchant* with Dustin Hoffman in 1989. Like the presence of the street urchins who pelt Shylock with stones, spitting is inspired by the text: Shylock complains in I.iii. that Antonio has voided his rheum upon his beard, and Antonio threatens to do so again. That very scene bears witness to Shylock's complaint. As he exits, Antonio spits forcefully in his direction, making spiteful a line – 'Hie thee, gentle Jew' (I.iii.170) – that might have been delivered more genteelly. Indeed, spitting punctuates most of the key moments of victimisation in the play. It begins at the outset when, silent and silhouetted upstage, Tubal stands alone. Salerio and Solanio enter across the bridge and, unprovoked, spit on him as they pass. That one simple action sets the tone for the whole play. They spit on him again when he enters to talk to Shylock in III.i, this time baiting him as well with a chorus of 'Jew, Jew, Jew!' Their authority in this scene, as we have observed, has been challenged by Shylock, who vows to 'better the instruction'; thus their hatred is displaced on to the less threatening Tubal. Shylock, bemoaning the theft of his ducats but having successfully fended off his Christian aggressors, gently wipes the spit off Tubal's beard in one of the production's rare moments of tenderness.

It is fitting, then, that when Shylock has gained the upper hand and leads Antonio off to jail, he abuses him in kind. Shylock will have none of Solanio's pleas for mercy: 'I'll not be made a soft and dull-eyed fool, / ... To Christian intercessors' (III.iii.14–16); and as a full stop, he spits. Before leaving, he spits again at the manacled Antonio: the Christians have taught him such behaviour. The gaoler and Solanio draw swords, but Shylock, confident of the law's protection, exits laughing. The scene concludes with Solanio spitting in the direction of Shylock's exit, just as Antonio has done in I.iii.

By such means, Alexander dramatises both the reciprocity and the violence of prejudice. Shylock imitates what he has learned from the Christians; thus he should be no more culpable than they are. The production challenges us, however, by pitting our ethical abhorrence of racism against our visceral response to those who are alien to us – by setting our rational tolerance at odds with those fears that feed racism. This unsettling disjunction is strikingly demonstrated at the trial, when Shylock, now with the authority of the law behind him, instructs the entire court on the nature of prejudice. Called upon to justify his insistence on the bond, he replies that prejudice needs no rationale: 'So can I give no reason, nor I will not, / More than a lodged hate and a certain loathing / I bear Antonio' (IV.i.59–61). The law is amoral: it legitimates prejudice by denying the need for rational cause and protecting what is emotionally based. If the law sanctions it, one can hate with impunity. To illustrate the point, Shylock seizes from the ranks of onlookers a black attendant and holds the young man directly before him, face out, for the whole court – and audience – to see. Pointing him first to one side, then the other, he poses an embarrassing question:

> You have among you many a purchased slave,
> Which, like your asses and your dogs and mules,
> You use in abject and in slavish parts,
> Because you bought them. Shall I say to you,
> 'Let them be free! Marry them to your heirs!'
>
> (90–4)

Shylock's logic is disturbingly clear. If Venetians need no cultural sanction for denying slaves a place in their daughters' beds, so, it would follow, Shylock needs no sanction for claiming his pound of Christian flesh. So too, it would ironically follow, Venetians need no sanction for anti-Semitism: it is simply an accepted clause in the social contract, beyond the need for moral justification. Shylock thus explains to the court the rules of a closed society which have victimised him, and which he now intends to turn against his oppressors.

Alexander's staging invests the text with remarkable topicality, creating 'that special sense of discomfort and uneasy excitement which you experience when an apparently remote argument unexpectedly cuts close to the bone' (*Sunday Times*, 3 May 1987). Cutting through all pretence of social morality, it illustrates the universality of racial intolerance and exposes the mechanisms by which prejudice is made legitimate. In effect, Alexander magnifies anti-Semitism by having us view it through the lens of discrimination against blacks, a form of racism that strikes contemporary audiences with a force that anti-Semitism has largely lost. Drawing on his experience as a South African, Sher makes us face the question of moral culpability squarely: for as he holds the slave in front of him, we see Shylock and the slave as one. Visually, the two victims of racism merge, and we project on to Shylock the anti-black prejudices that have become so insidious and commonplace in Western culture – prejudices that Alexander's overwhelmingly white middle-class audience, without realising it, may share. The potency of the stage image depends on our identification with the oppressors; we are placed in a position of complicity with a group of Venetians whose moral hypocrisy we might otherwise judge from a safe distance.

Alexander tested our complicity in other ways as well. Our attitudes towards the Venetians themselves, for example, may have been coloured by more subtle prejudices that he skilfully drew out and manipulated, for the Venetians were characterised by a homosexuality which many in the audience found objectionable and which inevitably complicated their responses to the Venetians' Jewbaiting. Ironically, in a production that presumed to expose the nature of racial prejudice, Alexander encouraged his audience to indulge prejudices of a different but equally insidious sort. Homosexuality, of course, is latent in the text, and recent productions have used it increasingly to explain Antonio's otherwise unaccountable melancholy. In no production, however, has it been so pervasive or served so overtly as a metaphor for social alienation: comments by no fewer than fifteen reviewers attest to its importance.

Alexander dramatises a homosexual relationship in the very first meeting of Antonio and Bassanio, where Antonio reveals the love of a world-weary man for a disingenuous youth. Elegantly attired in a satin doublet of Caroline style, he asks with distaste what 'lady' it is to whom Bassanio has sworn a secret pilgrimage, turning his back on the handsome young man as he does so. Reviewers had no doubt about his sexual orientation: he is 'a solidly middle-aged homosexual' according to Frank Rich (*New York Times*, 16 June 1987), 'a man hopelessly in love with Bassanio' (*Sunday Telegraph*, 3 May 1987), 'a repressed homosexual' (*Time Out*, 6 May 1987), and a 'tormented closet gay' (*Guardian*, 1 May 1987) whose 'homosexual passion' for Bassanio is 'touchingly signalled' in the opening scene (*Daily Telegraph*, 29 April 1988).

Bassanio, for playing on the older man's love, was condemned as a 'bisexual opportunist' (*The Listener*, 14 May 1987) who 'appears to exist on the instincts of a successful rent boy' (*Daily Mail*, 30 April 1987). The accusations are not unfounded. When he speaks of coming freshly off from his debts, confiding 'To you, Antonio, / I owe the most in money and in love' (I.i.129–30), he lays one hand casually on Antonio's shoulder, the other on his chest, fingering his ruffled collar. In response, Antonio places both hands on Bassanio's shoulders, leaving them there just a moment too long to signify mere friendship, and John Carlisle's rich, ironic bass teases an unwonted sexual innuendo out of 'My purse, my person, my extremest means / Lie all unlocked to your occasions' (137–8). When Bassanio begins to sing Portia's praises, Antonio moves away from him to sit on a mooring post downstage, but Bassanio knows the art of manipulation. On 'O my Antonio, had I but the means' (172), he approaches his benefactor from behind, goes down on one knee and places a hand on his shoulder; when Antonio, jealously unmoved, says he cannot raise the present sum, Bassanio moves his right arm around Antonio's waist. That does the trick. 'Therefore go forth, / Try what my credit can in Venice do' (178–9), Antonio says as he rises; but he is not pleased. The words 'fair Portia' (181) are spit out of his mouth like tart wine. The men embrace, but before they release each other, Antonio plants a kiss, full and frank, on Bassanio's lips. Bassanio steps back, surprised but not offended, as indeed he should not be: his behaviour has provoked that kiss.

Critical responses to this scene reveal as much about the critics – and their gender – as about the scene itself. Noting 'the passion of Antonio's kiss', Martin Hoyle in the *Financial Times* commented that the overtly homosexual bias of the production brought to mind 'Germaine Greer's recent remarks on the basic homosexuality of the English' (27 April 1988). If Hoyle's response was self-consciously and even defensively male (note how he takes these men as his countrymen, not even pretending to see them as Venetian), Mary Harron approached the scene with a woman's concerns in mind. Remarking that Bassanio was 'presented more blatantly than usual as Antonio's former lover', she wrote in the *Observer* that 'there is much sexual tension and pathos in the opening scene between these two, creating a thread of suspense every time Portia sees them together, as we wonder – how much does she know?' (3 May 1987). Attempting critical objectivity, Paul Taylor of the *Independent* protested that homosexuality precluded a 'straight' reading of the text; for, he asked, how can Christian magnanimity be taken seriously 'if Antonio's generous funding of Bassanio's wife-hunting is overplayed as the selfish stratagem by which a depressed homosexual manages to keep an emotional hold over – and wrest a few impassioned kisses from – the friend he is bound to lose?' (28 April 1988). How, indeed? The discomfort apparent in such responses was felt by many in the audience as well. One had only to listen to comments during the interval to recognise that Alexander's ploy had worked: viewers were at once fascinated and repelled by the strategies with which Antonio and Bassanio advanced their selfish ends.

By mirroring this unrequited love of an older man for a youth, the relationship between Salerio and Solanio suggested that homosexuality makes the whole world kin. It is significant that reviewers bothered to mention these minor characters at all: the *London Daily News* found them 'a wimpish lot, tending to bisexuality' (30 April 1987); the *London Evening Standard*, 'decadent, cruel ... and rather mixed up about their homosexual longings' (30 April 1987). Salerio, a middle-aged courtier more fashionably dressed than Antonio, hungers for Solanio, his effete young protégé who sports a plumed hat and is rather heavily made-up. Together, they embody the values of a jaded Venetian culture. Their grilling of Antonio in I.i, for example, seems aimed at getting Antonio to confess not why he is so sad, but who his new lover may be: 'Why then, you are in love' (I.i.46) is spoken with particular relish. Later, when Salerio describes Antonio's leave-taking from Bassanio, his intentions towards the younger man undermine the pathos of his account. Kneeling beside Solanio, who is lying provocatively centre stage, Salerio grows passionate as he recounts how Antonio, 'his eye being big with tears, / Turning his face ... put his hand behind him, / And with affection wondrous sensible / ... wrung Bassanio's hand' (II.viii.47–50). As if in sympathy, Salerio reaches for Solanio's hand and reclines next to him, apparently ready to make a sexual advance; but his young paramour abruptly rises and, in effect, spurns him. Such sexual game-playing continues in III.i, when they lament Antonio's ill luck. Solanio has been weeping, presumably in grief for his friend. When Salerio leans down to kiss away the tears, Solanio wipes the kiss off his cheek, once again rejecting the older man's attentions. Steve Grant in *Time Out* thought it a 'positive idea ... to have Salerio lust unsuccessfully after a somewhat petulant Solanio' (4 May 1988), for their interaction reinforces the sexual tension running through Antonio's scenes with Bassanio. In Salerio and Solanio, however, homosexuality is reduced to type, and their behaviour courts the disfavour of an unsympathetic viewer.

In the homophobic view of many in a bourgeois Stratford or London audience, Alexander's Venetians would seem particularly repugnant because the 'business' they have with each other, the mercantile self-interest commonly ascribed to them in the play, is dramatised through the dynamics of homosexual gamesmanship. Sexual commerce among these men employs the logic of capitalism, and audiences inured to exploitative business practices – audiences hesitant to call Bassanio morally bankrupt simply because he exploits a friend to win an heiress – may nonetheless disapprove of those practices when they serve homosexual ends. Such disapproval is implicit in some of the reviews quoted above. Alexander panders to popular prejudices: he makes us queasy about siding with the Venetians against Shylock not only because they are so calculatedly dishonest with one another, but because their dishonesty is bound up in stereotypes of homosexual behaviour that culturally 'enlightened' audiences have been taught to disavow. As in the trial scene, the production plays our ethical tolerance against our irrational responses to otherness, and by so doing makes those responses an issue we must confront. We may resent Alexander for soliciting our disapproval of these men, just as we may resent his daring us to dislike Shylock; for by identifying homosexuality as one source of that disapproval, he puts us in a position of complicity with the very closed-mindedness that the production ostensibly would have us repudiate. The critic who protested that 'Antonio's crush on Bassanio is amplified so that effeteness becomes a cheap token of the gentiles' malignity' proves my point (*The Listener*, 14 May 1987).

Antonio, in fact, is the only member of this Venetian community who commanded much critical respect. Tall, thin, patrician, and gravelly voiced, John Carlisle portrays him with tragic longing as Portia's unsuccessful rival for Bassanio's affections. The staging highlights that rivalry. At the conclusion of I.i, for example, after Bassanio has departed, Antonio stands alone midstage, with his back to the audience, while the stage is cleared and reset for Belmont; Portia sweeps on and stands beside him, facing out to greet all comers. The tableau is brief, but telling. A similar tableau, with Antonio and Portia standing on stage together, occurs at the intersection of II.vi and II.vii; but here the ambiguity of Antonio's sexual identity makes the suggestion of their rivalry more intriguing. In II.vi, after the revellers have gone, a solitary figure in a long black cloak enters downstage right; the figure is hooded and holds the mask of a young woman to its face. The text indicates that this is Antonio, come in search of Gratiano to tell him that the ship is about to sail for Belmont. In this production, however, we do not know the identity – or the gender – of the silent masked figure: it is simply a reveller come too late. When the figure lowers the mask, however, and Gratiano asks in surprise, 'Signor Antonio?' (II.vi.62), the audience may share his surprise, for Alexander uses transvestism unexpectedly – and powerfully – as a metaphor for self-alienation. Critics saw Antonio as a man 'out of love with himself' (*Sunday Telegraph*, 3 May 1987), 'whose melancholy amounts almost to a yearning for death' (*Daily Telegraph*, 29 April 1988); as 'a sad-to-be-gay merchant' (*Guardian*, 28 April 1988) who 'would actually prefer death to restricted life' (*Guardian*, 1 May 1987).

As someone who knows the pain of alienation, Antonio may understand the cause and intensity of Shylock's lust for his pound of flesh: a culturally conditioned self-hatred that causes the outsider to lash out at one more vulnerable than himself. Their mutual understanding is conveyed at the trial in a bit of business following Antonio's exhortation to 'Let me have judgement, and the Jew his will' (IV.i.83). The two antagonists circle one another at centre stage, the victim and his prey eyeing each other suspiciously. When, in desperation, Bassanio offers six thousand ducats for three, Antonio and Shylock stop to share a laugh at his naïveté. They know what motivates an alien to act as he does, and it is not money. This idea of self-hatred, of course, risks feeding a bourgeois audience's notion of homosexual neurosis. Indeed, Alexander may have had some such thing in mind; for clearly, at the trial, Antonio sees martyrdom as a way to bind Bassanio to him emotionally for ever. When Bassanio says, 'What, man, courage yet!' (111), Antonio pushes him to the floor with unanticipated fury and, standing over him, spits out his confession, 'I am a tainted wether of the flock, / Meetest for death' (114–15). Then, in a sudden reversal, he tenderly raises Bassanio and completes the speech: 'You cannot better be employed, Bassanio, / Than to live still and write mine epitaph' (117–18). In effect, he compels the young man's consent in this as he has not been able to in an affair of the heart. His subsequent speech to Bassanio, 'bid [Portia] be judge / Whether Bassanio had not once a love' (272–3), is accompanied by an embrace more passionate than any other in the play, Bassanio burying his head in his lover's shoulder, and Antonio stroking the hair and neck of his young friend.

Such intimacy prompts Shylock's dismissive – and knowing – aside, 'These be the Christian husbands!' (291). The Jew, till now himself the powerless object of so much derision, turns his scorn on men whose scarcely concealed sexual orientation could make them as scorned as he. Bassanio certainly takes the line as an accusation: breaking from Antonio, he spits viciously in Shylock's beard. His motive for doing so is obviously defensive. Furthermore, it suggests that those who spat on Shylock earlier may also have done so defensively, projecting their own alienation on to one who is a likely victim because more obviously alien than they. Their anti-Semitism thus would seem to derive in part from their homosexuality, as a form of transference. David Nathan, writing in the *Jewish Chronicle*, makes this connection: the 'self-hatred' Antonio feels for being 'homosexually drawn to Bassanio', he suggests, 'adds to the depth of his anti-Semitism' (8 May 1987). Anthony Deneslow asserts more judgementally that 'we can have little sympathy' for those Venetians who, because they are 'homosexually-touched' (curious phrase), 'hiss and spit at their victim' (BBC Radio London, 30 April 1988). In Alexander's production, therefore, alienation is not limited to the Jews. It infects the whole society – a society whose notions of class, whose rules of conduct in sex as in business, even whose religion, alienates men from one another and, worse, from themselves.

The violence with which these men use Shylock as a scapegoat is most brutal at the trial. Their ringleader Gratiano distils all the brute bullying of which we know his society to be capable. When, for instance, Shylock announces, 'I stand here for law' (IV.i.142), Gratiano rushes at him and spits directly in his face: no one objects. Later, when Shylock praises Portia as 'A Daniel come to judgment' (219), Gratiano leads Bassanio and Solanio in a chorus of 'Jew, Jew, Jew!', bearing down on him like dogs baying for *his* flesh until Portia calls them off (*Spectator*, 9 May 1987). Once Shylock has lost his case, however, their aggression is unleashed. When Portia instructs Shylock to get 'down, therefore, and beg mercy of the Duke' (359), Bassanio and Gratiano wrestle him to the floor, Bassanio pinning his arms while Gratiano stands with his foot planted firmly on Shylock's back. From this position, the Duke's mercy must surely sound strained to Shylock. Even more strained is that of Antonio who, now unbound, strides centre stage to pick up the knife Shylock has dropped and, volunteering to return half of his goods provided Shylock presently turn Christian, hurls it into the floor – on the word 'Christian' – at the very spot where Shylock performed his blood ritual. In essence, he strikes at Shylock's heart: he may speak of mercy, but he achieves revenge. In victory, these Christians are as merciless and barbaric as Shylock was in demanding the bond.

With disturbing accuracy, then, Alexander dramatises how alienation born of ideological difference leads inexorably to violence. In doing so, he makes credible and immediate a folkloric plot which often, on the stage, strains credibility. What conditions, after all, could lead a man to cut out the heart of another? Confronting us with modern cultural analogues for the racism Shakespeare knew, assaulting us with stereotypes of religious fanaticism, black servitude, and homosexuality, he adroitly manipulates our moral perspectives: he appeals to popular prejudices here, upsets them there, and by so doing would make us aware of how deeply we are implicated in perpetuating social conditions that cause minorities to feel alienated. There is, of course, no guarantee that encouraging an audience to indulge its prejudices will lead to the self-awareness Alexander intends: one cannot control audience response. To attempt to sensitise people to their own prejudices by causing them to *feel* those prejudices entails risk. Antony Sher attests to this risk when he complains that audiences applauded his defeat at the trial and thereby illustrated the very racism that the production sought to overcome: 'The problem ... is that we may appeal in exactly the wrong way to any racists in the audience.' In ways perhaps deeper than Alexander had anticipated, therefore, his *Merchant* functioned as a contemporary parable of culturally sanctioned hatred.

Kit Surrey's expressive set sharpens the production's focus on ideological kinship and conflict. The playing space is uncluttered, almost bare: a platform of dark wooden planks suggests a Venetian quay or landing stage, with gondola poles resting against the proscenium arch on each side of it; dank mist rises around it as from a canal, and at each corner is a mooring post on which actors may sit. Upstage centre, a narrow bridge leads off the platform; most entrances and exits are made across it. And looming high overhead, spanning the stage, is a wooden bridge evocative of the Bridge of Sighs – a bridge 'that creates an immediate sense of intrigue, of conversations overheard', a bridge that captures the brooding menace of a Venice 'all gloomy shadows and smoky golden light' (*Observer*, 3 May 1987). In this virtually empty space all the

Venetian scenes are played; and though Surrey was criticised for not having sufficiently distinguished the ducal court from the Rialto – one literal-minded critic complained that the trial was 'set, unsatisfactorily, out of doors' (*Sunday Telegraph*, 3 May 1987) – this lack of distinct locations makes a metaphoric point: the proceedings at court are only 'the floating continuation of sectarian strife in the streets' (*Financial Times*, 30 April 1987).

If the open space itself is neutral, the backdrop is not. Surrey stripped the stage of the Royal Shakespeare Theatre right back to its brick wall (a wall recreated for the London revival). The plaster on it is cracking – this is clearly meant to suggest an old edifice – and it is adorned with two opposing images: slightly to the right of centre, a Byzantine icon depicting the Madonna in gold leaf; slightly to the left, scrawled in yellow chalk, a Star of David. This opposition potently expresses the play's ideological conflict. The Madonna indicates that the wall belongs to a church – the Church of Rome, locus of ecclesiastical power and hegemony; on its wall, Judaism is reduced to an obscene graffito which hints at institutionalised prejudice. The identification of the wall with the Church is confirmed when, as the play begins, bells toll and a *Kyrie* is intoned. Clearly, this production will take Roman Catholicism seriously as the culturally and politically dominant force it was: the ecclesiastical attire and silver crucifix worn by the Duke at the trial are not fortuitous.

This visual representation of ideological conflict is picked up in the attire of other characters. Most of the Venetians wear large crucifixes around their necks. The largest and most ostentatious are sported by Salerio and Solanio, who also cross themselves frequently when speaking of Antonio's misfortune. We needn't regard such behaviour as hypocritical; it is habitual. In so far as they typify the attitudes of their church, they may indeed be 'good Christians' in the tradition of those Roman Catholics (even the Pope himself) who tolerated the anti-Semitic policies of Adolf Hitler. Memories of Hitler's purges inform our response to the Jews' costuming too. Tubal, in the play's opening tableau, stands with his back to the audience; on his coat is emblazoned a yellow Star of David, the badge of all his tribe. Similarly, in II.v, before leaving to dine with the Christians, Shylock dons a black coat which, when he turns to go, reveals a Star of David just like Tubal's. As Victoria Radin reminds us, Jews who lived in the Venetian Ghetto during the Renaissance were forced to wear such insignias (*New Statesman*, 13 May 1988); the costuming is thus as historically authentic as it is evocative of the Holocaust. Either way, these Jews are 'marked' men.

Alexander employs religious symbols to define Jessica's plight as well. Behind Shylock's back, Lancelot Gobbo hands her a golden crucifix on a chain, a gift from Lorenzo. Lorenzo has given it to Lancelot in II.iv when he says 'Hold here, take this' (19). The line is usually interpreted as a reference to money; but as so often in this production, religion takes the place of currency. The ideology of the marketplace is transferred to the Church. Jessica hides the crucifix from her father but kneels to kiss it once he has gone: it becomes the crucial symbol of her desire – and failure – to be assimilated into the Christian community.

A crucifix dangling from a chain is the final taunt Shylock suffers before being thrust out of the court after the trial: it is the mocking gesture of a closed society for whom Christianity signifies power and exclusion, not mercy and acceptance. The gesture has been anticipated when Antonio, in III.iii, dangles the chain by which he is being taken to prison in front of the gaoler, who instinctively crosses himself. Antonio himself is on the end of the chain, as one who suffers martyrdom, a role he plays nearly to death at the trial; like the Jews in the play, he knows the pain of unfulfilled desire. When Jessica arrives at Belmont, therefore, the crucifix and chain have accumulated considerable meaning. She carries them with her, along with a book of prayer from which she reads, as tokens of her cultural assimilation. But in fact, she is not accepted at all. Pointedly isolated by hosts who do not make her feel welcome – Nerissa ignores the request to 'cheer yond stranger, bid her welcome' (III.ii.236) by skirting around her – and baited by a Lancelot Gobbo who actually makes her fear damnation as Shylock's daughter (III.v), she is divided from the Christians by an accent similar to her father's, by her hair (long dark curls, like his), and by her Semitic looks and coloration. Even her costume betrays a difference: although the green Turkish harem suit she wore in Venice has been replaced by a white dress that would seem to signify her assimilation in Belmont, beneath it she still wears the red skirt she wore as an overskirt in Venice. It marks her as the Jew's daughter yet. Visually, she retains vestiges of her Judaism despite those tokens of Christianity she embraces; for the insiders at Belmont, therefore, she remains an outsider – 'Lorenzo and his infidel' (III.ii.217).

Act V reveals the influence of Jonathan Miller's emphasis on disharmony, particularly in Jessica's relationship to the Christians. Here, as they all enter the house to celebrate their nuptials, Jessica runs after Lorenzo, eager to take part and thereby to deny her obvious difference from them. On her way, however, she accidentally drops the crucifix she has been carrying. She breaks from Lorenzo to fetch it; but Antonio, who has spied it first, snatches it up in one fell swoop (a visual echo of what he has done with Shylock's knife at the trial) and, seeing her kneel down to get it, dangles it before her, just out of reach. The lights fade on the disquieting tableau of Jessica extending a hand to receive what can never be hers. In Miller's production, Antonio empathised with Jessica as one who, like her, knew what is was to feel isolated. In Alexander's, however, Antonio 'works off his own frustrated resentment by trying to exacerbate hers' (*Independent*, 28 April 1988). By taunting her with the crucifix – just as Solanio has done to Shylock at the trial – he reiterates the bitter lesson that no Jew may ever be permitted entry into the smug club of Christians for whom religion has more to do with power than faith.

When a production is so centrally concerned with issues of racial prejudice, male bonding and institutionalised power, one might expect the female world of Belmont to be overshadowed. In fact, Alexander's Belmont is ideologically of a piece with his Venice; its inhabitants subscribe to the same patriarchal assumptions and prejudices that the Venetians do. Belmont is a place where women honour tradition, where a dead father's will counts for more than a living daughter's wish, where the goal of every woman is to give herself and all her goods to the man she loves, and where Christian duty may be honoured more in the breach than the observance.

Some critics complained that this Belmont lacked magic, that it was too spare, too much like Venice: they wanted a green world to pose alternatives to the mercantile values of Venice. But that was not Alexander's aim. Ethically, his Belmont occupies the same space as Venice, and Kit Surrey's bare set helps to enforce the idea (much as an Elizabethan stage would have) that the worlds are reflections of one another – 'Belmont, it would seem, is just across the lagoon from the watery Republic' (*London Daily News*,

30 April 1987). Belmont basks in a warmer light than Venice, and the stage is softened by a beige oriental rug that is rolled out to cover much of the platform. A Bible on an ornate stand, upstage right, on which each suitor must swear his oath, symbolises the divine inspiration ascribed to Portia's father; and on the back wall, the Madonna is now lighted with votary candles, the Star of David visible only in shadow. Such minimal changes in the set ensured fluid scene changes and encouraged audiences to draw comparisons between the two worlds and their inhabitants.

If the men of Venice sported their Catholicism cavalierly, the women of Belmont take religion more dutifully. Dressed like 'Dresden shepherdesses' (*Independent*, 1 May 1987), their gowns adorned with large bejewelled crucifixes, they clearly have been educated at a convent school. They believe unblinkingly in male prerogatives: they cross themselves every time God is mentioned, and Portia never questions the will of her father. For her, God and the father are one and the same, a power to be honoured and obeyed. This faith in patriarchal authority allows Portia to endure the casket lottery obediently – but not without protest. She ridicules anyone whose manners differ from her own, be he English, French, German, or Neapolitan. Male critics were quick to point out in Deborah Findlay's portrayal an 'unusual disdain' for her suitors uncharacteristic of most Portias (*London Daily News*, 30 April 1987). She is 'as nasty as she ought to be but so rarely is', wrote the critic of the *Financial Times* (30 April 1987); and others concurred, calling her 'tart' and 'astringent' (*Guardian*, 1 May 1987; 28 April 1988), 'icy and fastidious' (*Daily Mail*, 30 April 1987), 'hard-sharp' and 'unsentimental' (*London Evening Standard*, 30 April 1987), and 'sharp, impatient … bossy, dully energetic [and] determined' (*Sunday Times*, 3 May 1987).

Portia is especially disdainful of the Prince of Morocco, but Alexander complicates the audience's response by making him a stereotype worthy of her disdain. Morocco woos Portia with all the arrogance of a man who regards women as chattels. Entering with a flourish, all in white save a turquoise sash, he grandly removes his cape and hands it to her to hold: as a woman, she of course would be his servant. He then puts on a bravura display of male potency, brandishing his scimitar so as to intimidate her: 'The best-regarded virgins of our clime / Have loved it' (II.i.10–11) carries more than a hint of sexual ravishment and draws a knowing giggle from the audience. Then, as he begins to sing Portia's praises in the tradition of a sonneteer – 'From the four corners of the earth they come / To kiss this shrine, this mortal breathing saint' (II.vii.39–40) – he seizes her hand to kiss and, in the course of the speech, ardently works his way up her arm. Though visibly shuddering at his touch, she does not withdraw her arm: she is bound by rules of decorum, even if he is not. Little wonder, then, that she expresses joy when he chooses wrong. Her disdain for him is deserved, and therefore the audience is inclined to forgive Portia her aversion to 'all of his complexion' (79). Indeed, the comic stereotype of a violently sexist African would seem to invite and condone a racist response in the audience as well.

Yet Alexander makes this gentle riddance problematic by casting a young black actor as Portia's servant Balthasar. When she dismisses everyone of a dark complexion, he flashes her a look of disapproval and mutters 'Tsk'. On the three occasions I saw this production, members of the audience responded to this moment uncomfortably, as if Balthasar were accusing them, and not just Portia, of racism. In a sense, he does. For by making us cognisant that she has openly spurned Morocco *as a black*, Balthasar forces us to recognise our own complicity too: by laughing at Morocco as a 'type' unsuitable to marry into the white world of aristocratic values, we have been guilty of a racist response. It is such complicity that makes Shylock's attack on culturally approved racism at the trial so effective. As he holds up the black attendant for all to see – 'Marry [him] to your heirs' – he does not speak in the abstract: he speaks directly to Portia and to everyone like her.

Portia, however, is blind to her own bigotry. She would no more have recognised her insensitivity to Balthasar than the xenophobia implicit in her dismissal of the suitors Nerissa lists in I.ii. That her prejudices are unconscious is revealed in the way she treats Jessica. Superficially, her *noblesse oblige* singles her out for Jessica's particular praise: 'the poor rude world / Hath not her fellow' (III.v.70–1). Yet Portia betrays a condescension towards Jessica through tone of voice. When Jessica wishes her 'all heart's content' at the monastery, Portia replies 'I thank you for your wish, and am well pleased / To wish it back on you' (III.iv.42–4) in the kind of patronising sing-song that one might use when speaking to a child. Unlike the Venetians, Portia *appears* to be sincere in her Christian convictions: like the rich churchgoer who heartily believes in charity for the poor but has no doubt of her own social superiority or of the value of her good works, she *means* well. Her limitations are those of the affluent bourgeoisie who advocate tolerance and open-mindedness even as they (often unawares) practise discrimination. 'No other production' of *The Merchant*, writes John Peter, 'has brought out so clearly ... this fatal schizophrenia of Western civilisation' (*Sunday Times*, 3 May 1987).

Paradoxically, Portia's ignorance of her own prejudices makes it easier to credit her sincerity and to accept the romance plot at face value. A good Catholic, she will adhere strictly to the letter of the law, and though she panics at the thought of being won by a suitor she abhors, she will not, like Joan Plowright's Portia, use guile to subvert her father's will. She plays her assigned role straight. Her voice registers a plangent fear in 'O me, the word "choose"!' (I.ii.19) yet rises to ecstatic crescendos at news that Bassanio has come to try his fortune. Credulous, dutiful, unselfconscious, she is very much a young woman in love. There is passion in her relationship with Bassanio, and the intensity of their attraction bids us to get caught up in the fiction of the three caskets and, at least for the moment, to put our moral misgivings aside – even to the point of accepting Bassanio as a suitor fully worthy of her.

Their climactic scene together does justice to the plot's fairy-tale premises by creating genuine suspense: will the handsome prince win the princess bride or be condemned forever to a life of celibacy? Bassanio comes on stage nervous with anticipation, pacing back and forth and breathing like an athlete about to run a race. His eagerness is matched by Portia's. She, now pretty in pink, enters breathlessly to him and, with comic zeal, holds him back from the caskets on the line, 'I pray you tarry' (III.ii.1); there is further laughter when she adds, 'I would detain you here some month or two' (9). And detain him she does, with her own crisis of conscience. 'I could teach you / How to choose right' (10–11), she admits, speaking the line with gravity, as if weighing the price of sin and, suddenly ashamed of herself, opting for obedience to her father instead: 'but then I am forsworn. / So will I never be' (11–12). All the while, Bassanio grows increasingly restive, trying to sneak a look at the caskets over her shoulder.

His complaint, 'Let me choose, / For as I am, I live upon the rack' (24–5), thus takes on a comic dimension because their youthful exuberance is working at cross-purposes: she has physically restrained him from discovering his own destiny, and hers. We momentarily forget that this Bassanio is motivated in part by desire for Portia's money and may be sexually linked to Antonio as well: here, he is simply a young man in love, vigorous and hot. When Portia tells him, 'If you do love me, you will find me out' (41), he strides downstage, 'squaring up to the caskets on which his fate depends as if to a feat of supreme athleticism', according to Stanley Wells (*Shakespeare Survey* 41 (1988), 165), the anxiety palpable as he sinks to his knees before them and flexes his arms like a wrestler.

The analogy to an athletic feat is apt. Portia, now standing with her back to Bassanio, raises her right arm when he rejects the gold and her left when he rejects the silver: together, her outstretched arms signal victory to the crowd of spectators behind her. Bassanio's exclamation when he opens the lead casket, 'What find I here? / Fair Portia's counterfeit!' (114–15), thus provokes a trumpet fanfare and a spontaneous cheer from the crowd. Such acclaim prompts him to say that he feels like an athlete contending for a prize, who, 'Hearing applause and universal shout / Giddy in spirit, still gaz[es] in a doubt / Whether those peals of praise be his or no' (143–5): the staging brings Bassanio's simile to life. Portia, going to him, lays his doubt to rest, and he claims the prize with two kisses – tentative, awkward kisses that reveal his inexperience in love. In seeking a contemporary analogue for the hero and heroine of romance, therefore, Alexander happily landed on the athlete and the cheerleader. By allowing us to regard Portia and Bassanio in this way – as athletic, exuberant, and innocent – he involves us emotionally in their plot much as we might feel involved at a football match, and thereby momentarily deflects our critical judgement of their values.

Innocence characterises everything Portia does. It is especially evident in her attitudes towards marriage and money. The speech in which she offers herself to Bassanio – 'You see me, Lord Bassanio, where I stand, / Such as I am' (149–50) – is spoken with a firm conviction that Bassanio has every right to her and her wealth, and she, no rights at all. This is an unironic Portia whose notions of women's subservience to men are deeply ingrained. Bassanio, more interested in her person than her speech, tries to stop her lips with a kiss when she exalts him as 'her lord, her governor, her king' (165), but she holds him off until she has formally relinquished all her power: 'Myself, and what is mine, to you and yours / Is now converted' (166–7). Furthermore, she treats her inheritance as if it were play money. This is certainly the case when, on hearing that Bassanio is in debt to Antonio for three thousand ducats, she rises, smiles, then asks off-handedly, 'What, no more?' (297). Her ensuing lines betray the smug confidence of one for whom money has always been a remedy for everything: 'Pay him six thousand ... Double six thousand, and then treble that' (298–9). Her magnanimity is tinged with the superciliousness of one who has never known want.

Portia simply does not understand the nature of the bond: this becomes abundantly clear at the trial, where she matter-of-factly instructs Shylock in the need for charity, reading him a lesson as if by rote – 'The quality of mercy is not *strained*' – and naively assuming that he will see things her way. For such a Portia, the sentiments of this great speech are not rhapsodic – here is no music in her soul – but perfunctory, commonplace, even mundane. Her delivery, according to Maureen Paton (*Daily Express*, 29 April 1988), resembles that of a Sunday School teacher lecturing on Christian obligations to a recalcitrant pupil. If Portia honours these obligations, then so should Shylock: of this she has no doubt. Such cultural solipsism betrays the narrowness of her ideology; for however well intentioned, she is insensible of what others feel or think. Her morality is untried in the crucible of the world. And in this, Bassanio is her match. When he offers Shylock double the money – *her* money – to let Antonio go, he demonstrates how oblivious he is to what is really at stake at the trial.

In Alexander's interpretation, then, Portia and Bassanio become the children of Thatcher's Britain and Reagan's America. Secure in their privilege and cavalier in their prejudices, they pursue material goals mindless of anything but their own desert. They are Christians in form but not in substance: charity and mercy, for them, are not spiritual duties but social obligations, manifestations of a modern *noblesse oblige*. Such, Alexander seems to suggest (with a political bias for which young RSC directors are noted), is the legacy of conservative governments: an affirmation that the monied classes may do as they please with scant regard for the rights and beliefs of those they tread on. In a significant way, his Belmontese lovers display the naive confidence of bright young people who prospered in the 1980s, and their behaviour is made to seem excusable, even engaging, by the earnestness of their convictions.

The materialism of their marriage is brilliantly represented by the caskets themselves: gold, silver, and lead boxes in the shape of miniature Palladian villas (see Figure 8). Presumably they are replicas of the 'fair mansion' in which Portia lives and which she will happily turn over to her husband: 'This house, these servants, and this same myself / Are yours, my lord's' (170–1). These caskets, then, signify the true prize – Portia's inheritance – that inspired Bassanio's quest in the first place, a quest whose material goals Alexander has only briefly allowed us to forget. When Bassanio wins Portia, he wins the house too, and all that goes with it. Their romance is thus a means to a most material end. The exquisite little villas, strategically placed at the front of the stage, keep insisting on their own importance; in tangible terms, they promise Bassanio access to the power Portia's father once held. By visually reinforcing the ways in which money and class underpin their romance, therefore, Alexander advances a socialist interpretation of Shakespeare's text inspired by the obsessive materialism of his own society.

The three caskets, furthermore, are placed on a large crane that bears a remarkable resemblance to scales. Rising through a trap in the platform, these giant scales ask us to consider the relative value of each metal – gold, silver and lead – but here they are balanced, each casket apparently of equal weight. Metaphorically, then, these scales imply the risk of choice – of weighing options, of calculating profit and loss. They remind us of how business is done in the souk where Shylock, scales by his side, has bargained for his pound of flesh; and they anticipate the trial, where he will bring those scales to weigh Antonio's forfeiture. Scales thus become a symbol for the kindred impulses that motivate gamblers in commerce and in love, in Venice and in Belmont. They may weigh flesh or caskets: either way, they signify the means by which human beings achieve power over one another. Ultimately, they signify the scales of a dubious justice that will bring Shylock down.

With an expressive force born of great visual economy, therefore, Alexander uses stage images to symbolise the ideologies of

Cultural stereotyping and audience response 155

Figure 8 'What demi-god / Hath come so near creation?' Bassanio (Nicholas Farrell) to Portia (Deborah Findlay) in the RSC production of 1987. Courtesy of Joe Cocks Studio.

Venice and Belmont. The Madonna icon, Bible and prayer book, crucifixes, and chains all express the power of institutionalised religion, just as the graffito Star of David and yellow badges signify the impotence of those victimised by that religion. Miniature Palladian villas and scales represent the material world for which Venetians are willing to hazard all they have; and costuming defines characters' standing within, or without, that world. In short, Alexander uses such images to define the culturally sanctioned bigotry and violence he finds implicit in Shakespeare's text. Dominated by the Church, the playworld he creates assumes that male hegemony and class privilege are God-given rights. That world promotes material acquisition, condones anti-Semitism and other forms of racism, values women only as they provide men with access to power, and fosters homosexual cliquishness. Such a world conditions its victims to respond in understandable ways: Shylock to seek violent revenge, Jessica to crave an assimilation she cannot have, Portia and Nerissa unquestioningly to capitulate to male authority. The problem Alexander creates for his audience is how to balance a rational appraisal of this world against an affective response to those who people it.

Modern audiences, their memories of the Holocaust still fresh, are more than willing to embrace the comforting vision of Shylock as a patrician Jew established by Irving over a century ago and recently recreated by Olivier. That tradition offers us a chance to identify with an isolated and persecuted alien, to deplore the narrowmindedness of a Venetian society that exploits and rejects him, and from a safe distance to congratulate ourselves on our own – and Shakespeare's – moral enlightenment. Such productions make bigotry a failing of individuals: the Venetians simply have made the wrong moral choices, choices we would never repeat. Alexander's *Merchant* calls precisely that conception of bigotry into question: it assumes that, for all our good intentions, for all our rhetoric of tolerance, deeply ingrained and unacknowledged cultural stereotypes continue to shape our responses to racial, religious, and sexual otherness. In this production, bigotry is portrayed as an ideological system that influences people at fundamental levels, preserving cultural difference because the alien serves to define, by his very exclusion, the normalcy and homogeneity of the rest of society. To declare oneself free of the influence of ideology – a classic gesture of Western humanism – is to indulge a dangerous fiction: Alexander will have none of it. By making visceral his bourgeois audience's discomfort with swarthy Semites and closet queens, he dramatises the subtle and finally violent effects of ideology and thereby denies us the smug satisfaction that moral distance would allow.

VII

Shylock and the pressures of history

In performance, perhaps no play by Shakespeare has been subject to the pressures of history – or, in the words of Jonathan Miller, 'held hostage to contemporary issues' (*New York Times*, 22 February 1981) – more forcibly than *The Merchant of Venice*. Particularly since Irving's landmark production of 1879, treatment of Shylock has focused the attention of Western audiences on the question of whether the play is anti-Semitic. Does Shakespeare, in Shylock, promote a comic Jewish stereotype or overturn that stereotype with a broader appeal to humanist values? Does he pander to Elizabethan prejudice against Jews as bloodthirsty villains, or expose the Christians as hypocrites and the Jew as their victim? In light of these insistent questions, no production of *The Merchant* can be politically or socially disinterested. In the twentieth century, the play has aroused more passion and prompted more theatrical extremism than any other Shakespearean comedy. Political regimes have been known to appropriate the play to further their own agendas: most notoriously, during the 1930s the Third Reich exploited it as comic propaganda against those Jews who – hook-nosed devils all, intent on bringing Germany to financial ruin – were being herded toward the Final Solution (Wulf, pp. 280–3), even as the play was staged in Palestine in 1936 by expatriate German-Jewish director Leopold Jessner to document the history of oppression against which European Jews like himself had struggled (Oz, pp. 167–71). Such extremes indicate how pervasively historical and cultural determinants have shaped the meanings of *The Merchant*.

Fear that the play might arouse anti-Semitic feeling has been especially pronounced in North America, where virtually any production may be greeted with irate letters to editors and protests by Jewish groups. The mere announcement that PBS intended to air the BBC *Merchant* in 1981 elicited calls for its cancellation. Morris Schappes, editor of *Jewish Currents*, argued that the very least PBS could do in compensation would be 'to mount swiftly an educational effort to demonstrate the evil of anti-Semitism today' (*New York Times*, 27 January 1981); and the Anti-Defamation League of the B'nai B'rith, citing a recent upsurge in anti-Semitic incidents, accused the producers of abdicating those 'social responsibilities demanded when staging a controversial presentation with an inherent potential for harm' (*New York Times*, 22 February 1981). Such protests have had long-term consequences for staging *The Merchant* in North America: seldom since the Holocaust has a production treated Shylock unsympathetically. As John Houseman admitted of his years as director of the American Shakespeare Theatre, 'we would not have had the nerve to do that play if we hadn't a completely sympathetic Shylock' (R. Cooper, pp. 46–7).

Occasionally critics have objected to a director's apparent capitulation. Michael Langham, for instance, was accused of bowing to pressure from the Canadian Jewish Congress to drop several offensive passages from his distinguished production for the Stratford, Ontario, Festival in 1989. A furore arose particularly over his excision of Shylock's forced conversion to Christianity (*The Toronto Star*, 18 May 1989). Langham, explaining that he had made the same cuts in a production for the Folger Shakespeare Library in Washington the previous year, claimed that he had omitted Shylock's conversion not because any Jewish group had pressured him to do so, but because, for modern audiences, 'this compulsory rejection of the Jewish faith takes on the odor of brutal racism'. It would, he said, have risked making Shylock 'a martyred victim', thus nullifying the impact of Portia's mercy and the Christian affirmations of Act V. Yet there is a curious paradox in Langham's self-defence: his ostensible reason for omitting Shylock's conversion – that it might draw sympathy to the Jew and away from the Christians – is antithetical to the reason directors usually give, that the conversion might provoke an anti-Semitic backlash in the audience. Reviewers were unconvinced. Some regarded Langham's cuts (which also included Portia's racist remarks about Morocco and Lancelot Gobbo's teasing Jessica about being damned as a Jew) as tantamount to 'self-censorship ... a regrettable nod in the direction of the book-burners' (*Elmira Independent*, 14 July 1989); and their complaints probably were justified, for such omissions suppress the potential of the play to confront audiences with images of racial intolerance that may be a part of their cultural history.

The controversy surrounding Langham's production brings into focus the problem of how to stage an acceptable *Merchant* for contemporary audiences. Wary, perhaps, of being accused of insensitivity to Jewish feeling, directors have frequently sanitised the text, exorcising the play's more blatant racism and offering, in place of the comic stage Jew in vogue between the wars, a Shylock more befitting a post-Holocaust sensibility. Certainly this was the case in Germany after 1945, where the play was tactfully rehabilitated by directors — many of whom had suffered under the Third Reich — who offered a Shylock of such tragic dignity that he 'came nearer to Lessing's *Nathan* than to Shakespeare's revenge-craving usurer' and thus allowed the Nazi propaganda piece once again to enter the repertory as 'a sensitive reflector of a nation's consciousness of guilt' (Verch, pp. 84–8). In Israel, too, heroic portrayals of Shylock have served as touchstones in the forging of a national Jewish identity. The one attempt by an Israeli director to portray Shylock as a medievalised Jew, shrewd, grasping, and currish (Tel Aviv, 1972) was roundly attacked by the nationalistic press as a throwback to the vicious stereotype that had made 'Shylock' a household word (Oz, pp. 173–5).

The idea of interpreting *The Merchant* as a tragedy of Jewish oppression first took root in England. It was nourished by the Victorians' fascination with alien cultures and blossomed in productions by Henry Irving and his disciples. Such interpretations, despite challenges by Poel, Komisarjevsky, and others to reclaim the play as comedy, lasted well into the twentieth century; and recently they have flowered again in productions which have paid homage, directly or indirectly, to their Victorian forebears. In his Berlin production of 1963, for example, Erwin Piscator deliberately recreated the contrasts of Irving's *Merchant* between a sober Renaissance Ghetto and a comically light-hearted Belmont — and, more tellingly, between a profoundly human Shylock, played by veteran Jewish tragedian Ernst Deutsch, and the frivolously amoral Christians whose discrimination against him culminated in his tragic collapse at the trial and subsequent heroic exit in the manner of Irving

(Verch, p. 87). Piscator's staging anticipated Jonathan Miller's self-consciously 'Victorian' *Merchant* for the National Theatre in 1970 in which Laurence Olivier, as we have seen, played Shylock as a direct descendant of Irving and George Arliss – a very gentle Jew indeed. In America, Victorian stage traditions have been resuscitated most successfully by Morris Carnovsky, who performed the role with remarkable fidelity to Irving on several occasions, arguing that Shylock was a decent man with great nobility and loftiness of character (Carnovsky, pp. 21–8). In one notable production at Stratford, Connecticut (1957), Carnovsky allowed his bid for tragic pathos to contest the spirited comedy of Katherine Hepburn's Portia – much as Irving's had contested Ellen Terry's – even to the point of borrowing Irving's most famous melodramatic interpolation for the first-act curtain. Returning home from dining with the Christians, he spied a mask left by a reveller, grew apprehensive, then shoved it aside when he noticed that the door of his house was ajar: as he entered the house – to discover that Jessica had fled – the curtain fell (R. Cooper, p. 47). This traditional appeal for audience sympathy had been abandoned in Britain before the war; typically, in America it lingered.

Other American productions have contended with the Jewish question without resorting to such antiquated stage traditions. In a revival at Lincoln Center in 1973, director Ellis Rabb, sensitive to the risks of staging *The Merchant* before a heavily Jewish New York audience, chose to foreground modes of cultural alienation that were at once recognisable but heavily stylised. His Venice recalled the world of Fellini's *La Dolce Vita*, all cocktail bars, sunglasses, beach chairs, and bikinis (*Daily News*, 5 March 1973). Belmont itself became a yacht at anchor, a pleasure-toy of the idle rich. Rabb thus created 'an atmosphere charged with languorous hedonism, decadence, and voluptuous money lust' (*Newsweek*, 19 March 1973); and contributing to that atmosphere were James Tilton's black-and-white projections of a Venice crumbling, decaying, and sinking into the sea, 'a visual metaphor for contemporary civilisation' (*After Dark*, May 1973, pp. 43–4). Such stylisation yielded a *Verfremdungseffekt* characteristic of Rabb's whole approach to the play. His actors conveyed boredom, ennui, and alienation from one another and from the roles they played. The prickly homosexual relationship between Antonio and Bassanio, for example, clearly affected Bassanio's marriage to Portia who, as a sophisticated older woman, was keenly aware that her young husband was bound to another man. Even the trial was 'twisted to serve the bisexual romantic triangulation imposed on the text' (*Christian Science Monitor*, 5 March 1973). Jessica quarrelled with Lorenzo, who drunkenly slapped her during the love duet opening Act V – to Clive Barnes they seemed 'more like Edward Albee haters than Shakespearean lovers' (*New York Times*, 5 March 1973); and the game of rings, which in a conventional production brings the lovers full circle, instead underscored loss, suspicion, and the unlikelihood that these marriages would last.

In striking contrast to this degenerate group, Sydney Walker's unsentimental, business-like Shylock was dignified not so much by heroic acting as by sober restraint. In a dark suit, grey gloves, and Homburg, he resembled, in the eyes of one critic, Bernard Baruch (*Newsweek*, 19 March 1973); and for most, 'his sincerity, austerity, uprightness, and moral perception formed an edifying contrast to the triviality and shallowness of the Christians' (*New York Times*, 11 March 1973). The word 'edifying' alerts us to Rabb's Brechtian didacticism, and nowhere was his intention clearer than in an interpolated masque leading up to Jessica's elopement. Such masques, as we have seen, provided festive and often spectacular interludes in nineteenth-century *Merchants* – comic revelry that enhanced the pathos of Shylock's return to an empty house. Rabb, on the other hand, used his masque to illustrate the violent effects of religious persecution on minorities – Jews and women. He staged it as a Black Mass, 'a phantasmagorical, sacrilegious orgy' of men in drag during which a large cross was borne across the stage by an erotically suffering Christ. At its climax, when Jessica approached the cross to signal her conversion, 'the revelers leaped at her and tore her blouse off – presumably in order to show her, and us, just what it was she had really converted to' (*New York Times*, 11 March 1973). This atavistic attack on Jessica, a far cry from what Shakespeare's text suggests her elopement with a Christian might be, vividly demonstrates how Rabb used *The Merchant* to indict a decadent society (American, perhaps?) that would rape anyone who dared resist its pleasures.

Those who believe in an 'essentialist' Shakespeare – a recoverable and authoritative historical standard against which performances should be measured – may of course object that such interpolations distort the play by imposing contemporary concerns on it. Indeed, critics complained that, by disparaging the Christians and ennobling the Jews, Rabb's production, like Miller's, actually reversed the sympathies Shakespeare's text cultivates. As I have tried to suggest, however, the complexities of that text, and our uncertainty of how it was originally performed, should preclude us from making any such judgements. Furthermore, events of the past century have attached new meanings to events within the play and have compelled audiences to view *The Merchant* through the lens of Jewish history. Arnold Wesker, whose anti-establishment plays such as *Chips with Everything* have won him a wide following in London and New York, posed a question that has vexed many directors: how much historical burden can Shakespeare's text be made to bear? Finding the play inescapably anti-Semitic – 'because here is a Jew who against all humanity persists in claiming his pound of flesh' (*New York Times*, 22 February 1981) – Wesker implied that productions such as Miller's and Rabb's encumbered the text with more cultural baggage than it could comfortably carry. Yet, as a Jew, he was sympathetic with their aims; recalling his response to Miller's production, he admitted that 'when Portia suddenly got to the bit about having a pound of flesh but no blood, it flashed on me that the kind of Jew I know would stand up and say "Thank God!"' (*Guardian Weekend*, 29 August 1981, p. 9). And so, like a modern-day Granville, he took it upon himself to fit the play to the temper of the times.

His adaptation, simply titled *The Merchant*, had its English-speaking première in New York in 1977. Directed by John Dexter, it featured a genially cultured Shylock (originally played by Zero Mostel, who died during the tryout) who, as a scholar, a collector of rare books, and a patron of the arts, has a humanist's faith that knowledge – the wisdom of the ancients – can save mankind from itself: 'Knowledge, like underground springs, fresh and constant there, till one day – up! Bubbling! For dying men to drink, for survivors from dark and terrible times. I love it!' (1.6, p. 233). Wesker's depiction of the Ghetto smells of the library. It is so doggedly authentic, so full of self-conscious references to the Venice of 1563 – to the new science, to printing presses and men of letters, to art and architecture, and to expatriate Portuguese Jews who sought refuge there – that the play at times resembles a scholarly apologia for Jewish culture with

Shylock serving as Wesker's mouthpiece. In effect, Wesker revised Shakespeare's text to meet the criteria of the late nineteenth-century naturalism that Miller had attempted to impose on it; and where Miller had found the text resistant to such imposition, Wesker skirted the problem by rewriting it as a 'problem play' in the vein of Ibsen – the play Miller perhaps wished Shakespeare had written.

The dramatic fulcrum of Wesker's *Merchant* is the relationship between Shylock and Antonio. As in Miller's production, they are two genteel old men who physically resemble one another; but where in Shakespeare they are antagonists, Wesker makes them fellows in enlightenment who cross accepted social (and Ghetto) boundaries to indulge their friendship. When Antonio needs to borrow three thousand ducats to supply an arrogant godson whom he barely knows, Shylock wants to lend them without security, as an act of friendship. Antonio, however, sensible that Jews need the protection of the law, insists on drawing up a bond; therefore Shylock – perhaps taking his lead from Olivier's Shylock, who proposed the bond not in spite but in sport – suggests that they sign an agreement so absurd that it will mock the Venetian law which refuses to sanction friendship between Jews and Christians. Shylock thus makes a political point, and Antonio concurs with it: 'the bond is their protest against the oppressive laws of Venice and, beyond that, against the whole, well-attested history of European persecution of Jews, occurring most viciously at the time of the play's action in Portugal' (Sinfield, pp. 137–8).

When the bond is forfeit, of course neither man wants to abide by its terms. Both try to raise the sum to pay it off; failing that, they may comfort themselves that the court will, if they wish, relieve them of the bond. But Wesker allows no easy solution. He creates a moral dilemma that hinges on Shylock's responsibility to (and for) the Jewish community – and, in so doing, he demonstrates an awareness that for four centuries Shylock has been made to shoulder that responsibility. In a climactic scene, Shylock's sister Rivka reminds him that there is more at stake than Antonio's friendship. As she defines his dilemma,

> To save a citizen's life the court *will* relieve you of your bond. You do *know* that don't you? ... They will even let you bend the law and lend him further ducats for repayment when the hour is passed. You do *know* that, don't you? ... More! They'll wait days, weeks, even

months. But – and here your moral problem begins – not everyone in the Ghetto will agree to the bending of the law ... Some may. Some may even beg you to do that rather than have the blood of a Christian on their hands. But others will say, no! Having bent the law for us, how often will they bend it for themselves and then we'll live in even greater uncertainties than before. They'll be divided, as you are, my clever brother. Who to save – your poor people or your poor friend? You can't see that? ... It's not only your problem now, it's the community's.

(2.3, pp. 242–3)

What follows is an irony worthy of Ibsen. Irritated by Shylock's avoidance of choice, Antonio himself forces Shylock to recognise that for the sake of defending the rights of Jews – Jews who fear the consequences of legal precedent – they must hold to the terms of the bond, even though it will mean death for both of them: Antonio's at the hands of Shylock, and Shylock's at the hands of the court. Antonio affirms his understanding of Shylock's dilemma in a remarkable show of unity with him. 'Your yellow hat belongs to both of us,' he says. 'I'm party to the mockery as well' (p. 246).

This revision of the bond plot redeems Shylock from his barbaric lust for a pound of Christian flesh – a motive from which no production of Shakespeare can, according to Wesker, fully exculpate him. It dramatically fulfils the desire of many recent directors to rewrite the play as a tragedy of Jewish oppression. In his most daring appropriation of Shakespeare's text, Wesker places 'Hath not a Jew eyes' – his only direct quotation of Shakespeare – in the mouth of Lorenzo, a supercilious pedant (much like Miller's) who delivers it at the trial purportedly to defend the 'humanity' of Jews while condemning only their *practice* of usury, thereby drawing a specious distinction between doer and deed which for generations has served to mask racial prejudice. Shylock is justifiably incensed by Lorenzo's presumption: 'I will not have my humanity mocked and apologised for. If I am unexceptionally like any man then I need no exceptional portraiture. I merit no special pleas, no special cautions, no special gratitudes. My humanity is my right, not your bestowed and gracious privilege' (2.5, p. 259).

In its context in *The Merchant of Venice*, as Alan Sinfield argues, this famous speech seems 'to manifest the transcendent humanism which is otherwise hard to find in the play' (p. 139); but Wesker's Shylock, by condemning it as a condescending plea for a humanity which should be taken for granted, reveals the tragic irony of the use to which not only the speech, but the whole of *The Merchant of Venice* has been put by ostensibly tolerant societies. Wesker glosses Shakespeare's lines as themselves a contribution to anti-Semitic mythology. By incorporating them in a new context which encourages us to hear them as such, he both acknowledges and unsettles Shakespeare's cultural authority.

If Wesker, however indirectly, exposes Shakespeare's text as both a product and a cause of anti-Semitism, others have more blatantly implicated *The Merchant of Venice* in the history of Jewish oppression by calling into question the purposes for which it has been performed. German director George Tabori's production for the Stockbridge (Massachusetts) Playhouse in 1966 is a case in point. Though Tabori used Shakespeare's text, his production was even more revisionary than Wesker's: it devastatingly indicted the play as a weapon used by hegemonic societies against the Jews. Influenced by Peter Weiss's violently meta-theatrical *Marat/Sade* (1964), Tabori staged *The Merchant* as a play within a play, performed by the inmates of a German concentration camp before an audience of Nazi soldiers for whom the play presumably provided good anti-Semitic entertainment. As Shylock, Alvin Epstein wore the false nose and red beard that characterised the devilish Jew of Mystery plays and stage Shylocks of the Third Reich. According to one reviewer, however, 'the role was conceived with a double edge: on the surface, Epstein was a craven caricature of the Jew as comic villain, complete with whining accent and exaggerated hand gestures ... but just beneath the top layer of this Jewish Uncle Tom was a hostile inmate of a prison camp desperately seeking revenge' (*Judaism* 16 (1967), 463). At certain moments, Epstein would remove the nose, drop the accent, and begin in his own persona, that of inmate, to address Shakespeare's lines antagonistically to the Nazi officers who had been strategically placed on stage and among the audience. 'When it became apparent that the nameless inmate playing Shylock was ready to go at the German guards with his bare hands the rest of the acting company had to ... restrain him' (*Judaism*, p. 464) – a disturbing image of Jews suppressing Jews. Such violation of theatrical decorum reached a climax during the trial scene, when Shylock, suddenly discovered to be wielding a real knife, assaulted a prison guard: in the ensuing scuffle, he was pinned down by the guards and killed – the probable fate, audiences were well aware, of all the inmates performing the play. An improvised curtain of potato sacks was then hastily drawn across the stage.

Shorn of Belmont, magic, and moonlight, Tabori's *Merchant* focused exclusively on the degradation to which Jews were subjected in being forced to perform a play that, as an artefact of historical anti-Semitism, may have contributed to their present victimisation. The actors thus became victims of both Shakespeare's play and the Aryan oppressors who watched it. According to Michael Shapiro, Tabori revealed 'the potential Holocaust' which history has shown 'lurking at the heart of the play' (*Shofar*, p. 8). Shakespeare's text was viewed in light of – and was made to bear a responsibility for – historical events. By refashioning it as political theatre, Tabori eerily recalled its use in Hitler's Germany to fuel anti-Jewish sentiment.

Tabori's production imaginatively invoked and contained the most odious moment in *The Merchant*'s stage history. The Pirandellian device by which he confused the inner play – Shakespeare's play – with the outer play (the plight of the Jewish inmates) distanced the audience by fixing the historical moment of performance, but at the same time encouraged the audience to respond to *The Merchant* itself as a cultural document with political and social resonances. When Tabori restaged it in his native Germany twelve years later (1978), those resonances grew even stronger. Here, the performance venue was not a theatre but the former boiler room of the Munich Kammerspiele; the camp was identified as nearby Dachau; and the role of Shylock was shared among thirteen different inmates, who thus formed a *group* of German actors collectively 'struggling with and acting out' the guilt of Germany's anti-Semitic past (Verch, p. 89). Tabori succeeded in recreating for *The Merchant* a historical context that apparently, for German audiences, lent the play great contemporary significance. Jerome McGann has observed that the 'focus upon history as constituted in what we call "the past" only achieves its critical fulfilment when that study of the past reveals its significance in and for the present and the future' (p. 25). Tabori's Munich production, according to Maria Verch, achieved such fulfilment: of all recent stagings of *The Merchant* in Germany, it 'was the one which had moved furthest from its Shakespearean source and nearest to a psycho-analytic medium in its approach to the unresolved problems of the past' (p. 89).

One may object, of course, that a production so far removed from its Shakespearean source is no longer *The Merchant of Venice*, but the director's play. In a sense, however, isn't *any* production of *The Merchant* the director's play? Irving's, Komisarjevsky's, Miller's, Rabb's, and Alexander's all have likewise been called 'unfaithful' to Shakespeare; but this, of course, begs the question of whose Shakespeare they have been unfaithful to. Because Shakespeare has traditionally, and certainly since Irving, been constructed as a purveyor of liberal humanist values, directors have resorted to the various means detailed in this volume – from cutting and updating on the one hand, to recreating what they imagine to have been the original conditions of performance on the other – to make *The Merchant* reflect those values. They have intervened to save 'their' Shakespeare from the embarrassing stigma of anti-Semitism. Tabori, therefore, may be regarded as having simply moved further along the scale of directorial intervention; and in so far as he intervened to have Shakespeare speak to his nation's consciousness, he revitalised *The Merchant* and invested it with a topical power it otherwise might have lacked.

If such intervention allows a play to speak in new ways to its audience, would Shakespeare have complained? He knew the extent to which any successful production depends on the receptivity of audiences to the material being dramatised; as playwright, actor, and sharer, he knew that the proof of a play was in performance – what drew audiences to the theatre. And for four hundred years *The Merchant* has drawn audiences. It has worn masks in which they have seen themselves; it has spoken to them in many voices on matters of race, religion, gender, and social value; it has served as a Rorschach test of cultural difference. For better and worse, it has entered our historical consciousness as no other Shakespearean comedy has, converging with the pressures of history to yield meanings Shakespeare could never have imagined. Such meanings have sometimes been said to distort the play; seldom, however, has the play suffered on that account. Its adaptability, in fact, may above all else explain why, when the fortunes of other comedies have waxed and waned, the popularity of *The Merchant* has remained constant.

Part II

Segue

The Merchant of Venice: pressures of war, ideology, and the crises of late capitalism

Some thirty years ago, James C. Bulman finished his study of the major performances of *The Merchant of Venice* for this series with a chapter which anticipated the global turn in Shakespeare performance scholarship. In this spirit, the chapters that follow include a diversity of traditions, opening up the British focus of Part I. We discuss primarily continental European theatre productions (Max Reinhardt's and Peter Zadek's influential long-term engagements with the play, Leopold Jessner's daring staging, Robert Sturua's postmodern satirical take), as well as work done in Britain and the United States (Trevor Nunn's celebrated production for the National Theatre, Rupert Goold's and Edward Hall's radical re-envisionings of the play, Daniel Sullivan's Broadway production), and international collaborations (the site-specific theatre work of Compagnia de' Colombari and the transnational medium of film, from New Zealand to Hollywood, including early film adaptations). Two of these productions were accompanied by legal trials of the play; the interactions of theatre and legal discourses on *The Merchant* are analysed in the final chapter. On a number of occasions, including a part of this Segue, we throw a bridge to the period before the Second World War, which marked a watershed in the stage history of the play. The Segue also maps trends in the performance history of the play from the 1930s through the 2010s.

Why the European focus? This Venetian play of Shakespeare's was one of the first to have travelled from England to continental Europe, where it has had a notable stage life for nearly four hundred years (Limon, p. 117; Stříbrný, p. 13). Looking at Shakespeare from the vantage point of non-English speaking cultures with widely differing histories enables a discussion of diverse theatrical and cinematic traditions, re-interpretations, and appropriations – i.e., the inclusion of 'more alternative Shakespeares' (Delabastita, p. 113).

Fully aware that 'no production of *The Merchant* can be politically or socially disinterested', we follow in Bulman's steps in analysing key performances as shaped by 'the pressures of history'. These pressures, creatively dramatised both onstage and on the big screen, have included ethnic and religious intolerance, political overturns, war, economic turmoil, gender, racial, and sexual bias, and migration-induced social controversies. Central to the interpretive work in Part II has been a discussion of the use of the play to foreground relationships with the social Other in specific cultural and historical milieux.

To map the larger historical context, political and theatrical, for the major productions discussed in the subsequent chapters, this Segue charts key developments in theatrical approaches to the play, from the rise of Nazi ideology to its hegemonic status in the 1930s, through the collapse of communism in the 1990s, to the fallout of the 2008 global financial crisis, the immigration waves in Europe peaking in 2015, and the global political radicalisation during the first two decades of the twenty-first century. Directly or obliquely, the stage and screen life of *The Merchant* has been entangled with these social upheavals and ideological collisions. Thus Reinhardt's multiple productions over the first three decades of the twentieth century may appear politically disengaged, but their theatrical aesthetic acquires new dimensions when considered in their turbulent political context (see Part II, Chapter I).

A process of subtle and not-so-subtle political signification marks the life of the play in Germany during the Third Reich (1933–45). Since the late 1990s, the persistent assertion that *The Merchant* was the favourite play of the Nazi regime, weaponised by its propaganda machine, has been challenged by Shakespeare theatre criticism (Hortmann, p. 135). In fact, the National Socialists initially banned the play from the stage (Ackermann, p. 36) and proscribed it from inclusion in public library collections (Symington, p. 245). Accordingly, the number of new productions in Germany dropped dramatically. While in 1927 *The Merchant of Venice* was the most performed Shakespeare play on the German stage, in 1941 it had plummeted to twenty-first place, even though Shakespeare remained a repertoire staple (Ackermann and Schülting, p. 46). It seems that the authorities were apprehensive of the play's subversive potential (Márkus, p. 149, Ackermann, p. 38). Theatre professionals, in turn, were uncertain whether 'the Jewish subject would be acceptable to the authorities and, more pertinently, how to perform it: as a *Stürmer* caricature, which many directors considered tasteless, or in a pro-Shylock sense, which would have been suicidal' (Hortmann, p. 135).[1] In addition, the racial laws of 1935 rendered the marriage of the Christian Lorenzo and the converted Jewess, Jessica, untenable (Bonnell, *German Life and Letters*, p. 171). The single production of the play authorised for staging in Berlin in 1942 used a heavily revised text. In this rabidly anti-Semitic appropriation, performed at the Rose Theater, a grotesque Shylock was played by active National Socialist Party member Georg August Koch; the triple victory of romance in the happy ending was secured by making Jessica the Jew's adopted daughter. Director Paul Rose used the commedia dell'arte form for anti-Semitic agitation, creating a propagandist *Volksfest* of dance, music, and audience participation. Especially disconcerting was the timing of the production, which coincided with the first deportations of Berlin Jews to the concentration camps (Márcus, pp. 148–50).

As the Jewish genocide gathered momentum, the number of productions of the play throughout the Reich rose almost to 1933 levels (Ackermann and Schülting, p. 50). This dreadful dynamic was on stark display during the run of the hugely popular 1943 production at the Vienna Burgtheater, directed by Lothar Müthel, with Werner Krauss as Shylock. Krauss had performed the part in Berlin in 1921, under Reinhardt's direction, but in Vienna he offered a different interpretation. His earlier, ferocious Shylock was replaced by a comically deflated character: 'an odd and funny lout who, in the trial scene, fails to grasp why the Doge and the judge should have anything against him' (Herbert Ihering, qtd. in Ackermann, p. 50). Unlike the heavy adaptation of the play at the Berlin Rose Theater, Müthel's production advertised itself as 'authentic' Shakespeare, with no significant alterations and few textual cuts. Its ideological value derived from presenting it as an unadulterated Shakespearean comedy, in which the villain, Shylock, had been diminished and depleted of pathos and humanity. This empty shell of a character drew the imperious laughter of the Viennese spectators, who were no doubt aware that the city's 200,000 Jews (one in ten citizens) had been expelled, deported, and exterminated (Ackermann, p. 55). The production was an effective vehicle of ideology, more insidious than the blatant propaganda of the Nazi mass media (Ackermann and Schülting, p. 53).

In the newly established Soviet Union (1922), on the opposite side of the ideological divide that defined Europe after the First World War, *The Merchant of Venice* vanished from the stage for nearly seventy years (Bartoshevich). With the expansion of the Soviet sphere of influence after the Second World War, productions plummeted in all East European countries, too, although the play had been popular there before. This had to do with post-Holocaust sensitivity; but more to the point, the near-disappearance of the play was caused by the need to fall into step with the Soviet model and suppress discourses about ethnic difference or conflict (Sokolova, *Shakespeare Survey*, pp. 89–90). Only a handful of stagings followed the prescribed Marxist paradigm of class struggle, which entailed diminished sympathy for the financier Shylock. One such rare production, directed by Hugo Klajn, appeared at the Belgrade National Theatre in 1964 (Nikolić, pp. 96–7).

During the 1930s and 1940s, the grip of fascist ideology on theatre life was weaker in countries allied with Germany, as can be gauged by production choices and their critical reception. In 1938, Bulgarian director Hrisan Tsankov heavily adapted *The Merchant*, giving it an ethical and expressly philo-Semitic treatment at the National Theatre in Sofia. Tsankov, who had trained with Reinhardt in the 1920s, had supported his colleague publicly when the Nazi government expropriated his theatres (Sokolova, *Shakespeare in between*, pp. 48–9). Along with a number of Bulgarian intellectuals and politicians, he had also taken a public stance against anti-Semitism (Piti, p. 198). Shylock was performed by Lubomir Zolotovich as a loving father and a man deeply scarred by adversity. In the trial scene, his love for Jessica and concern for her future stopped him from exacting the pound of flesh (Piti, *Nova kambana*, 20 April 1938). Reviewers were alert to the topicality of the subject and highly approved of the changes. One even suggested that 'Shakespeare would not have objected', but rather, 'sighed with relief [...] that his play has retained its truly humane essence' (Nadya Bolgar, *Vestnik na zhenata*, 30 March 1938). Others concurred that these changes fulfilled a moral duty, and Zolotovich spoke of his desire to convey 'what it feels like to belong to a persecuted race' (*Zarya*, 12 March 1938). Tsankov staged *The Merchant* before the legal codification of anti-Semitism in Bulgaria, which might partially account for the openly positive reception of the production. The critical reaction points to the way theatre taps into larger and enduring social sentiments, too: in 1943, when Jewish deportations started, these same attitudes enabled a coalition of politicians and clergy to put a partial halt to them, in spite of intense pressure from Nazi Germany.

The reaction to the 1940 production of the play at the Hungarian National Theatre, directed by Béla Both, which appeared *after* the passing of anti-Jewish laws in Hungary, complicates the discussion of resistance to fascist ideology. In the Budapest production, Tamás Major played Shylock as a 'relatively complex, at times even poignant' character, offsetting Both's overall comedic approach. Reviewers were split over the resulting tension between comedy and pathos. Some empathised with Shylock's 'drama of solitude and isolation'; others revelled in the contrast between the joyous world of the Christians and 'the miserly and bloodthirsty Jewish merchant' (Márkus, pp. 151, 152). It appears that this production was read both subversively and in accordance with fascist ideology, the critics' diverging views reflecting the fluidity of the political context. Such ambiguity would no longer be possible after the deportations of Budapest's Jews in 1944.

Some seventeen months before the end of the war, in January 1944, a philo-Semitic and anti-Nazi *Merchant* was staged in neutral Sweden. Alf Söberg's production at the National Theatre in Stockholm was impacted by the increasing knowledge of the tragic fate of Jews throughout Europe and by the presence of thousands of Jewish refugees from Denmark in the country. The production was hugely popular: it attracted more than 60,000 people, including the royal family, and generated a radio play (Sorelius, p. 203). Shylock, performed by the young star Holger Löwenadler, spoke the unaccented Swedish of someone born and bred in the country. Consequently, his rage against the Christians' casual rejection was more than justified. In the trial scene, the Venetians, who often hid behind white expressionless masks, behaved like *Hitlerjugend* thugs – another way of eliciting sympathy for Shylock (pp. 199–20).

The conversion was omitted, as was Graziano's subsequent insult. Critical reception split in a way different from that in Hungary. Some deplored the choice to mount *The Merchant* in the presence of the refugees from Denmark; others complained that the romantic and comic elements of the production overpowered Shylock's tragedy (p. 202).

During the rise of fascism and the Second World War, European productions of *The Merchant of Venice* refracted dominant ideology in complex ways, ranging from collaborationist to oppositional. They preserved the comic matrix made popular by Reinhardt over the first thirty years of the twentieth century, but no longer portrayed Shylock in a Romantic mode. Instead, versions of the Jewish moneylender ranged from a comically deflated mask to a father who chose his daughter's happiness over revenge, or to a sympathy-eliciting man rejected by a cold Christian world. Furthermore, the reception of these productions was often divergent within their own countries, with reviewers bringing to bear on them their own received ideas of Shakespeare, their biases and allegiances, as well as the general unease characteristic of a period of intense political conflict.

In the post-Holocaust world, *The Merchant of Venice* shed its comic trappings and refocused on Shylock's tragedy and moral righteousness within a depraved Christian Venice. While West German productions during the Konrad Adenauer era (1949–63) – a period when the country recovered from the Nazi dictatorship and the devastation of the war – were dominated by what has been described as the facile philo-Semitism of post-war expiation of guilt (Ackermann and Schülting, pp. 66–7), in European countries with totalitarian regimes, stretching from the Iberian to the Balkan peninsulas and into the heart of continental Europe, the play largely disappeared from the stage. Whatever the political system, *The Merchant*'s propensity for raising uneasy questions about living with the Other proved a stumbling block in its theatrical fortunes.

In the 1970s–1980s, with the rise of economic globalisation, the cult of consumerism, and the concomitant cultural shift away from communitarian priorities and toward unabashed self-interest, *The Merchant of Venice* acquired a new significance. The next notable trend in post-Holocaust European performances of the play came in the form of its economic interpretation (Bayerdörfer, p. 208). Several significant productions from the final decades of the twentieth century were set in the new centres of global finance. Capturing the pernicious effects of banking capitalism on the social fabric, these modern-dress productions privileged the economic clash above the play's ethnic and religious conflicts. In an influential staging for the Vienna Burgtheater in 1988, German-Jewish-British director Peter Zadek broke the post-war mould of victimised Shylocks to present the character as a successful banker, indistinguishable from his competitors in the cut-throat world of late capitalism (see Part II, Chapter II). By the early 1990s, the economic approach had become mainstream. In Spain, Carlos Plaza put on a production at Madrid's Centro Dramático Nacional in 1992, which critiqued a money-obsessed society riddled with class divisions and villainising Others (Gregor, pp. 115–16). (This approach was redeployed on the Spanish stage in 2015, in Eduardo Vasco's Madrid production, which engaged with the austerity measures imposed by the World Bank on the country, labelled as a 'financial holocaust' (Fischer, p. 318).) Economic concerns were centre-stage in David Thacker's 1993 modern-dress production for the Royal Shakespeare Company (RSC), where Shylock (David Calder) started out as one of the financial sharks from the City, but abandoned his efforts at assimilation and adopted a clear-cut Jewish identity and dress style at the trial. The character followed a similar line of development in Rupert Goold's 2009 RSC production, revived at the Almeida Theatre in London in 2011 (see Part II, Chapter V). The economic interpretation was reprised in 2010 in Daniel Sullivan's Public Theatre production, first staged in New York's Central Park and later on Broadway (see Part II, Chapter V).

Toward the end of the twentieth century, new adaptations of the play began linking the economic conflict to racism and interracial conflicts. In 1994, Peter Sellars, 'the Wunderkind and *enfant terrible*' of US theatre, put on a paradigm-shifting, if uneven, production at the Goodman Theatre in Chicago which has had a lasting influence on global stages (Thompson, p. i). It embodied his lifelong commitment to 'the stage as a public arena for discussion of dissent and debate' (Delgado, p. 477). The highly topicalised production appeared in the wake of documented police violence against the African-American Rodney King, the controversial acquittal of the white policemen involved in King's beating, and the ensuing racial uprising in Los Angeles – events which foreshadowed the circumstances leading to the Black Lives Matter movement in the early twenty-first century (Thompson, p. xv). Sellars set out to explore 'the economic roots of racism' and re-envisioned Venice as the Los Angeles neighbourhood of Venice Beach, and Belmont as the exclusive Bel Air enclave, where former President Ronald Reagan used to live. Furthermore, Sellars extended 'the metaphor and the reality of anti-Semitism ... to include parallel struggles' (Pettengill, p. 20). Mirroring the racial makeup of the LA uprising, he cast African-American actors in the parts of the Jews, Latino actors as the Venetians, and Asian-Americans, the model immigrant class in the US, as the denizens of Belmont. The clowns were white: Lancelot Gobbo was played by Philip Seymour Hoffman as an embittered yuppie whose father harassed him about his lifestyle, and Old Gobbo (performed by Del Close, doubling as the Duke) had *chosen* to live as a homeless man.[2] Racial conflicts intersected with class and sexual identities: Shylock (Paul Butler) was 'an African-American moneylender at odds with a clique of racist gay and bisexual Latinos' (Kate Bassett, *The Times*, 25 October 1994). These casting choices may have inadvertently reinforced racial stereotypes; however, as David Richards noted, this 'splintered view of *The Merchant of Venice*' showed 'something disturbing about American [racial] malaise in the 1990s' ('Sellars' Merchant of Venice Beach', *New York Times*, 18 October 1994).

Sellars's new vision of the play found an innovative expression in the heavy mediatisation of the dramatic action. The production opened with Antonio (Geno Silva) broadcasting his sadness in front of a microphone, surrounded by monitors mounted at different levels around the proscenium and on the stage. They showed shots of the ocean denoting the Venice Beach setting, urban youths playing basketball, speeding cars, and politically charged footage from the Rodney King beating and the race upheaval it unleashed. The documentary approach dissolved the boundary between theatre fiction and reportage. In the court scene, the use of cameras invited parallels with the Rodney King trial, which had kept the American public glued to their TV sets two years before. Extreme close-ups of Butler delivering the 'Hath not a Jew eyes' speech directly to the camera 'with stunning simplicity and tremendous emotional weight' were multiplied on the monitors (Richard Christiansen,

'Provocative Merchant', *Chicago Tribune*, 11 October 1994). This sharpened the spectators' experience of his 'intense stare [which mingled] decades of pain and repression with the anger of the moment' (Pettengill, p. 117). Augmented through multiple screens, Shylock's desire for revenge translated as Black anger accumulated over the course of American history. This interpretation was sustained in the trial scene when Butler once again delivered 'You have among you many a purchased slave' (IV.i.89) directly to the camera, adding four repetitions of 'Let them be free' (93) – one of the most powerful moments of the production (O'Connor, p. 234).

Critics on both sides of the Atlantic were mostly outraged by Sellars's overtly ideological and mediatised approach; traditional theatregoers in Chicago voted with their feet at the interval. However, the play found an enthusiastic audience among the Chicago teenagers who saw it through the Goodman Theatre educational programme. Sellars's *Merchant* sold out in London and was warmly received in Hamburg and Paris, where audiences have long had an exposure to avant-garde theatre, and it has since acquired iconic status among academic critics.

While Sellars critiqued late American capitalism and its entanglement with racism, productions in Eastern Europe from the end of the twentieth century resonated with a monumental socio-economic shift that upended the lives of millions. The collapse of the communist system, which began with the fall of the Berlin Wall in 1989 and continued precipitously over the following decade, opened up new political vistas, but also destroyed social support networks, unleashed financial shocks, and caused mass impoverishment. Criminal oligarchies fought for political power, corrupting moral and legal systems. When *The Merchant* returned to East European stages after a long hiatus, it reflected the rupture, trauma, and even hopelessness brought by this chaotic social transition. East European *Merchants* presented intolerant, violent, loveless new-capitalist worlds with few sympathetic characters, where Shylock rarely survived, and where identities, including gender and sexuality, were challenged. Productions thus dramatised wider and more complex sets of othering phobias.

In 1992, Zdravko Mitkov's production at the 'Ivan Vazov' National Theatre in Sofia breathed with the giddy atmosphere of early post-communism, with its rapacious reparcelling of assets and utter disregard of moral values. The play reflected a historical moment when conflicting political philosophies clashed over the principles of Bulgaria's new constitution, as well as the status of 'property and the morality of its confiscation and restitution' (Pancheva, p. 252). Paranoia about manipulations of all kinds engulfed Bulgarian society. In the production, Venice was a modern city bustling with young, smart-suited fortune-seekers, dominated by a Coca-Cola sign on the glass façade of a high-rise which dwarfed Shylock's house next door. In the cold, white space of Belmont, Portia and Nerissa orchestrated unromantic marriages as a cover-up for their lesbian relationship. Manipulation was endemic: Bassanio (Andrei Batashov) chose the right casket thanks to a serial con, in which Lancelot (Georgi Mamalev) impersonated Morocco, and Gratiano (Yuri Angelov) Arragon. In spite of Shylock's conspicuous Orthodox costuming, critics did not suggest that the production engaged with issues of anti-Semitism. Rather, they noted the audience's strong identification with Shylock, and his transformation from an ethnic to an ethical sign. Performed by Stefan Danailov, a charismatic star of Bulgarian theatre and cinema, Shylock was the sole character with moral integrity, ultimately defeated through devious manipulation of the law. The play ended with an image of a Belmont suffused in Chekhovian melancholy, where a heavily pregnant Jessica stood apart from Lorenzo, lost in the coldness of this space.

While *The Merchant* has since disappeared from the Bulgarian stages, signalling perhaps a lack of interest in reckoning with the moral burdens of history, in post-communist Hungary no fewer than fifteen productions were staged between 1989 and 2019 (Pikli, p. 153). Clearly, theatre professionals there saw *The Merchant* as a vehicle for depicting the social and moral crises of the transition. Among the most significant was a 1998 staging at the studio Tivoli Theatre in Budapest by young actor-director Róbert Alföldy. He portrayed Venice as a rocking city of yuppies, obsessed with sex, fashion brands, and money. This was the generation that had reached adulthood 'in the new wild capitalism of Hungary' (Szucs, p. 301). Like the young Venetians in Mitkov's production, they relied on brutality, lies, and manipulation to get ahead. The casket contest in Alföldy's staging of the play was another con job: Bassanio (Péter Bozsó) changed disguises as the other suitors, performing ugly stereotypes of otherness to ascertain the winning choice. The Venetians were not only con men, but violent thugs – misogynist, homophobic, and bigoted. At the end of the trial, the entire court, from the guards to the Duke, swarmed upon Shylock and beat him to death under Portia's impassive gaze (performed by Kati Egri). His body remained on stage, invisible to the lovers in Act V, which also abounded in violence. As the Christian gang in Dr Martens boots marched back to Belmont, they found Lorenzo raping Jessica. In a final display of aggressive cupidity, Bassanio and Gratiano (Kornél Mundruczó), fearful that their hard-won 'golden fleece' may have been jeopardised by giving away their wedding rings, roughed up their wives before a horrified Portia could produce the explanatory letters.

Shylock, performed by Zoltán Rátóti, was a study in the social creation of the Other. A yuppie type himself, physically similar to Antonio, he was spat upon, slighted, and humiliated for no apparent reason. By the trial scene, he had transformed into a vengeful and raging religious zealot. Like Sellars, Alföldy used cinematic techniques, though to different effect: surveillance cameras captured selected scenes and projected them on large screens, magnifying images of horrific violence and faces contorted in grotesque expressions of hatred. The role of the media in whipping up hatred against the Other was dramatised in III.i, where the pained articulation of the 'Hath not a Jew eyes' speech was caricatured by on-screen distortions of Shylock's face. His beating to death in the courtroom was also projected on screen. As some audience members laughed at the mockery of Shylock's plea for humanity and most gawked silently at the murderous violence, the mediatised aesthetic was harnessed to offer a harsh commentary on 'the rise of anti-Semitism as a symptom of larger societal issues which plague [post-communist] Hungarian society: xenophobia, lack of openness and curiosity, and a hatred of the unconventional or alien' (Szucs, p. 300). At the same time, Alföldy's production exonerated neither hegemonic nor minority cultures from responsibility for social disintegration. It subtly suggested that Shylock had become a mirror image of Antonio, thus relativising the roles of victim and perpetrator.

Across the border, director László Bocsárdi staged *The Merchant* for the Hungarian Theatre in Romania in 2010. His production, which went on to tour Romania and Hungary, 'extended the

Stranger's case beyond the Jew's' (Cinpoeş, 135) by including intelligent women and gay people among the Others who were perceived to threaten the alleged homogeneity of Venetian (Romanian) society. It also concerned itself with legal manipulation and questionable methods of wealth accumulation, issues relevant to the historical moment. A provocative feature of the production was its integration of the audience, which was seated on stage, as part of the world of the play. They were thus cast as the xenophobic, homophobic, misogynist citizens of Venice, on whose behalf Portia made her plea to Shylock (Cinpoeş, pp. 136–7).

Similar social concerns underpinned Egon Savin's 2004 production at the Belgrade National Theatre in Serbia. Staged in the wake of the wars leading to the collapse of Yugoslavia, it represented otherness in terms of ethnicity, gender, and sexuality. The production stressed Shylock's Jewishness, his shrewd grasp of the law, as well as his endangered status as a ghettoised Other in a 1920s Venice teetering on the brink of fascism (Nikolić, p. 97). A rare and much praised cross-cast Portia was performed by the male star of Serbian theatre Dragan Mićanović, who gave the character seductive sophistication in both her female and male personations. Savin's production probed the condition of the numerous minorities created in the new national formations after the demise of Yugoslavia, a country where society '*was* and *was not* truly multicultural' (p. 98). The play's conclusion was ominous: as Portia's servants in brown uniforms came to take away a homosexual Antonio, it became clear that the merchant and the Jew were equally vulnerable to vigilantes ready to enforce their notion of moral order and national unity. The issues dramatised in this post-Yugoslav, post-communist production recalled the approach taken in Sturua's *Shylock* (2000), staged in the aftermath of the dissolution of the Soviet Union (see Part II, Chapter V).

Two postmodern takes on *The Merchant* from post-communist Europe appropriated the play as a collage of absurdist narratives with disturbing satirical shifts in point of view (a formal quality shared with Sturua's *Shylock*). The first of these radical rewritings of Shakespeare's play was part of Krzsystof Warlikowski's *African Tales after Shakespeare* (2011) – a transformation of *King Lear*, *Othello*, and *The Merchant of Venice* collaged with passages by South-African-Australian novelist J. M. Coetzee and

Lebanese-Canadian writer Wajdi Mouawad. Next came *The Merchant of Venice* developed by the Mohácsi brothers – director-playwright János, dramaturge-playwright István, and set designer András – performed at the National Theatre in Budapest in 2013. The Mohácsis rewrote the play in colloquial prose, adding new scenes and rehearsal-room improvisations to create an East European world of acquisitiveness, moral decay, rampant xenophobia, homophobia, and misogyny. Casual anti-Semitic jokes were thrown about as part of 'infantile, often vulgar circus fun' (Pikli, p. 158). The outrageously absurdist characters of Morocco and Arragon became the object of crass laughter by on-stage and off-stage audiences alike. The 'half-blood' Morocco, whose face was painted half white and brown, was met with monkey sounds; 'the Great Mogul of Arragon was a lesbian' (Pikli, p. 162). Neither of these Others survived: Morocco was drowned in a canal, and Arragon committed suicide. Nor was Shylock (Sándor Gáspár) exempt from the greed and racism endemic to Venice. In an added scene, in which he was Portia's fourth suitor, he held his nose in disgust at Morocco's supposed stench. The Mohácsis created a distorted, but recognisable funhouse-mirror image of Hungarian life permeated by conservative government propaganda since the anti-liberal government takeover in 2010 (Pikli, p. 153). Ominously, their production mixed absurdist humour with the erasure of otherness, including Jewishness. Jessica and Shylock were the last Jews left in Venice; he bemoaned her elopement as death – not only of a daughter but of the future of the Jewish line. Shylock's baptism in the trial scene, when he was given the name Peter (adding insult to injury), marked the end of Jewishness in the present (pp. 161–2). Undeniably, the Mohácsi brothers' appropriation of *The Merchant* took considerable political and formal risks. While these risks appealed to theatregoers, the critics chafed at the fragmentary nature of the narrative and what they saw as an 'excessively "journalistic" approach' (p. 167). Though the production played to packed houses, it was allowed to run for two-and-a-half months only and was taken down when a new conservative management of the National Theatre was installed. Once again, the stage history of the play was affected by a change in the political climate.

Warlikowski was no less a risk-taker in his appropriation of *The Merchant* in the third of his *African Tales*. The play opened at Théâtre de la Place in Liège (Belgium), had a Polish premiere at Nowy Theatre in Warsaw, and enjoyed an impressive theatre-festival life. It was part of the director's life-long commitment to expose 'what is perceived as different, other and even hostile in Polish culture' (Niziołek, p. 9). 'African', in the play's title, was an epithet signifying cultural marginalisation and exclusion; *The Merchant* 'tale', in particular, invited national soul-searching about the Polish relationship with the Holocaust. Warlikowski deployed complex intertextuality and a web of images from popular culture, transcending the national. Prominent among them were visual borrowings from Art Spiegelman's graphic novel *Maus*, disturbingly deployed in the scene when Shylock decides to exact his bond (III.i). In the transformed trial scene, Antonio's anti-Semitic rant probed the nature of anti-Semitism and xenophobia as compensating for existential fears of change, old age, and rejection. In the final movement of *The Merchant* section of *African Tales*, Portia (Małgorzata Hajewska-Krzysztofik) slowly and painfully ingested and then vomited a pound of flesh-like-substance in the same spot where Antonio delivered his rant earlier. Having thus literally eaten the terms of the bond, she addressed the audience with a not-guilty verdict for Shylock's homoerotic desire for his enemy's flesh. Portia's own otherness was underscored in the resolution of the dramatic action. Instead of marrying Bassanio, she committed herself to God and delivered a long soliloquy, which seemed to compare her situation to that of the Jew (Sakowska, p. 76). While this Portia avoided the misery of marrying into the established homosexual relationship of Bassanio and Antonio, the play offered no way out of female subjugation, pointing to the backlash of conservative gender ideologies pervasive in Poland and elsewhere in Eastern Europe in the early twenty-first century.

Post-communist productions and transformations of Shakespeare's play dramatised anti-Semitism as one of multiple forms of othering. They placed Venice in a cut-throat capitalist world recognisable to their audience and sometimes encompassing it, and largely replaced comedy and romance with biting satire, unromantic liaisons, and violence. Across the Atlantic, Aaron Posner took a more light-handed but no less incisive approach to the American dynamic of racial, religious, ethnic, and gender systems of oppression, which he dramatised in his adaptation of

Shakespeare's play, *District Merchants*, staged at the Folger Theatre in Washington, DC, under the direction of Michael John Garcés. It was produced in 2016, two years after civil unrest erupted in Ferguson, Missouri, in the aftermath of the fatal shooting of African-American Michael Brown by a white police officer. The often-violent clashes between police and protesters opened a new chapter in the long battle for civil rights in the United States and transformed the Black Lives Matter political project into a national movement. At the same time, the Ferguson unrest fuelled white rage and energised American white-supremacist groups and politicians.

Posner's creative transformation of Shakespeare's play, set mostly in the nation's capital in the decade after the Civil War, engaged with a similar historical fulcrum, when the country was poised between renewing its commitment to equality and justice, and perpetuating divisions and injustices under the dead weight of prejudice and acquisitiveness. The play's characters frequently broke the fourth wall to address their frustrations, hopes, and animosities directly to the audience, using subtle humour to evoke historical parallels between the 1870s and the 2010s. *District Merchants* represented the intersections of three versions of the American dream: Shylock's as a 'foreign-born refugee, a religious minority, and an ethnic "Other"' (Greenberg, p. 352); Antoine's (as Antonio was renamed in the play) as a freeborn African-American entrepreneur pursuing new opportunities in the metropolis alongside the freedmen flocking to this 'gateway from bondage to freedom', among them his protégé Benjamin Bassanio (p. 353); Portia's and Jessica's as white women eager for 'social and personal authority' beyond the bounds of their patriarchal households (p. 353). None of these characters belonged to the white male urban elite born entitled to living the American dream; for most, its pursuit entailed 'squabbling over the same crumbs' (Geoffrey Himes, 'Sending the Bard back for Rewrite', *Washington Post*, 27 May 2016). Along these lines, the main conflict between Shakespeare's Venetian merchant and the Jewish Other was reshaped as 'the alternately symbiotic and tense relationship of American Blacks and Jews, and their separate, powerful claims to the story of oppression' (Peter Marks, 'Shylock Goes to Washington', *Washington Post*, 8 June 2016). While Posner's 'uneasy comedy' (as the play's subtitle stated) eschewed stage violence, it was haunted by memories of pogroms and lynchings and remained clear-eyed about the ubiquity of microaggressions and prejudice. Nobody was forced to convert, but many chose 'passing', that is, taking on socially privileged identities, as they chased the American dream. The sensitive and ambitious Bassanio (Seth Rue) passed for white as he courted the Boston heiress Portia (Figure 9); the self-assured entrepreneur Antoine (Craig Wallace) passed for a 'race man' dedicated to helping the Black community while quietly adding his own commission onto loans arranged with his business partner Shylock; smart and spirited Portia (Maren Bush) passed for a male student at Harvard Law School. At the trial, Portia's exuberant, sharp, and psychologically astute Black servant Nessa (Celeste Jones) became the judge, while Shylock's equally exuberant, sharp, and psychologically astute Black servant Lancelot (Akeem Davis) took on the part of his attorney – a theatrical passing justified, as the characters explained jokingly to the audience, by the insufficient number in the company of white men accustomed to arguing 'with supercilious superiority'. The one character who refused to pass was Shylock

Figure 9 Seth Rue as Bassanio, Maren Bush as Portia, and Celeste Jones as Nessa in *District Merchants* by Aaron Posner, directed by Michael John Garcés, Folger Theatre, 2016.

(Matthew Boston). Battered by the loss of his entire family and by ugly daily humiliations, he had walked away from the trial with his dream of fairness and equality crushed, yet returned at the end of the play to address the audience and extend good wishes to those to whom life had been kinder. There were none such on stage, however. Antoine was broke, though his spirit was not broken. The young lovers had come clean to each other about their deceptions and prejudices; reeling with disillusionment, they paused before pledging commitment to each other, though they appeared eager to connect. Hope for the future, still alive, flickered somewhat dimly in this American revisioning of *The Merchant*.

After the terrorist acts of 11 September 2001, whose aftermath exposed unresolved conflicts and anxieties in Western democracies, productions of the play in European countries with imperial legacies started reshaping the post-Holocaust tradition to confront audiences with xenophobia, nationalism, and the resentment they breed. French, Dutch, and German stagings of *The Merchant* from the first two decades of the twenty-first century shifted attention to Islamophobia as a new form of racism, brought to the fore secondary and newly invented characters to introduce the perspectives of the underprivileged and the invisible, and probed the shaping and erasure of identity in multicultural societies under stress. As in the United States and Eastern Europe, actors breached the fourth wall and challenged audience complacency. Shakespeare, too, was brought to book, and his position as the gold standard of European culture was questioned.

When Andrei Şerban's production opened at the Comédie Française in Paris just four days after 9/11, it brought an end to the ninety-six-year absence of the play from the boards of the foremost French theatre.[3] Staged by a Romanian-American director, this *Merchant* marked a radical departure from the French tradition of setting the play in a distant historical past. The dramatic action unfolded in the here-and-now of the audience, echoing with anxieties about resurgent anti-Semitism and fears of racial and Islamic Others within the French nation, fears amplified in the new age of global terrorism. Şerban's production focused on the barriers outsiders faced while navigating their lives, the compromises they made, and the losses they suffered. Shylock, performed by Polish-born Andrzej Seweryn, presented himself to the outside world as the miserly and stubborn Jew from French comic drama and cinema, provoking audience discomfort about silent complicity in such stereotyping. When alone, he was a hard-working businessman; his French, too, was impeccable, except for moments of heightened emotion, when foreign cadences slipped in. He was aware of Jessica's desire to become a Christian and tossed her a bag of money before leaving for dinner with Antonio. Though he was dressed as a successful businessman, like Antonio, to whom he bore a close resemblance, this did not stop the Christians from mocking and beating him in the trial scene. In Act V, his body lay on the stage as a barely noticeable object around which the denizens of Belmont moved.

Şerban's production paid close attention to the fate of the play's other Others, Morocco and Arragon. Like Shylock, they were disdained and ignored by the Venetians, except for a single anonymous dark-skinned servant (D'Jazzy) who offered them compassion. She turned out to be the 'Moor' whom Lancelot was accused of impregnating (III.v.36) and was in turn ignored and degraded not only by her mistress Portia, but also by Jessica, herself a target of ethnic othering. The scenes with the foreign suitors were staged behind a scrim as a sort of shadow theatre for on-stage and off-stage spectators. Both suitors collapsed after failing the casket test, as Shylock often does in performance. Arragon was given an exit worthy of the Jewish character, as he staggered through the audience. At the end, these strangers came out to beg money from Portia, hat-in-hand, while she barely registered their presence. Like Shylock's disregarded body on the ground, they had become 'ghosts of Portia's past, … the nomads and migrants one tries, or even chooses, not to see' (Valls-Russell, *Shakespeare's Others*, p. 116). To drive home the discomforting overlap between Venice and modern-day Paris, Şerban repeatedly broke the fourth wall by placing Venetian characters in the auditorium. In these instances, as well as during Shylock's long final exit through the audience, the silence was deafening.

The intensifying political debates on multiculturalism and immigration in the aftermath of local terrorist acts in Holland (2002 and 2004) and Paris (2006, 2011, and 2015) informed Aram Adriaanse's 2008 production, *The Arab of Amsterdam*, staged at

De Nieuwe Amsterdam theatre in the Netherlands, and *Business in Venice*, directed by Jacques Vincey in 2017 at the Théâtre Olympia in Tours, France. These creative adaptations of Shakespeare's play dramatised the pressures upon individual identity in Western democracies where the social fabric has been fraying; they showed characters donning and doffing social roles, conforming to imposed identities, and resolutely embracing familiar ones. Shylock was a thoroughly isolated character in both productions, much more so than he is in Shakespeare's play. The challenge offered in *The Arab of Amsterdam* and *Business in Venice* extended not only to their audiences, but to Shakespeare's emblematic cultural status – something that had not been done since the 1936 Literary Trial of *The Merchant* at the Habima Theatre in Tel Aviv (see Part II, Chapter VII).

Adriaanse's production came after the assassinations of populist nativist Dutch politician Pim Fortuyn (2002) and of racially and religiously provocative film-maker Theo van Gogh (2004) – murders that 'dramatically changed the tone of the multiculturalist debate in Holland and revealed a growing polarisation of Dutch society' on issues of immigration and integration (Heijes, *Shakespeare's Others*, p. 172). In the intertextual hybrid of Justus Van Oel's prose adaptation, the Shylock character, renamed Rafi (played by the Egyptian-Dutch actor Sabri Saad El Hamus), was the sole outsider, as Morocco and Arragon were dropped from the play. What was lost in the number of Others, however, was gained through the complexity of the protagonist's identity as Other, for Rafi introduced himself in the prologue as a 'Jewish Arab, an Arab Jew'. A political refugee in Amsterdam, he had carved out a respectable lifestyle as the owner of a small chain of shawarma snack bars, but was despised as an Arab by Dutch drug trafficker Antonio and his cohort. Dutch xenophobia was not that different from the anti-Semitism Rafi had faced as a Jewish Arab student in Iraq, where his professor had forced him to write a thesis about Shylock – something Rafi experienced as a humiliating pressure to apologise 'on behalf of an invented Jew ... to satisfy a group of sniggering students' (van Oel, qtd. in Heijes, *Shakespeare's Others*, p. 180). Upon arrival in the Netherlands, he was met with a different form of anti-Semitism, which downplayed the trauma of the Holocaust and went as far as negating Jewishness: 'you are not a Jew, Jews don't exist, you just suffer from hallucinations, from paranoia' (p. 181). To reveal the intractable situation of the Other in a self-congratulatory 'peaceful' society rife with bias, the production employed Shylock's famous speech from III.i twice: Rafi first spoke the words as a Jew and then substituted 'Arab' for 'Jew' – a provocation in the tense social context of the time. The production closed with a heavily revised trial scene, in which Rafi, and not Portia, chose to stop the impending butchery, though fully aware that this act of mercy would not staunch Antonio's hatred. Shakespeare himself appeared as a defendant in the trial, accused of drawing interest from 'anti-Semitic start-up capital' (van Oel, qtd. in Heijes, *Shakespeare's Others*, p. 183). The production, which was highly praised for its confrontation of anti-Semitism, xenophobia, and Islamophobia, ended on 'a tentative note of hope' (p. 184) in spite of the anti-immigration backlash in the Netherlands.

Business in Venice – a free translation of Shakespeare's play by Vanasay Khamphommala with several interpolated scenes – likewise appeared in the wake of domestic terrorist acts: the 2006 torture and murder of Ilan Haimi, a young Jewish Parisian of Moroccan descent, by a gang calling itself 'The Barbarians'; the 2011 firebombing of the satirical magazine *Charlie Hebdo* and the 2015 murder of twelve of its staff members; and the subsequent deadly siege of a kosher supermarket in a Paris suburb by a terrorist claiming allegiance to ISIS. Like *The Arab of Amsterdam*, the play had a contemporary setting; like Sellars's production of *The Merchant*, it shed light on the economic roots of racism. Shylock (performed by the director Vincey) was the owner of a nondescript supermarket, a thoroughly utilitarian site invaded by an urban gang of young Venetians who swarmed it in the opening act, trading anti-Semitic jokes and sporting offensive carnival costumes, and later returned to loot it. The youths were ruthless in their violence and devoid of identity markers; 'they could be Christian, Muslim, non-believer, left-wing, right-wing, non-political', with a collective identity bond generated through nasty stereotyping of the Other (Valls-Russell, *Shakespeare's Others*, p. 118). After stripping bare Shylock's supermarket, they took off with Jessica, having defaced the back wall with 'JUIF' (Jew), scribbled in pink. Given Shylock's portrayal as a secular Jew integrated to the point of invisibility, the anti-Semitic vandalism was a dramatisation of a process described by Jean-Paul Sartre: 'it is the anti-Semite who creates the Jew' (qtd. Valls-Russell, *Shakespeare's Others*, p. 119). To take over Belmont, the Venetians substituted subterfuge for violence. Bassanio (Thomas Gonzalez) 'won' the marriage lottery by appearing three times in the reality-show hosted by the cold, glamorous Portia (Océane Mozas). He first disguised himself as a caricature of Morocco (a Prince of Zanzibar), then as Arragon (an Asian Prince of Siam), before finally getting to the correct casket. But it soon became clear that these wannabe Jasons, who still wore pieces of their crass carnival costumes on their Belmont adventure, were no match for the master of disguises Portia. 'Shedding her blond wig and white lace gown, Mozas' Portia ... emerge[d] as a dark-haired, trouser-clad businesswoman', who after winning the trial made it clear that she would run her world 'on her (economic?) terms' (Valls-Russell, *Shakespeare Bulletin*, p. 323). In this world of fake and hollow identities, Shylock was the only character who never wore a mask and held onto core convictions; abandoned by his daughter, he found prosperity meaningless. Without Tubal, a Jewish community, or a synagogue, he was also profoundly isolated. The production rattled audiences with close encounters with present-day anti-Semitic violence and questioned 'the postmodern juggling with identities at a time when French society seems to be losing faith in the Republican ideal of a social contract' (p. 122). Like *The Arab of Amsterdam*, it challenged Shakespeare's iconic status. In the prologue, an actor dressed in orange and wearing the ginger wig of the stage Jew of yesteryear shuffled along under the weight of a tray loaded with meat slabs to complain about his miserable pay. He asked for money from 'the tight-fisted bunch of ... [Jews]' and the 'cathos' (Catholics) withholding their charity – the audience members sitting there, supporting the theatre business in Shakespeare (p. 121).

Nowhere was theatre more directly entangled with politics than in Germany during the refugee crisis of 2015–16. When over a million migrants and refugees flooded Europe, the largest number of them were officially accepted by Germany. Many theatres joined in welcome actions encouraged by the government.

The postmodern, strongly mediatised, and metatheatrical adaptation of *The Merchant of Venice* directed by Nicolas Stemann at the Kammerspiele in Munich was part of this *Willkommenskultur* (culture of welcome) (Boecker, pp. 208–11). It directly addressed the problem facing Germany while testing the effectiveness of postdramatic theatre as a vehicle of political expression. Stemann's *Merchant* put Shakespeare's text on trial by projecting it on large screens and having six actors of diverse backgrounds read and react to the lines of the play's twenty-odd characters with little attempt to make them distinct. Words of abuse against Shylock blazed in bold red letters on the monitors. The severing of the connection between character and performer in this rehearsal-style performance opened up possibilities for metacommentary and the inclusion of unsettling contemporary references, simultaneously undercutting 'the notion of bounded identities on which prejudice is grounded' (Fowler, p. 52). Every actor got to be the merchant *and* the Jew at some point of the play. For instance, Shylock's iconic speech, 'Hath not a Jew eyes', was first spoken by a chorus of the cast members; each of them then reworked a section to voice their particular social disenfranchisement as, respectively, a Muslim, a Roma, a Jewish homosexual, a woman. In a characteristically subversive move, the scene ended with a retort by the white male heterosexual, 'I am fed up with all this shit' (Boecker, p. 219). 'Hath not a Jew' was reiterated later on, spoken simultaneously in German and untranslated Arabic – a subtle reminder that some pleas for empathy remain unheeded. In spite of the alienating effect of severing the connection between performer and character, the production did not lack in affective power. One such emotionally gripping choice was the staging of the trial scene resolution, in which Shylock's lines were not spoken, only projected on the screen (Figure 10). The character was thus stripped of embodiment and transformed into sheer text. Yet this was a text impervious to erasure. Shylock's final words, 'I ask you to allow me to leave. I do not feel well', were displayed on the onstage monitors for the duration of the fifth act, haunting the festivities in Belmont. This was a silent, accusatory reminder of those excluded from the economic boom. Still, for some the Kammerspiele *Merchant* precluded empathy and created

Figure 10 The 'Resolution' of the trial in *The Merchant of Venice*, directed by Nicolas Stemann, Munich Kammerspiele, 2015.

a world that 'resembled right-wing dystopias' (Boecker, p. 219). For others, in the context of the refugee crisis, the production was indicative of the crisis of 'Enlightenment values and Western Euro- and ethno-centrism' (Fowler, 59).

As this overview of the developments in staging *The Merchant of Venice* suggests, Shakespeare's play has come to resonate with multiple histories of oppression. Its performances have been revising and fragmenting its 'classic' text, challenging it directly or appropriating it in order to speak to the intersecting stories of victimisation of Black and Brown people, Muslims, immigrants, women, and queer people. Such radical transformations have used Shakespeare's playtext as a source for new narratives, not unlike Shakespeare's use of his own sources. No doubt, the stage life of *The Merchant* remains buoyant and provocative. However reimagined, the play continues to be a 'mote' that troubles the eye with its powers of interrogation. The questions its recent productions pose clearly mark the crossroads at which the cultures of late capitalism find themselves.

Notes

1 The notorious *Der Stürmer* (Attacker/Striker) (1923–45) was a virulently anti-Semitic weekly tabloid, a significant organ of Nazi propaganda.
2 We follow John Drakakis's Arden 3 edition of *The Merchant of Venice* in references to the play, except for cases of different textual choices in specific productions.
3 Şerban had staged *The Merchant* at the American Repertory Theater at Harvard University in 1998 with the same designer and composer but a different cast. The Paris production also entailed a number of directorial changes.

I

Magical spectacles and nightmarish times: Max Reinhardt's productions of *The Merchant of Venice*

The year 1905 saw the last performance of Irving's *Merchant of Venice* at the Lyceum Theatre, marking the beginning of the decline of a noble tradition of grandiloquent, tragic Shylocks. In the same year, Max Reinhardt (1873–1943), the young artistic director of Deutsches Theater in Berlin, who would acquire this most prestigious of Germany's theatre venues a year later, transformed Shakespeare's play into a festive celebration of Venice and love. Reinhardt had achieved artistic and financial success a few months earlier with his production of *A Midsummer Night's Dream*, which had propelled him to national prominence. By 1930, his *Dream* would be performed 427 times, and his *Merchant*, 363 (Rothe, p. i). Notable, too, is how these German Shakespeare productions crisscrossed Europe. Between 1906 and 1924, Reinhardt's *Merchant* was seen in Prague, Budapest, Vienna, Brussels, Munich, Bucharest, Copenhagen, Oslo, and Stockholm (Styan, *Max Reinhardt*, p. 61). In 1934, it was staged, in a new Italian translation by Paola Ojetti, as the festive finale of the first Theatre Biennale in Venice. Over the course of three decades, Reinhardt's productions in general, and of *The Merchant* in particular, shaped the work of an entire European generation of theatre practitioners, including architects, playwrights, musicians, dancers, actors, directors, and critics.

Reinhardt was born into an Austrian-Jewish family in Vienna, the capital of the Austro-Hungarian empire and for a long time the grand centre of German-language theatre, literature, and music. As Amos Elon, another Jewish Viennese who would become one of Israel's leading journalists, has suggested, 'Nowhere on the continent was it easier to be "European"' (p. 223). Two years before Reinhardt's birth, German unification had created a new political entity, Imperial Germany. Soon it became the industrial powerhouse of Europe, which fuelled its territorial ambitions, while its capital, Berlin, began to vie for cultural prominence with both Vienna and Paris. Crucial to the process of German national consolidation in the Imperial era was the role of *Kultur*, reliant on the medium of the German language. In addition to Germany and Switzerland, in the nineteenth and early twentieth centuries, German was spoken throughout Austro-Hungary, which included a large part of Central Europe extending to the Balkans, in parts of Romania, and in large areas along the Baltic coast. The rise of Germany as an industrial and cultural power attracted artists like Reinhardt to develop their talents in its booming capital. The presence of large German-speaking populations across the continent ensured in turn that Reinhardt's work could be shown in its original language far afield.

It was in Berlin, between 1905 and 1933, that Reinhardt became the most influential director of his time. There, too, he tasted the bitter fruit of humiliation and defeat. He lived and worked through the disintegration of Austro-Hungary in the aftermath of the First World War, the rise and fall of the German Empire, and the birth of the Weimar Republic, witnessing its hope and volatility, its hyperinflation and revolutionary unrest, and its collapse into the Nazi Third Reich. The arc of Reinhardt's creative career maps the jarring contradictions of the times. Recognised by his contemporaries as Europe's most influential director, with honorary degrees from Tübingen, Erfurt, and Königsberg, he was forced to abandon his life's work and sign off his theatre empire to the Nazi government because he was a Jew. The last incarnation of his vision for *The Merchant*, staged after he was effectively exiled from Germany, was celebrated as an incomparable theatre event even as the production was appropriated for the ends of Mussolini's cultural politics. Reinhardt emigrated to the United States and died in 1942. Yet throughout his artistic life, whatever political and economic obstacles lay in his way, he found in theatre a *raison d'être*.

Having started as an actor in Salzburg, Austria, Reinhardt was brought to Berlin by Otto Brahm, the powerful director of the Deutsches Theater and a proponent of stage naturalism. Here Reinhardt played Tubal in Brahm's 1894 production of *The Merchant*. By 1902, he had given up acting to embark on the then-novel career of a full-time stage director. It was in this capacity that his 1905 *Dream* earned him the reputation of 'the great rediscoverer ... of Shakespeare for the modern German theatre', a success so spectacular that it enabled him to buy the Deutsches Theater (Wolfgang Drews, qtd. in Bonnell, *Shylock in Germany*, p. 47).

The beginning of the twentieth century was a time of transformation in theatre art, and Reinhard, who joked that his cradle was the top gallery of Vienna's Burgtheater, became one of its driving forces. Theorists and practitioners were calling for the retheatricalisation of theatre and for the 'unification of actors and spectators into a festive community' (Fischer-Lichte, p. 167). At the same time, radicals such as Adolphe Appia (1862–1928) and Edward Gordon Craig (1872–1966) spearheaded a conceptual and visual revolution. Theirs was a reaction against the dominance of naturalism and a launching forward into a theatre of forms and light. They conceived of the stage as an autonomous abstract space wherein a dynamic plasticity of forms could be achieved by way of music, rhythm, scenography, and, particularly, the expressiveness of lighting. The latter they considered 'a core of the drama' (MacGowan, p. 81). For these theatre innovators, the actor's body was an integral part of a larger system of signs. Placed among and against 'platforms, ramps, staircases ... in which shadowy areas contrasted with lighted ones', the body expressed 'the confrontation between man and the real volumes of the stage space' (Hortmann, p. 45). The rhythmical and gestural expressiveness of the actor grew to be more important than psychological characterisation.

In this transformative climate, Reinhardt first formulated his ideals regarding theatre at a famed 1902 meeting in a Berlin café. They were set down by Arthur Kahane, his future dramaturge, in the form of a Manifesto. Its central tenets included: a return to theatre's festive origins; the importance of the classics; the essential recognition of theatre space as autonomous; the centrality of the director; and the inclusion of the audience in this parallel world through deploying all forms of theatricality. The Manifesto also stipulated the need for three types of space to achieve Reinhardt's vision. The main auditorium of the Deutsches Theater, seating 600, would be his 'large [stage] for the classics'. He also envisioned 'a smaller, intimate stage for the modern poets' chamber art'. Finally, he needed 'a very large theater for a great art of monumental effects, a festival theater, which is detached from everyday life ... in the spirit of the Greeks' (Hostetter, p. 187). All this became reality when he added to the Deutsches Theater the Kammerspiele, seating about 230 spectators, and later remodelled a former circus building (Schumann Circus) as the Grosses Schauspielhaus, with 3,200 seats radiating out from a gigantic thrust stage to involve spectators in a communal 'theatre of totality' (Schnapp, p. 92). Committed to the idea of theatre inclusiveness, Reinhardt also produced plays in large public spaces such as the Salzburg Cathedral Square, the Boboli Gardens in Florence, Olympia Hall in London, and Salzburg's Imperial Riding School. The 1934 open-air production of *The Merchant* in Campo San Trovaso, as a special event of the first Theatre Biennale in Venice, was among the final incarnations of his expansive vision for the theatre. In one of the grimly ironic twists of twentieth-century history, this innovation was initiated by Mussolini's government as part of a fascist cultural programme aiming to dilute 'the social and formal boundaries of European elite culture' (Stone, p. 184) and transform 'the Biennale's visitors from arts connoisseurs to cultural consumers' (p. 187).

Unlike his radically and ideologically minded theatre contemporaries, Reinhardt never committed 'to a set literary program' or a single style. In his Manifesto, he had stated that he would not reject naturalism, because it represented the 'highest art form of our time'. However, he continuously searched for 'younger energies developing new methods' (Hostetter, p. 184). For some of his productions, such as those of *The Merchant*, he modified Brahm's picture-frame stage, reorganising the space within the frame and extending the apron. For others, such as the acclaimed *Oedipus Rex* (1910), he created a stripped-down abstract space structured by platforms and stairs. Reinhardt combined theatre tradition with innovations in form, light, and accessibility, to create worlds that were self-sufficient, exquisitely elegant, fluid, and rich. His contemporary, the theatre critic Siegfried Jacobsohn, noted that Reinhardt did not 'create a "natural" milieu' in his productions, but 'through the complete transformation of things, illuminated the inner being of the drama' (qtd. in S. Williams, p. 124). Reinhardt's *Regiebücher* (director's notebooks) reveal a meticulous working-out of mise-en-scène, intonation, and gesture, all in the service of a specific vision. Copious colour-coded notes in the *Regiebuch* of *The Merchant*, for instance, map the evolution of his take on the play from 1905 to 1934 and its adaptation to a range of theatre spaces. These notes made his productions readily transferable, which was part of his enormous success as a theatre entrepreneur. However, as he wrote to his friend, the composer E. W. Korngold, 'the basic material is not what I have written down ... but the living human being' – that is, the actors and the spectators (qtd. in Hortmann, p. 37). Reinhardt deployed a rich palette of theatrical tools both old and new to 'bring people joy', to 'lead [them] from the misery of everyday life into an atmosphere of bright and pure beauty', and to replace the drudgery of daily hardships with 'a heightened sense of life' (Hostetter, p. 183). Audiences responded. As the foreign correspondent of the London *Observer* (21 December 1913) noted regarding the revival of productions for Reinhardt's Shakespeare Cycle (a seven-play cycle in the 1913–14 season, which was Reinhardt's first go at producing a festival), he could do 'three months of [Shakespeare] at the height of the season with prospects of sold out houses thrice a week'.

Unabashedly delighting in theatricality, Reinhardt pioneered the use of sensory effects to enfold the audience within the world of the play and sought new ways of reshaping theatre space. Thus, the magic of Renaissance Venice was conveyed by the deployment of a revolutionary piece of theatre technology – the *Drehbühne* (stage revolve). It created hitherto-unseen fluidity between scenes, but more importantly, Reinhardt turned it into a meaningful element of the action. Apart from redrawing the spatial geography within the frame – a structural element that he later dispensed with – the revolve enabled a filmic illusion of depth and multiple perspectives. Other means contributing to an immersive theatre experience included the use of the cyclorama, projections, impressionistic and expressionistic lighting, olfactory cues, choreographed group movement, atmospheric sound, and music. This is how audiences experienced the opening of his ground-breaking *A Midsummer Night's Dream* in 1905: 'With the first sounds of Mendelssohn's overture, the red velvet curtain fluttered and slowly parted. Pine fragrance wafted over the audience. The forest, huge, almost endless, shot through with moonlight, floated before the gaze' (Stern, *Bühnenbildner*, p. 121). It had become the central character of the production, 'sway[ing] into a dance, [the trees'] roots willfully tripp[ing] the lovers' (Hortmann, p. 33).

Similarly, an animated Venice was at the centre of *The Merchant*. In both Emil Orlik's 1905 and Ernst Stern's 1913 designs a canal traversed the revolve along the diagonal. As Stern recalls in his memoir, 'the movement flowed on in an uninterrupted stream of action and, in addition, the set gave glimpses through the scene beyond' (*My Life, My Stage*, pp. 71–2). Characters moved about the city with cinematic fluidity; that same fluidity characterised the transitions between Venice and Belmont. Critics immediately recognised Reinhardt's directorial concept as novel: the protagonist of the play was Venice, the place of carnivals, whose festive nature was established from the opening. It was a 'singing, humming city with ... elegance and the effervescent joy of life' (Kahane, p. 83). Spectators felt as if they had been 'transported into a fairy-tale land' (Bonnell, *Shylock in Germany*, p. 52).

The stage pictures, costumes, and gestures reminded the Danish critic Georg Brandes of Carpaccio, Giovanni Bellini, and Paolo Veronese (quoted in Styan, *Max Reinhardt*, p. 61). For the 1934 Biennale production in Venice, a working-class neighbourhood was refashioned as a Renaissance stage-dream (Figure 11). Reinhardt's collaborator, architect Duilio Torres, transformed the back entrance of an ancient boatshed into the façade of Portia's palazzo, complete with a grand staircase and a loggia; the adjacent campo was glamorised with the addition of arched garden portals, a pleasure-house, and newly built walkways with white-stone balustrades (*Gazetta di Venezia*, 3 June 1934) (Figure 12). To unify the design, the existing houses and walkways were painted in delicate hues of grey, pink, and yellow, harmonising with the 'iridescent' Renaissance-style costumes by Titina Rota, whose feathered hats, ornate damasks, and velvets suggested a world where poverty was non-existent or at least invisible (Damerini, p. 301).

Critics anticipating Reinhardt's production at the Biennale were apprehensive about maintaining the rhythm and fluidity of action without a stage revolve. The layout of Campo San Trovaso, however, allowed him to retain the Rio degli Ognissanti canal as a main scenic axis, while conveying a sense of movement by bringing groups of characters to the acting space in gondolas and in a grand ship in the case of the Doge. The canal kept the audience at a distance from Shylock's abode and from the pleasure-house and gardens frequented by Antonio and his friends. Portia's Belmont was

Magical spectacles and nightmarish times 201

Figure 11 Campo San Trovaso before its transformation for Max Reinhardt's 1934 production of *The Merchant of Venice* for the first Theatre Biennale of Venice, with the bridge over the Rio degli Ognissanti in the middle, and the back entrance to the *squero* (boat-building shed) on the left.

Figure 12 Scenic design by Duilio Torres for Max Reinhardt's production for the 1934 Theatre Biennale of Venice.

on the audience's side, inviting identification with her world. Ballet numbers, and the precisely orchestrated trial scene, unfolded at arm's length from the spectators.

The site, 'part sacred destination and part meadow overshadowed by old acacias', added a pastoral atmosphere difficult to achieve in a theatre auditorium (Damerini, p. 299). Writing on opening night, another critic singled out two stars: the music and the canal (*Il Gazzettino*, 18 July 1934). The dramatic location of each scene was defined through meticulously calculated lighting design, which according to one reviewer created a 'hallucinatory truthfulness' (*Le Monde Illustré*, 28 July 1934).

Music was vital to the atmosphere and characterisation in *The Merchant* from the very beginning. In 1905, conductor Bruno Walter detected the undertow of an ominous march blending in with Engelbert Humperdinck's joyful music (Styan, *Max Reinhardt*, p. 61). By 1934, in Venice, music had gained in scope and significance. Accordingly, advertising materials gave the name of composer Victor de Sabata the same prominence as that of the director. Sabata created an almost operatic score, which included sections for orchestra, dance, chorus, and solo voices. Like its Berlin predecessors, the production opened with an 'overture' of the city's awakening, complete with gondoliers' songs, animal sounds, and church bells. It was followed by the theme of Antonio's melancholy, which cued his entry and, at the end, underscored his loneliness after the departure of the newlyweds. Spectators were further entertained by galliards, madrigals, and serenades. Racial, ethnic, and class hierarchies bore unambiguous musical expressions: a 'grotesque march' announced Morocco's arrival; Arragon's was accompanied by a guitar frenzy; triumphant fanfare introduced the Duke. The calculatedly delayed arrival of the Prince of Piemonte, who was a member of the audience, created another spectacular moment when play and reality merged (*Gazetta di Venezia*, 19 July 1934; *Il Gazzettino*, 18 July 1934).

A signature element of Reinhardt's performances was the *Massenregie*: the detailed choreography of crowd movement and voice, painstakingly worked out in his notes. This technique, which included the development of silent action to introduce scenes, achieved large-scale effects and nuanced shifts of mood. Thus Arragon's arrival in Belmont unfolded in an elaborate crowd scene involving blaring trumpets to announce his approach, followed by his musical theme, flag-raising, lantern-bearers, a ceremonial presentation of gifts, hat-flourishing, and knee-bending, as well as three tenors serenading Portia (Tollini, p. 200).

The emotional climax of the court scene was enhanced by textual additions and the meticulous orchestration of voices balanced by fraught silence. The sheer number of participants made it clear that the stakes at trial were social, not personal; it also demonstrated how much the odds were stacked against Shylock and the depth of his conviction (Figure 13). The *Regiebuch* indicates added lines for the Duke, Antonio's friends, and no fewer than three judges, intended to create an uproar of desperation. After a precisely timed interval, Shylock spoke 'plainly, unemotionally'; Portia was equally self-possessed, 'quietly shaking her head' (qtd. in Styan, *Max Reinhardt*, p. 63). The exchanges between Portia and Shylock were precisely timed, so that they could be clearly audible; emotional pressure reached a boiling point during 'a full three-quarter-of-a-minute pause' following Portia's command to 'Tarry a little'

Figure 13 The court scene in Max Reinhardt's production for the 1934 Theatre Biennale of Venice.

(Hortmann, p. 36). The notes specify that her next statement, 'there is something else' (IV.i.301), was to unleash among the court audience a 'cry of relief ... as with one voice', followed by laughter (qtd. in Styan, *Max Reinhardt*, p. 64). The spectators, seamlessly integrated in the scene as part of the court audience, likely joined in.

These silences and moments of stasis stood out against the fast rhythm of the production. Critic Heinrich Hart noted the 'racing, romping, wriggling, storming from beginning to end' (qtd. in Fischer-Lichte, p. 174), a frantic movement antithetical to psychological realism. Many Italian reviewers were put off by the burlesque comedy of Morocco, Arragon, and Lancelot Gobbo, sharing reservations expressed by German critics of Reinhardt's early productions of *The Merchant* (Fischer-Lichte, pp. 173–4). Gino Damerini found that the calculated movement of the ensemble, the extravagant costumes, and the play of light 'threatened, at certain moments, the compact comedy and risked ... shifting the interest toward the choreographed additions' rather than the play itself (pp. 301–2).

The divided critical response mirrored the range of attitudes to the shift from a predominantly literary theatre, dominated by star actors and heavy with psychological realism, to a theatre that prioritised action over characterisation and foregrounded the performative nature of acting (Fischer-Lichte, pp. 174–5). Reviewers who appreciated Reinhardt's 'powerful orchestration' seemed intent on severing their commentaries about an evening of magical escapism from any references to the gathering storm of anti-Semitic politics in Europe (Guido Marta, *Rivista 'Lidel'*, Milan, August 1934). The exception was an anonymous writer who rejoiced in the victory of Portia's 'higher will' over a 'perverse man, conquered by the lowest instincts of his race'. Conveniently forgetting the 'race' of the play's 'supreme director', the reviewer went on to extol the achievement of Europe's most famous Jewish theatre artist:

> he has taken the highs and lows [of the play], turned them into scenes, framed them with music and light, strung them together with threads of poetry, alternated dances with colourful parades ..., [and] created carnival riot from the volatile impulses of the crowd. His production has the grace and splendour of the grand-scale choreography of Russian ballet without overpowering, betraying, or profaning the comedy.
>
> (*Gazetta di Venezia*, 19 July 1934)

Like a good fairy-tale, Reinhardt's *Merchant* mixed enchantment with anxiety and fear, with Shylock's dark sobriety offsetting light-hearted Venetian joyousness in a chiaroscuro effect. According to Styan, Shylock was the first complex Shakespearean character Reinhardt encountered, and the director gave him detailed attention (p. 62). If Venice was painted with impressionistic brush strokes, Reinhardt's *Regiebuch* captured a Shylock etched with expressive sharpness – 'stonelike', 'sinister', and 'rigidly controlled' (qtd. in Styan, *Max Reinhardt*, p. 63). Set apart from the romanticised aesthetic harmony of Venice, he was neither weighed down by psychologically realistic suffering nor elevated as a tragic hero. Rather, Reinhardt allowed the part to accommodate a variety of acting styles in his differently sized and configured theatres. His habit of studying actors' mannerisms and incorporating them in the productions allowed different individualities to shine. Characterisation ranged 'from the cruel Shylock of Werner Krauss to that of Albert Bassermann, Alexander Moissi or Rudolph Schildkraut in which pathos was rather overstressed' (Marek, p. 87).

Shylock's contrast to Venetian glamour and festivity was differently rendered by each actor. Among the poised, perfumed, immaculately turned-out Venetians in the 1905 production, Schildkraut – Reinhardt's earliest Shylock – performed the Levantine Jew with a turban, bad teeth, and an angular, self-deprecatory stoop. Fritz Kortner, who played the part in Vienna in 1924, remembered Schildkraut's Shylock as 'an underdeveloped giant with protruding goiter-like eyes' (qtd. in Blackadder, p. 65); a Shylock who 'smells of onion and garlic' (Malkin, p. 204). Yet Schildkraut did not match the grotesque appearance of his character with an exaggerated acting style. He delivered a psychologically sensitive Shylock who changed with the dramatic action (Bonnell, *Shylock in Germany*, p. 49).

In the context of evolving Jewish assimilation in Austrian and German culture, some critics saw Schildkraut's deeply melancholic hero as conveying not just Jewish suffering, but the suffering of any marginalised person (Malkin, p. 206). This was communicated in no small part through added stage business. Like Irving, Reinhardt followed Jessica's elaborately orchestrated elopement by a pantomimic scene of Shylock's return to his deserted house. This was certainly an opportunity to provoke sympathy for the character, but the contrast also suggested how ill-fitting Shylock was in refined

Venetian society. The *Massenregie* of ballet and harmonised singing during the elopement could not be more different from Shylock's humming of an old Shabbat song, or the way he moved. Schildkraut shuffled clumsily on stage, only to dash wildly up and down the steps of the house and then back to the bridge upon discovering that his daughter and his money had gone missing (Marx, p. 651). In the end, this mildly comic, patient, diminutive foreigner turned into an almost unwilling revenger, egged on by the insults and physical abuse of the Christians. After his forced conversion, he exited 'in mournful agony', mouthing the words of the Shema Yisrael ('Hear, O Israel') prayer (Tollini, p. 68). Performing for 150 nights in the 1905–6 season alone, Schildkraut's Shylock was widely celebrated (Bonnell, *Shylock in Germany*, p. 47).

In 1913, when Reinhardt staged *The Merchant* for the Shakespeare Cycle, the part of Shylock was played alternatively by Schildkraut and Albert Bassermann who brought another angle to the contrast between the character and Venice. Tall and aristocratic in stature, Bassermann was a furious archetypal revenger. Julius Bab, one of the important critical voices of the era and himself Jewish, compared him to 'the wolf from the fairy tale'. Bassermann's Shylock, with extravagantly bushy grey beard, outsized side-locks, wild eyebrows, flowing robes, and unconstrained movement, cut 'an almost grotesque and in any case a gruesome figure' which Bab believed well-suited to the fairy-tale world (qtd. in Bonnell, *Shylock in Germany*, p. 53). Although he and others lamented the lack of character development, all were impressed by his fierce determination (p. 54, n. 263). Bassermann, admired as Germany's premier actor at the time, was dedicated to this rendition of the character, so much so that he refused to include much of the pantomimic business of Shylock's return to his empty house (Tollini, p. 68 and n. 152). He stood tall in the trial scene and left it with clenched fists. For this production, designer Ernst Stern had extended the stage over the first three orchestra rows to bring Shylock within discomfiting proximity to the audience (Tollini, p. 69).

Subsequent actors developed a further assortment of vocal and visual means of portrayal. In 1918 Shylock was played by Alexander Moissi (Albanian-Italian-Jewish in origin), whose androgynous appearance and exotic accent were frequently discussed in the press. He gave Shylock a 'voluptuous sing-song voice', a treatment considered by critic Herbert Ihering to be experimental if a bit superficial (Bonnell, *Shylock in Germany*, p. 68). In the following year Moissi was replaced by Paul Wegener, whose Shylock had a false nose and resembled an 'an ungainly troll' or 'a wicked uncle out of a fairy tale' (p. 93). Fritz Kortner, who performed the part in 1924 on the stage of Reinhardt's Theater in der Josefstadt in Vienna, objected to the direction of playing the character as more human and developed a demonically expressionistic Shylock. Demonism was suggested through Kortner's 'thrusting gestures and trumpeting voice', although he himself did not feel he had gone far enough (Malkin, p. 199). 'My performances', writes Kortner, 'didn't express the ethical fervor of the character and the play; the volcanic eruption; the unarticulated *schrei* [scream] of rage at not being able to make oneself understood' (qtd. in Malkin, pp. 213–14). In Venice in 1934, Memo Benassi performed a dignified, even haughty Shylock; tragic in his isolation, he was visually set apart from Venetian society through his makeup. Benassi unleashed the scream of rage twice – in the interpolated scene when he discovers Jessica's elopement, and in the Tubal scene.

Perhaps the most expressionistic Shylock in Reinhardt's productions was Werner Krauss, who performed the role in 1921 at the Grosses Schauspielhaus, nicknamed 'the Theatre of the Five Thousand'. Krauss had played an applauded Lancelot Gobbo at the Deutsches Theater, and gained international acclaim as Dr Caligari in Robert Wiener's film noir released the previous year. His Shylock was a 'red, ugly, joking devil ... a spookily deformed nightmare' (Marx, p. 654). Reinhardt's assistant director Walther Volbach recalls his aggressively overblown acting style: the 'broad, plump steps, sometimes almost hopping' across the wide stage of the Grosses Schauspielhaus; the 'yelling, grotesque quality' of his speech with its excessive accentuation of words (pp. 24–5). Matching the grotesque physicality of Krauss's acting style was the intensified physical violence against Shylock. To a degree, such unrestrained physical acting was necessitated by the huge proportions of the performance space. According to reviewer Alfred Kerr, the production amplified Shylock's misfortune and underscored how his lack of mercy paled in comparison to Antonio's ruthless profiteering when he took away both Shylock's money and his religion (Hostetter, p. 150). For others, in the enormous new theatre where crowds laughed at the slapstick humour levelled against Shylock – a dehumanised evil clown – the mirth of Reinhardt's Venetian world began to acquire a sinister tinge. Noting the jeers that Krauss's Shylock received from certain segments of the audience, theatre critic Emil Faktor wondered 'whether this play is really a good choice in our days of racism' (Marx, p. 654).

It is difficult, from a post-Second World War perspective, to make sense of Reinhardt's thirty years of sustaining and elaborating a vision of *The Merchant* as an apolitically festive play. His persistence is even more astounding when we recall the challenges he and his theatre weathered. How was he able to continue projecting a refined theatrical vision of joy in increasingly ominous historical circumstances? In 1915, Reinhardt wrote that art is 'a truly neutral country whose goods ought to be exchanged at all times, irrespective of nationality' (Hortmann, p. 43). Theatre and art were for him 'a second world', different from the real one, a place for imaginative recreation and liberation from the mundane (S. Williams, p. 124). Even in 1932, when he ceded the directorship of the Berlin Deutsches Theater, he listed the theatre's independence as his major achievement in his letter to the Nazi government: 'The Deutsches Theater is the only theater of cultural rank in the world that ... has maintained itself without subvention of any kind and therefore free from any political and partisan connection' (qtd. in Kvam, pp. 357–8).

Stylistic purists labelled Reinhardt eclectic; politically minded critics and artists called him bourgeois; others dismissed him as a 'creator of spectacles' (Brooks, p. 1). However, his audiences never deserted him, not in the darkest hour, for he gave them a shelter of fragile beauty in a nightmarish world. Deeply immersed in his art and at the same time a businessman with a widely successful brand, Reinhardt, an assimilated Jew, had grown up in an extraordinary period of Jewish integration into German society. So when Hitler and the Nazis rose to power in the 1930s, though writ large, the signs were hard to read. As Amos Elon explains,

> The moment was one of paradox, of surging Nazism and increasing assimilation, of anti-Semitic outrages and growing prominence for Jews in every field of Weimar culture ... Max Reinhardt, showered with honorary doctorates ..., was directing Hugo von Hofmannsthal's Christian morality play *Everyman* on the steps of

Salzburg cathedral. Jews mistook such prominence as an index of their successful integration. The few who suspected otherwise must have repressed their concerns.

(p. 386)

Apart from Reinhardt's huge personal loss and the subsequent loss of his theatre art to the world, what is tragic from the longer perspective of history is that Reinhardt's theatre of spectacle would prove indispensable to the cultural agenda of rising totalitarianism. Five weeks after Hitler came to power on 20 January 1933, Reinhardt left Germany for good. On 16 June 1933, hours before the opening of his Oxford production of *A Midsummer Night's Dream*, he responded to a memorandum from the German government by giving up ownership of his theatre in Berlin. He wrote:

> I have only one choice remaining, to offer to Germany the possession of my life's work ... The decision to sever myself conclusively from the Deutsches Theater does not come easily for me. With this possession I lose not only the fruit of a thirty-seven-year career; more important, I lose the place that I have built up for a lifetime and in which I myself have grown. I lose my home.

(qtd. in Kvam, p. 367)

He spent most of the next four years in a whirlwind of international productions across Europe and the United States, while holding on to his theatre and home in Vienna. In 1937, as the annexation of Austria by the German Reich became imminent, he departed for the US. His properties in Vienna were confiscated in the following year. Paradoxically, even as the Nazi government of Germany took 'the prop' of Reinhardt's art, the fascist administration of the Venetian Biennale continued to show *The Merchant of Venice* in his absence, including it again in an extraordinary 1935 edition of the Biennale.

A play envisioned as a festive celebration of theatre and love had been hijacked for the goals of fascist cultural politics. Mussolini's direction was to 'stress the consumption of "the Venetian experience"' (Stone, p. 191). Accordingly, Reinhardt's *Merchant* was packaged with gondola rides and other cultural 'goods' to be acquired from 'a supermarket of events and exhibitions' (p. 195). His reliably transferable productions that had brought mass audiences to stadium-sized theatres and open public spaces, and had democratised high culture, proved easy to co-opt by the very ideologies that destroyed his theatre and forced him into exile. As Karl Kraus aptly put it, 'Kitsch is death in disguise: it replaces ethics with aesthetics' (qtd. in Elon, p. 330) – and, one might add, with consumption. While Reinhardt worked toward the creation of a far-reaching community based on humanist principles and the common enjoyment of life, the fascist cultural-political powers of the 1930s would use his theatre art to totalise divisiveness.

II

Peter Zadek's challenges to the post-war German legacy of *The Merchant of Venice*

It is hard to imagine a starker contrast in approaches to *The Merchant of Venice* than that between the stagings of Max Reinhardt and Peter Zadek, two Jewish artists who were paragons of German (and European) director's theatre during, respectively, the first and third part of the twentieth century. Whereas Reinhardt's quasi-utopian vision of *The Merchant* as a festive play enfolded spectators in a world of theatre magic away from daily drudgery and nightmarish political developments, Zadek (1926–2009) was intent on provoking the discomfort of traditional middle-class, season-ticket-holding theatregoers and providing raucous fun for new, young, and working-class audiences. Whether he deployed an aesthetic of excess and calculated discrepancy within and between characters, or cool irony and performative restraint, his theatre constantly defied expectations, and demanded that spectators keep reconsidering their responses to the very end of the performance. His productions of *The Merchant* offered vibrant (some critics would say, kitschy) entertainment while rattling received ideas about the representation of Shylock on the German post-war stage, as well as constructions of German and European cultural identity implicit in these representations.

Like Reinhardt, Zadek kept revisiting *The Merchant* throughout a career in which Shakespeare figured prominently, from *Measure for Measure*, his first major production in Ulm done as revue entertainment (1960), through 'brutal vaudeville' renditions of *King Lear* in Bochum (1974) and *Othello* in Hamburg (1976), to a Berlin *Hamlet* with a female lead set in a world choking on a surfeit of garbage (1999). His engagement with *The Merchant* dated back to his youth in Britain, where his family had fled in

1934, when Zadek was 7. In 1947, soon after venturing into theatre studies at the Old Vic School in London, he staged the play with a touring company in the English Midlands. His German productions for the Städtische Bühnen in Ulm (1961) and the Schauspielhaus Bochum (1972) declared an early commitment to theatrical showmanship, radical innovation, and spontaneity, earning him a reputation as 'the most flamboyantly outrageous of avant-garde directors' (Hortmann, p. 253). Zadek's most influential production of the play opened at the Vienna Burgtheater in 1988 during a season commemorating its centennial, which coincided with the fiftieth anniversary of Austria's annexation to Hitler's Reich (Honegger, p. 122). This fourth *Merchant* drew considerable critical attention during a 1990 festival tour in Paris; it was revived by the famed Berliner Ensemble in 1994, shortly after German reunification; the following year, Zadek brought it to the UK, where he had cut his teeth as a director, as a highlight of the Edinburgh Festival. In both concept and circulation, this was *The Merchant* as a European, even global play. Once again, his revision surprised audiences with its dispassionate, aloof characterisation in both the romantic and the bond plots – their matter-of-fact style underscored by farcical comedy in the scenes with Lancelot Gobbo, Morocco, and Arragon. Each of Zadek's German-language *Merchants* matched iconoclastic theatre expression with what Gitta Honegger has called his 'polemical contrariness' regarding dominant cultural-political models of processing German and European anti-Semitism and xenophobia (p. 120).

Zadek has been forthcoming about his personal connection to the play: 'basically every 15 years I investigate and describe my own situation' (Lange, p. 54). The nature of his 'situation', of course, was affected by the growing national and international acclaim that his theatre work received, and by shifts in the public discourse about Germany's Nazi past, which vacillated between a conciliatory 'warding off' of Holocaust memories and a 'vigorous culture of memory' (Aleida Assmann, qtd. in Feinberg, *Unlikely History*, p. 241). Zadek started staging his German *Merchants* during a period when the 'latent anti-Semitism and hypocritical philo-Semitism' of the war generation during Adenauer's chancellorship (1949–63) met the wave of leftist anti-Zionism of the 1970s (Feinberg, *Jews and Theater*, p. 285). What remained constant was his life-long self-identification as a cultural Other, a position that appears to have fed his capacity for cultural insight as well as his iconoclasm. It is no coincidence, Marvin Carlson points out, 'that the first volume of his autobiography (published in 1998), although written in German, bore an English title which not only underlined Zadek's English background, but his status as an outsider – *My Way*' (*Theatre Research International*, p. 234). In England, Zadek 'was an outsider on two counts: as a Jew and a German among the English and as somebody strongly anglicised among the other refugees' (Raab, p. 858). He returned to his native Germany in the late 1950s, bringing with him the experience of the invigorating rhythm of British regional theatre, with its weekly repertoire changes, as well as the daring freedom of London's alternative stages. On the negative side, his command of German was poor. As he explained in an interview, 'during the war, we didn't speak German at home' (Quadri, p. 129), and since his entire formal education took place in the UK, he retained an accent throughout his life. In fact, his first rehearsals in Cologne were conducted through an interpreter. Although the German of his early childhood soon resurfaced, actors sometimes disregarded his directions offered in a polite Anglo-German lilt, and he 'had to learn to shout' (Hugh Rorrison, *Guardian*, 3 August 2009).

However loud Zadek may have been in the rehearsal room, his tactical interventions in the cultural politics of German theatre were no less boisterous. *The Merchant* he staged in Ulm in 1961 was the first to push against the 'philo-Semitic' approach to the play that had risen to prominence during the foundational decade of the Federal Republic of Germany – an era 'politically and culturally defined by a generation who were already adults when National Socialism rose to power' (Ackermann, p. 366). At a time when, reeling from post-war destruction, disorientation, and guilt, many Germans turned to the theatre (and the churches) for some form of solace, this ambivalent historical approach sidestepped enduring anti-Semitic sentiments and steered clear of Jewish stereotypes deployed in recent Nazi propaganda. Marcus Moninger famously declared that *The Merchant* 'has been offering a stage for the drama of German postwar society's dealings with Auschwitz' (p. 230), but philo-Semitic *Merchants* were rather evasive in such dealings.

According to Zeno Ackermann's astute unpacking of Moninger's fraught theatre metaphor, they were often driven by the desire 'to simply "play away" (that is, to continue performing as if nothing had happened) in order to secretly "play away" (to displace from consideration) the past, the victims of the Holocaust, and the guilty involvement of many Germans' (p. 369). Alleviating cultural anxieties about recent history, Shakespeare's play was cast as the tragedy of a wise, honourable, suffering Shylock, reminiscent of Henry Irving's Great Tradition – an 'expiation' Shylock who satisfied 'a deep need for making historical amends' (Hortmann, p. 255).

Influential philo-Semitic stagings included the 1956 Stuttgart production directed by Werner Kraut, with Erich Ponto as Shylock, and the 1957 Düsseldorf production directed by Karl Heinz Stroux, with Ernst Deutsch as Shylock. By 1967, Deutsch would reprise the part of the noble Jew, self-assured, silently suffering, deeply religious, in three more major productions (Ackermann and Schülting, p. 77). Before performing Shylock, Ponto and Deutsch, theatre and film stars from the Weimar era, had both played the Jewish merchant Nathan the Wise, the principal character in Gotthold Ephraim Lessing's eponymous play (1779) – a canonical German text and a plea for human and inter-religious tolerance. Having been banned by the Nazis, *Nathan the Wise* was chosen for the reopening of the Deutsches Theater in September 1945 – four months after the war and twelve years after Reinhardt had been forced to give up its ownership to Hitler's government (Feinberg, *Jews and Theater*, p. 277). Ponto and Deutsch had also performed Otto Frank in the hugely popular stage adaptation of *The Diary of Anne Frank*, the hit of the German theatre during the 1956–57 season (Ackermann and Schülting, p. 66). Their portrayals of Shylock, then, brought into play a phenomenon described by Carlson as 'ghosting': the audience experiences of a stage character as shaped by their recollection of the actor's previous roles or public persona (*The Haunted Stage*, pp. 7–9). In the case of Deutsch, the first Jewish actor to perform the part on a German-speaking stage after the war, Shylock's portrayal was also ghosted by his personal experience as a refugee from Hitler's regime who had lost family members in the Holocaust. 'This actor will be unable to forget the unbelievable trials that his people had to undergo', wrote a reviewer for the West German daily *Der Mittag* (qtd. in Ackermann and Schülting, p. 76). Another critic of a touring production with Deutsch suggested that when audiences applauded his performance, it seemed that they 'wanted to compensate him for what he had suffered from the Venetians' (qtd. in Ackermann and Schülting, p. 80). Apparently, an affective response to a performance conflating Shakespeare's character with Lessing's and with Holocaust victims was perceived as somehow capable of assuaging historical guilt.

In 1961, Zadek became the first German director to challenge this reverential approach to Shylock and, along with it, the taboo of othering Shylock through the use of stereotypically Jewish physical and language performance markers. The risk he took was considerable. The world was awaiting the beginning of the trial of Adolf Eichmann, one of the architects of the 'Final Solution', who in May 1960 had been extracted by Mossad agents from Argentina, triggering massive anti-Semitic protests there, organised by far-right groups. In 1960 again, Hans Schüller, manager of Nationaltheater Mannheim, had cancelled rehearsals of *The Merchant* in reaction to a wave of anti-Semitic graffiti on synagogues and Jewish cemeteries throughout Germany. He justified the decision thus: 'The play was misused by various directors and theatre managers of the Hitler era for anti-Jewish propaganda and could, for this reason, despite the full appreciation of the ingenuity of its author, shock Jewish members of the audience, as has already happened elsewhere' (qtd. in Ackermann and Schülting, p. 88). Zadek embraced the play's capacity to shock – not the handful of Jews living in Ulm, but the German audiences of this rapidly growing industrial city. He gave them a grotesque, bloodthirsty villain from the Ghetto, 'a truly vicious character, who was nasty to his daughter'. Norbert Kappen, who played Shylock, protested during rehearsals: 'I am German, I can't play an unsympathetic Jew, it makes me sick.' But that was precisely what Zadek wanted: 'When an actor really has that feeling of deep, stifling, sincere malaise, he gives it to the [audience]. It is not perversity, it is precisely what we must aim at' (Colette Godard, *Guardian*, 5 October 1990). The reviewer for *Stuttgarter Zeitung* noted the kitschy set of Belmont in the final 'reconciliation' scene, decked with 'paper flowers and Baroque putti reminiscent of the poetry of *A Midsummer Night's Dream*' (Hellmuth Karasek, qtd. in Ackermann, p. 393). The contrast between the cliché of the evil Jew and the saccharine artifice of reconciliation from which he was excluded demanded a confrontation not only with the past, but also with the way German theatre dealt with historical memory. The slim critical response, however, does not indicate whether the production achieved this effect.

What the Ulm audience was not aware of was that Zadek's provocation was an instance of intercultural translation. He had first encountered *The Merchant* on the English stage, an experience he describes in his autobiography as profoundly unsettling. In 1938, his parents took the 11-year-old boy to a production of the play at the Queen's Theatre in London, with John Gielgud performing Shylock. (Gielgud co-directed the play with Glen Byam Shaw.) 'Never before in my life', writes Zadek, 'had I seen a Jew as mean as the one played by Gielgud. I remember how my parents struggled to explain this Shylock to me' (p. 106). 'Remorseless, toothless – utterly revolting in the remnants of a ginger wig', according to a reviewer for *The Daily Express* (qtd. in Nahshon, p. 146), this was a Shylock akin to J. R. R. Tolkien's Gollum.[1] His repulsive fawning, grubbiness, compulsive viciousness, and exaggerated accent and gesturing were the stuff of grotesque figuration. Gielgud would later explain that his portrayal was driven by historicist faithfulness to the image of the Elizabethan comic villain and by an unwillingness to politicise the play by connecting a sympathetic Shylock with the unfolding tragedy of the Jews in Nazi Germany (Shapiro, pp. 28–9). Decades later, in his Ulm 'translation' of the play, Zadek reprised this 'comic and exaggerated ... horror figure' (Zadek and Leverett) by giving his audience the Nazi appropriation of the Elizabethan comic villain, ghosted by the memory of his own childhood malaise *and* that of the actor who performed the part.

The provocation, Zadek decided, was worth repeating, if the ghost of anti-Semitic prejudice was to be exorcised. He launched his appointment as Artistic Director of the Schauspielhaus in the mining town of Bochum with a season that included a wildly popular musical-revue version of Hans Fallada's small-town life novel, *Little Man, What Now?* and *The Merchant* staged as a 'burlesque Venetian carnival', with Shylock as 'a frightening as well as ridiculous cardboard ogre' (Hortmann, p. 257). Not only did this production scandalise the press, but, as designer Götz Loepelmann recalls, it also prompted anti-Semitic graffiti on the theatre walls and even a bomb threat to the theatre. Between these vehement reactions and the financial success of the production – more than 23,000 tickets were sold for the thirty-one performances of its run from December 1972 to June 1973 (Ackermann and Schülting, p. 119) – it was clear that Zadek succeeded in his mission to engage a new, young, working-class audience with the theatre tradition of the city. Provocation and entertainment proved useful, if risky, tactics for the success of his 'people's theatre' (*Volkstheater*) project.[2] He had offered an invitation for full, unrestrained emotional participation to the 90 per cent of the population who did not attend theatre – something the director deemed instrumental for the moral growth of society. In an interview given early in his Bochum appointment, he declared:

> The theatre that I am slowly developing is not at all a political, an ideological theatre, but a moral theatre. In every human relationship I consider it most important to place before everyone completely personal decisions (in life, in art, and anywhere else) and always to keep insisting that these choices be made.
> (qtd. in Carlson, *Theatre Research*, 2007, p. 237)

The choice with which this *Merchant* confronted Bochum theatregoers was not easy: could they sympathise with and applaud a non-sentimentalised Shylock, a character who was 'about to become a murderer' (Godard, *Guardian*, 5 October 1990); or would they be incited to anti-Semitic actions?

By 1972, Zadek's audiences were better prepared to engage with this question than at the time of his first German production of the play. Three years earlier, German TV had broadcast a film adaptation of *The Merchant* directed by Otto Schenk, in which the 76-year-old Jewish actor Fritz Kortner, who had returned from emigration, played Shylock. Kortner, who had performed the part three times before the war (including under Reinhardt's direction in Vienna in 1924), brought into the living-rooms of his viewers 'a misfit, an old Jew, unkempt, shabby, and unrefined, driven by his growing hatred: a killjoy from a different age' (Ackermann and Schülting, p. 102). This was *The Merchant* as a revenge-tragedy of a Holocaust survivor. Controversy ensued; a TV panel aired by West German Broadcasting debated whether 'the Jew may be evil again'. Critics feared that Kortner's portrayal 'would not only confirm the anti-Semitic prejudices of the older generation, but would also encourage the emerging anti-Zionism of leftist groups, ... that many spectators would see their anti-Semitic prejudices reconfirmed and embodied (rather than played) by a Jew' (Schülting, *World-Wide Shakespeares*, pp. 294–5).

Zadek's artistic response to the controversy was to outdo the portrayal of the 'evil Jew' in Schenk's film. Played by Hans Mahnke, who, in Zadek's description, 'made very good use of the methods of a grand old actor', this Shylock amalgamated anti-Semitic clichés: 'ugly and sinister, with a dwindled goat-beard and blinking beady eyes, he slobbered, shuffled his feet, lisped, and spoke distorted German with a "Jewish' accent"' (Feinberg, *Jews and Theater*, p. 283). His exaggerated speech contours along with the combination of sly sycophancy and unrestrained malice in his physical actions – he 'dragged Antonio around on a rope like cattle' (Verch, p. 88) – recalled Veit Harlan's notorious Nazi propaganda film, *Jud Süß* (1940). Zadek wanted a Shylock who scraped the dirt from his toenails (Raab, p. 865); he instructed his designer Götz Loepelmann to make Mahnke's ragged sackcloth caftan 'stinky and filthy and dirty and ugly'. Machine oil and soot from the theatre's garage were used for this purpose. 'And the Germans fought to see him', Loepelmann reminisced in an interview.

Several critics branded Zadek's take on Shylock a 'scandalous distortion' (qtd. in Feinberg, *Jews and Theater*, p. 284). Yet the outrageous repulsiveness of the character was only part of the whole picture. In a production in which the golden youth of Venice strutted on ridiculous high platform shoes and acted like farcical popinjays, Shylock, according to a reviewer for *Süddeutsche Zeitung*, was 'the only human being' (qtd. in Ackermann and Schülting, p. 109). In the outcome of the trial scene, 'his naked human vulnerability also aroused pity, when his bare feet were still heard tapping the floorboards after he had left the court in defeat' (Verch, pp. 88–9). As Zadek believed, 'the character who is still sympathetic at the end of the play is Shylock' (Godard, *Guardian*, 5 October 1990). But he needed to put both his actors and the audience through 'a kind of purgatorial process' (qtd. in Hortmann, p. 257), to shine a light on the demons of anti-Semitism in their most disturbing forms in order to expel them. Many critics doubted that this effect was achieved.

In a 1980 interview, Zadek explained that he had approached the Bochum production of the play in the spirit of 'a not too refined, rather brutal, rather outspoken *Volkstheater*', though he may have tried too hard (Zadek and Leverett, pp. 109–10). Shylock was a figure familiar to the wider audiences that Zadek was attracting; he looked, moved, and smelled like clichés imprinted onto German cultural memory. The director shrank the historical distance of language and used the set design to bring theatregoers close to the world of the play. He replaced August Schlegel's poetic translation (1799) with a modern-prose rendition by Karsten Schälike (Ackermann and Schülting, p. 107). The set design of the French scenographer René Allio – a criss-crossing maze of long wooden plankways suggesting the bridges of Venice – extended into the auditorium, allowing the action to unfold both literally and metaphorically in the face of the spectator (Ackermann and Schülting, p. 109). Nor was the social engagement with the 'evil Jew' limited to the theatre auditorium. An enormous poster over the main entrance of the Schauspielhaus featured cutout caricatures of Mahnke's Shylock – hook-nosed, crooked, open-mouthed – aiming a dagger at the bared chest of Günther Lüders's Antonio. The latter, erect and stoic, had his gaze fixed to the heavens in the posture of St Sebastian awaiting his martyrdom, a connection drawn by the reproduction in the theatre programme of Andrea Mantegna's Renaissance painting of the saint. Not only did these allegorical figures breach the divide between theatrical and everyday space, they invited the physical engagement of Bochum's citizens. An illustration of journalist Franco Quadri's conversation with Zadek shows two children play-acting the poster scene in front of the theatre on a sunny day (p. 138). Passers-by could animate the cutouts by pulling on a rope attached to Shylock's knife-holding hand (Ackermann and Schülting, p. 108), thus turning the grotesquery of the malignant Jew into a product literally hand-made by the citizens of Bochum.

The provocation with which Zadek confronted his spectators was delivered through a similarly jarring theatre language of 'disjunction and "de-centering"' (Hortmann, p. 259). Aesthetically as well as ethically, he refused to develop a cohesive Shakespearean product for easy consumption. Rather, by provoking his audiences, he pushed them to take positions on the play's characters and conflicts, and then to reconsider these very positions. Somehow, he succeeded in doing all this with his signature madcap playfulness. Costumes were 'wildly eclectic' (Hortmann, p. 262); comic action distracted the audience (Ackermann and Schülting, p. 107). The discomfiting scenes with Shylock were disrupted by the antics of Ulrich Wildgruber's Lancelot Gobbo, who delivered the part in a rustic Swabian accent that was practically unintelligible to the Northern German audience. Portia (Rosel Zech) performed three different character types: the Belmont doll, the bride of sugary romances, and the farcical judge so hyper-focused on performing masculinity in the trial scene that she mangled speech and physical action (Verch, p. 89; Ackermann and Schülting, p. 108). Mahnke's over-the-top Shylock counterpointed Lüders's 'subtle, intimate' Antonio. The contrast allowed for 'a strong sympathy for Antonio [to be] developed', which Zadek then problematised by inserting non-Shakespearean material that gave Shylock an indisputable logical advantage over Portia's argument about the 'drop of Christian blood' (Zadek and Leverett, p. 110). In the insertion, from Richard Hengist Horn's 1838 'Dramatic Reverie', Shylock countered Portia's warning against shedding blood while cutting the pound of flesh by declaring that 'blood is liquid flesh' (Shakespeare, *New Variorum*, p. 400). In this way, along with the blow that Zadek dealt to the philo-Semitic brand of *The Merchant*, he upended time-honoured theatrical conventions of moralistic didacticism and the 'German obsession ... with theatre as "high art"' (Honneger, p. 117).

In 1988, Zadek put on another striking staging of *The Merchant* at the Vienna Burgtheater, where Lothar Müthel's 1943 production, with Werner Krauss as Shylock, had fuelled the anti-Semitic propaganda of the Nazi regime. In spite of the memory-ridden local context of the double anniversary, of Austria's annexation by the German Reich (1938) and the Burgtheater's centennial, the director took a decisively presentist approach, one with a global outlook to boot. Yet again, Zadek defied expectations; neither did he engage with the specific occasion, nor did he indulge in his signature eclectic, over-the-top style. Sidestepping the earlier ludic provocations amalgamating anti-Semitic stereotypes, he transformed the play into a disciplined study of the corporate operators of the global financial marketplace, with all their pragmatism, competitiveness, and insidious evasions of 'the Jewish question'. Inspired by the portrayal of the calculated ruthlessness of the world of high finance in Oliver Stone's 1987 film *Wall Street*, Zadek created a *Merchant* for the Thatcher-Reagan-Kohl era of economic deregulation and 'increasing "globalization" of economic and cultural exchange' (Ackermann and Schülting, p. 162). At the same time, he offered a firm artistic retort to the rise of right-wing populism and national conservatism evident in the electoral success of Jörg Haider's Austrian Freedom Party (FPÖ) (Ackermann and Schülting, p. 110). To the pan-German vision of cultural identity promoted by the FPÖ in the 1980s, at a time when Haider was laying the foundation of an anti-immigration 'Austria first' initiative, Zadek contrasted a world in which it was impossible to ward off Shylock because 'the boundary between self and its others [had] become blurred' (Schülting, p. 69). He may have lost in an overreaching gamble, the director clarified, 'but he will be back, he will start up a new business. He is not finished, I am sure of that' (Godard, *Guardian*, 5 October 1990).

This production of *The Merchant* has been widely viewed as setting the pace in the years to come for the economic interpretation of the play. As discussed in the Segue, productions deploying this approach present the ethnic and religious conflict between Shylock and Antonio as rooted in struggles for economic survival that flared during a historical change from the financial paradigm of money-hoarding to that of commercial capital venture (Hortmann, p. 259). Zadek was not the first to foreground economic competitiveness between Christians and Jews over religious and ethnic intolerance. In 1971, Jonathan Miller minimised the visual differences between the Venetian mercantile class and the public persona of Laurence Olivier's Rothschild-like Shylock in an extremely popular National Theatre production in London, televised in 1973 (see Part I, Chapter IV). In West Germany, Peter Palitzsch's Düsseldorf production with Stefan Wigger as Shylock (1981) likewise downplayed markers of ethnic and religious difference to focus on the economic antagonism between Shylock and Antonio, an approach also embraced in the rare East German productions of the play (Ackermann and Schülting, p. 126). Yet in all earlier examples of the economic turn in *Merchant* productions, Shylock was dramatically isolated and ultimately expelled from the Christian world. One recalls Olivier's blood-curdling off-stage keening after his final exit and Wigger's freezing on stage after the line 'What judgement shall I dread, doing no wrong' (IV.i.88) for the duration of the intermission, as well as the crucifixion pose he held against his black-fronted house as the lovers warily claimed their new life in Belmont. Not so in Zadek's 1988 production.

Here, Shylock (Gert Voss) was one of the financiers of New York, Tokyo, Milan, or Frankfurt. Tall, blue-eyed, well-heeled, and charismatic, he was virtually indistinguishable from the rest in looks, mannerisms, and profiteering drive. Indeed, Portia (Eva Mattes) was genuinely confused in the trial scene, when she asked, 'Which is the merchant here, and which the Jew?' (IV.i.170), and mistook the rather uptight, bespectacled Antonio (Ignaz Kirchner) for Shylock, causing the merchant to drop his cigar from his mouth. Titles of reviews referred to the world of high finance as multiculturally integrated: 'Zadek takes Shylock to the world of Wall Street', 'Shylock among the stock brokers', 'The profiteers of Trump Tower' (qtd. in Ackermann and Schülting, p. 167). In a world where keeping up with the international press appeared to be the order of the day, Shakespeare's play about loans and bonds shed light, in the words of a reviewer for the Edinburgh Festival revival, on 'the Mammon in *all* of us' (Roger Savage, *Times Literary Supplement*, 8 September 1995; emphasis added).

In Wilfried Minks's stage design, Venice was the atrium of an office tower, its cold-coloured glass-and-metal emptiness dwarfing the human body. Most exits and entrances were through a huge lift upstage, its giant sliding doors engraved with the Venetian lions of St Mark, its motion matching the ups and downs of the characters' fortunes. Belmont seemed to be a different world, bathed in soft orange light, but scene transitions suggested that the difference between the two locales was a matter of window dressing. To transform the office tower into Portia's estate, neo-expressionist canvas drops, painted in broad strokes, came down to cover the lift doors. The bold compositions and ostentatious size of the drops (painted by Johannes Grützke, who also designed the costumes) spoke as loudly about the power of money as the cold towers of Venice did.

The characters' station in the world of business and finance was signalled by smart suits and office-party gear (and an elegant line of cocktail dresses for Portia), as well as by symbolic props, such as the ubiquitous newspapers, cigars, the large portaphones of the time, briefcases, and portable audio recorders. Jessica, too, was introduced as part and parcel of the business world, not within Shylock's domestic space. Until her elopement, she wore a pencil skirt and heeled pumps; clutching a leather portfolio under her arm, she addressed her father with the eager deference of a young administrative assistant. Antonio and his friends projected the casual entitlement of the rich: for instance, the opening scene was re-envisioned as a press interview, during which Salarino and Salanio patiently waited for Antonio to complete his morning exercise routine – cigar in mouth – with his personal trainer. And certainly nobody raised their voices, except the Gobbos, the outrageously pantomimic Morocco (performed by Ignaz Kirchner in incongruous blackface and a gaudy robe flung over a white-collar shirt), and Arragon (a moustachioed Gert Voss in black shades and full Francoist uniform). The provocative double casting of Morocco and Arragon as alter-egos ghosting Antonio and Shylock, respectively, was another subversive dramatisation of the blurring of racial and ethnic differences in a world ruled by corporate greed, though it was not discussed in the production's reception.

Among the suave Venetians, Gert Voss's Shylock was the epitome of cool (Figure 14). Self-assured and swift-spoken, a connoisseur of hard-hitting irony, he easily maintained emotional control over Bassanio and Antonio while negotiating the 3,000-ducat loan. When he explained, casually, that he had been publicly berated and spat upon, it was hard to imagine Antonio spitting on his gold-pinned, cream-coloured cravat. In fact, when Gratiano did spit next to Shylock in the trial scene, Bassanio quickly knelt to clean any stray drops that could have landed on the banker's impeccably tailored trousers. Voss underplayed his part throughout. The 'Hath not a Jew eyes' speech, for instance, he delivered in a quiet, matter-of-fact manner, as an argument he had mulled over for a long time. His preparations to exact the pound of flesh were carried out with sardonic practicality. Setting down his briefcase, he took out a large knife and sharpened it on both soles, balancing first on one foot and then on the other. When asked, 'Are there balance here to weigh / The flesh?' (IV.i.251–2), he opened the briefcase again, took out his

Figure 14 Gert Voss as Shylock in Peter Zadek's production for the Vienna Burgtheater, 1988.

portable scales and calmly assembled them on the floor. With the same calm purposefulness, without batting an eyelid at losing his principal, he placed the knife and the scales back into the briefcase when it became clear that shedding Antonio's blood would cost him his life.

Though emotionally controlled, Voss's Shylock was not emotionally stunted. To Tubal, he revealed how much Jessica had hurt him, accompanying his curse against his daughter with a Jewish ritual gesture, raising both hands and bringing them down sharply, as tears welled up in his eyes (Beyerdörfer, p. 216) (Figure 15). As Ackermann and Schülting suggest, Zadek created a Shylock who showed to the world a fascinating and impenetrable mask (p. 170). What was behind the mask was not for the business world to know, nor for the general public for that matter. A reviewer for the *Stuttgarter Zeitung* wrote that this was 'not a Shylock for us but a Shylock for Shylock' (qtd. in Ackermann and Schülting, p. 169). At the end of the trial scene, on his knees as he was commanded, he once again donned the mask that had long served him as a declaration of excellence in the financial district. Holding the pose, he verified the date on his watch, took his time writing out two checks, handed them over to Antonio and 'Balthazar' with the utmost dignity, put on his classy Homberg, and smirked, declaring, 'I am content'. This exit seriously disturbed the 'Venetians'. This was not a Shylock who was about to catch the next boat to America, nor fade into insignificance, nor yet disappear down a gloomy corridor. 'We know that somewhere he still has an account', Zadek mused in a conversation with Olivier Ortolani (qtd. in Honegger, p. 122). He will be back, and he will be meticulously equipped for the next merciless fight with his competitors.

Some critics saw as a cop-out Zadek's choice to drop the familiar performance markers of Jewishness and portray Shylock as an assimilated Jew in a homogenised world of high finance. Writing immediately after opening night for *Die Süddeutsche Zeitung*, C. B. Sucher protested, 'He robbed the Jews of their Jewishness ... Zadek avoids the explosive nature of the text. After the performance, nobody asks how anti-Semitic Shakespeare's play really is? [sic] It is highly unlikely that Zadek's play will have abolished any anti-Semitic prejudices' (qtd. in Beyerdörfer, p. 218). Theatre scholar Marvin Carlson concurred, though in milder terms: 'The

Figure 15 Gert Voss as Shylock and Pavel Landovský as Tubal in Peter Zadek's production for the Vienna Burgtheater, 1988.

Jewish question disappeared entirely from the production, to be replaced by a modern capitalistic lust for financial gain' (*Theatre Research*, p. 239). Others, however, have argued that Zadek did not avoid 'the Jewish question'. Rather, he confronted anti-Semitism in its more insidious manifestations even as he pushed against naturalised notions of a Jewish identity as victimhood, a mentality for which he had little patience (see Bayerdörfer, p. 217; Honneger, p. 121). Far from creating some kind of post-ethnic utopia, Zadek's production brought out the privilege of being born to the 'insiders club' and thus reaping profit at the expense of Shylock's loss, like the not particularly sharp Bassanio (Paulus Manker), who barely managed to choose correctly in Portia's lottery, or the sheltered Portia. Nor did the director shy away from alluding to Holocaust memories in the production's homogenised world of high finance. As Bayerdörfer points out, 'the actions of a carnival group during the kidnapping scene remind us of a pogrom during which Jessica is almost raped by Lorenzo's gang' (p. 216). At the same time, the always-provocative director mused that the headline for his version of Shylock should be 'perpetrator rather than victim'. He explained:

> What interested me in Shylock was this sudden change into an almost perfect cynic. What he really is telling them is 'Kiss my ass, all of you with your stupid attitude. I am making money here and if you don't like it, too bad. And if you kick my ass, I'll kick back, only more strongly.' That's a simple story. And somewhat scary. In my perception, of course, it has to do with Israel ... This interplay between victim and perpetrator suddenly doesn't function anymore with regard to Israel. They don't want to be victims, but perpetrators.
>
> (qtd. in Honegger, p. 121)

Zadek has always succeeded in rattling his audiences, whether in Austria, Germany, France, or Great Britain, by undercutting philo-Semitic approaches to Shakespeare's play, recalling anti-Semitic stereotypes, and succeeding in entertaining spectators with palatable, playful, provocative irony. His 1988 production of *The Merchant* managed to do this in a masterfully dispassionate, almost nonchalant way.

Notes

1 Tolkien's novel, *The Hobbit*, was published in September 1937 to much critical acclaim and may have influenced Gielgud's portrayal of Shylock, although no direct connections were drawn by the theatre critics of the time.
2 A concept difficult to translate into English, *Volkstheater* is described by Marvin Carlson as 'a theatre not devoted to specific political education, but rather as a centre of community social life' (*Theatre Research*, p. 237).

III

A post-Holocaust balancing act: *The Merchant of Venice* directed by Trevor Nunn at the National Theatre, London (1999)

Dear Trevor,

What a thrill! Your *Merchant* is one of the best theatre productions I've ever seen. It illuminates every aspect of this normally patchy and unsatisfactory play and discovers an underlining coherence and human meaning that binds it all into a whole. Extraordinary Goodman! Rarest of all, it becomes contemporary not by modernising, but by revealing the natural life within the text.

With congratulations and love, Peter

(Brook, p. 294)

The author of this supreme accolade is none other than Peter Brook, one of the greatest European directors of the twentieth century. The note captures something essential to Trevor Nunn's (1940–) talent – his capacity to create worlds that make the behaviour of characters viable, their life in the text 'natural'. Brook also signals the particular difficulty of dealing with the play. Whether 'patchy and unsatisfactory' in his words, or more strongly put, 'split, sundered, schizoid' (Nevo, p. 120), post-Holocaust interpretative collisions over *The Merchant* have affected responses to its performances (Bulman, *Shakespeare in Performance*, p. 27).

In 1999, Nunn was not only one of the most prominent and versatile British directors, but also someone whose work at the RSC (1964–86) had modernised and energised twentieth-century Shakespearean performance in Britain. In his critical biography, Russell Jackson points out Nunn's 'enthusiasm for exciting theatricality', his taste for the 'grand theatrical gesture' coupled with a 'Leavisite' 'attention to the subtlety of verse and prose' (pp. 16–18). By the time he directed *The Merchant*, Nunn was well known for his 'thoroughly worked out interpretative approach', which involved textual interventions (Jackson, p. 2) of the kind practised at the RSC in the 1970s and 1980s by John Barton, with whom Nunn had a long professional partnership.

His arrival as Artistic Director at the National Theatre (NT) in 1997 brought to the helm of the principal publicly funded national institution a director of experience, energy, and high professionalism, equally skilled at putting on Shakespeare and popular musicals. Though not all applauded the choice, it proved to be a 'perfect casting' for running such a complex organisation. The NT, with its 'three auditoria, an educational arm and an international venue, with responsibilities not only to London but to the rest of the country and ... overseas', needs a director who can 'deal with government ministers and Arts Council officials one moment, and then speak the language of the coalface to actors and technicians the next' (Thelma Holt, *Independent*, 7 March 1996). Undoubtedly, Nunn was such a man, ready to do what his predecessor in the job, Richard Eyre, has described as 'National Service' in the title of his memoir. During his tenure, Nunn initiated structural changes to the houses, created an ensemble, and in his five seasons, 'won more theatre awards than the NT had ever won before, or ... since' (Andrew Dickson, Interview with Trevor Nunn, *Independent*, 18 November 2011).

The Merchant of Venice was one of the few Shakespeare plays he had not directed, and he faced this challenge by working *within* and *with* the post-Holocaust performance tradition. Since the middle of the twentieth century, when Tyrone Guthrie removed the play from the Renaissance setting, foregrounded homosexual attraction, presented the Christians as unpleasant, and Shylock as a thriving merchant, directors' interpretations of the play have embraced the pressures of history and social concerns. George Tabori's 1966 production tightened the focus on anti-Semitic crimes (Part I, Chapter VII); Peter Zadek, in turn, rejected a victimised tragic Shylock (Part II, Chapter II); feminist stagings foregrounded patriarchal constraints and women's agency; productions began to home in on the racism in Belmont; social commentary blossomed through casting choices and the creative development of minor characters. Without being presentist, Nunn's production can be said to have resonated with the tensions of Third Way politics, brought in by New Labour in

1997. While Britain's stabilised economy allowed for social investment and opened up hopeful vistas, the unleashing of frenzied consumerism, the rise of political spin, celebrity culture, and media power soon dulled the shine of new promises (*Encyclopaedia Britannica*, 'Tony Blair Biography', 'The Tony Blair Government (1997–2007)'. At the same time, the self-congratulatory and facile multiculturalism of the New Labour government window-dressed a simmering hostility to social change within the political establishment and beyond. Nunn's production, although set in the 1930s Weimar Republic, resonated with the feverish pitch of life in the early internet era and the mentality of living dangerously among the first bursting bubbles of the dot-com economy.

As only the second production of *The Merchant* at the NT, Nunn's inevitably invites a conversation with the first, directed in 1970 by Jonathan Miller (Part I, Chapter IV). Miller's late Victorian England had unveiled the entrenched prejudice underneath the veneer of British upper-class manners. For his purposes, Nunn chose the febrile interim between the two World Wars, drawing a closer connection with the Holocaust. His Venice was a very *Mittel*-European place, teetering on the brink of one of the great tragedies of the twentieth century. The Jewish Miller had cast Laurence Olivier, the most prominent non-Jewish actor of the day, as Shylock. In order to emphasise 'the absurdity of racial prejudice', Olivier performed the character as an assimilated businessman, barely distinguishable from the other merchants (Miller, *Subsequent Performances*, pp. 155–6).[1] Nunn gave the part to Henry Goodman, a British Jewish actor who as a boy had been chased by anti-Semites in the East End of London, thus placing embodied Jewishness on the stage.[2] Goodman's Shylock was a shrewd financier with deep cultural roots, who viewed the Christians with barely disguised resentment. Like Miller, Nunn demystified Belmont and envisioned a bitterly disillusioned Jessica at the finale. At the same time, both NT stagings belong to the tradition extending back to Henry Irving and beyond in their grand and fundamentally tragic central character, their psychological realism, and their willingness to tamper with the text for their own purposes. In 2001, Nunn's production was recorded on DVD under the direction of Chris Hunt.

Nunn felt a genuine unease about the play in the post-Holocaust context (Interview for PBS Masterpiece Theatre). His reservations were partly influenced by the views of the respected British theatre critic David Nathan, who considered it offensive (Ann Hedges, *Houston Chronicle*, 8 October 2001). Nunn might have also been worried by Nathan's negative review of a 1997 RSC production (O'Rourke, p. 287). A conversation with Goodman about how to resolve what was seen as a major difficulty – how not to allow Shylock's behaviour to be seen as representative of Jews in general – enabled the director to overcome his misgivings (*Jewish Chronicle*, 25 February 2000). Nunn's success can be judged by Nathan's enthusiastic review of the production, which included a reference to the earlier rejection of the play. The development of the role of Tubal to counterbalance Shylock's fatal decision was, according to the critic, a 'masterstroke' which helped avoid generalisations about Jews (*Jewish Chronicle*, 25 June 1999). However, proving that a major production of *The Merchant of Venice* is never plain-sailing, dramatist Arnold Wesker, who in the wake of Miller's production had written that Shakespeare's play was 'inescapably anti-Semitic' (Part 1, Chapter VII), published a new attack, titled 'Shame on you, Shakespeare' (*Independent*, 21 July 1999). A quick riposte which appeared on the following day countered by referring to Nunn's staging, saying that Wesker's argument 'was made foolish by the production running currently at the National Theatre' (Tom Morris, *Independent*, 22 July 1999).

Among a spate of overwhelmingly positive reviews, the influential critic Michael Billington singled out Nunn's mastery of creating a 'specific, emotional and social context' (*Guardian*, 18 June 1999) for the actions of characters, aligning the production with those by Bill Alexander (see Part I, Chapter VI), Peter Zadek, and Peter Sellars (see Part II, Segue). Other critics praised the director's 'fidelity to the shifting moods of the play' (Matt Wolf, *Variety*, 4 August 1999) and his interpretation, 'subtle and alive to all sides' (Paul Taylor, *Independent*, 18 June 1999). In a perspicacious piece, Alistair Macaulay summed up Nunn's directorial thinking as 'neither traditional, nor radical', yet 'fresh at every turn', noting at the same time the director's 'embarrassed determination to realign Shakespeare's sociological attitudes to ones that will ingratiate today' (*Financial Times*, 22 June 1999). Some critics commented on the 'shaky' and 'slow' start (John Gross, *Sunday Telegraph*, 20 June 1999; Sheridan Morley, *Spectator*, 26 June 1999) and on the excessive length of the production (three and a half hours). John Gross found Shylock's mouthing of 'the most sacred Jewish prayer, the Shema' in preparation for cutting Antonio's flesh, 'offensive' (*Sunday Telegraph*, 20 June 1999), while Billington thought that the narrative flow of the production was 'clogged' by 'a mass of novelistic detail' (*Guardian*, 1 February 2000). In her overall evaluation of the achievements of the season, Susanna Clapp, who reviewed *The Merchant* favourably, nevertheless put it behind two other productions in her list of theatrical highlights (*Observer*, 20 June 1999). However, these were cavils in a flow of positive reviews. Accordingly, in the autumn of 1999 the production was transferred from the chamber Cottesloe Theatre to the large Olivier auditorium; in 2000, Trevor Nunn received the Best Director Olivier Award for the show.

Venice, created for the production, conjured up a recognisable society in which characters faced painful existential situations. Along with the rabid anti-Semitism among the Venetians, it uncovered a web of societal hierarchies and probed latent and overt xenophobia, racism, and patriarchal attitudes. A sympathetic Shylock, performed with psychological realism by Henry Goodman, was driven to extremes by a hostile world. New insights into social interactions were produced through textual cuts and additions, line and scene transpositions, stage design, and meaningful casting; the agency and plight of minor characters came to the fore, illuminating the complex fabric of interpersonal relations.

When *The Merchant* premiered on 17 June 1999 at the Cottesloe Theatre, the intimacy of the small house was further enhanced by placing the audience on both sides of a traverse, which reduced the seating to 200 and facilitated full immersion in the action. Venice, as designed by Hildegard Bechtler, was not a world of canals and bridges, which were still visible in Miller's production. Instead, she chose a socially evocative and temporally grounded Central European 1930s style. The city on the stage could be Berlin, Vienna, Prague, any place in Europe that bore memories of the Jazz Age and its horrible aftermath. The element most emblematic of the period was the floor, an inspiration for which Bechtler found in an 'abstract painting which had … [a] deliberate thirties patterning, almost like a swastika' ('Shakespeare at the National Theatre'). The irregular cream, tan, and black floor was thus inspired by an artwork with a dark underbelly; costumes invoked photographs of Berlin cabaret life in the period.

The closeness of stage and audience allowed access to every minute detail and served well the psychological acting style. Placed at the opposite ends of the traverse, Shylock's and Portia's houses were connected by the checked pavement used for all indoor and outdoor spaces in Venice and Belmont. Shylock's home loomed in dark grey flats. Portia's space was an art nouveau world of white and gold. A Gustav Klimt piece, showing supplicant female bodies from his 'Beethoven Frieze' (1902), signalled her wealth, and the tension between sexual desire and romantic remoteness (Figure 16).

When the production transferred to the stage of the 1,150-seater Olivier auditorium, spatial continuity was secured by the revolve, with the two houses positioned on obverse sides. Transferring a chamber piece to a larger space can be tricky, but the new round of reviews confirmed the success. John Peter found that the larger stage allowed for more detail and enhanced Shylock's loneliness (*Sunday Times*, 9 January 2000). Belmont housed the central panel from Klimt's artwork, showing a gold-clad knight summoned to take up the fight for happiness (the central theme of Beethoven's

Figure 16 Derbhle Crotty as Portia and Alexander Hanson as Bassanio in Trevor Nunn's production for the National Theatre, London, 1999.

Ninth Symphony). Its presence in Portia's home symbolised her predicament and 'mingled brilliantly with the psychological insight into [her] personality and character' (John Peter, *Sunday Times*, 9 January 2000). In the casket scene, the image stood for Bassanio, the 'Hercules' (III.ii.60) who performed the heroic labour of releasing Portia from her maidenly bonds. The period-specific ambience was enhanced by the sound design, the peaceful chirruping of birds and violin strings of Belmont juxtaposed with the rumba dances of the restless cabaret culture of Venice. Shylock's home, in turn, offered a sense of Jewish life and sound with Leah's photograph forming an emotional centre for the domestic scenes.

Scene and text transpositions created new situations and unexpected twists to character relationships. Lancelot's complaint about 'My master, the Jew' and the conflict between his conscience and the fiend (II.ii.1–28) became a stand-up cabaret act, raucously applauded by the on-stage audience, with an unscripted appearance of Shylock at its finale. The transposition of Morocco's first appearance highlighted the racism of Belmont. 'Mislike me not for my complexion' (II.i.1), came as a response to Portia's 'If he have the condition of a saint and the complexion of a devil, I had rather he should shrive me than wive me' (I.ii.124–6), words which Morocco had overheard as he entered for their first encounter. Whether prince or Jew, in Venice or in Belmont, the Other was always confronted with one of the many faces of prejudice. Among Nunn's contribution to *The Merchant*, critics included the creation of a society 'ruled insidiously by a casual sense of evil' (Michael Phillips, *Los Angeles Times*, 6 October 2001).

Casting, too, was pointedly employed. Just as Shylock's ethnicity was embodied by Goodman, and the Prince of Morocco's by Chu Omambala, the ethnicity of minor characters was also brought to the fore. Michael Coveney noted the social and racial implications of the casting of the two Gobbos as black men (*Daily Mail*, 18 June 1999). Lancelot (Andrew French) and old Gobbo (Oscar James) were servants, the lowest of the low in society, the son trying to rise in the world as an entertainer in the Weimar 1930s by amusing the white crowd at the expense of the Jew. Perhaps unintentionally, this approach produced another momentary flash: with a black Lancelot on stage, Shylock's 'what says that fool of Hagar's offspring...?' (II.v.42) added a casual racial element to *his* prejudice.

In a superficially multicultural Venice, black and white people rubbed shoulders in cafés, suggesting a level of social mobility. Peter De Jersey as Salerio portrayed a man of colour moving in the higher echelons of Venetian life, which gave the audience the chance to observe his slow disillusionment, similar to that of Jessica. Smart, elegant, and suave, De Jersey's character was a foil to his thuggish white mates, Gratiano (Richard Henders) and Solanio (Mark Umbers). Fashionably indifferent, he drifted along, apparently as one of their set. In his review, Robert Smallwood noted that Salerio began to move away from the group, the first sign coming in III.i when he helped release the much older Shylock from the grip of the 'implacably racist Solanio'. In the trial scene, along with Portia, he was shocked by Antonio's demand for conversion; 'appalled by the behaviour of his fellow Christians', he intervened to restrain the 'loathsome Gratiano' (Smallwood, pp. 269–70; Fischer, p. 26).

Key to Nunn's interpretative approach was his choice to lay bare the instabilities and weaknesses of all characters, which allowed for shifts of empathy. The action opened with David Bamber's melancholy Antonio playing the piano in a swish Venetian café. The Northern inflections in his voice alerted British audiences to his difference from the metropolitan set (Smallwood, p. 268). A rich man from the industrial North, sexually repressed and uncertain in his social graces, he was both a cash-cow and an object of mockery. Salerio and Solanio had a bit of private fun mocking his accent, but no compunction in sneaking out and leaving him to pay their hefty bill. Like a Gatsby without the style and glamour, this Antonio was a paying outsider desperate to prove his credentials; his repressed yearnings for Bassanio felt as 'more of a chronic embarrassment than adoration' (Nicholas de Jong, *Evening Standard*, 18 September 1999). On occasion, in I.i, he would furtively run his fingers through Bassanio's hair when he had his back to him. John Drakakis notes Antonio's general instability, which culminated in the trial scene where he alternated between a 'suffering victim and eager sacrifice' for his love (p. 152). The idea of doubly-othering Antonio as a gay man and misfit among the metropolitan set helped make sense of his intense hatred for the other Other – Shylock. His pathological distaste for the Jew showed in the bond scene (which took place in the café), where he chose to sit as far away as possible from

Shylock. At the trial he carried a small Bible to help him 'suffer with a quietness of spirit' Shylock's 'tyranny and rage' (IV.i.11–12).

Alexander Hanson performed a 'most complex' Bassanio (Matt Wolf, *Variety*, 4 August 1999). He was 'quite a decent sort', which allowed for a genuine emotional relationship with Portia (Michael Billington, *Country Life*, 1 July 1999, p. 121). An impeccably mannered and turned-out aristocrat, 'his decency adrift in a Venice of thwarted loyalties', this Bassanio was riven with unease (Matt Wolf, *Variety*, 4 April 1999). Hanson conveyed the embarrassment of asking for help from a man whose advances he could not reciprocate, which gave the impression that this was not the first time he had tried to woo an heiress (Nicholas de Jong, *Evening Standard*, 18 September 1999). Like Portia, he rode on compromise, but unlike his young companions, he had a cultivated sense of what nobility is supposed to be, which made his choice in the casket scene convincing. In the end, he fully realised what he owed his wife, and distanced himself from his companions – a move strengthened by line transposition. 'Speak not so grossly' (V.i.266), a line which belongs to Portia, became his reprimand to Gratiano for the rude remark about cuckoldry (265). Hanson's manner showed genuine contrition and commitment to honour his new pledge 'never more [to] break an oath with [her]' (248), a promise which came as a visible shock to Antonio.

Behind the front of steely politeness, Henry Goodman's darkly scintillating Shylock hid the vulnerability of a widower with a grown-up daughter on his hands. In the world of the play, he was another lonely Other, sustained by his financial clout, faith, and family. Though socially at ease in public, he was always on the alert. While indulging himself in telling the story of Laban's sheep with relish and humour, he also made sure he paid for his coffee and left a tip. Nunn's cutting of lines that could be seen as ethnic stereotyping, like Shylock's 'dreams of moneybags' (II.v.18) and his reference to Lancelot as 'a huge feeder' (44), also helped shape a sympathetic character, to which Goodman's sense of humour contributed enormously.

Right from their first encounter, it was clear that Shylock and Antonio were old adversaries. The loan deal would have fallen through had Bassanio not intervened. While Antonio flaunted his religiosity as part of a display of superiority and aggression,

Shylock's religious traditionalism was announced by the tzitzit under his jacket; his mannerisms and Yiddish accent, in turn, signalled his otherness.

Shylock had another side hidden from the world, which the production meticulously developed. Textual augmentation and scenic detail conjured up a patriarchal domesticity at a breaking point. Yiddish conversation and Hebrew prayer divulged a heart-wrenching emptiness in his life, visualised by Leah's photograph, set between two candles. Giving Shylock a domestic history is a theatrical tradition to which Nunn added richly emotive details. In II.v, before leaving the house for dinner with the Christians, father and daughter sang Eshet Chayil ('A Woman of Virtue'), the Sabbath prayer by which husband and children pay tribute to the mother of the house (Edelman, p. 265). Shylock's love for Jessica was intensely possessive. It made sense as part of his patriarchal attitudes but also psychologically. He was a man who did not know how to deal with his grown-up daughter. Susan Fischer perceptively describes his state of embarrassed overreaction as 'he alternatively smacked and hugged [Jessica], kissed the picture of his departed spouse, and put his hand on his forehead in a medley of fear, love and disgust' (p. 26).[3] Making Jessica the mainstay of his world was a step towards explaining the events after her elopement. Upon his return home, instead of the received stage business of a hectic search for his daughter, Nunn underscored the portent of the moment by silence. As Shylock knocked on the door, the lights went out, a dog barked, and darkness hid distress.

In III.i, Goodman's acting conveyed both the pain of a man who had lost everything dearest to him and a determination to stand up to Solanio's racist insults. The decision to take revenge came only after Tubal's news about Jessica's spending spree combined with that about Antonio's losses. This was an unpremeditated decision, one made at a moment of extreme pressure, as underscored by the transposition of 'If I can catch him once upon the hip' (I.iii.42–3). Jewish loss was further suggested by astutely chosen visual detail. Tubal appeared carrying a cardboard suitcase, which evoked associations with the displacement of European Jews in the immediate aftermath of the period when the production was set. John Nolan's 'unsympathetic and unkempt' character was another social Other. A social inferior to the banker who had sent him to look for his daughter; he dutifully presented receipts for his expenses (Fischer, p. 26).

On the other side of the play's symmetries, the production engaged with Portia's predicament through similarly delicate layering touches. Nunn gave Portia a household of sympathetic female servants while transposed lines fleshed out Balthazar's character, meaningfully doubled by John Nolan who also played Tubal. Derbhle Crotty's 'luscious and intense' character, clad in slinky dresses and fashioned as a mirror image of one of Klimt's supplicants, was desperate to break her bondage and find a husband to her own liking (Susannah Clapp, *Observer*, 20 June 1999). After the embarrassment of her first encounter with Morocco, the scene of his casket choice went some way to shift the audience's view of her. In the event, her reactions suggested that had Chu Omambala's classy Morocco (who might have attended an expensive private school in England) chosen right, Portia might not have been unhappy to become his wife (Smallwood, p. 268). Her words, 'May all of his complexion choose me so' (II.vii.79) were played against her actual feelings, and came across as a self-protective gesture before her servants (Sokolova, *Shakespeare Closely Read*, p. 106). Though partly diffused through the comedy of her embarrassment vis-à-vis Morocco, Portia's ingrained cultural superiority was punctured again in the scene with Arragon, where she made another *faux pas*. Assuming that the foppish Spaniard did not understand her language, she tried to explain with gestures what the test required, only to discover that he spoke quite good, although accented, English.

The other daughter, Gabrielle Jourdan's Jessica, followed a clear path of distress, guilt, and an increasing sense of displacement. Her flight from home was in equal measure an act of love for Lorenzo and a youthful rebellion against a desperately conflicted parent and his domestic oppression. A transposition of the text, 'O, Lorenzo, / If thou keep promise I shall end this strife, / Become a Christian, and thy loving wife' (II.iii.19–21), to the moment after Shylock slapped her before leaving for dinner in II.v was used to strengthen the case for her elopement. Even as she said the words, she clung to Leah's photograph.

Unprepared as she was for life outside the house, Jessica was overpowered by a sense of bereavement which grew to a frenetic pitch shortly after her arrival in Belmont. In spite of Portia's gentleness to her (not often seen in modern performance) and the loving care with which Daniel Evans's Lorenzo treated her, she felt uprooted and adrift. In V.i she lay on the checked stage floor as if crucified, while Lorenzo tried to calm her down. The end of the production homed in on her. For the finale, Nunn cut Gratiano's speech and gave Portia a collage of lines, starting with, 'This night methinks is but the daylight sick; / It looks a little paler' (V.i.124–5). In the ensuing lull, Jessica's disconsolate singing of Eshet Chayil tore the silence. Stunned, Portia responded with an evasive 'It is almost morning' (295). In the distance, a peal of thunder was heard, or was it the opening salvo of the war that would soon obliterate the Jews of Europe?

Unlike the other principal characters, Shylock and Portia meet only once, at the trial. In Nunn's rendition, this 'most morally harrowing' moment gathered into focus all the conflicts and let shine the director's ability to balance atmosphere and individual character reactions (John Peter, *Sunday Times*, 27 June 1999). Christians in uniform-like grey suits, aggressive and menacing, filled the stage. Like football hooligans, they applauded their own or rushed to attack Shylock and even Portia/Balthazar when she pronounced the initial verdict. The Duke (David Burt) kept losing his temper with Shylock. The courtroom was bursting with anti-Semitic energy, and Goodman's acting was alive to the vibes of aggression, but also to gentler persuasion. Portia's 'quality of mercy' speech was revelatory in this respect (IV.i.180). She took a chair, sat in front of Shylock, and spoke directly and privately to him. As Smallwood noted,

> never before ... [had] a member of the Christian community spoken to him with this degree of immediacy and it was curiously welcome. At the end he agonised for several tense painful seconds of almost unbearable suspense before a returning awareness of the Gratiano mob rekindled his resolve and he just managed to find the strength to say, 'My deeds upon my head'.
>
> (p. 269)

Edelman counted an 'astonishing' twenty-eight seconds before these fatal words were pronounced (p. 225).[4] The emotional intensity and volatility of the scene made it into 'a courtroom thriller, worthy of John Grisham' (Sheridan Morley, *Spectator* 26 June 1999).

Shylock's 'deeply and disturbingly perturbed' internal state became evident in his deliberate preparations for cutting the pound of flesh (David Nathan, *Jewish Chronicle*, 25 June 1999). Like Antonio who was pitifully quivering in the chair, mouthing the Lord's Prayer, Shylock said a prayer, then shakily approached his antagonist, only to stagger back to compose himself. Intent as he was on the deed, he was finding it hard to kill another human being. His defeat was meticulously orchestrated as well. Made to sit in the chair where Antonio had been tied until a moment before, Goodman's character recognised the statute quoted by Portia so much so that he joined in reciting it 'with weary, contemptuous familiarity', realising that there was no escape from *that* law (Smallwood, p. 270).

The brilliant execution of the scene included several novel *coups de théâtre*. As Ralph Berry maintains, Tubal is 'one of the key tests of an intelligent production of *The Merchant*', he is 'the sketch for a Jewish chorus .... [expressing] the attitude of the Jewish community toward Shylock' (p. 53). By bringing him into the courtroom, Nunn was following theatrical predecessors, but, as usual, made a point all his own. When Shylock decided to cut Antonio's flesh, Tubal got up and slowly walked out, making it clear that, as a Jew, he could not accept the bloodshed. In the morally blind world of Jew-baiting Christians, an act of moral judgement was delivered by a socially marginalised Other.

High tension swirled around Portia/Balthazar as well. Crotty's bespectacled character had no idea how to save Antonio.[5] She only thought of the clause about the 'drop of Christian blood' when Shylock tied a white cloth around his waist to protect his clothes from Antonio's blood. Portia's legal victory, however, was tarnished by the shock of observing Bassanio's friends' behaviour, and two further events. She had not expected Antonio's demand for conversion and was perturbed by it; furthermore, her presence in the courtroom had allowed her to see through the relationship between her husband and Antonio. No doubt she had more work to do to secure the bond of marriage, which she competently executed in Act V. The emotional rollercoaster of the trial scene concluded with a view of the pair of scales, brought in by Shylock, tipped one way by his kippah and tzitzit which he had angrily thrown on them, the gestures tantamount to tearing off pieces of his own flesh. This image foreclosed all comic possibilities and solidified the orchestration of events in Act V.

Trevor Nunn created 'a rare *Merchant* ... that must be labelled with its director's name' (Edelman, p. 284). Even more so, his production proved responsive to the rich colours of the play, its human relationships, its social tensions, and its challenges of class, race, and patriarchal oppression. It echoed with the larger sensibilities of a post-Holocaust culture, offered a polyphonic reading of the play and memorable performances, and justly deserves a place in the production history of *The Merchant of Venice*. It captured a tenuous moment of peace before the historical catastrophes of the twentieth century.

Notes

1 Jonathan Miller writes that the idea of setting the play in the nineteenth century was Olivier's, though their conceptions of the character were diametrically opposite. Olivier imagined Shylock in the received tradition 'as a grotesque, ornamentally Jewish figure'. He bought a 'pair of very expensive dentures, a big hook nose and ringlets', most of which were scrapped as he warmed up to Miller's interest in exploring bias in spite of apparent similarity. Only the dentures were eventually used, since Olivier 'had invested such a large amount of money that [Miller] did not feel justified to ask him to surrender them' (p. 107).
2 The part earned Goodman an Olivier Award for Best Actor in 2000.
3 Some of the business, including Shylock's slapping of Jessica, can be traced back to John Barton's productions for the Royal Shakespeare Company (1976, 1978, and 1981), but also to film (see Part II, Chapter VI).
4 Jonathan Miller seems to be the first to have conceived of the scene as private, setting it in a small office.
5 Judi Dench also played Portia as taken aback by Shylock's rejection of the argument about mercy and only thinking of an escape clause at the last minute in the 1971 RSC production of *The Merchant* directed by Terry Hands (see Part I, Chapter I).

IV

Desperate outsiders in a money-drunk world: *The Merchant of Venice* directed by Daniel Sullivan (2010) and Rupert Goold (2011)

The beginning of the second decade of the twenty-first century saw high-profile productions of *The Merchant of Venice* on two of the most popular US and UK stages, both supported by public funding. In the summer of 2010, Daniel Sullivan (1940–) directed the play for the Delacorte stage of the Public Theater in New York City's Central Park; the production starred Al Pacino in his second take on Shylock's role after the 2004 film directed by Michael Radford (see Part II, Chapter VI). In November 2010 it transferred to the Broadhurst Theatre on Broadway for a two-month run, with some cast alterations. In the summer of 2011, Rupert Goold (1972–) staged the play for the Royal Shakespeare Company in Stratford-upon-Avon, with Patrick Stewart revisiting the part of Shylock after his 'tough and unsentimental' performance of the character under John Barton's direction at the Other Place, the RSC chamber stage, in 1979 (Gilbert, *Shakespeare at Stratford*, p. 21). Shortly after assuming artistic directorship of the Almeida Theatre in London, Goold revived his *Merchant* there, this time with Ian McDiarmid as Shylock (2014).

In addition to the star status of the actors performing Shylock, the commercial and artistic success of these productions was due in no small part to provocative decisions about characterisation and genre. Both directors gave the Belmont heiress the attention they afforded to Shylock; both asked audiences to revise their first initial impressions of these characters. Although both productions flirted with crowd-pleasing spectacles (Sullivan's with vaudeville numbers, Goold's with the genre of the TV reality show), by the end they established a poignant continuity between the trials of Portia and Shylock. This dynamic meant that, while Sullivan and Goold ultimately expunged the romance from the comedy in the manner embraced by many post-Holocaust productions, they only did so after enticing the audience with a good measure of glamour and comedic cheer. Without resorting to explicit topicality (one might even say, by carefully sidestepping it), they focused on the morally corrosive power of money in a cold, profit-driven world – a long-established didactic approach to the play which resonated with the widespread social anxiety and desperation felt in the aftermath of the 2008 stock market crash.

The Merchant in New York: provocation without outrage

Daniel Sullivan's production was only the second *Merchant of Venice* on the Delacorte stage, after Joseph Papp's 1962 production at the new home of the New York Shakespeare Festival (later renamed Free Shakespeare in the Park). The huge 1,892-seat amphitheatre seated audiences of diverse cultural, racial, and economic backgrounds. Papp cast a popular movie star, George C. Scott, as Shylock, who endowed the character with dignity and righteous anger – the mandatory North American approach after the Second World War.[1] Nonetheless, fears that the play would ignite anti-Semitism among theatregoers caused outrage among the secular and religious Jewish leaders of New York City. The telecasting by CBS of the play's opening night proved so controversial that the network building was picketed by 'representatives of the Jewish War Veterans and its women's auxiliary' (Basso, p. 79).

No such furore met Sullivan's production in spite of its provocations. Pacino's Shylock was a man both 'sinned against and sinning' (Joe Dziemianowicz, *Daily News*, 16 November 2010). Byron Jennings's Antonio conveyed 'the wide range of love and disdain at his character's core'. 'Hamish Linklater [was] callous and romantic' as Bassanio (Christopher Byrne, *Villager*, 14–21 July 2010).[2] Lily Rabe's Portia morphed from 'a rich girl (with a trace of Katharine Hepburn's madcap heiresses)' and a penchant for wry, epigrammatic humour (Ben Brantley, *New York Times*, 1 July

2010) into 'a brutal woman who takes almost sadistic pleasure in toying with her adversary' (Erik Haagensen, *Back Stage*, 8 July 2010). Such ambiguous characterisation served the play's duality well; furthermore, the approach matched the audience's wariness of seemingly clear-cut resolutions in the age of Wall Street bubble-busting and bank bailouts. Money was at the cold heart of the play's Edwardian world: Shylock was inseparable from his moneyboxes – which bore an uncanny resemblance to the caskets in Belmont – while the actions of the Christian Venetians centred on a ticker-tape machine and a manual exchange board next to it. Sullivan sidestepped the opportunities for racial critique afforded by the playtext and solidified the reading of *The Merchant* as a Jewish play.

The critics, too, turned a blind eye to matters of race. With some caveats, they praised the production as 'supremely intelligent ... somber and stately' (David Cote, *Time Out New York*, 18 November 2010), sweeping the audience 'with ... hell-bent momentum' (Terry Teachout, *Wall Street Journal*, 15 November 2010). Among the harshest comments was Stephen Greenblatt's negative comparison of Pacino's Shylock to the psychological intensity with which Laurence Olivier (see Part I, Chapter IV), Antony Sher, and Henry Goodman (see Part II, Chapter III) had endowed the character: 'His Shylock had no inner life or psychic resources, no baffled search for a source of comfort, no deep pathos, no gleeful intelligence, no sly comedy ... But Pacino did convey one thing brilliantly: what Shylock calls "a lodged hate and a certain loathing" he feels for the Christian Antonio' (*New York Review of Books*, 30 September 2010).

Indeed, for over half of the play, Pacino delivered not representational but presentational intensity, not a psychologically conflicted character but a provocative stereotype – albeit one not quite as outrageous as those offered in Peter Zadek's productions (see Part II, Chapter II). Theatre critic Hilton Als saw Shylock as 'less a character than an idea' (*New Yorker*, 12 July 2010). Although he belonged to an Orthodox Jewish community, which Sullivan took some pains to establish, he was alone in playing up a vaudevillian ethnic caricature. Clad in an Orthodox costume, Pacino used a signature rasp and verbal cadences, emphatic gesticulation, and incessant nervous movement, which set him apart from the crisply dressed, poised, and (cautiously) polite Christian Venetians with their polished classical enunciations. His height was minimised by stooped posture. As Greenblatt pointed out, 'next to Byron Jennings's lean, anguished Antonio or Lily Rabe's statuesque Portia, he looked positively shrunken'. Yet there was a method to Shylock's unceremoniously stereotyping histrionics. They were sometimes deployed for his own amusement and that of the audience, sometimes as a coping mechanism in a life of humiliation, but mostly to rile up his Christian adversaries and goad them into exposing the viciousness beneath their polite appearance.

Shylock's first scene was at once a vaudeville Jewish skit and a commentary on the genre. His aversion to all things Christian was comically exaggerated by the swift crossing of his arms to avoid Bassanio's eager handshake when he agreed to consider the loan. The gesture turned out to be a set-up for the punch line in response to the dinner invitation: 'Yes, to smell pork'; a laughter-inviting pause was followed by a sarcastic jab, 'to eat of the habitation which your Prophet the Nazarite conjured the devil into' (I.iii.30–1). Unused to such snubs, Bassanio was visibly startled – unlike Shylock, who was unfazed when Antonio avoided shaking his hand upon arrival. Daringly, Shylock held out his hand and stared the merchant in the eye, then half-turned to the audience with a shrug of mock disbelief at Antonio's hesitation. After Antonio grudgingly accepted the handshake, Shylock faced the auditorium with a conspiratorial grin.

As Shylock proceeded to recount the spurning and spitting humiliations of his life-story, vaudeville humour mutated into social drama. Antonio lost both physical and verbal decorum and had to be restrained by Bassanio. In contrast, the manner in which Shylock offered the 'merry bond' as a conciliatory gesture demonstrated his self-possession. He clearly enjoyed the power play. As Sullivan explained, 'He's thinking [that] the fact that Antonio would go so far as to sign such a bond is going to get out there in public' and humiliate the merchant (Charlie Rose, 21 December 2010, https://charlierose.com/videos/25941). In this scene, as in the delivery of 'Hath not a Jew eyes' (III.i.53–66), where Shylock's alternations between taunting and rage drove Solanio to lunge at him, the obnoxious little man forced an outburst of otherwise covert anti-Semitism.

Often, Shylock's vaudeville humour was ratcheted up to crudeness. He mimicked for Antonio the procreation act in Jacob and Laban's story, mimed the bond's provision of cutting the merchant's 'fair flesh', and inserted a suggestive pause when specifying that the cut would be from 'what part of your body … pleaseth me' (I.iii.146, 147). Ending the 'merry bond' offer with lewd laughter, he turned to the audience to invite them to join in on his ridicule of Antonio's closeted homosexuality. Ensuing chuckles suggested that Shylock did not have an exclusive prerogative over homophobia. Later, similar insinuations, physical miming, and nasty jibes were exchanged by Salarino and Solanio when they discussed Antonio's parting with Bassanio. In the larger context of the production, Shylock's vulgar taunting divulged the hypocrisy of polite society across cultures.

After the loss of Jessica and his money, Shylock's obnoxiousness tipped into viciousness. As Ben Brantley observes, 'the lines between wrathful avarice and paternal anguish blur beyond reckoning', creating a 'mirror of … the very soul of the money-drunk society [he] serves and despises' (*New York Times*, 1 July 2010). In III.i, Tubal was visibly concerned about the self-destructive effect of Shylock's hair-raising curse on Jessica, 'I would my daughter were dead at my foot, and the jewels in her ear' (80–1), but his gesture of consolation was rebuffed. The deranged intensity of this harsh moment marked a turning point from presentational to emotionally representational performance of the character.

By the trial scene, Shylock had steeled himself. As he attempted to exact the pound of flesh, he asserted again and again his craving for recognition as the Venetians' equal before the law. While Pacino deployed the familiar exaggerated gestures and intonations, this time around they were coloured by unmistakable sadness. Recalling Jessica's Christian marriage, he choked up. As the moment to exact the penalty drew near, he appeared crushed by the burden of the horror he sought to unleash, silently praying for strength to deliver the blow. Joshua Furst described Pacino's performance in this scene as capturing 'a pain that can't be understood by those to whom much has been given in this world. It's not a pound of flesh he wants, but dignity' (*Forward*, 23 July 2010). Dignity, as Shylock's tired stubbornness suggested, cannot be bought with money.

For all his pettiness, unpleasantness, and viciousness, Pacino's Shylock had the appeal of a gruff New Yorker. 'Like the best of us', Hilton Als explained, 'he is amped up and perpetually paranoid' (*New Yorker*, 12 July 2010). Als went on to describe the cadences used by Pacino as audience-'appealing New York City diction, a combination of black, Jewish, and Puerto Rican rhythms'. While in the world of the play, these cadences distinguished Shylock from Jewish and Christian characters alike, the production nonetheless gave him a supportive Jewish community. Tubal, always vigilant, defused the situation when Shylock, incensed that Antonio's privilege had allowed him to leave the jail and plead for his mercy, burst into screaming and lunged at the merchant (III.iii). At the end of this scene, another Jewish friend blocked an irate Solanio, who was itching for a fight. Tubal was given a non-scripted family, portrayed as quite close to Shylock. In a rare directorial choice, the soliloquy explicating Shylock's hatred for Antonio was delivered as a lesson to a young apprentice in his counting house:

> I hate him for he is a Christian;
> But more, for that in low simplicity
> He lends out money gratis, and brings down
> The rate of usance here with us in Venice.
> If I can catch him once upon the hip
> I will feed fat the ancient grudge I bear him.
>
> (I.iii.38–43)

We later realise that the apprentice was Tubal's son. Greenblatt comments:

> The grudge is 'ancient' not merely because it extends back through all the years that Antonio has spat upon and cursed Shylock but because it extends ... through the long, painful centuries of Jewish-Christian relations. For the Jews these relations have led to the ghetto and the economic life that Sullivan sketches in the first moments of the play, when the Jews circle outside the gates of the bourse and are angrily shooed away.
>
> (*New York Review of Books*, 30 September 2010)

Sullivan's direction suggests that Shylock took pains to keep this bitter public memory alive. Indeed, the personal was clearly political in his unveiling of the levers of economic dominance afforded by Christian privilege.

While Pacino's Shylock never grew to be a hero, a directorial addition to the playtext secured his haunting status in Jewish and Christian cultural memory. Following a waterboarding-like baptism and subsequent abandonment by the 'godfathers' (IV.i.394), Tubal and his son helped Shylock to his feet. Reeling, he donned his kippah and, after a touching farewell to the boy who tried in vain to pull him back, lunged toward the Christians. Miriam Gilbert discusses the forced conversion as the erasure of the Other – the culmination of ostracising the Other from sites of economic power portrayed in the play's opening.[3] She writes: 'Certainly, in a post-Holocaust world, productions have increasingly forced audiences to confront not only Shylock the Jew, but the society that cannot tolerate him, and may even try, unsuccessfully, to eradicate him' (*The State of Play*, p. 41). Sullivan shows that such eradication is doomed in the long run. Even as Shylock departed on what felt like a suicide mission, his defiance was imprinted on the memory of the scene's witnesses. In this production, memory was inscribed in the site of the action as well. When the lights came up again, Jessica (Heather Kind) was shown wading in the pool that had served as her father's baptismal font, her melancholy quickly morphing into bitter aggravation as she parried Lorenzo's classical recitations of love.[4]

In the interview with Charlie Rose, Sullivan shared that Pacino's interest in revisiting Shylock after playing the part in Radford's film was driven by a desire to continue the exploration of the character's relationship with Portia in the trial scene.[5] Lily Rabe, critics concurred, performed a Portia who matched Pacino's Shylock in strength and interest. The production also unveiled parallels between these characters, whose trials, legal and moral, set them on a collision course.

Rabe's Portia had a histrionic streak similar to Shylock's, albeit of the amusing rather than the sardonic type. In several scenes she entered with dramatic aplomb, costumed in finely fitted gowns in shades of red, striking a pose. Her delight in playacting was announced from the moment she appeared in the first Belmont scene (I.ii) on top of a spiral staircase, 'posing for a photograph that will be part of the lottery her father devised to determine her husband' (Joe Dziemianowicz, *Daily News*, 16 November 2010). A vaudeville double act followed, in which she quickly established rapport with the audience as Nerissa listed the suitors. In an interview, Rabe shared that her initial unease about the scene dissipated when she approached it as 'a bit of a standup act' used to elicit audience laughter (Basso, p. 182).

In the next Belmont scene (a consolidation of the two scenes with Morocco), Portia switched roles from entertainer to entertained. Unlike the creative use of vaudeville-style numbers by Shylock to reveal and ridicule anti-Semitic attitudes, Morocco's show deployed straightforward racial stereotyping. It opened with a stick dance, the military-drill emulation developed on American plantations and popularised in nineteenth-century minstrel shows. It also featured practical jokes, abundant sexual innuendo, and high-pitched vocalising. The crude humour of this performance elicited gracious applause on Portia's part; later, she offered a well-trained display of empathy when Morocco read the verdict from the gold casket. With the deletion of Portia's comment about his complexion, she was free to wear her privilege politely, without the stain of overt racial prejudice. In expunging Portia's racism – a choice also made in Radford's film (see Part II, Chapter VI) – Sullivan followed a long tradition of focusing exclusively on the play's revelation of anti-Semitism, rather than on the many strands of xenophobia present in the plot.

Beyond Portia's theatrical strengths as both performer and gracious spectator, she was an adept director, with considerable sway over the staging of her suitors' casket choices. Both she and Nerissa were aware of what each one contained, as was evident from the way they custom-tailored the arrangement, foregrounding the casket that each suitor was supposed to choose. Portia and Nerissa were also humorously involved in the staging of Bassanio's choice. High on the spiral staircase, Portia directed the scene and indulged in another stand-up routine, cheering Bassanio on with a full-throttled 'Go, Hercules!' (III.ii.60), much to the delight of audiences both on- and off-stage. The musical number that followed was the last vaudeville element in the play: a barbershop-style quartet with Gratiano singing 'Tell me where is fancy bred', supported by three female servants.

Bassanio's savvily orchestrated choice of the correct casket was also the moment when Portia's light-hearted playacting shifted into emotional expressiveness. Her days of performing and devising comic entertainment to exert control over her life were over. From this moment on, her problem was Bassanio's authenticity. A second challenge cropped up during the trial. Elated by her newly won freedom, Portia (as Balthazar) entered the courtroom with the confidence afforded by her privilege and acting ability, never doubting the potency of her punch line, 'Then must the Jew be merciful' (IV.i.178). Shylock's retort, 'On what compulsion must I?' (179) took her by surprise; she needed to pause and collect herself for the mercy speech, which was met with utter indifference by Shylock. Flummoxed by the logic of the religious and ethnic Other who had himself never benefited from mercy, and betrayed by Antonio's and Bassanio's public commitment to each other, a seething Portia toyed briefly with Shylock before unleashing her rage and the violence of the law against the 'alien' (345). Like Shylock's desire for revenge, this rage was also destructive – to Shylock, certainly, but also to her foundational belief in mercy as the greatest good.

The fallout was evident in Sullivan's sombre staging of the final Belmont scene. After the rings were returned and the ventures believed lost were recovered, the bitter couples drifted silently apart. Jessica and Portia remained on stage 'in solitary spotlights, contemplating the huge, hard grasp of outsiderness' (Linda Winer, *Newsday*, 15 November 2010). The pool that doubled as Shylock's baptismal font shimmered with haunting memories.

Whatever their individual fates, all characters appeared trapped in Mark Wendland's mammoth set of concentric metal railings. In the play's opening, these railings divided those with access to the heart of the economic power from the outsiders without such access. By the end, the metal bars looked like a prison where all were inmates.

Rupert Goold's *Merchant* in Las Vegas: to 'provoke and unprovoke'

After a string of Shakespeare productions praised for their edgy modernity and inventive relocations brought Rupert Goold to prominence during the early 2000s, his *Merchant of Venice* (2011, revived in 2014) strongly divided critics.[6] Concept-driven, like his enthusiastically received *Tempest* (2006), *Macbeth* (2007), and *Romeo and Juliet* (2010), it drew critical fire which at times acquired a personal and political edge. Critics either loved it or hated it. In language foreshadowing the culture wars of the incipient decade, the director was lambasted for his 'egomaniacal showiness', the production was branded 'as worthless as fool's gold', and the RSC was condemned as a 'left-wing' theatre (Quentin Letts, *Daily Mail*, 20 May 2011). For Charles Spencer, the chosen setting became emblematic of the attraction and the failure of the production: 'this unusually entertaining' production felt 'false and hollow – just like Las Vegas itself' (*Daily Telegraph*, 20 May 2011). Even voices appreciative of Goold's exuberant directorial thinking concluded that 'extremes ... flatten out subtleties' (Libby Purves, *The Times*, 20 May 2011). In measured tones, Michael Billington reminded his readers that Goold was not the first to connect the play with capitalism; but unlike Peter Zadek and David Thacker, who had translated it to the banking world (see Part II, Segue), he had relocated it to other sites of frenzied capitalism – the gambling tables of Las Vegas casinos and the reality TV games of self-indulgent consumerism (*Guardian*, 20 May 2011). Paul Taylor took the occasion to point to an earlier example of the play's transposition to the USA, Peter Sellars's critically divisive 1994 production (see Segue). He concluded that Goold's was a pertinent choice because 'few non-fully criminal places on earth could expose Christian superiority about money more vividly than this glittering excrescence in the Nevada desert' (*Independent*, 24 May 2011). Though critical opinion had misgivings about the execution of the concept, in the end it largely approved of this post-Holocaust-with-a-difference reading of *The Merchant*, a production that 'purists may balk [at]' but were unlikely to be able to resist (John Nathan, *Jewish Chronicle*, 26 May 2011). In addition to the unconventional setting and the American accents, critics singled out numerous allusions to films, such as *Batman and Robin* (1997),

Fear and Loathing in Las Vegas (1998), and *Legally Blonde* (2001). All noted the novelty of turning the casket scenes into a reality TV show.[7] The focus on 'Portia's tragedy' (Kate Bassett, *Independent on Sunday*, 22 May 2011), which placed her at 'the heart of the play' (Neil Norman, *Daily Express*, 20 May 2011), also drew critical approval. For Miriam Gilbert, the final foregrounding and isolation of Portia 'was the stunning interpretation of the RSC's 2011 production' (*State*, p. 30). All were impressed by Patrick Stewart as Shylock. Alan Dessen saw his character as 'the polar opposite of the stage tradition stretching back to Sir Henry Irving' of performing the play as Shylock's tragedy. Rather, Stewart created a character who 'had been bested but not broken' (*Shakespeare Bulletin*, p. 46).

Goold's theatre frequently avails itself of the language of contemporary popular culture and film. His long-time collaborator, Adam Cork, has commented on the director's interest in the innovative use of film language in the theatre medium (Cork, qtd. in Grochala, pp. 3–4). Goold's *Merchant* continued his sustained reimagining of the classics, begun in the 1990s and in the work he did with Headlong (2005–13), a company which 'changed the course of British drama' (Matt Trueman, *Telegraph*, 26 March 2019). Some have seen the influence of contemporary European theatre in Goold's impulse to re-envision old plays (Ben Power, qtd. in Grochala, p. 1). Others have aligned him with Bill Alexander, John Barton, and Jonathan Miller, pointing out the balance he strikes between the close reading of the texts and his novel settings and aesthetic solutions (Grochala, pp. 2–3). According to Sarah Grochala, 'the familiar social worlds or genre tropes the director layers onto texts act as lenses enabling the audience to see the text more clearly' (pp. 2–3). The 'lens' used in *The Merchant* was suggested by Patrick Stewart, who had already agreed to play Shylock. In an interview, Stewart remembers what happened:

> [I]n the early 2000s, I was talking to the screenwriter and playwright John Logan on the set of the *Star Trek* films. *The Merchant* came up ... Three weeks later, a script turned up. It was a brilliant concept: the play was set in contemporary Las Vegas. The language was intact, but everything else was updated ... It was wonderful. You realise how much the play is about money: everything has a price, even love.
>
> (Interview by Andrew Dickson, *Guardian*, 22 August 2016)

Though the funding for that production disappeared weeks from the beginning of filming, the idea stayed with Stewart, who shared it with Goold.[8] With Logan's permission, Las Vegas, complete with a Lancelot Gobbo as an Elvis impersonator, appeared on the RSC stage in 2011 and in the Almeida Theatre, where Goold reprised the production, in 2014.

The set, created by Tom Scutt, ushered the audience into a floodlit casino with elegantly curving symmetrical stairs leading into a gaming area, complete with golden palm trees, fruit machines and roulette tables. High on the back wall of this temple of excess, a skimpily clothed female figure held her arms open against a gaming wheel, inviting punters to 'give and hazard all [they] have' (II.vii.16). With the aid of Rick Fisher's lighting and blithe, filmic transitions, the space beguilingly transformed into a TV studio, Portia's and Shylock's homes, or a slaughterhouse basement. New spaces were conjured up in the blink of an eye: a car, a lift, a private corner; screens magnified the faces of the contestants for Portia's wealth; aerialists filled the space above. An unstable world swirled and dazzled (Figure 17).

The play started with an extended pre-show, a frequent choice in recent productions of *The Merchant* (Gilbert, *State*, p. 18), which established the atmosphere and created a continuum between auditorium and stage. As audiences drifted into the theatre, the vast RSC thrust stage slowly filled with gamblers, scantily dressed high-heeled waitresses, and hangers on. At one of the tables, Scott Handy's Antonio was obviously losing money. People seemed to be recruited from among the crowd in the auditorium to join a game on the stage; later, these were recognised as Morocco and Arragon. The audience space blended with that of the stage on several occasions in the course of the play.

With an explosion of light and colour and a booming 'Viva Las Vegas' performed by an Elvis impersonator later identified as Lancelot Gobbo, the casino world came to life. The lyrics of Elvis's song burst with the febrile excitement of 'neon flashin'', 'pretty girls ... livin' the devil may care', with the dream promised by the 'blackjack and poker and the roulette wheel', and the fizzle of 'hopes down the drain'. The lyrics offered a key to the play's world. Following this opening salvo, a sustained line of musical cues underpinned

Figure 17 Tom Scutt's casino set with Rebecca Brewer as Stephanie (front left), Susannah Fielding as Portia (rear left), Emily Plumtree as Nerissa (rear right), and Merry Holden as Conscience (front right) in Rupert Goold's revival of *The Merchant of Venice* at the Almeida Theatre, London, 2014.

the action. Lancelot (Jamie Beamish) made his decision to leave Shylock against the background of another Elvis hit, 'It's Now or Never'; he strummed 'Are You Lonesome Tonight' to the lovesick Jessica; the same tune underscored Portia's solitary dance, which provided the searing closing image of the production. In contrast to the Elvis hits that spoke of the desires of the young denizens of Venice and Belmont, Shylock's musical line articulated his otherness. Like his accent, the aural world surrounding him was Central European. Along with the stately sound of Wagner's *Parsifal* one could hear traditional Jewish melodies. Jessica's predicament was marked by the strains of Liu's self-sacrificial aria from Puccini's opera *Turandot*, another story about marriage by lottery. The cinematic use of music signalled shifts in emotional tone and 'guided the audience response' (Rogers, p. 733).

American accents (challenging for the British cast) were used to ground the play in specific social milieux. As hostesses in *Destiny*, the reality TV show standing for the casket lottery (Figure 18), Portia and Nerissa performed with the 'ditziness' of stereotypical Californian 'Valley Girls'; off-air, they reverted to their normal Southern accents (Prescott, p. 252). Locked by 'Mah daddy's will' into an insipid contest in which she was herself the prize, Susannah Fielding's Portia was in a situation not dissimilar to that of Britney Spears ('Directing Shakespeare', 7 July 2016, www.youtube.com/watch?v=2VwH8ZNRVZs&list=RDCMUCWXfkNfLqo-gVaJJ_ujqWTQ&start_radio=1&rv=2VwH8ZNRVZs&t=0).Though she hated every moment of it, she performed with professional aplomb, likely because she had been groomed for the part from childhood by an ambitious father (Prescott, p. 252). A similar idea emerged in the scenes involving Morocco and Arragon, where a small, dolled up girl sat on the stage, silently watching the proceedings. Was she too being groomed? Placing her downstage-centre seemed to suggest as much, while also underscoring the play-within-a-play nature of the casket scenes.

Costumes and acting styles were exaggerated to the point of garishness. Portia sported a flared pink miniskirt, platform shoes, and a stiff Dolly Parton-style blond wig. Her suitors – a black boxer in golden shorts, an absurd Mexican, and a no less ludicrous Hercules-Bassanio – all wore costumes 'that invited mockery, recalling the willing humiliation the contestants endured on shows such as *The Price Is Right*' (O'Connor, p. 27). Portia gave vent to her true feelings the moment the 'Off-Air' sign lit up. Her Southern accent added subtext to her racist remark about Morocco's skin colour, and brought out her 'nastier qualities' (O'Connor, p. 27). These became evident in her condescending treatment of Jessica and her assault on Shylock in the trial scene. The Southern belle switched effortlessly between acting the 'unlessoned girl' (III.ii.159), the racist, and the Jew-basher, while also revealing a woman who craved love, something the audience was invited to empathise with.

The absurdity of deciding the future of a modern young woman by way of a game show elicited a margin of pathos, which Fielding captured in Portia's speech to Bassanio, in III.ii. Her wig and platform shoes removed, a much smaller, dark-haired, vulnerable-looking girl appeared 'such as [she is]' (150) under the mask, with a deep-seated desire for love. After the garishness of the lottery, Portia's shedding of the TV persona created a moment of genuine

Figure 18 The 'Destiny' TV show hosted by Portia (Susannah Fielding) and Nerissa (Emily Plumtree) in Rupert Goold's production for the Royal Shakespeare Company, Stratford-upon-Avon, 2011.

audience empathy, as it also involved a chilling recognition that Bassanio (Richard Riddel) was not particularly interested in her. He planted a small peck on her cheek for the 'loving kiss' she expected, and mostly stood apart (III.ii.138). The blocking foreshadowed the even larger distance gaping between them in the last scene.

Within this world of gross superficiality, greed, and betrayal, Patrick Stewart's suave, cultured Shylock 'seemed to inhabit another production', as a negative review put it (Charles Spencer, *Daily Telegraph*, 20 May 2011). Noting and interpreting this disjunction, Coen Heijes contends that the production presented a Shylock whose culture and character were 'unintelligible to the world around him' (p. 97) – a major difference with previous interpretations of the part.

Externally indistinguishable from the Christians, Stewart's Shylock belonged to the upper echelons of the business world. Equally at ease in the casino and the office, he negotiated his encounters with the Venetians with a sense of quiet superiority and controlled disdain. His aside, 'How like a fawning publican he looks' (I.iii.37), often cut in performance, was preserved, though substituting 'politician' for 'publican'; his menacing hiss in delivering 'Hath not a Jew eyes' (III.i.53–73) left 'no question about the motives behind the supposedly merry bond' (Dessen, *Shakespeare Bulletin*, p. 45). His slight European accent and impossible wish to keep his daughter away from the world in which he made his money hinted at ancestral memories; Jessica's elopement rekindled his allegiance to tradition. Neither his smart grey suits, nor the golf putts in his enormous office, nor his irony could erase the humiliation of having been spat upon. In III.i, the ingrained anti-Semitism of Venice was made overt through the reactions of the minor characters, as 'Aidan Kelly's Mafia-like ... Solanio greeted Shylock with a hiss ... [of] the kind heard in gas chambers' (John Nathan, *Jewish Chronicle*, 26 May 2011). Shylock's answer to this was a ferocious 'If you prick ussss do we not bleed?' (58). From there, the way to the synagogue and the fatal oath lay wide open. The release of the pent-up tension, once Shylock sent Tubal for an officer, found physical expression in a dance performed by Stewart, which anticipated Portia's solitary twirl in the final moments of the production. In an interview, the actor explained that it expressed 'the anger, the determination, trying to hide the sadness by stamping it away, the potential for violence, the Jewishness, being human with all of these contradictory human emotions' (Heijes, *Multicultural Shakespeares*, p. 97).[9]

These contradictions came to a head in the trial scene, which was set in a basement of what seemed like an abattoir, with animal carcasses visible through plastic sheeting. Justice was to be delivered by a Mafioso-type Duke and his henchmen. Both Shylock and Portia were uneasy in this setting, and both appeared transformed for the occasion. Now dressed in a kippah and tallit, Shylock pronounced his name as 'Sheelak', and read his demands out of a printed document. He laced his speech with imitations of the sounds of the animals mentioned in it. This may have helped to disguise his emotions, but he was clearly in pain when he refused to show mercy. Despite her male persona, Portia was completely unprepared for the dark cellar and gave a shortened and rather self-consciously unconvincing version of the mercy speech. She was shocked by the terms of the bond and by her husband's physical closeness with Antonio. Observing with mounting horror Shylock's elaborate preparations to apply a butcher's knife to the merchant's flesh, she recognised in Antonio's passivity and readiness to die for his 'love' (IV.i.274), the depth of her husband's betrayal. Nor did her legal masterstroke of citing the Alien Act yield the desired effect on Shylock. When he realised he had lost, he pulled out a gun, though it was quickly wrenched from his hand by the guards.

The moment of Antonio's vindictive mercy showed two dejected men kneeling against each other: Shylock, following Portia's command to get down and 'beg mercy of the Duke' (IV.i.359), and Antonio, slumped down after being released from his ordeal. With a grand gesture, Stewart stood up, threw his kippah and tallit down, trampled on them, and was pelted by a gob of spittle from Gratiano. History had come full circle: whether in a suit or religious garb, the Other was once again reviled and humiliated. But this Other knew he was going to make it yet again and left with a 'sneaky smile' on his face (Dessen, *Shakespeare Bulletin*, p. 47). A Hispanic janitor, another 'purchased slave' of capitalism (IV.i.80), stuffed what had been sacred into a black bin bag. The action reminded the audience that Venice and Belmont relied on the service of Others – people who could be used, scapegoated, or kicked out when, like Shylock, they became threatening (Davidhazi, pp. 272–5).

While the final act of the production preserved a modicum of peace in Lorenzo and Jessica's love duet and offered a brief moment of shared emotion, the endgame after the return of the men was deeply disturbing. Gratiano roughed up Nerissa when he thought he might have lost her to another man. Portia sat on the sofa (the one from the *Destiny* show) squeezed between Antonio and Bassanio, who held hands behind her back. As she promised to 'answer all things faithfully' (V.i.299), she got up and pulled her blond wig and platform shoes from her travel bag, but only managed to put one shoe on. Twirling slowly on one heel, limping on the other leg, wig in hand, she was the epitome of dejection. Elvis's 'Are You Lonesome Tonight' filled the air. Its words, as Gilbert has observed, were richly resonant with the moment: 'someone said that the world's a stage' ... 'You read your line so cleverly and never missed a cue', 'Now the stage is bare' (*State*, pp. 33–4).

On one side of the stage stood Lorenzo and Jessica. On the other, Nerissa left unanswered Gratiano's call to join him in bed. Indeed, she was on her way out.

While Goold's production of *The Merchant* was memorable for its spectacular theatricality, bold reimagining of the setting, excellent performances, and for bringing Portia's plight to the fore, some of the criticism levelled against it needs to be borne in mind. As Prescott contends, this was a piece of theatre that 'was never entirely in control of its own political effects': Portia and Nerissa were 'unnervingly confected to titillate the male gaze', while the 'displays of taboo behaviours' in the scenes involving the suitors 'missed their mark' (pp. 252–3). The representation of Jewishness in turning a suave Shylock into a murderous religious fanatic also raised a few eyebrows (John Nathan, *Jewish Chronicle*, 18 December 2014). One can indeed relate to the question of whether a place closer to home than Las Vegas would have helped strike a deeper and more resonant chord with the British audience. Instead of viewing the inanities of capitalist excess, greed, and xenophobia as somehow inherent in other Western societies, a closer look into contemporary British society might have produced, if not a more spectacular, then surely a more topical reading of this problematic Shakespeare play.

Notes

1 The Anglo-American post-war tradition of staging Shylock as a noble and heroic character continued in major performances by Sydney Walker in Ellis Rabb's 1973 production at the Lincoln Center (see Part I, Chapter VII), by Paul Butler in Peter Sellars's 1994 touring production (see Part II, Segue), by Hal Holbrook in Michael Kahn's 1999 production for the Shakespeare Theater in Washington, DC, and by F. Murray Abraham in Darko Tresnjak's 2007 production for New York's Theatre for a New Audience.
2 Linklater was replaced by David Harbour when the play transferred to Broadway.
3 Another prominent production featuring a conversion scene was Shakespeare's Globe's *Merchant of Venice* directed by Jonathan Munby (2015) with Jonathan Pryce as Shylock (Gilbert, *State*, pp. 36–7).
4 Keith Warner's 2013 production of André Tchaikowsky's eponymous opera (1968–82) for the Bregenz Festival, Austria, made a similar use of design to introduce a bitter overtone to Jessica's and Lorenzo's relationship in Belmont by relating it to Shylock's devastating defeat. In this case, an enamoured Jessica splashed her face in the water filling the tomb-sized silver casket into which Shylock had silently submerged himself minutes before.
5 Portia's lines in the trial scene were substantially cut in Michael Radford's film.
6 By the time he did *Macbeth* at the Chichester Festival (2007), Goold had directed *Romeo and Juliet* (1998), *Othello* (2003), and *Hamlet* (2005); he would go on to stage *King Lear* in 2008.
7 An earlier presentation of Portia's lottery as a game show was in the 1999 production of the play directed by Andrey Zhitinkin for the Mossovet Theatre, Moscow.
8 Stewart had already starred in two acclaimed Shakespeare productions under Goold's direction: *The Tempest*, RSC (2006), and *Macbeth*, Chichester Festival Theatre/West End, London/New York (2007)/DVD (2011).

9 In 1970, Laurence Olivier had performed a similar dance in Jonathan Miller's production, which was 'inspired by the little jig of triumph done by Adolf Hitler in a railway carriage in Compiègne when he heard that France had surrendered', and which Olivier had seen in a newsreel (Part I, Chapter IV).

V

Crises of the new millennium: *The Merchant of Venice* directed by Robert Sturua (2000) and Edward Hall (2009)

The first decade of the twenty-first century was bookended by two unconventional productions of *The Merchant of Venice*, both loudly resonant with the tensions and fears caused by major socio-political and financial catastrophes. Robert Sturua's *Shylock* at the Et Cetera Theatre in Moscow was staged after the collapse of the Soviet Union, in the depths of the post-communist crisis. Nine years later, Edward Hall's all-male touring company put on the play for British and American audiences in the throes of the global financial crisis of 2008. Devoid of moralising or sentimentality, these productions offered astute diagnoses of the social traumas of their historical moments. Sturua (1938–) transformed the genre of romantic comedy into a darkly satirical carnival; Hall (1966–) replaced comedy with vicious drama. Both productions focused on ruthless power struggles, laid bare the connection between money and violence, blocked the path to hope, and allowed hatred to triumph. An unforgiving, claustrophobic, xenophobic, money-obsessed Venice, light-years removed from Reinhardt's festive city of canals, became the central character once again. Both stagings deployed a distinctly postmodern approach: they featured metatheatrical and metacinematic elements, framing, *da capo* endings; they cut and reshuffled the playtext, and multiplied intertextual and intratextual quotations. The play's antagonists, Antonio and Shylock, were portrayed as mirror images of each other.

Sacred cows, golden piggy banks, and scapegoats

Sturua is regarded as the greatest postmodern director of the Soviet period still active in the post-Soviet world, with a life-long interest in Shakespeare and an impressive international reputation. Explorations of power dynamics have been central to his distinguished theatre career. It began in the 1970s, in his native Tbilisi, at the Shota Rustaveli Dramatic Theatre with which he has been connected for over half a century. Sturua's exuberantly theatrical style developed as a resistance to the dominant psychological tradition of the Soviet stage. While the roots of his inspiration can be traced back to the Georgian folk tradition, his artistic vocabulary has been influenced by Mikhail Bakhtin's formalist ideas and Brecht's epic theatre (Ivanov, pp. 28–9). Sturua's striking worlds oscillate between carnival and tragedy, comedy and farce; expressionistically abstract, rich in movement and dance, they are suffused with music. He has adapted more than half of Shakespeare's plays, teasing out themes that resound with modern audiences. Convinced by the events in the 1990s that at the moment 'making political theatre ... is impossible, while making theatre for sheer entertainment is immoral', his subsequent Shakespeare work has mixed entertainment with reflection (qtd. in Gavrilova, p. 40).

Sturua is interested in 'the impersonal structure of power' (Shatirishvili, p. 49), the arbitrary resolution of power struggles, and the irrelevance of ethical considerations to their outcome (Ivanov, p. 28), ideas of profound significance during the sociopolitical upheavals of the post-Soviet 1990s. The wild capitalist appropriation of the assets of the former communist state caused large swathes of the population to be severely impoverished amidst the rise of warring criminal oligarchies. Along with this cut-throat reparcelling of the economy, territorial conflicts erupted on the fringes of the former Soviet Union, some between Russia and its former republics, others among and within the newly formed independent states. Violent nationalisms weaponised religious differences, as in the Chechen and Nagorno-Karabakh wars of the 1990s. Historian Robert E. Hamilton notes that, though the post-Soviet transition is often described as peaceful, it was in fact accompanied by considerable violence: during the first post-communist decade, more than 130,000 people lost their lives while ethnic violence resulted in massive internal displacement.[1]

In such circumstances, the former Soviet citizen Robert Sturua found himself in the position of an immigrant in Moscow, sharing in the predicament of thousands of people who, as new borders were drawn, became Others in what used to be their own country. There, at the Et Cetera Theatre, he put on a cut and reassembled version of Shakespeare's *Merchant*, titled *Shylock*,[2] billing it as an exploration of 'the irrational impulse of xenophobia' (Oleg Zintsov, *Vedomosti*, 25 April 2000). In the context of raging ethnic conflicts, his production acquired resonances well beyond the relationship between Christians and Jews. As Sturua explained:

> The anti-Semitic and anti-Christian attitudes in *The Merchant of Venice* are just a starting point for reflection. The beginning of the twenty-first century has come to show that we all dislike the Other; we all suffer from the same malaise, but we don't want to talk about it ... We keep it under wraps, until [hatred] ... suddenly erupts. If we want to be cured, we should talk about it all the time.
>
> (qtd. in Gurski)

In 2000, Sturua's *Shylock*, along with Andrey Zhitinkin's production of *The Merchant of Venice* (also in Moscow), made history for another reason as well. Their appearance marked the end of a seventy-year gap in the performance life of the play which had practically disappeared from Soviet stages since the 1920s, though it had been popular before (Bartoshevich, Kommersant. ru, 17 April 2015; Sokolova, 'Mingled Yarn', pp. 88–9). In the vigorous critical discourse that ensued, these revivals were seen as grappling with ingrained Russian xenophobia, aggressively rampant during the post-Soviet ethnic wars of the 1990s (Dina Kirnarskaya, *Moskovskie novosti*, 21–27 December 1999; Roman Dolzhansky, Kommersant.ru, 25 April 2000). Thus, the influential critic Natalia Kaminskaya hailed the play's return as a sign of civic maturity and as inviting a public conversation about Russia's past and present. In her view, *The Merchant* compelled the audience to think about the dubious rewards 'we reap by searching for [Others] in the crowd and by trying to conceal ... prosaic ends behind lofty religious arguments and state interests' ('A Shylock Who Could be Called Shamil', *Kultura*, 9–15 December 1999). She praised Sturua's *Shylock* for empowering the theatre to speak about interethnic hatred unleashed by the division of the former Union (Kaminskaya, 'There's no justice here on earth', *Kultura*, 27 April 2000). Taking a longer view of Sturua's development and vision, Grigory Zaslavsky discerned in *Shylock* an indication of the director's mounting social pessimism: 'there is no room for hope', 'hatred triumphs', and the situation is 'more tragic than in the most tragic of *Hamlets*' (*Nezavisimaya gazeta*, 24 April 2000).

In a typical postmodernist fashion, Sturua adapted the text of Shakespeare's play to his needs by employing deep cuts and rearrangement, and by using stage props to give body to elements of Shakespeare's language. He transformed the narrative into a surrealist, eternally repetitive black comedy about the irrationality of human behaviour in the face of difference, which underlies ethnic hatred. Characters were reduced to a basic trait, like marionettes, and set into motion in a blatantly theatrical space. The pathos of their situation emerged in the interactions with their environment, which in the production's fantasy world was shaped by musical cues, rhythmical group movements, signature gestures, and emblematic properties. Sometimes realities merged; striking scenic pictures crystallised into fleeting visual allegories.

The production's theatricality was declared from the outset, when a conspiratorial-looking clown invited the audience to pay attention and opened the stage curtain. 'Venice' – created by Sturua's long-time collaborator, set designer Georgi Aleksi-Meskhishvili – comprised two asymmetrical white panels placed at an angle. One was the site of an office with a view of artificial trees; the other, with a balcony recess in the middle, was half-covered by a roughly sketched wrought-iron gate. The set blended inside and outside, private and public, mundane and absurd. Familiar objects appeared and disappeared, sometimes evoking elements of René Magritte's paintings – a cloud, cigar, bowler hat, apple, umbrella. In an openly metatheatrical gesture, a low platform, complete with a trapdoor, was placed downstage; there, literally, 'every man [played] a part' (I.i.78). To enter the action, characters were often introduced by name and then stepped onto the platform to do their scene, while those secondary to the action remained on the lower ground. Characters emerging through the trapdoor inhabited another time-space, brought bad news, or were mysterious and malicious. The heads of golden dummies – a cow, pig, and calf – peered from the left wing. At times, they were pushed forward, then pulled back. Were these dumb beasts the idols of a world obsessed with money, or primeval emblems of human qualities? In the course of the production, the pig came to signify the Christians' obsession with Shylock's Jewishness, or a piggy bank with readily accessible (Jewish) capital that they craved. Once the money was depleted, another animal symbol was introduced. At the riotous end of the court scene, Shylock was mounted backwards on the cow, a reference to an ancient Georgian ritual of shaming and scapegoating (Kaminskaya, 'There's no justice here on earth', *Kultura*, 27 April 2000).

An enigmatic 'Manipulator', a Borsalino-wearing Mafioso type in a black mac, hovered in the background, adding to the action a touch of cinematic *noir*. With the flick of a remote control, he brought to each office screen an image of a burning candle. From then on, he appeared to be in control, silently stage-managing the handing out of crucial properties: a magic wand that would become the temporary sign of a character's dominance over a situation, a red quill for signing the bond, a menorah with burning candles and a moth-eaten tallit that gave a religious aura to Shylock's desperate decision. This character spread rumours about ships lost at sea, gossiped about the absconding Jessica, and maliciously mouthed the news of Shylock being chased down the streets by jeering boys.

The soundscape of the play was multi-ethnic and cinematic. Ghiya Kancheli's score had a ritualistic power (Zaslavsky, *Nezavisimaya gazeta*, 24 April 2000); sound effects drew attention to the dreamlike quality of the action (an eerie rumbling sound opened the play), to moments of insight (a deep piano chord unlocked Bassanio's revelation about the right casket), and to heightened moments of emotion (falling in love was marked by a strike on a triangle).

The two main characters, Antonio and Shylock, mirrored each other. Scene One opened with Antonio (Viktor Verzhbitsky) on a high ladder. Dressed in an Oriental gown and pointy slippers he absent-mindedly perused books on an upper shelf, while two office clerks – Salanio and Salerio, one of them wearing a kippah – assiduously worked on stock exchange data at the desks next to him. The same pair inhabited Shylock's professional and domestic space. Antonio's first gesture was to point to the golden dummies that had moved forward, as if emblematising the turmoil in his mind. He was a man who cared little about money markets and was haunted by vague existential anxieties.

Antonio was more of an onlooker than agent in his emotionally empty life. Everything in it – money-making, friendship, love, even death – bore evidence of apathy and detachment, including his pining over Bassanio's portrait. As he cradled the portrait while lying in the middle of the platform, his homoerotic desire was made more apparent by the smirks of his office clerks rather than by his own emotion. The dreamy vagueness that characterised him was also visible in the interactions with his young friend. After Bassanio and his followers appeared marching in a military formation, and a thuggish Gratiano left his gun behind to test the authenticity of the merchant's 'melancholy', Antonio toyed with the idea of shooting himself, if for no other reason than to gauge Bassanio's reaction (Alexei Osipov). The latter easily wrestled the gun out of his hand and proceeded to rhapsodise about Portia, while the merchant feebly attempted to undermine his enthusiasm. 'From her eyes / I did receive fair speechless messages' (I.i.164) elicited a mocking echo, 'Speechless?'. Still, he conjured up Portia (Anastasiya Kormilitsina), who entered climbing over the office desks and proceeded to the platform upon the stage for Act 1, Scene 2. Thus Portia, whose story Bassanio read from a newspaper personal ad, was immediately associated with money-trading. In an added silent scene, Antonio organised Bassanio's theatrical dressing up for the journey to Belmont, which transformed the young man into a comic mannequin. Antonio also hovered by the platform for the scenes with Portia's suitors, offering her emotional succour from the parallel world he inhabited.

A most startling demonstration of Antonio's emotional vacuity occurred at the trial. There, he restlessly demanded the end of the proceedings and walked casually to the gurney where Shylock stood ready to take the pound of flesh with a scalpel. The declaration of his love to Bassanio and his self-sacrificial speeches were pitifully truncated. Portia's question, 'You, merchant, have you anything to say?', received an uninterested, 'But little ... I am prepared' (IV.i.259–260), which elicited a stunned response from Shylock: 'And that is all?'

Since Antonio had no emotional depth, his hatred for Shylock appeared essentially baseless. Given his lack of business acumen, his antagonism to the Jew seemed primarily driven by irrational xenophobia, embodied by the golden pig, the ultimate anti-Semitic symbol that came into prominent view as the production progressed. As religious references were mostly cut, including Shylock's 'I hate him for he is a Christian' (I.iii.38), what emerged as motivation was prejudice inherited from the depths of history. The choice of the Russian word 'zhid', a slur for 'Jew', in the translation, also pointed in this direction.

Both Venice and Belmont were rife with xenophobia. While racist language was whittled out of Portia's text, the endemic racism was unmistakable: Morocco's mention of his complexion was met by a guffaw from one of the clerks (II.i.1); together with all her household, Portia joined gleefully in reciting 'Thus hath the candle singed the moth' after Arragon's departure (II.ix.78). Most blatantly, as the Lady of Belmont welcomed Jessica to her home, she unceremoniously discarded the bouquet she had brought her. This microaggression was a visual manifestation of her attitude toward Jews, made evident earlier when she joined in the public laughter elicited by the report of Shylock's humiliation in the streets of Venice.

In the spiritually and emotionally empty Venetian world, religion-as-otherness was always an empty signifier of difference: crosses hung on chains around the necks of characters without a shred of spirituality about them, kippahs were used to mop up spilled coffee. Yet the constant visual presence of the golden pig suggested that cupidity, rather than religion, lay at the heart of Venetian anti-Semitism. Sturua transposed the line about the effect of new Christians on 'the price of hogs' (III.v.21–2) by turning it into a joke cracked by the Jewish office clerk, eliciting uneasy laughter from the audience. In the course of events, superficial differences were blown up to fully fledged aggression. The New Russians who tagged along with rich-boy Bassanio were a bunch of no-goods, led by a Gratiano who crossed himself with his gun in hand. During Jessica's elopement, they wore black balaclavas, like B-movie bank robbers. Gratiano hastened to tear off the star of David necklace she was wearing and put a cross around her neck (another moment underscored by a music cue).

With their focus on the brash machismo of the foreign suitors, the casket scenes with Morocco and Arragon (both performed by Vladimir Skvortsov) loudly proclaimed the crassness of the contenders for her hand. One was a travesty of a sheikh, the other, of a general. Both wielded weapons and aggressively invaded Portia's personal space. Even among the other marionette-like characters, these caricatures looked absurd. Critic Natalia Ligazhevska interpreted their overblown militarised masculinities as images of currently raging nationalisms, which, for all their differences, fundamentally resemble each other (*Shakespeare Gazette*, 9 August 2001). In this sense they were no different from Gratiano's thugs and just as ready to beat and humiliate. The Morocco of this production exited with an unmistakable terrorist threat: 'I will return, with fire!'

Unsurprisingly then, Portia, who was left profoundly distressed by these experiences, found superficially urbane Bassanio so irresistibly attractive that she fainted in his arms as soon as he entered. It all would have looked like the beginning of a romance had not the pivotal III.ii scene involved a number of drastic interruptions. First, as Portia recovered in Bassanio's arms and a musical love theme began to swell, a 'power cut' caused mayhem on the stage, the curtain closed, and the interval was announced. After it, the scene resumed *in medias res*, only to be interrupted twice by Portia who tried to stop Bassanio from making a hasty choice. In a characteristic transposition, the next interruption was caused by Antonio's appearance, during which he recited 'Tell me where is fancy bred' (III.ii.63) from his parallel world, showing halfway through the trapdoor. The words sounded as a farewell to his own love and portentously prefigured his demise. The speech ended with the tolling of a bell, which cued Bassanio's realisation which of the caskets to choose. It also crucially visualised the connection between the events in Belmont and Antonio; the next character who emerged from the trapdoor brought the news of the merchant's arrest. After the almost divine revelation which prompted him how to choose, Bassanio gave a shortened version of 'So many outward things be not themselves' (III.ii.73). To underline the improbability of such words coming from the mouth of a fake like him, he once again stopped short of picking the casket, still unsure whether he was choosing correctly. The scene was interrupted yet again as Bassanio passed out on the platform, which enabled Portia to slip him the key to the lead casket before leaving the stage. His coming to, key in hand, gave a dream-like quality to the discovery of its contents, while allowing the audience a view of the theatrical mechanics that helped him achieve his dream. As a background to the farcical action, upstage stood the golden pig – a reminder of how Bassanio's 'outward shows' were financed (III.ii.73). All this left little doubt that the affair with Portia, to say nothing of that of Nerissa and Gratiano, was profoundly anti-romantic.

If the spiritually impoverished Antonio was an insider born to a world of ingrained xenophobia, Shylock was all about trying to fit in. Aleksandr Kalyagin's Chaplinesque, bowler-hatted character negotiated the various obstacles of space and dramatic action with the rotund charm of a roly-poly toy, bouncing back after every hit. The world he inhabited was characterised by what Péter Dávidházi describes as the manipulative use of the Other, both for gain and as a scapegoat, which endowed the character with an archetypal, biblical quality (pp. 269–79). Yet Kalyagin's balanced acting never allowed the audience to forget the human being behind the mask of the clown. He created an emotionally complex character across a spectrum of states, ranging from comic absurdity to heart-rending pathos.

Clad in a 1930s black suit, exuding professional confidence and well-being, Shylock was introduced as the apparent opposite of pale, abstracted Antonio. On his entry into the office, in I.iii, the screens exploded with stock-market data, the computer keyboards clattered even more loudly, and the office clerks beavered away at their work. 'The boss' had all his needs immediately attended to: a cup of coffee, a lit match for his cigar, a carefully folded umbrella and bowler hat stowed away. At all times, Shylock kept a close eye on the market movements. The cuts in his long aside revealed that, for him, the conflict with Antonio was economic, not religious. Before turning to the audience to share his grudge against Antonio 'for bring[ing] down / The rate of usance' (40–1), Shylock momentarily enquired about 'anything new' on the mart; the clerk promptly handed him a long printout of data. With this property conspicuously held high, he gave vent to his desire to 'catch [Antonio] … upon the hip' (43), the paper pointing to the meticulous attention with which he documented his transactions. A paper trail travelled through the production and featured prominently in the court scene, where Shylock came prepared with multiple copies of the bond. When Portia tore up one of them, he promptly produced another. Unlike Antonio's carelessness, strict accounting was Shylock's sole guarantee of his status as a Venetian.

The way I.iii was blocked on the little platform closely mirrored I.i, including the same office with the same two clerks. In the opening scene, Antonio force-fed one of them his soup, in a suggestive externalisation of 'My wind, cooling my broth' (22). This insulting joke (making the clerk eat his own words) was replicated in the way Shylock treated the other clerk in I.iii. When Bassanio with ineffectual servility tried to offer Shylock a light for his cigar, he tripped against the edge of the platform and spilled Shylock's coffee. Unceremoniously, Shylock grabbed the clerk's kippah and wiped his trousers with it. While he was playing fast and loose with the symbol of his own religion, the golden pig again appeared upstage. Shylock's blindness to this symbol of prejudice became clear when he nearly sat on the pig during the signing of the bond. As the blocking of the action suggested, avoiding collision with stereotypes was impossible, though Shylock could deftly navigate among them.

Shylock's comically dysfunctional relationship with his teenaged daughter Jessica (Maria Skosyreva) was rendered through a silent scene in which her doting daddy presented her with a pile of books, a moment mirroring Antonio's exertions around dressing up Bassanio for Belmont. Neither of the young people was interested in what the old had to offer. Bassanio showed more interest in the girl helping with the clothes; Jessica absconded with Lorenzo.

The aftermath of Jessica's elopement, III.i, was the emotional centre of the production; like the Belmont scene (III.ii), it was subverted by interruptions. In a touch of brilliance recalling the pathos of a Chaplin film, Kalyagin's Shylock staggered back to his office beaten, dishevelled, his umbrella broken, a star of David chalked on his back. The mask of the affluent businessman-clown had slipped; underneath showed the bruised face of the little man-clown, powerless, humiliated, and alone. That was the moment when the Manipulator brought out from the trap a moth-eaten tallit and handed Shylock a menorah. His face lit only by its candles, Kalyagin delivered 'Hath not a Jew eyes' (III.i.53) as if waking up from a nightmare only to step into another dream (Figure 19).

The Manipulator then reappeared from below, bringing the message about Antonio's 'ill luck' (III.i.89), which pushed the abused man over the edge. At the same time, he offered Shylock a symbolic prop to help him master the situation, a conductor's

Figure 19 Alexander Kalyagin as Shylock in Robert Sturua's production for the Et Cetera Theatre, Moscow, 2000.

baton, which Shylock hesitated to take. At this crucial moment, Sturua homed in on the way religion can be manipulated in the service of hatred and retaliation. Yet it was clear that the much-abused Shylock did not harbour a personal malice; what he wanted was to be a Venetian and exercise his right to enforce the terms of the bond, as guaranteed by the law. The baton came into his hand only briefly during the trial.

The frequently deleted jailor scene (III.iii) was transformed into a silent sequence in which Shylock brought wine and crystal goblets to Antonio's prison cell, an ironic alternative vision of their relationship. While the two men drank together in perfect harmony, the chasm between them was marked by a symbolic property placed on the edge of the table. An apple with a scalpel protruding from it offered a visual metaphor for the apple of discord and the tool to be used in exacting the punishment.

The court scene was a charade of justice presided over by a senile Duke (Lyudmila Dmitrieva). Her smudged, pallid makeup and laboured, mechanical movements presented a legal system in a state of putrefaction. Comatose in her mantle of gold, she brought to mind the line of octogenarian political leaders during the long agony of the Soviet era. In the meantime, the baton of power had passed from Shylock to Portia, who used it to accentuate her trial speeches. However, the moment the word 'alien' was pronounced, the trimmings of the law were pushed aside and violence erupted. The pig – the emblem the Other and his use for gain – was moved towards the audience, while the Christian mob upstage berated, beat, and mounted Shylock backwards on the golden cow. Close-ups of the violence were projected on the screens. In a desperate attempt to stop the turmoil, Antonio shouted, 'Let him become a Christian!' to no avail. It was the Duke, barely awake from her slumber, who stopped the mayhem by announcing the supreme value in Venice: lunch.

Instead of Act V, a *da capo* ending brought Antonio and Shylock together onstage. Antonio settled down to meditate on the platform, Shylock made a slow entrance through the brightly lit upstage door, umbrella in hand. The two men looked at each other as if wondering whether they were in or out of their roles, whether the play had ended or they were to repeat it once again. A brief exchange consisting of a collage of quotations from Portia's small talk with Lorenzo in V.i marked their final positions: 'What a night!', exclaimed Shylock; 'This night, methinks, is but the daylight sick' (124), responded Antonio. 'No', objected Shylock, "tis a day / Such as the day is when the sun is hid' (125–6). This medley of echoed sentiments suggested the characters' basic similarity and the arbitrariness of their conflict. In a darker turn, the Manipulator conjured up the image of a single candle on each of the screens, just as he had done at the opening of the play; and a chorus intoned, 'Oh Heavenly Salvation'. The single light seemed to underscore the outcome of the conversion, a new uniformity contrasted with the multiple lights of the menorah. As in a Beckett play, the spectators were faced at the end with two bewildered characters and a number of unanswered questions. Is a resolution to the conflict ever possible? Who is in control of our lives? What are the 'dark forces' driving divisions? *Quo vadis*, Russia?

Reflecting on the history of the play fifteen years after this production opened, Aleksey Bartoshevich noted that *The Merchant of Venice* had once again disappeared from the Russian stage. For him, this was a symptom of the acuteness of Russia's national problems. As the director noted, 'to be able to talk about evil is to fight evil' (qtd. in Dina Kirnarskaya, *Moskovskie novosti*, 21–27 December 1999). In the meantime, Sturua's *Shylock* has received numerous accolades at festivals and continues to live in a free-access HD recording on the Et Cetera theatre site.[3]

A prison called Venice

The Merchant of Venice has often been called Shylock's play, but in its 2009 production by Propeller, the main character was the prison where the action was set. Largely erasing the romance from the play, the creative team built a world modelled on 'filmed prison dramas such as "Oz" and "The Shawshank Redemption" in terms of place, physical action and the objects that might be used in a contemporary prison' (Pavelka). An unforgiving Venice sharpened the play's action and characters in this version directed by Edward Hall – founder of the all-male touring ensemble known for novel perspectives and accessible performances of Shakespeare's plays, exuberant physical and musical aesthetics, and a collaborative production process.

Propeller's male Venice Penitentiary could be located anywhere, though it was, beyond doubt, a contemporary institution. The choice, Sokolova argues, 'showed how violence can turn all groups into ghettoised communities. It spoke of irredeemable physical and mental entrapment, in a space where Christians, Jews, and Muslims, white and black, were incarcerated together' (*Shakespeare Bulletin*, p. 93). Alice Dailey concurs: 'It is not merely Venice that is a prison, Propeller suggested, but the systems of commodification that order human relations in a broader commercial world' (p. 510). Some critics chafed against this approach to the play, calling it an 'extravagant directorial interpolation' (Dominic Cavendish, 3 February 2009); others complained that Hall's concept-driven staging missed an opportunity to engage with a contemporary 'culture of quantification' exacerbated during the global recession of 2008–9 (Ilya Khodosh, *Berkshire Review for the Arts*, 21 June 2009). Perhaps, in the convulsions of the worst global financial crisis since the Great

Depression, they had trouble stomaching Propeller's bold metaphor for a self-destructive market society 'held prisoner by its own greed' (Sokolova, *Shakespeare Bulletin*, p. 94). Among those who endorsed the prison metaphor was Lyn Gardner. She went on to point out the modernist and postmodernist literary connections in Propeller's play: 'the ritualized play-acting of Genet's *The Maids*, particularly in the casket scenes; the confined agony of Sartre's *Huis Clos*, where hell is other people from whom no escape is possible' (*Guardian*, 2 February 2009).

The prison of Propeller's Venice was at once a repressive mechanism and a ferocious social body. A constant reminder of its repressive nature was Michael Pavelka's daunting yet versatile set. The tiered metal cells 'literalized the lex talionis' (Rutter, *Shakespeare Survey* 63, p. 364). The U-shaped acting space bounded by the cells functioned, in turn, as a prison yard where shady deals and violent encounters between rival gangs took place; a drab dining hall providing the sole occasion for excitement; a chapel where a bewildered Jessica attended her first Christian service after running away with Lorenzo. With relentless regularity, this acting space was a site of tedious janitorial toil. The seemingly fixed prison world, Pavelka explains, was animated by human movement and conveyed pent-up emotions and violence:

> The set's metal structure created a framework that actors could vertically scale and also gave them aural percussive possibilities that punctuated the dialogue with rhythmic hammering and door slamming ... Designing for Propeller involves empowering actors with control of their performance environment, so the set was ergonomically engineered to be manipulated by bodies rather than relying on automated technologies.

An integral part of the design, the soundscape functioned as both a vehicle for institutional regimentation and a means by which the gangs asserted power. On the one hand, the action was regularly interrupted 'by the imperious sound of prison bells or whistles' which summoned the men to mind-numbing rags-and-buckets toil (Sokol, p. 210). On the other hand, the inmates' taunts and metal banging proclaimed a violent group identity. This identity was explicitly tied to religion whenever the gangs broke out into song. The Christians intoned 'Onward, Christian soldiers', banging plates on the cell bars when Shylock crossed the stage for the dinner with Antonio. In turn, Shylock's identity was suggested through the traditional music of the Kol Nidrei prayer from the Day of Atonement, which is about the renouncing of old bonds (Adam Feldman, *Time Out New York*, 14–20 May 2009).

The ferocity and regimentation of the prison, a human-architectural hybrid, were on stark display from the opening tableau of inmates in greyish uniforms seated or stooped in their cages. The auditory signature of the prison was immediately established, raucous voices straining to overpower the banging on cell bars, which eventually settled into rhythmic drumming. With a sharp click, the cell doors opened, but before chaos could ensue, a warden in a pristine white suit – later identified as the Duke (Babou Ceesay) – strutted confidently to the centre, prompting the prisoners to line up on his two sides as he yelled a modification of Portia's opening line at the trial, 'Which is the Christian here, and which the Jew?' Two prisoners stepped out of the line, distinguished only by the knitted cap worn by one of them – Richard Clothier's Shylock.[4] In key moments of the play, the Duke/warden appeared on the top of the prison's metal body to direct the Christian fervour of his charges, while turning a blind eye to the deals conducted in the yard.

The Duke was not the only character with access to surveillance vantage points. Scene blocking emphasised the degree to which lives in the Venice Penitentiary were lived in the public eye. Since there was no way for the inmates to leave, when cast members were not participating in a scene, they kept close watch from their cells on the power clashes and the transactions of money and flesh. Across from them, theatregoers – some of whom were seated onstage when the play showed at the Brooklyn Academy of Music in New York – watched both the action and the inmates' responses to it. There was no avoiding surveillance, starkly exposed by Ben Ormerod's institutional lighting. As reviewers made clear, this metatheatrical choice, combined with the level of violence used in the production, tested the stamina of audience members and critics.

Pavelka's metal set, fixed yet allowing for manipulation, also allowed for cinematic-style zooming and deep-focus effects. The zooming highlighted vestiges of privacy and freedom in Venice; the deep focus disclosed how precarious and provisional they were. Thus Portia and Nerissa indulged in a parody of the 'princely

Figure 20 Kelsey Brookfield as Portia in the production of Propeller and Watermill Theatre Newbury, directed by Edward Hall. Liverpool Playhouse, Liverpool, 2009.

suitors' (I.ii.33) while strutting in the centre-stage opening, with the 'princes' hungrily reaching in through the bars of their locked cells. 'Zooming in' on the 'women' in this central space, which was ruled by them with toughness and witty banter, showed their superior status. This status came with pleasures and privileges unavailable to others: they were exempt from menial labour, handled large sums of money, and flaunted flashy (if shabby) drag. Both wore corsets and heels; Nerissa sported ripped fishnet hose and nipples framed by men's suspenders, while Portia, in tight cropped pants, wore a curled blond wig and later donned a fringed golden scarf – an emblem of the Golden Fleece (Figure 20). In the prison context, the choice of men to feminise themselves can be a submissive survival strategy. Such was the case of Jon Trenchard's Jessica, 'a jailbird skivvy in a headscarf', who scrubbed the toilet in Shylock's cell (Michael Coveney, *Independent*, 24 February 2009). Portia and Nerissa, however, acted as independent, 'fierce transvestites' (Roseanne Wells, PlayShakespeare.com, 7 January 2011). The casket lottery, staged under the protection of the Duke, allowed them to revel in their acting flair while pocketing a considerable cash bonus. Bassanio's 'winning' guess was secured by a bribe of 3,000 ducats paid to Nerissa. Conversely, the suitors' tight enclosures indicated their disadvantaged status in the prison system, as well as their psychological imprisonment by greed and desire.

However, the balance of power was reversed when Morocco, Arragon, and Bassanio came to make their choice (II.vii, II.ix, and III.ii, respectively). In these scenes, Portia was locked into one of the mobile cages, now wheeled to centre stage from the flanks of the U-shaped metal structure. In front of her, the casket lottery was taking place; behind her hung the Duke's white jacket. It stood for the will of the 'father' under whose auspices the casket lottery took place. All three layers were visible to the audience. While the father/Duke provided security and a measure of freedom for the 'women', the deep focus of the casket scenes revealed how readily his emblematic presence could tighten the vice of institutional power, some of which was held by the warden, and some delegated to those prisoners who were able to raise money for the casket lottery.

Asked about his view of Portia, actor Kelsey Brookfield explained, 'I saw her as someone who was under incredible scrutiny' (qtd. in Basso, p. 162). On top of the constant surveillance that all the characters endured, Portia's racial difference – she was the only black prisoner – must have made her plight still more unbearable. The Duke watched Bassanio's casket choice from on high – a scene which Brookfield's acting imbued with yearning for romance, only to have Portia's hopes dashed. The dramatic call, 'Go, Hercules!' (III.ii.60) was followed by a moving *a cappella* rendition of 'Tell me where is fancy bred', which boosted expectations for a romantic climax. Yet, as Roseanne Wells reported, Portia displayed 'only half-hearted affection toward Bassanio after he [had] won her' (PlayShakespeare.com, 7 January 2011). S/he held Bassanio at an arm's length when he reached for the kiss stipulated in the 'gentle scroll' (III.ii.139). Moving to centre stage, Portia poignantly announced the commitment of 'her gentle spirit' to the direction of this new 'lord ... governor ... king' (163–5), at the same time taking off the wig and high heels. Bassanio appeared stunned by this invitation to enter a commitment devoid of deals and role-playing. Nor did the Duke allow for such a commitment. Before Portia and Bassanio (and Nerissa and Gratiano) could solemnise their vows with a kiss, a shrill whistle announced the end of romantic playacting and the start of labour duty. The couples dropped to their knees and began scrubbing the floor, discussing marriage plans to the work rhythm set by a prison guard. So much for fantasies of romance and freedom in the Venice Penitentiary.

Employing a deep focus on characters restricted to the mobile cages and zooming in on them when they occupied the larger field of action centre-stage yielded surprising insights into the characters of Antonio and Shylock. Bob Barrett's Antonio, 'a big shot, mafia don-type in tired spats', entered the dramatic action in conversation with his friend Salerio, portrayed by Sam Swainsbury (Wells, PlayShakespeare.com, 7 January 2011). The merchant moved confidently through the crowded central yard, among prisoners engaged in furtive money transactions, guard-bribing, and casual gambling; he strutted his grounds unperturbed by the 'undercurrent of incipient violence' in the prison world to which the global commerce of Shakespeare's character had been reduced (Dailey, p. 512). His centrally located cage initially appeared to be a site of private privilege, where he shared a physical relationship with a half-clothed Bassanio. However, the deep focus on the action in the cell revealed how Antonio's sexual desire weakened his hold on power. Thriving under Antonio's protection, Bassanio ran his own money scheme from the back door without the merchant noticing, even while telling him about Portia. The blocking of the scene, with Bassanio upstage behind Antonio and both men facing the audience, revealed the young man's expert sexual manipulation. He caressed the merchant as he began to spin the tale of the 'lady richly left' (I.i.161), but abruptly broke contact when Antonio explained that he was short on cash. In the meantime, spectators 'were privy to a range of gestures and facial expressions that communicated the young man's selfish and disingenuous manipulation of the smitten, gullible, but unsympathetically imperious "merchant"' (Dailey, p. 512). Antonio's offer of his line of credit, coming promptly after Bassanio severed physical contact, left no doubt about the tight spot in which desire had imprisoned the tough master of the prison yard.

Shylock, on the other hand, was consistently associated with the open space in the middle of the stage. There he unleashed the full range of his dramatic power, commanding the attention of off-stage and on-stage audiences alike. The latter included the prison guard on Shylock's payroll, who appeared promptly whenever Shylock was threatened. Not that this fearless and 'powerfully physical Shylock' was in dire need of paid protection (Mentz, p. 679). Far from being the aged, victimised Jew of post-Second World War theatre tradition, Clothier's Shylock flaunted his intellectual superiority when telling the Jacob and Laban story (I.iii.74–93). This was a Shylock in the mode of Peter Zadek, aggressive and independent (see Part II, Chapter II). The game he played with Antonio and his thugs was dangerous, just as he liked it. He was jumped by the merchant's men and ended up with Antonio's shiv against his throat. However, Shylock knew that his life was not in danger, although he gave the appearance that his consideration of the loan was the result of violent coercion. Antonio needed his money, and besides, Shylock could count on the protection not only of the guard who promptly broke up the skirmish, but of the Duke himself who appeared at the top of the cells at the sound of the whistle. When these protectors left, Shylock, undeterred, continued to flex his financial muscle and demonstrated remarkable physical alacrity to boot. His sneering account of Antonio's anti-Semitic assaults provoked the merchant and his thugs into another violent attack, which Shylock managed to avoid by leaping into the safety of a cell, buying time for the guard to return. The 'merry sport' proposal for the collateral was the culmination of this daredevil improvisation. In the outcome of the scene, not only did Shylock remain unscathed by Antonio and his mates, he also managed to get them to laugh about the innuendo regarding the pound of Antonio's flesh, which was apparently the object of prison gossip.

Like the fortunes of the 2008–9 financial markets, Shylock's risky investment in Antonio's humiliation yielded poor returns. The downward turn of affairs for both characters was signalled by an added silent ritual of sealing the bond. It was conducted at the threshold of Antonio's cell, a mobile cage brought to centre-stage. The deadly seriousness of the deal became apparent when the two men cut their palms before shaking hands, their mingled blood trickling into a bucket. The ritual symbolised the volatile balance of power between the 'two types of "big men" operating within the prison system: those who are violent and those who can procure things others cannot' (Poltrack, p. 280). In the tight space of the cell, Shylock and Antonio were further constrained by prisoners who had scaled it from the outside. The resulting triple enclosure of iron, the inmates' bodies, and the larger surveillance economy of the prison (including the gaze of the audience) created a pressure-cooker situation where compromise or going back on the deal was tantamount to a surrender of power, livelihood, life.

The balance of power was upset by Jessica's flight from 'the house of Shylock'. In the context of the prison setting, this was not just a betrayal of family and faith, but a devastating blow to Shylock's financial and social status. The theft of the money he had stashed in the filthy water tank of the commode in his cell, which Jessica had dutifully scrubbed in an earlier scene, left him without the means to protect his life. Like a wounded animal, Shylock stumbled across the prison yard while the Christian mob abused him verbally and physically. His ruthlessness fuelled by survival instinct, he knocked down Salerio and tied him to the bars of a cell door – 'to bait fish withal' (III.i.48). He then proceeded to punctuate the famous 'Hath not a Jew eyes' speech – the summit of a venerable performance tradition of humanising Shylock – with a series of violent acts, culminating in gouging out Salerio's eye. The mob returned, summoned by his screams of agony, but Shylock managed to hold them off, wildly swinging a chair until an equally ferocious Tubal came to his rescue. There was no doubt that, even having lost their financial clout, Shylock and his 'tribe' were more than capable of retooling to 'better the instruction' of Christian violence (66).

The trial scene pitched the power of money against legally protected violence. Six thousand ducats rained down upon the court when Bassanio emptied a money bag from the top of the cells, double payment for the outstanding loan. Shylock whistled at the sight but proceeded with his preparations for cutting the pound of flesh. Portia's moneyed privilege enabled 'her' to don an attorney suit beyond which nobody looked to ascertain identity; 'her' honey-tongued plea for mercy rang with new urgency in the prison context. From his position as both recipient and perpetrator of horrific violence, Shylock laughed it off. As he lunged, grunting, to bury his knife into the cross tattooed over Antonio's heart, Portia took a mad gamble on what was *not* written in the legal agreement: 'This bond doth give thee here no jot of blood: / The words expressly are "a pound of flesh"' (IV.i.303–4). The speculation paid off, though for a moment it seemed that Shylock was about to strike down the young attorney. However ridiculous the legal fiction was, it served the interests of the moneyed (under)class. Antonio, now the only 'big man' in the prisoner hierarchy, swiftly embraced the opportunity to conjoin anti-Semitism and profit when he topped his demand for Shylock's conversion with a stipulation that the Christian Lorenzo and Jessica would inherit what was left of Shylock's Jewish fortune. This blow left Shylock wriggling on the floor, barely able to whisper the agreement that allowed him to live. He was absent-mindedly kicked out by one of Antonio's men. 'The action is to try to destroy him without killing him', reflected Hall on the conversion scene. 'It's a fate worse than death' (qtd. in Basso, p. 170).

Back in bleak Belmont, a sullen homecoming devolved into a spat between the 'wives' and the vow-betraying 'husbands'. Nerissa and Portia turned out to be almost as adept as Shylock at using chairs as assault weapons in a violent domestic dispute, which also involved harsh twisting of noses, penises, and nipples. These were characters doomed to violence in a claustrophobic prison where money could buy them only a temporary breathing space. At the end, prompted by the shrill whistle, the inmates lined up on the three sides of the yard, and the white-suited 'Duke' echoed the line with which the production opened, 'Which is the Christian here and which the Jew'. In the repressive world of the production, it was impossible to tell. Antonio had become Mr Money; Shylock – now with nothing to lose – wore a cross around his neck. In Hall's vision of the play, as in Sturua's, the cycle of violence was about to start again.

Notes

1 As we were putting the finishing touches on this text in 2022, Russia mounted its most devastating attack yet, on independent Ukraine, laying a claim to Ukrainian sovereign territory. The number of victims has grown exponentially while millions of refugees have fled to Europe and across the world.
2 In the Russian reception, the play has often been named after its Jewish protagonist.
3 The production can be viewed at www.youtube.com/watch?v=H1zW7Gr_4fY
4 In the sixty-minute *Pocket Merchant* version of the play, staged in 2013 for educational purposes, the actors took on their identities when the Duke tossed a crucifix medallion to Antonio and a cap to Shylock. The choice emphasised even more clearly the social construction of these warring religious identities.

VI

The Merchant of Venice on film

The history of *The Merchant of Venice* on film is truly a global one. It started with a spate of silent shorts and has produced four feature-length cinematic adaptations: *The Jew of Mestri* (Germany, 1923), *The Merchant of Venice* (France and Italy, 1953), *The Maori Merchant of Venice* (New Zealand, 2001), and *William Shakespeare's Merchant of Venice* (UK and USA, 2004). From the beginning, these films used and developed existing theatre conventions. In addition, whether referencing or fully engaging with current cultural-political and social trauma, they also cited and reshaped important cinematic genres.

Glamour and villainy, pathos and rehabilitation: from the silents to mid-century film drama

The Merchant of Venice was a popular choice among global filmmakers of the silent era. As early as 1905, Shylock's name was featured in the title of George Méliès's film *Un miroir de Venise (Une mésaventure de Shylock)* – now lost, like many others. While this Shakespeare reference was likely a shorthand for establishing a familiar context for Méliès's signature trick photography (Ugenti, p. 130), silent films with speeches or scenes from *The Merchant* quickly followed in the USA, Italy, France, and the UK. Among the silent *Merchant* films were two firsts in cinema history: the first woman-directed feature-length film, released by Universal in 1914, co-written and co-directed by Lois Weber and Phillips Smalley, who also starred as Portia and Shylock; and the first animated Shakespeare film, Anson Dyer's 1919 burlesque adaptation, also the first to set the story in the film's own era. Here Antonio is an ice-cream seller, and Shylock loses his court case because he lacks sufficient ration coupons for a pound of flesh (Lanier, p. 177).

An outstanding achievement of the silent era is Peter Paul Felner's (1884–1927) German production, *Der Kaufmann von Venedig* (1923), released in English-speaking countries as *The Jew of Mestri*. Shot largely on location in Venice, it purports to bring audiences to the source of Shakespeare's play, Giovanni Fiorentino's novella *Il Pecorone (The Simpleton)*. The film positions itself as a 'subsequent performance' to the two previous narratives; it transforms the plots of both novella and play, sidestepping the fairy-tale elements and resonating with the hedonism and economic anxiety of Weimar Germany. With mounting melodramatic pathos, it unveils Shylock's motivations for pursuing revenge. The result, in Elio Ugenti's evaluation, is a sustained focus on Shylock's character, 'second only to that assigned to it by Orson Welles in his 196[9] unfinished [television] adaptation of *The Merchant*' (p. 140).

Mordecai (Shylock) was performed by Werner Krauss, one of the stars of German theatre. Only two years earlier, Krauss had played a cruel and physically grotesque Shylock in one of Reinhardt's productions. Felner's film, however, gives the character psychological dynamism and complicates the reasons for Shylock's decision to exact the bond. He is devastated by two deaths, one real, one metaphorical. His beloved wife, Leah, dies of a heart attack caused by the callousness of the spendthrift Giannetto (Bassanio) and his mates; then, he loses his daughter to the Christians, and grief nearly causes him to succumb to heart failure. In a poignant gesture, after much painful hesitation, he lights a ritual candle and sits Shiva for Rachela (Jessica) – a symbol of her death as a Jew, which would be borrowed by later theatre performances. Rachela later returns home to plead forgiveness for Benito (Antonio) before the trial, only to encounter her father's haunting emotional vacancy, as if he himself has died internally. Nor is Mordecai the instigator of the bond; it is publicised by Giannetto in an attempt to procure funding for his lavish lifestyle. Using it as a revenge ploy is Tubal's idea, motivated by his mortification at Rachela's rejection of his son. Mordecai thus stands out as a man more sinned against than sinning, beset by family tragedy and goaded into revenge by his friends. In spite of generally moulding him around a stereotype, the film invites understanding and empathy for him. Nor is Mordecai punished by conversion; instead, his eventual fate is heartbreaking loneliness. The film builds a telling contrast between a Jewish life, based on tradition but defied by young love, and the profligate lifestyle of the Christian Venetians and inhabitants of Belmont, where the rich Beatrice (Portia, played by Henny Porten, Germany's first film star) holds court and flirts with her suitors, free of the constraints of the casket lottery. Douglas Lanier suggests that it is possible to view Krauss's Mordecai 'as a tragic, sympathetic victim of bourgeois decadents'. Although the calculated obsequiousness of the character in the bond scene undermines such a reading, Mordecai's plight among the dissolute Christians 'would have resonated in economically devastated Weimar Germany' (p. 179). In some ways, Felner's film anticipated the shift to the character's emotional acquittal, prevalent in theatre and film productions after the Second World War. Along with the display of the splendours of Venice, the new medium opened space for a fuller representation of Jewish domesticity, custom, and community, as well as for developing minor characters such as Tubal. Importantly, the film endows the character equivalents of the play's Portia and Jessica with equally proactive parts as courageous women fighting for personal and social autonomy. There was a generational divide between these characters, driven by the independence values of the 'New Woman' trend popularised by British-American writer Henry James (1843–1916), and Shylock's wife Leah, who affirmed to her daughter that suffering is 'the fate of all women of our tribe'.

The commercialisation of sound cinema in the late 1920s overlapped with the rise of racialist anti-Semitic ideologies; accordingly, most filmmakers in Europe and America grew wary of *The Merchant*. Between the release in 1927 of Widgey Newman's *Merchant of Venice* – the first Shakespeare talkie, a nine-minute static version of an Old Vic production presenting a caricature of Shylock with added anti-Semitic dialogue – and the Second World War, only three screen adaptations of the play were produced. These films, now lost, were all made in India, and engaged in a cultural context distant from the rise of fascism. Directed by M. Udvadia (1927), D. N. Madhok (1937), and J. J. Madan (1941), respectively, they focused on 'the cycle of poverty and economic barriers to aspiration rather than religious or caste prejudice' (Lanier, p. 181). During the war, Veit Harlan, Joseph Goebbels's favourite director, was at work on a *Merchant* film designed to supplement his notorious *Jud Süß* (1940) in the Nazi propagandist arsenal, but the 1944 bombings of Berlin put an end to the production (Guneratne, pp. 400–2).

In the wake of the Holocaust, producers were understandably unwilling to take on a text embroiled in the traumas of recent history. The exception was a lavish 1953 French-Italian drama, *Le Marchand de Venise*, directed and partly written by Pierre Billon (1901–81). Shot on location in Venice and at the Turin studios, it provided entertainment sought by audiences living in the dire economic conditions of post-Second World War Europe by intensifying Bassanio's romantic pursuit of Portia and matching it with the passionate love affair of Jessica and Lorenzo. At the same time, Shylock is treated as the absolute protagonist, contrasted not only to an 'unsympathetic, pretentious, and cynical' Antonio but to all of the overbearing and class-entitled Christians (Ugenti, p. 143). The gravitas with which Michel Simon's Shylock moves and speaks is similar to the portrayals of 'the noble Jew' by Erich Ponto and Ernst Deutsch in 1950s–1960s Germany, memorably foregrounding his character's no-nonsense, working-class attitude. This Shylock refuses to be a victim, and the film never slips into stereotype or melodrama.

Shylock's moral stature and steadfastness are clearly declared in the added narrative – a device which would be reprised in both of the twenty-first-century full-feature films. Without explicit modernisation, the prologue nonetheless evokes anti-Semitic abuse during the Nazi occupation. In the opening sequence, Shylock visits a bordello to extricate his brother's daughter who has bought her independence from her father by prostituting for the Christians. Less than a decade after the war, the allusion to the Nazis' and their collaborators' sexual exploitation of Jewish women as the price of survival would have been transparent for movie-goers (Lanier, p. 182). Further allusions to anti-Semitic violence from the era occur in the sequence when Shylock returns to his home to find it apparently burgled, the window wide open, Jessica possibly abducted. Beside himself, he dashes out, gasping 'my daughter, my little daughter', only to be hounded by torch-bearing revellers in grotesque masks who swarm him on a bridge – an image heavy with terrifying war memories. Only when Jessica passes by in a gondola with Lorenzo and taunts her father does he realise, with a mix of relief and dejection, that she has eloped.

The film's surprising ending uses a family reconciliation trope from Jewish cinema. Closing the cinematic frame, Portia (Andrée Debar) visits Shylock's house and reveals that she was the lawyer who won the case, suggesting that he, too, could don the mask of a Christian to transform from a usurer into a banker. Stunned, Shylock responds with a dignified delivery of 'Hath not a Jew eyes' (III.i.53ff.), which visibly shakes Portia. She promises to intercede with the Duke to revoke the forced baptism, as long as Shylock forgives Jessica. The romantic plot and Shylock's are brought together in a close-up of Shylock's hand putting into Portia's necklace – an old gift to Jessica left behind when she eloped. Integrating tropes from film romance (the triumph of true love) and Jewish cinema (family reconciliation), the film ends with a recognition of women's intellectual and sexual agency and a promise of civic and legal Jewish rehabilitation – a significant choice in the aftermath of the war (Ugenti, p. 145).

It would take nearly fifty years for a new feature-length cinematic *The Merchant* to appear, interweaving trauma narratives from two widely different cultures as well as the genre conventions of heritage and drama film.

Cultural hybridity on the terms of the colonised: Don Selwyn's *Te Tangata Whai Rawa O Weniti*, or *The Maori Merchant of Venice* (2001)

The Merchant was reintroduced to the big screen in 2001 after a decade of fundraising effort by Don C. Selwyn (1935–2007), a New Zealand actor, stage and screen director, and pioneer of the Māori film and television industry.[1] This was another first in cinema history: his *Merchant* was the first Māori feature film. He had directed a stage production of *The Merchant* for the 1990 Spring Festival in Auckland, using Pei Te (Pete) Hurinui Jones's translation into *te reo kohatu* – the formal, highly metaphoric register of the Māori language. *Te reo* is distinct from the contemporary vernacular, which bears the effects of New Zealand's settler colonialism, having been inundated by slightly modified English words and reverse translations in the mould of English syntactic patterns. With an almost entirely Māori cast and multicultural crew, the film primarily targeted an indigenous audience by showcasing the oratorial aspects of a language threatened by extinction hoping to promote its study.[2] The film's language politics are clearly announced in its title, first given as *Te Tangata Whai Rawa O Weniti*, then translated immediately as *The Maori Merchant of Venice*. Shakespeare's playtext is compressed and slightly modernised in the film's subtitles, its poetic qualities and ornate rhetoric replaced by serviceable prose for the benefit of monolingual English speakers. Across the linguistic divide, the primary target audience of the film indulge fully in the exuberant undulations of Māori speech. Characters acquire Māori names: Shylock became Hairoka, Portia Pohia, Antonio Anatonio, Jessica Tiehika, Bassanio Patanio. The effect is an appropriation of Shakespeare's cultural authority in a Māori heritage film. As Selwyn said, 'When I was going to school they brought Shakespeare in to colonize me. Now that I've put it into Māori language I've colonized Shakespeare' ('Don Selwyn, Actor, Director').

A heritage drama with an opulent mise-en-scène, alternating between the breezy coastline and colourful markets of Venice/Weniti and the luxuriously designed, verdant Belmont/Peremona, *The Maori Merchant* offers manifold arthouse pleasures. Yet this heritage drama is devoid of the nostalgic tropes of the genre. The past is represented as clearly heterotopic in Selwyn's film, its multilingual programme grounded in the routes of colonisation, exile, and deferred homecoming, as well as in ongoing cultural rerooting. Along with the unique redistribution of rhetorical modes across linguistic boundaries, the film also reimagines the world of Shakespeare's play as a series of convergences of heterogeneous cultural, political, and historical trajectories. This Māori 'Fourth World' integrates European and Māori cultural narratives and signifiers. Its characters traverse borders between water and land, the natural and the social world, art and commerce, law and religion, myth, fiction, and history, as well as historical distinctions between early modern Europe and nineteenth-century and contemporary New Zealand. Such revisioning of Shakespeare's play as an alternative New Zealand history not only reshapes the heritage film genre, but also questions and upends prescribed social hierarchies and concepts. For Western audiences, this invites a productive estrangement and a new understanding of the important social questions Shakespeare's play raises about justice, revenge, and honour. Specifically, *The Maori Merchant of Venice* recontextualises the impact of the Holocaust through a major event in New Zealand's history of colonisation, charting a comparative consideration of two deep traumas in global history (Fitzpatrick, pp. 169–71).

Cultural hybridity is made apparent as early as the soundtrack of the prologue sequences, which 'morphs from the lush romantic score composed by Clive Cockburn relying heavily on the sounds of violins to the Māori *waiata*, traditional songs composed by the late Hirini Melbourne' (Houlahan, p. 143). Hybridity characterises both of the play's locales, though each has its distinct balance between dominant and minority culture. In Weniti (Venice), Māori actors in breeches, jerkins, and ruffs man tall ships and stroll past convincingly European neo-Renaissance façades; the trial scene is shot in a neo-Gothic church. Yet most of the bond scene takes place in a gallery with paintings commemorating Māori loss of land and the dark legacy of settler-colonialism. Peremona (Belmont) is a cultural hybrid of a different sort. It is located deep in the moonlit New Zealand bush, where 'children of the mist' – the mythic first dwellers of the islands – somersault through the air and take flight among the trees (Royal). Water is as important to Peremona as to Weniti, but here it is not a venue of maritime trade; Peremona's waterfalls and fountains, as well as Pohia's (Ngarimu Daniels) almost ritualistic watering of the ferns in her parlour, are all part of this world's natural fecundity rather than a resource for money-making ventures. Here, European art and costumes have been collected with discernment, functioning as exotic affirmations of Pohia's princely status. The awkward postures and incongruous costumes of her European suitors – especially Arakona (Arragon) with his white wig, hose, and feathered hat – accentuate the association of the Europeans with comic Otherness. The absurdity of the European nobleman is further offset by the solemnity of Morako's (Morocco) arrival. The furnishings of Pohia's parlour include harps, books, and sofas, but its aesthetic is dominated by Polynesian masks, decorative oars, shells, and carved wooden statues – the latter standing guard over the three caskets. Although Pohia's 'fondness for the free-flowing

European clothing [was] akin to that adopted in formal nineteenth-century portraits of Māori aristocrats', the main allegiance of her household is to Māori identity (Houlahan, p. 143). This is signalled not only through the intricate decorative elements of the women's costuming, which features flax bodices, prized feather necklaces, and shawls curling around the shoulder in the *koru* pattern of New Zealand's coiled fern, but more importantly through strict adherence to Māori ceremony. The latter is on display in the welcoming of Morako, complete with a conch signal, a female dance and welcoming cry, and a warrior challenge dance (McDougall, p. 99). In contrast, during the trial scene this realm's 'high-born "ariki tapairu" or princess' (Houlahan, p. 143) and cultural custodian delivers to the Venetian merchants a carefully prepared case for Christian values. Still, the film ends with an image of a heavy closed door decorated with Māori carvings, suggesting that whatever balance of hybridity marks the identities of the couples behind it, they have preserved or embraced the Māori tradition.

Time and again, Selwyn's film revisits the crossing and dissolution of spatial boundaries. The significance of transience in the cinematic narrative is declared in the opening sequence. The first shot is a close-up on Hairoka's (Waihoroi Shortland) feet as he climbs a wind-swept staircase in an unidentified urban space, the wistful violins of the extradiegetic music yielding to a voice-over of the opening of 'Hath not a Jew eyes'. The camera pans up Hairoka's body and focuses briefly on his intent face, eyes riveted on a threatening sky that seems to respond to his cue of 'passions' with a vicious thunderbolt. His voice carries into the next shot, which cuts to a tempest tossing a ship on the ocean – presumably one of Anatonio's argosies. The boundary between the social and the natural world dissipates as Hairoka appears to commune with the elements. So, too, does the boundary between the voiced trauma of Shakespeare's character and the historical trauma of colonialism, of which the ship is a metaphorical reminder, as well as a gesture to silent films of *The Tempest* – the ultimate Shakespearean colonialist text.

To the visual imagery of spatial border crossing, the bond scene (I.iii) adds the convergence of historical trajectories. The gallery/art studio in which it takes place features paintings by prominent Māori artist Selwyn Muru who appears in a cameo performance working on a canvas. Adjacent to a bustling marketplace catering to consumers' appetites for food and entertainment, this is a quiet space of creation and reflection, which Hairoka enters right after he declares the limits of his social interactions as a Jew in Christian Weniti: 'I will buy and sell with you, talk and walk with you, but I will not eat, or pray with you.'[3] His confrontation with Anatonio over the terms of the bond may take place away from the public eye, yet it unfolds in the eye of history as brought to life in Muru's paintings. When Hairoka proclaims the abuse he has endured, he is surrounded by art bearing visual witness to the memory of the violence and dispossession of the Māori during the Land Wars of 1860s–1880s. The paintings depict places, people, and events around the village at Parihaka, an inter-tribal pacifist community established by the prophets Te Whiti-o-Rongomai and Tohu Kākahi to resist the European settlers' land-grab. The settlement was destroyed by British troops, who also had the peaceful protesters and their leaders jailed and exiled to the South Island (Ministry for Culture and Heritage). Thus Hairoka's declaration, 'Cursed be my tribe if I forgive him', uttered in front of a painting of Parihaka's spiritual guardian, the owl Kaitaki, resounds with the frustration and anger of dispossessed and brutalised Māori people.[4] The film's editing drives home the local significance of the line. It is spoken after a cut to a frame showing Patanio (Te Rangihau Gilbert) and Anatonio (Scott Morrison) in which they flank a painting with Mount Taranaki towering above the remains of Parihaka. In another two-shot, Hairoka is framed delivering a full-throttled retort to his public shaming on the Rialto, positioned alongside a portrait of a Māori warrior; their two faces mirror each other in indignant expression (Figure 21).

As the scene unfolds, the history of Jewish persecution is overtaken by that of Māori colonialisation. After Anatonio dares Hairoka to 'exact the penalty' from his 'enemy' should the loan be forfeited, the scene, so far private, gradually transforms into a public one. As Hairoka, still with the portrait of the Māori warrior by his shoulder, introduces the penalty as 'a pound of your flesh, cut off in a part of your body, that I choose', a kippah-wearing man and his female companion enter behind him and remain in an animated discussion of another painting; more people follow shortly after. Anatonio laughs off the terms of the 'penalty', but Patanio appears

Figure 21 Waihoroi Shortland as Hairoka (Shylock) next to a painting of the owl Kaitaki by Selwyn Muru, in Don Selwyn's film, *Te Tangata Whai Rawa O Weniti*, or *The Maori Merchant of Venice* (2001).

petrified, and with good reason. Once personal humiliation is recast as a war-like confrontation between merchants and tribes (Hairoka's and the indigenous tribes represented on the canvases), talk of the victor's claim to human flesh begins to resonate with an ancient Māori cultural practice associated with revenge and conceptualised as defence or increase of *mana* (authority, honour, prestige) (Barber, p. 280; Bowden, pp. 95–6). Absorption of the offender's body by the victor was supposed to recuperate loss of *mana* inflicted by an insult. In this context, the pound of flesh demanded by Hairoka hints at his readiness to avenge his own wounded honour and that of his tribe. His first blow is an insult to Anatonio of the kind considered most degrading by the Māori: associating a person with food (Bowden, p. 94), and moreover food that is 'not so valuable ... as flesh of mutton, beef or goats'.[5]

In the alternative history presented in the film, where the golden city of Renaissance commerce is enfolded in Polynesian flora and cultural heritage, the dramatic action is haunted by juxtaposed notions of justice, revenge, and honour. Still, the convergence of New Zealand colonial history and the global history of persecution and genocide would have remained unintelligible to international audiences without Selwyn's remarkable visual epilogue to the bond scene. As Anatonio and Patanio exit the gallery, the camera cuts to the painting that the artist has been working on and zooms in on the inscription 'HO/LO/CAU/ST', tilted halfway down an abstract composition in red, grey, and black. Panning up, it captures 'HOLOCAUST' at the top of the canvas, too. The inscriptions transform the painting – and through it, the film – into a convergence of two cultural traumas: the Jewish genocide by the Nazis and the decimation of the Māori by British settler-colonialism. For New Zealanders at the time of the film's release, this was a clear endorsement of Māori parliamentarian Tariana Turia's public and controversial statement in 2000 regarding 'the holocaust suffered by indigenous people including Māori as a result of colonial contact and behaviour' (quoted in Silverstone, p. 138). Shooting the scene after Turia was castigated by the Prime Minister, Selwyn chose to add this controversial political perspective to his film.

Hairoka's desire for retaliation, productively estranged through the cultural lens of Māori experience, acquires an unmistakable social dimension. As Valerie Wayne contends, 'he wants justice, compensation, a restoration of mana for personal *and* collective suffering' (p. 425, emphasis added). Jessica's elopement adds fuel to the fire, but hardly to the extent it does in the European performance tradition. Nor does Hairoka allow others to direct his actions, as in Felner's film. The social overtones of his revenge are most explicit in the trial scene (IV.i). Shot in the historic Church of the Holy Sepulchre in Auckland, the scene matches defendant, plaintiff, and head of the state with symbolic props. Hairoka is consistently shown with the scales of justice by his side; Anatonio, in the pulpit, wears the 'red cross of martyrdom' on his tunic (Houlahan, p. 147); the Duke, in the apse, is backed by a golden crucifix. Though Hairoka is positioned below these figures of towering authority and below Pohia, who speaks from a tall lectern, he is closest to the court audience, to whom he addresses his plea for justice directly, turning his back on the bench. As in the bond scene, he is not alone. Not only is he flanked by his counsel that includes Tupara (Tubal) and an honourable elder, he literally has the backing of half the assembly. Separated by the aisle, Jews and Christians, all of them Māori, are intensely focused on the argument, augmenting the rhetoric of each side with emphatic gestures.

In the end, Pohia wins the case for the Christian side. Yet even after Anatonio extends the humiliating 'mercy' of conversion, Hairoka remains undaunted. In spite of the church setting, no conversion takes place; Hairoka takes off his kippah, kisses it, and, turning for a slow exit, puts it back on. He is followed at a respectful distance by the two elders of his counsel. As the camera tracks the party of justice/honour/revenge, it captures a range of expressions on the Christian side of the assembly, from smug and gloating to ashamed and pitiful – a tentative emotional erasure of the scar of social division between Māori Christians and Māori Jews. At the church door, Shylock's silver-haired counsel member turns back with an accusation burning with the memory of Parihaka's destruction by the British: 'Eaten by fire! All thieves, rogues!' When he exits, the camera cuts to the Jewish part of the audience, Hairoka's monologue sounding off-screen: 'If a Christian wrong a Jew, what should his sufferance be by Christian example? Why, revenge!' The rhetorical question, asked in the language and context of Māori culture, points to the tangled and unresolved problems of Māori honour (*mana*), inheritance, and restorative justice. Outside the church, Hairoka climbs another staircase as his monologue continues in voice-over. As in the prologue, he crosses into a new realm, a space and history yet to be defined.

Created as a vehicle for reviving Māori language and, arguably, *mana*, Selwyn's *Te Tangata* celebrates cultural resilience and adaptability even as it remains unflinching in its portrayal of loss. Having echoed Hairoka's opening speech about the right to defend one's honour when it comes under attack at the end of the trial scene, the film closes with Tiehika's (Reikura Morgan) interior speech, recollecting her words as she last watched her father leave their house: 'Farewell, and if my fortune be not crossed, I have a father left. You ... a daughter lost'. She recalls her farewell to family and belief with tenderness, but does not fixate on the past. The final images suggest that her new life can flourish.[6] Even though Tiehika stands before a door about to close behind her, the association of Pohia's house with the circulation of water and harmonising music suffuses the conclusion with hope, akin to the ending of Billon's film, though rare in modern theatre productions of *The Merchant*. The ending bears testament to Sirkka Ahonen's point that 'the identity of a community is not an immutable essence, but rather a dynamic process, deriving its elements from stories told and retold, in the course of intersubjective mediation' (p. 179). Heterogeneous historical trajectories converge in this cinematic adaptation of *The Merchant of Venice* as Hairoka, Pohia, and Tiehika traverse real and imaginary borders and experience loss, danger, and bitterness but also demonstrate courage and resilience, create new alliances, and discover the possibility of growth around the verdant tree of Māori life symbolised by the rich carvings on the door that closes in the final frame of the film.

Shylock and the time-to-be: Michael Radford's *William Shakespeare's The Merchant of Venice* (2004)

While the low-budget *Māori Merchant of Venice* passed almost unnoticed by the cinema industry, the first Hollywood adaptation of the play, *William Shakespeare's The Merchant of Venice* (2004) directed by Michael Radford (1946–), attracted media attention before its premiere and has remained in the critical limelight. Unsurprisingly, the reactions it elicited were strong. At that point, the post-Holocaust baggage of the play was compounded by a post-9/11 (2001) siege mentality, the ongoing military intervention in Iraq, and heated debates over the representation of Jews in the wake of Mel Gibson's film *The Passion of the Christ* (2004) (Drew, p. 52). In public statements, Radford had related his film to a larger agenda of intolerance (*Groucho Reviews*, 11 December 2004). Some objected to such broad interpretations of 'stories of anti-Jewish hatred ... [as] parables for racism or intolerance' (Jonathan Freedland, *Guardian*, 9 September 2004). Radford strongly disagreed with the suggestion that he had failed to engage with anti-Semitism and reiterated his belief that the play is 'actually about humanity' (Jan Lisa Huttner, *FF2 Media*, 6 January 2005).

The conundrum posed by post-Holocaust interpretations of *The Merchant* is well summed up by Milla Cozart Riggio: 'We appear to have three options: to denounce the play as anti-Semitic and to reject it; to excuse its anti-Semitism on the basis of the inescapable prejudice of "Shakespeare's age"; or – most commonly – to protect Shylock's humanity at all costs, mainly at the expense of the Christians in the play' (p. 173). Radford rejected the idea of the play's anti-Semitism (*Groucho Reviews*, 11 December 2004), placed the action in 'Shakespeare's age' (hence the title), and conceived Shylock as a tragic minority character driven to desperation by the hypocrisy of the morally corrupt Venetians.

The first responses in the UK were mixed though generally positive. To Peter Bradshaw, this was an 'unpretentious screen revival ... raised above the commonplace by a brilliant performance from Al Pacino as Shylock' (*Guardian*, 3 December 2004). Nigel Andrews concurred that 'Pacino was born to play Shylock', but wished for 'a more imaginative midwife' than Radford (*Financial Times*, 2 December 2004). In the US, reactions ranged from critical affirmation to full-throttled lambasting. Desson Thomson praised the film for engaging in 'a profound, subtextual dialogue with bigotry' (*Washington Post*, 28 January 2005); A. O. Scott – for being 'judiciously trimmed', and for 'succeed[ing] in rendering the complexities with clarity and vigor' (*New York Times*, 29 December 2004). The eminent Roger Ebert praised the film overall, but found fault with its 'peculiar construction', which he compared to 'channel-surfing between a teen romance and a dark abyss of loss and grief' (*Chicago Sun-Times*, 20 January 2005). Ron Rosenbaum, one of the harshest critics of the film, objected to its strategies of evasion, calling out its 'sanitized version of history' and Al Pacino's portrayal of 'an inoffensive, defanged, P.C. Shylock ... a heroically suffering Everyman' (*Jewish World Review*, 6 December 2004). Film scholar Thomas Cartelli has argued that the film privileges Belmont's 'norms of desired social behavior ... thus muting the redistribution of complicities that might otherwise shadow Belmont's revels and qualify the virtue of Portia's mercifixion of Shylock in Venice' (p. 61). The critic contends that the film offers a flattering version of a youth culture of class, manners, and beauty, as if lifted from the pages of *Vogue* and *Seventeen* (p. 68). Whatever their disagreements about the film, most critics considered Pacino a towering Shylock.

Shot in seven hectic weeks on location in Venice and on set in Luxembourg, with a CGI set borrowed from *The Lord of the Rings* for Portia's island of Belmont, the film offers high production values and an interpretation which places it 'squarely in the middle of mainstream readings of the work' (Philip Kennicott, *Washington Post*, 28 January 2005). From the late twentieth-century theatre tradition, it borrows a tragic Shylock, anti-Semitic Venetians, a homosexual Antonio (Bulman, *Shakespeare in Performance*, p. 38), a more prominent Jessica (Gilbert, *The Merchant of Venice: The State of Play*, pp. 17–18), and a darkened ending. Catering to Hollywood's international-marketing demands, it adds comic levity in the romantic line by occluding the xenophobia of Belmont's polite society (Pittman, p. 21).

In the hands of experienced filmmaker Radford, who is also the scriptwriter, the story is streamlined and disambiguated, told through the rich visual language of heritage film. Only the fourth feature-length film of the play, and the third made after the Holocaust, Radford's *Merchant* engages in a dialogue with both pre- and post-Holocaust film adaptations. Like Felner's and Billon's films, it utilises the natural beauty of the location; unlike them, it does not romanticise it. Benoît Delhomme's camera is tightly focused on a Venice of passageways and indoor spaces, peopled by bustling life. The splendours of the Serenissima fade through blue camera filters into the perpetual gloom of inclement weather. The colour palette and atmosphere of the Venetian scenes evoke the memorable contrast of grey and red in Steven Spielberg's *Schindler's List* (1994), here hyped up in hue. Other images, too, recall the 1930s rather than the 1590s. In effect, the film functions as 'a memorial: its construction of a Shakespearean past is tunnelled through a more immediate legacy, with the inevitable result that its pre-images are also its after-images' (Burnett, p. 105).

An establishing shot introduces Venice as a place where a railing friar stirs up religious violence against the Jews. Sacred Jewish books burn; a dense grey multitude surrounds a tiny group of Jews, distinguished by their red caps; on the Rialto bridge, the incensed crowd throws a Jew into the waters of the Grand Canal. Visuals alternate with textual scrolls akin to the title cards of silent cinema, describing the assault on Jews in a non-Shakespearean Venice. Cameo sequences introduce the viewer to the main characters and basic conflicts: Antonio spits on Shylock; Bassanio nonchalantly glides past in a gondola surrounded by a merry, drinking company; Lorenzo gains access to the Ghetto after curfew. Another sequence reveals Shylock and Antonio's religious lives: one appears in the warm glow of a synagogue full of men and women (the only women in Venice who are not prostitutes); the other kneels down in a church dominated by a sword-like cross, the camera carefully isolating him from other male worshippers.

A motif, recurring across narrative strands, features hands in close-up, expressing the desires and values of the characters: some handle money; others messages, gloves, meat, keys, rings. This specifically cinematic ploy, occasionally used in both Felner's and Billon's films, is here consistently employed to provide commentary. Money furtively changing hands between Jews and Venetians in the opening frames re-emerges as a shower of coins cascading from Bassanio's hand during his spending spree before departing for Belmont. Leah's ring, seen on Jessica's hand in the opening shots, is still tantalisingly there, as revealed in a final close-up (evidence that Tubal's report that she had traded the ring for a monkey was erroneous).

Venice is a decadent, sexualised, and aggressive place. There is no doubt of the moral corruption of its Christian inhabitants. Two of the play's minor characters, Salerio (John Sessions) and Solanio (Gregor Fisher), emblematise this quality. Though fervently kneeling at prayer in the opening sequence, they are gluttons, drunks, and brothel regulars; close-ups of their ring-wearing hands (were they married men?) show them kneading the flesh of prostitutes. Nor are the Venetian youth who descend upon Belmont to prey on its riches an attractive lot either. Gratiano (Kris Marshall) is a loud-mouthed, violent profligate, Solanio's drinking mate, and Bassanio's companion on boys' nights out. Bassanio (Joseph Fiennes), though better mannered and higher born, is a full member of this dubious company. Likely because of concerns for the rating, the film restricted the portrayal of Antonio's homosexuality to delicately suggestive visuals and Jeremy Irons's perpetual expression of pained reserve. Bassanio asks Antonio for money in the dark recesses of the latter's house and under the canopy of a four-poster bed, the only bed visible in a film about sexual desire. He appears as a crafty, exploitative manipulator who pouts when Antonio mentions that his fortunes are at sea, but, tellingly, gives him a kiss on the mouth when he gets what he came for.

More oblique is the film's portrayal of Venetian (Christian) racism. In the opening sequence on the Rialto bridge, a careful viewer could discern a black man jostled around with the group of Jews. Another black person appears in the crowd behind Shylock in the trial scene, almost shadowing his movements; close at hand, a black 'purchased slave' (IV.i. 89) fans his Venetian master, an image somewhat reminiscent of the decorative function of Portia's black page in Felner's silent film. Such fleeting moments, however, do not add up to a consistent critical exploration of race, while the obfuscation of the racism of the mistress of Belmont is a more deliberate directorial choice (Pittman, p. 21). The Princes of Morocco (David Harewood) and Arragon (Antonio Gil) provide bizarre instances of comic relief. One is an Eddie Murphy type Hollywood cliché of an African with an entourage of turbaned buffoons, the other a gargoyle of a man whose attendants appear to have come out of a caricature of Velázquez's 'Las Meninas". Along with the other ridiculous foreigners, these characters are used to justify Portia's unwillingness to marry a non-Venetian, while her racist lines are strategically cut.

Within the narratives of religious intolerance and racist bigotry, the central conflict between Shylock and Antonio is in the hands of two large acting personalities, Al Pacino and Jeremy Irons. The characters' animosity (mutual in Shakespeare's text) is here more one-sided, evident in Antonio's ugly act of spitting on Shylock in the opening sequence. The two men are, however, portrayed as similarly isolated and chronically depressed. For Pacino's New York Yiddish-accented Shylock, the problem is that he belongs to 'a struggling ethnic minority, whose will to survive at all costs leads to criminal excess and tragic over-reaching' (Drew, p. 54). If the slaughtered goat in the marketplace (where part of the bond scene is set) is anything to go by, Venice is a place of cut-throat relationships. Shylock's unease among the Venetians is clearly conveyed in the added scene of a riotous banquet in celebration of the loan. Ignored by all, jostled by a prostitute consorting with a reveller right next to him, eyed by those plotting his daughter's elopement, he barely suppresses his disgust, never touching the food or the wine. Close by, Antonio who feels similarly out of place mechanically stuffs himself with food (Figure 22).

Shylock is a man harassed, humiliated, and joyless, whose life is anchored in his small business, community, and family, however unsentimental his relationship with Jessica might be. Two great scenes offer a pattern for understanding how this oppressed man's 'affections [and] passions' (III.i.54) have been ignited.

Figure 22 Al Pacino as Shylock and Jeremy Irons as Antonio at the loan celebration banquet in Michael Radford's film, *William Shakespeare's The Merchant of Venice* (2004).

After Jessica's flight, a broken Shylock spots Salerio and Solanio enter a brothel and follows to get information about her. Though Radford's film does not suggest that the brothel involves the exploitation of Jewish women, as did Billon's, the choice underscores Christian hypocrisy and Jewish humiliation. Vented in a public walkway, with bare-breasted prostitutes hovering in the background, Shylock's exasperated 'Hath not a Jew eyes' (III.i.53 ff.) explodes under unbearable pressure. Pacino's restrained acting heats up with measured oratorical propulsion, climaxing in a logically unassailable 'shall we not revenge?' (60). Tubal's (Allan Corduner) expressionless delivery of one piece of bad news after another comprises a sequence where the spoken word is visualised as action. Wordless scenes of Venetian debauchery, featuring Jessica carousing and trading Leah's ring, flick across Shylock's fevered imagination, culminating in his unnaturally self-composed request, 'fee me an officer' (113–14). In the trial scene (shot at the Doge's Palace in Venice), Shylock again slowly gives way to his righteous rage, only to be callously undercut by Portia's manipulation of the proceedings. Publicly humiliated, he slumps to the ground with a pitiful wail. After Antonio calls for conversion, the crowded nature of the scene recalls the abuse of the anonymous Jew that opened the film. In the finale, the door of the synagogue is shut in Shylock's face. His rejection is complete.

While Shylock's representation is supposedly thoroughly historicised, the roles of Portia (Lynn Collins) and Jessica (Zuleikha Robinson) match modern expectations of female agency, a cinematic practice since Felner's *Jew of Mestri*. On the one hand, their common predicament as daughters under patriarchal control is conveyed by their being framed by doors and windows, like portraits. A combination of shots of the framed Portia and 'Portia's counterfeit' (III.ii.115) – her portrait from the casket – activates an interplay with the meaning of 'counterfeit' as both artistic and fraudulent imitation, a side of Portia's character which Radford hints at. The added sequence showing her visit the old lawyer Bellario before the trial enhances this characterisation. Clearly, she has planned how to spring the legal trap on Shylock. The court scene also allows Portia to observe the interactions between her husband and Antonio. Her delay to act while Shylock probes the merchant's breast with his knife to confirm where his blow will fall, is as much a torture of her husband's lover as it is a test of the limits of Shylock's vengefulness. At the end of the scene, her problem is elegantly summed up in a close-up of her hands clasping Antonio's gloves and her own wedding ring, received as payment for her legal services.

While Portia, a blond beauty styled after Botticelli's Primavera, agonises romantically in the splendours of a vast sun-lit palace, Jessica lives under gruff parental control in Shylock's 'sober house' (II.v.35), a cramped space with shuttered windows. As with Portia, shots of her face are portrait-like, framed by a window and a mirror. The dimness of her reflection anticipates her coming fate. When she arrives in Belmont with Lorenzo, though not hailed as an 'infidel' (III.ii.217), she fades away in the background. The tenuousness of her position is made clear through Portia's obvious neglect. The heiress disregards the new convert when she asks Lorenzo to look after the house, a moment shot in a convent, with Jessica in obliterating darkness. Upon Portia's return from Venice, however, a two-shot of the women offers a moment that seems to establish a degree of parity. Portia's 'This night, methinks, is but the daylight sick' (V.i.124–6), addressed to Jessica, sounds like a piece of polite trivia, but is also the first direct communication between them. Jessica's positioning and the attention the camera begins to pay to her reactions suggest her growing awareness of the ways Belmont operates.

The film ends with Jessica alone at sunrise, looking over the golden waters of the Venetian lagoon. In a last close-up, the camera rests on her hand with Leah's ring still there – the one that her father was told (and filmgoers believed) had been sold for a monkey. Like Portia's ring, which Antonio returned to Bassanio in an emotional two-shot, this ring too symbolises a severed connection: in Jessica's case, to her family and community. As the romance of the winners of the day builds to closure, heavy with erotic anticipation, Radford focuses on those excluded from the loving circles. A dejected Lancelot with a clown's bauble exits the room alone; a wistful Antonio stands by a window; a bare-headed Shylock is left alone outside the synagogue. While Jessica's way is not solitary (her Lorenzo is the most decent of the Venetian Christians, played by an affable Charlie Cox), she, too, is coming to terms with a profound loss for which no one can console her. The mood of the moment is captured in Jocelyn Pook's wistful musical rendition of verses from John Milton's *Paradise Lost* about Adam and Eve's banishment from Eden: 'They, hand in hand, with wandering steps and slow, through Eden took their solitary way.'

Radford's best films 'deal in ways tragic and benign ... with the cultural outsider' (Crowl, pp. 115–16) and so does his *Merchant of Venice*. However thoughtful its adaptation, the past as well as the present cast a shadow on the aesthetic choices made in its filming, a reminder of the pressures of history and marketing, not unlike those playing out in the exchanges between the Christian Venetians and their Others.

Notes

1 The world premiere of *The Maori Merchant of Venice* was on 15 February 2002 in Waikato, New Zealand (Cox, 92, note 6). However, distribution began in late 2001, using a slow release strategy among Māori-speaking audiences at charity events 'to benefit the Pei Te Hurinui Jones Trust, formed to fund creative writing in *te reo*' (Silverstone, p. 141). Funding was eventually provided by Te Māngai

Pāho, the state funding body for Māori-language broadcasting (Wayne, p. 426).

2 After playing in New Zealand movie theatres, Selwyn's film was broadcast in 2004 on the newly launched Māori Television channel; in the following year, it was included in the inaugural Wairoa Māori Film Festival (Silverstone, pp. 141–2). Its international circulation was limited to film festivals and academic events in 2002–5.

3 All quotations from *Te Tengata* are from the film subtitles.

4 Thank you to art historian Megan Tamati-Quennell of the Modern and Contemporary Māori and Indigenous Art Museum for the identification of the visual symbolism of Selwyn Muru's paintings. Personal communication, 2 September 2020.

5 Subtle though the allusion to cannibalism may be (especially for global audiences), it is not restricted to the bond scene. Not long after, when Morako makes his choice of the golden casket in Peremona, the 'carrion death' he discovers is a mummified head – a statement of the *mana* of the house of Pohia, perhaps, as well as an unmistakable threat, underscored by a percussion surge in the musical score.

6 Alternative, less hopeful interpretations of the ending have been offered by Gretchen E. Minton (p. 53) and Lanier (p. 190).

VII

The search for justice: *The Merchant of Venice* in Mandatory Palestine (1936) and the Venetian Ghetto (2016)

Among the plethora of interpretations of *The Merchant of Venice* in theatre and film productions across the globe, two stand out for their part in broader, intentional debates on the significance of 'the most famous fictional Jew in Western culture' at pivotal moments in history (Bassi, *New Places*, p. 164). These debates arose from the encounter of the play with the charged contexts of two productions – both of them in places of singular significance for Jewish history, spirituality, and cultural identity. The immediate cultural resonance of these productions was enhanced by mock trials that ran parallel with them and involved prominent intellectuals and legal professionals whose objective was to restore justice denied to Shylock. Yet, even as justice triumphed for this dramatic character, it was withheld from others. Shakespeare's problem comedy, it seems, keeps its interpreters, both on-stage and in the courtroom, chasing after this elusive ideal.

The first of these productions opened on 14 May 1936 in Tel Aviv, the fast-growing economic and cultural centre of Jewish life in what was then Mandatory Palestine. The first play in Hebrew at the new Habima Theatre (which would become the National Theatre of Israel in 1958), it was guest-directed by Leopold Jessner (1878–1945), a Jewish refugee from Nazi Germany. He had been one of Berlin's outstanding directors, a champion of the Expressionist movement whose 'politically oriented "topical theatre" or *Zeittheater* paved the way for the political theatre of Piscator and Brecht' (Feinberg, *Jews and the Making of Modern German Theatre*, p. 232). The play, which ran for forty-seven nights, created a media frenzy across ideological lines in the Palestinian press; it had drawn the ire of the American Anti-Defamation League before it even opened. To address the controversy provoked by the show, the Friends of Habima organised a Literary Trial held in the Ohel Shem Hall on 23 June 1936, at which lawyers, poets, and theatre professionals argued the question of Shakespeare's anti-Semitism, Habima's judgement in bringing 'an indefensible play' to the Land of Israel, and the feasibility and effect of Jessner's approach to Shylock (Zer-Zion, *Forum Modernes Theater*, p. 163). The trial proceedings were published in the theatre journal *Bamah* alongside a series of articles on the play and the production. Nor was this event easily forgotten. In 2012, the trial received a full-page summary in the Hebrew playbill of another Habima production, which would later travel to London to be performed in the Globe to Globe season (Zer-Zion, *Wrestling with Shylock*, p. 196).

The second production of the play in a locale significant to Jewish history was staged in 2016 in the Campo del Ghetto Nuovo in Venice. Titled *The Merchant in Venice*, it honoured the confluence of two anniversaries: 400 years since Shakespeare's death and 500 years since the establishment of the Venetian Jewish Ghetto, a site that gave us the word for ethnic urban segregation. Historically, the Ghetto was a contact zone between the Venetian Christians and the Ashkenazi, Sephardic, and Levantine Jews confined to this tiny island in the Cannaregio district of the city; moreover, it was a cradle of Jewish cultural and intellectual creativity of lasting global impact. To this day, it is home to five synagogues, one for each of the original immigrant communities. It is also a site of Holocaust remembrance (Bassi, *Shakespeare Survey*, pp. 67–71). This is where the international performing collective Compagnia de' Colombari, under the direction of its founder Karin Coonrod (1953–), staged its production, developed in consultation with the city's Jewish leaders and the Ghetto residents. The play ran in the Ghetto for six days, from 26 July to 1 August 2016 and was subsequently performed at the Theatre Festival of Bassano del Grappa and in Casa di Reclusione, a high-security men's prison in Padua. It was revived, with an altered cast, for a 2017–18 US campus tour at Montclair State University, Yale, and Dartmouth. This was a multi-national and multilingual production, born out of wide-ranging and sometimes tense conversations. The creative team hailed from Belgium, France, India, Italy, the USA, and the United Kingdom; although English was the main language of the performance, Italian, Venetian, Ladino, Yiddish, Judaeo-Venetian, Hebrew, German, French, and Spanish were also heard – languages resonant with the past and present of the performance site.

The Merchant in Venice developed as part of an international academic project titled *Shakespeare In and Beyond the Ghetto*.[1] It brought together students, scholars, and theatre artists from across the globe for lectures, symposia, workshops, spin-off productions, and an exhibition at the Doge's Palace on Venetian Jewish history. As highly anticipated as the performance itself was the 'Mock Appeal in the Matter of Shylock v. Antonio', heard by a bench of international lawyers presided over by US Supreme Court Justice Ruth Bader Ginsburg. This trial – a side show arguably more tightly orchestrated than the boisterous 1936 Literary Trial – took place on 27 July 2016, in the Tintoretto-frescoed Sala Capitolare (Chapter Hall) of the Scuola Grande di San Rocco. Like the Colombari production, it was transferred to the US, where it was reprised at the Law Library of Congress in 2017.[2]

The historical contexts of the Habima and Colombari productions of *The Merchant* bear uncanny similarities. Both were marked by surges in immigration, violence, and political radicalisation. With the 1935 Nuremberg Laws wreaking havoc among German Jews and the rapid increase of Jewish persecution in Central Europe, the number of new immigrants to Palestine in 1936 rose nearly fourteen-fold. This resulted in a dramatic shift in the demographic balance between Arabs and Jews, exacerbated cultural conflicts in addition to the obvious religious divide, and caused an economic downturn for under-skilled Arab labour, provoking in turn escalating waves of Arab violence. Starting in April 1936, Palestine saw 'not only strikes, shop closures, nationalist demonstrations, and violence against Jewish homes and businesses but also attacks on telephone lines, traffic, railroad bridges, and other targets controlled by the British colonial authorities' (Bayer, p. 67). To complicate matters further, tensions were also palpable within the Palestinian Jewish community. Its leadership was both eager to offer a safe haven to German Jews fleeing Nazi persecution and apprehensive about the influx of immigrants who had been assimilated into German culture, often had no knowledge of Hebrew, and were unfamiliar with Judaism – in other words, immigrants whose cultural integration and inclusion in the Zionist enterprise was bound to be slow and difficult (Zer-Zion, *Wrestling*, p. 177). Thus Habima mounted *The Merchant of Venice* under the pressure of 'growing nationalist sentiments [which] frayed traditional relationships that revolved around families, tribes, and clans' (Bayer, p. 67).

Along similar lines, 2016 was the sixth consecutive year of an immigration surge to Europe, and the peak year of unauthorised immigration.[3] Immigration had rapidly accelerated the year before, fuelled by armed conflicts in North Africa and the Middle East, notably the Syrian civil war (2011–). Although the immigration tide was nowhere near affecting the European demographic balance as Jewish immigration had done to Palestine in the 1930s, it put a strain on social resources, especially in leading destination countries, such as Germany, the United Kingdom, Italy, and France, and in the poorer, more recent members of the European Union. Coming on the heels of the global financial crash of 2008–9, the surge of immigrants with significant cultural differences, coupled with deadly terrorist attacks carried out by home-grown radical Islamist groups in Paris, Brussels, and Nice, 'stoked the flames of ethno-nationalisms, with their familiar forms of virulent racism, xenophobia and gender-role normativity, disguised as a return to traditional "patriotic" and family (i.e. patriarchal) values' (Sokolova and Valls-Russell, p. 8). The Colombari's *Merchant in Venice*, then, was developed 'at a specific geopolitical juncture in the history of Europe when the most sophisticated awareness and development of critical multicultural thinking coexist[ed] with the resurgence of populism, antisemitism, and racism as major political vectors' (Bassi, *The Merchant in Venice*, p. 35).

Performing 'the Jewish play' in places where formative strands of Jewish history met the political turbulence of the present was a study in conflicting interpretations. Jessner's proposal to stage *The Merchant* at the Habima Theatre in order to enhance its classical repertoire – and, with the added prestige of his name, its status – enabled the company to resolve some unfinished business. In Habima's early days, when it operated under the auspices of the Moscow Art Theatre, the famed Russian director Konstantin Stanislavsky embarked on a production of the play in which Habima actors were to play the Jews, members of the Armenian Studio of the Theatre were to play Morocco, Arragon, and their retinues, and Russian actors were to play the Venetians (Kouts, p. 108). Stanislavsky refused to take a stance on the conflict between the Venetians and their Others, asking the actors 'to persuade him which group was worthier'. The result, as reported by Habima actor Moshe Halevi, who was to play Shylock, was a near outbreak of violence: 'It seemed that the exercises exceeded mere "acting" and both groups seemed to be clamouring for blood' (Zer-Zion, *Wrestling*, p. 184).

Jessner, in contrast, brought a clear directorial vision to the play. The dramaturgical adaptation published in *Bamah* describes a sharpening of the conflict between Shylock 'as one of a People that has been oppressed for thousands of years' and 'the radiant Christian worlds of Venice and Belmont' – attractive, but unaccepting of Others and awash with amorality (qtd. in Zer-Zion, *Wrestling*, p. 185). Jessner's political interpretation of the play was theatre for a new Jewish homeland, where, he argued, it was to 'serve ... as a vehicle of propaganda for the *Eretz-Israeli-an* conception [that is, as propaganda supporting a sovereign Israeli state]' (qtd. in Bayer, p. 65). Accordingly, he cleansed Shylock of the caricature stylisation that played into the ideological rise of anti-Semitism in the 1920s and 1930s (see Part II, Segue) and gave his Jewish audience a Shylock of pride and dignity, devoid of 'the hard lines wrought by hatred, rancor, and cruelty' (*Setel Variety*, 10 June 1936). Two veteran Habima actors, Aharon Meskin and Shimon Finkel, performed the part on alternate nights. Meskin, a former Red Army soldier, gave a powerful, earthy Shylock (Figure 23), ghosted by the actor's celebrated performance in the title role of H. Levick's *The Golem*.[4] Finkel, who was trained in the German acting tradition and 'had in the past portrayed a series of German-Jewish protagonists who claimed equal rights, avenged insults, yet were eventually deceived by the false promise of emancipation', imbued the character with lofty nobility and with fatherly softness (Zer-Zion, *Wrestling*, p. 187) (Figure 24). Jessner's direction aimed to create 'a fighting Shylock who, although he falls defeated by the libelous machinations of his rivals and indeed ends tragically, ends not as sufferer, but as tragic hero' (qtd. in Zer-Zion, *Forum*, p. 171). The actors delivered. A reviewer for *HaBoker* wrote of his impression of Shylock as 'a great tragic figure ..., a sort of prince among the Jews ... More than being a persecuted Jew, he is a Doge of

Figure 23 Studio portrait of Aharon Meskin as Shylock in Leopold Jessner's production for the Habima Theatre, Tel Aviv, 1936.

Venice of sorts' (qtd. in Kouts, p. 111). The single surviving photograph from the production captures him climbing the diagonal of a wide staircase, moving higher than the Duke.[5] Book in hand, upright despite the yellow badge on the back of his traditional dark

Figure 24 Studio portrait of Shimon Finkel as Shylock in Leopold Jessner's production for the Habima Theatre, Tel Aviv, 1936.

robe, Shylock confidently approaches Balthazar/Portia, who stands before the image of Justice on the mural behind her (Figure 25). The description of the scene in *Bamah* captures the commanding dynamism of a character 'speaking ... in a thundering voice, while

Figure 25 The trial scene in Leopold Jessner's production for the Habima Theatre, Tel Aviv, 1936.

everybody froze as if suddenly hypnotized' (qtd. in Oz, p. 200). This was not a Jew from the Ghetto, but 'a court Jew on the cusp of the enlightenment' (Zer-Zion, *German-Jewish Experience*, p. 259).

The portrayal of Shylock as a hero full of righteous contempt for Venetian society was envisaged as support for the Zionist cause. Still, a loud chorus of voices challenged the suitability of the play for a Hebrew theatre dedicated to the formation of a new nation. The climax of the controversy came at the Literary Trial. The issue was the portrayal of the Venetian world as embodying an attractive humanistic ideal unattainable by Jews. Shylock's desire to revenge his exclusion resonated with the experience of Jessner and his generation of German Jews who had built the cultural legacy of their country only to be disenfranchised and exiled from it. However, such desire for revenge was at odds with the Zionist dream of renewal and transformation, accounting for the play's mixed reception (Zer-Zion, *Forum*, pp. 172–3). 'Our audience was slightly insulted by this performance' wrote poet Jacob Fichman in an otherwise positive review (qtd. in Kouts, p. 112). At the trial, another poet and a witness for the prosecution, Alexander Penn, declared Shylock puny and vicious, lacking the self-restraint that the Jewish community had demonstrated during the Arab revolt, and therefore perilous for the Zionist cause: 'for us, who came here to bring about a great spiritual-economical shift in our life, this show should have been a sharp reminder, an acute warning against all those petty Shylocks, those speculators and profiteers penetrating our country' (qtd. in Oz, p. 201). Literary critic Avraham Kariv, another witness for the prosecution, denounced Shylock's pursuit of justice as 'primitive vengeance unacceptable to a Jew', questioning the tragic stature of a character whose 'fall did not affirm any humanistic or Jewish value' (Zer-Zion, *Forum*, p. 174). Surprisingly, it was Shylock's nemesis, Portia – or rather, Habima's leading lady and Zionist icon Hanna Rovina as the lady of Belmont – who was seen as a tragic heroine for her sacrifice in playing against her Jewish sensibilities for the sake of art (Zer-Zion, *Wrestling* p. 190). The defence circumvented the Zionist pathos of the prosecution, deploying the cultural capital of a supra-generational community of dead and living German-Jewish intellectuals to support its argument for Shakespeare's canonical status and the play as an open metaphor rich for interpretation.[6]

The judges were convinced. They found Shakespeare innocent, Habima courageous to 'present a play that, with all its supreme artistic quality, is inherently dangerous for the national Hebrew stage', and Jessner not guilty in staging *The Merchant of Venice* in the spirit of the time (qtd. in Zer-Zion, *Forum*, p. 177). Yet the juridical endorsement had a limited effect. In spite of Jessner's dedicated support of amateur and professional Hebrew theatre, in spite of his ardour for new rituals connecting biblical stories of fighting and victorious Jews to the Jewish experience in Mandatory Palestine, in spite of his publicly professed desire to put down roots in the country, he was not invited to continue his work with Habima. After six months in the Land of Israel, he left for Vienna, where in June 1937, a few months before emigrating to the United States, he staged his last work in Europe (Feinberg, *Jews and the Making of Modern German Theatre*, p. 248). This was the dramatic documentary poem, *Chronicle of 1936* by Yiddish poet Malka Locker, performed by eighty young Jewish amateur actors. It ended with a vision of the persecuted Jews of Central Europe uniting with Zionist pioneers in the budding Jewish state – the very political entity that had rejected Jessner, associating him with a diasporic Shylock inconvenient for the Zionist leaders.

Eighty years after Habima staged *The Merchant of Venice* in Hebrew, Coonrod's international, multilingual Compagnia de' Colombari brought the play into 'creative collision' with a site overlaid with historical memories of exclusion, effacement, cultural negotiation, and spirituality, as well as with a host of transhistorical projections and fictionalisations (Bassi, *Shakespeare Survey*, p. 69). Subtly retitled *The Merchant in Venice*, the production integrated Shakespeare's play with a number of theatrical and musical traditions, including sixteenth-century Venetian rustic comedy, its close relative commedia dell'arte, opera, jazz, Jewish chants, and more; it transmuted a boisterous comedic opening into dark drama. Character construction was laid bare throughout: costumes changes were done in plain sight, actors switched between performing and observing the dramatic action, props (the improbable rings, Morocco's imposing scimitar) were exhibited in their artisanal Venetian glory before they were used. Most notably, Shylock was conceived as a mosaic of his roles in the five scenes in which he appears. Five actors of different nationalities, accents, ages, and genders portrayed him: first as the urbane negotiator in I.iii, performed by Mumbai-born Sorab Wadia; then as the overbearing, anxious father in II.v, by the Italian Adriano Iurissevich; as the father/mother bereft of a child in III.i, by Welsh Jenni Lea-Jones; as the frantic widower in III.iii, whose comedic portrayal by the Italian Andrea Brugnera recalled the stereotype of the caricature Jew (Rutter, *Shakespeare Survey* 70, p. 86); and finally, as the steel-minded avenger in IV.i, by New Yorker Ned Eisenberg. At key moments in the play, they came together as the unified body of the Other (Figure 26). What was lost in continuity was gained in multiplying otherness, opening up Shylock's character to a range of human experiences. Furthermore, since the five Shylocks also doubled as other characters – some casually or viciously anti-Semitic – the audience was privy to the unnervingly rapid dynamics of social alienation.

More poetic than ideologically driven, the production invited neither a backward look at Jewish history nor an anticipation of

Figure 26 The five Shylocks lament Jessica's flight in the Compagnia de' Colombari's production of *The Merchant in Venice*, directed by Karin Coonrod, 2016. Left to right: Ned Eisenberg, Andrea Brugnera, Adriano Iurissevich, Sorab Wadia, Jenni Lea-Jones.

Jewish (moral) victory. Rather, it called for introspection about our discomforts, fears, fascinations, and bonds with strangers: not only the Shylocks whose Jewishness was marked by elegant yellow sashes, but also Morocco and Arragon, who appeared in back-to-back scenes that opened with ethnic stereotyping but added touchingly realistic characterisation. Such introspection was facilitated by the self-consciousness of the audience attending a play in the inwardly looking campo of the Ghetto Nuovo. Spectators witnessed Shakespearean anti-Semitic slurs spewed in English, Italian, Spanish, French, and German not only under the gaze of the families dining by the windows of the ancient tenements surrounding the campo, but also as they faced the shuttered windows of the Ghetto's synagogues. In an added final scene, creative directing, music, and lighting were used to fashion a multi-media dialogue extending across time, languages, and the divide between fiction and reality. This dialogue was provoked by a reiteration of Shylock's refusal to justify his demand for the pound of flesh, spoken by all five actors performing the character: 'I [can] give no reason, nor I will not, / More than a lodged hate and certain loathing / I bear Antonio … / … Are you answered? (4.1.58–61). The rhetorical question, spoken as the actors advanced in a straight line toward the audience, was underscored by the sound of shofars. Traversing the campo, a frantic Jessica broke past the footlights and out of the space of the play to face Shylock's question alongside the audience. The word 'mercy' in English, Italian, and Hebrew lit up the walls of the Ghetto tenements. This was an open metaphor of the kind Jessner's defence counsel had referred to.

The projected writing on the walls angered some, puzzled others, and captivated many. Dario Calimani saw it as 'deviant and blasphemous', an invitation to the audience to take home the 'failed ideal' of Venetian Christian society (*Moked*/מוקד, 1 August 2016). Kent Cartwright pondered if the ending 'was meant to acknowledge the impasse to which our inhumanity threatens to take us' and offered 'a desperate call for an intervening mercy' (p. 151) – a reading Diane Henderson concurred with (p. 167). Carol Rutter wondered whether this ending, which 'resolved nothing', was an attempt to deflect Shylock's question and give the Ghetto the final word, or whether it was a prompt to continue wrestling with questions of justice and compassion that the play refuses to resolve (*Shakespeare Survey* 70, p. 88). Mindful of the diverse sacred and historical narratives informing the notion of mercy in different languages and cultures, we suggest that the charged dialogue in the final scene and the play's lack of resolution may have been a reminder of the difficulty of reconciling volatile meanings of 'mercy' and its supplement 'justice', in 2016.

The highly anticipated 'Mock Appeal' – another performative event with a setting of symbolic significance – aimed to restore mercy and justice to Shylock and ultimately demonstrated the contingency of these ideals. Tintoretto's breath-taking decorative scheme reminded attendees that mercy is foundational to both Jewish and Christian traditions. The ceiling panels in San Rocco's Sala Capitolare feature dramatic events from the Old Testament (most pertinent to the occasion, the Binding of Isaac), while paintings of scenes from the life of Christ adorn the long walls of the room. In the adjacent Salla dell'Albergo, the Virgin Mary appears in the Allegory of the Scuola della Misericordia – a merciful mother stretching her arms around the brothers of that confraternity. The connection between Justice and Mercy (or equity, in legal terms) was underscored in an opening speech by

Fabrizio Marrella, professor of international law at Ca' Foscari University; he also explained the significance of Astraea, the Greek virgin goddess of Justice, in the early modern civic myth of Venice. The last deity to live among mortals, Astraea is enshrined in a sculpture, standing today atop the Palazzo Ducale, sword and scales in her hands (Rutter, *The Merchant in Venice*, p. 176). The setting, not to mention the brilliance of the legal minds at the bench, promised a judicial outcome worthy of the goddess. Chief judge Ruth Bader Ginsburg contributed not only professional expertise but also theatrical acumen, which she had honed in a series of appeals by Shakespeare characters in the popular mock trials sponsored by the Shakespeare Theatre Company in Washington, DC.[7]

Yet the conflict was sanitised from the start. Contrary to Shylock's reiteration of his claim to a pound of Antonio's flesh declared at the end of Ghetto production of the play, it turned out that his demand had been relinquished in a pre-trial hearing. This dulled the edge of the controversy. The argument advanced by Mario Siragusa, Counsel for Antonio and the Republic of Venice, that Shylock had come to court prepared to murder for revenge, was dismissed, as Judge Ginsburg declared that the pound of flesh was a jest.[8] Thus managed, the 'principles of law ... entailed their own silence regarding the moral nuances of action and character' (Cartwright, p. 160). Once the basis for criminal action was removed, and after acknowledging how inappropriate it had been for the defendant Antonio to determine the penalty, justice was unanimously restored to Shylock. The conversion was annulled and the 3,000 ducats returned to him (without interest, since four centuries were deemed an excessive delay).

Yet, even as the appellant court denounced the transformation of the civil case against Shylock into a criminal one, it expanded its own prerogative to that of a criminal court. A new defendant, Portia, was summoned to answer for deploying the questionable Alien Act against Shylock and for 'perpetuating a hoax on the judiciary by pretending to be a judge'. In a disturbing instance of 'trading scapegoats', a split majority declared her ' "a liar and a hypocrite" who failed to render Shylock the mercy she required him to give Antonio, and [sentenced] her for criminal imposture'

(Rutter, *The Merchant in Venice*, p. 181). The penalty was to enrol in the Law School of the University of Padua.

Thankfully, this was not the final judgment on Portia. When the trial was revived at the Law Library of Congress in Washington, DC, her counsel, Teresa Miguel-Stearns, asked that Portia 'be discharged from the dispute and future related proceedings' and successfully argued that not only was Portia qualified to provide legal advice to the Duke – gender restrictions on the legal profession in sixteenth-century Venice notwithstanding – but that her navigation of the law had saved the lives of both Antonio and Shylock. This time, the overwhelmingly female bench decided in favour of both Shylock and Portia. He got the principal of the loan – 'as a substitutional remedy because he did not get the pound of flesh' – and an annulment of the conversion. She was warmly encouraged – *not* sentenced – to pursue studies at the Law School of Lake Forest University. It remains for future appeals of judgement carried and miscarried in *The Merchant of Venice* to seek justice-with-equity for the Gobbos, Morocco, Arragon, and Jessica. Apparently, the controversies regarding legal interpretations of the play are just as difficult to resolve as those regarding performative interpretation.

* * *

As the tumultuous stage history of *The Merchant of Venice* of which this book offers a taste suggests, 'the course' of this Shakespearean play about the Other 'never did run smooth' (*A Midsummer Night's Dream*, I.i.134). Its fortunes have been indelibly affected by the totalitarian regimes of twentieth-century fascism and communism. The delicate tissue of a festive romantic comedy was either shredded by the upheavals of history, or the play was quietly removed from the stage. The long shadow of the Holocaust still clouds the skies over Shakespeare's Venice, thrusting the fictional Jew to the centre of the action, and barring the way to a comic resolution. Nor is Shylock always a Jew in the productions of the new century; sometimes he is another Other suffering prejudice and injustice, voicing the grievances of other oppressed communities. Needless to say, all of the stage and film performances discussed here (whatever their own claims to authenticity) unfold at a cultural, textual, and aesthetic remove from Shakespeare's play. Few portray justice and social harmony as attainable.

The attempts of lawyers to wrestle with the legal conundrums of the fictional plot have likewise failed to deliver even-handed justice. Rather, these 'judgements' have divulged the limitations of historical legal systems and the biases of individual officers of the law.

If a metaphor is an appropriate way to end a complex story, perhaps we can think of *The Merchant* as a lens: polished by the tides of history, it starts to refract with a difference. The exceptional vitality of the play seems to suggest that the cruelty and beauty it juggles with capture something of the turbulent life of our societies, speak to our cruelty, cupidity, tribalism, intolerance, and the hatreds we endure and harbour. But what about the love that is in the play, that crosses tribal barriers and promises happiness? Adaptations of *The Merchant* in which Jessica is not subjected to paternal curses or Christian jibes are rare, while Antonio is never simply content with a monetary compensation. As the state of thinking about the play at the beginning of the twenty-first century seems to suggest, imagining such resolutions is nigh impossible. Instead, the lovers end up in a limbo of unhappiness, Shylock is defeated or turns into a mirror image of the Christians, Venice and Belmont transpire as places of cut-throat competitiveness, greed, anti-Semitism, racism, and xenophobia. The way the play is being adapted for stage and screen is symptomatic of persisting social malaises. Had the world been different, there would have been no need for this study in greed, with flesh as a global currency.

Notes

1 *Shakespeare In and Beyond the Ghetto* was the brainchild of Shaul Bassi, visionary project director of *The Merchant in Venice* and coordinator of the Venice Ghetto 500th-anniversary committee. The project was organised by Ca' Foscari University in collaboration with Fondazione Giorgio Cini and international partners, and funded by the Creative Europe Programme of the European Union as well as by private donors. The project's multifaceted nature has been captured in the collection *The Merchant in Venice: Shakespeare in the Ghetto*, edited by Shaul Bassi and Carol Chillington Rutter.
2 The recording is available at www.youtube.com/watch?v=ljFaVJ6RNpE

3 See Pew Research Center, 'Europe's unauthorized immigrant population peaks in 2016, then levels off', www.pewresearch.org/global/2019/11/13/europes-unauthorized-immigrant-population-peaks-in-2016-then-levels-off/
4 A rare video recording of Meskin's performance as Shylock can be seen at www.youtube.com/watch?v=zNalVT1EMhU&t=32s
5 The *Jessnertreppe* – a set of stairwells connecting various stage levels on a more or less bare stage – was developed by the director and his stage designer, Emil Pirchan, during Jessner's artistic directorship of the Berlin Staatstheater, Germany's national theatre. Along with an emblematic acting style emphasising a single facet of the character, this was a distinctive element of Jessner's politically grounded Expressionism.
6 Among the authorities 'summoned' by the theatre critic Dov Ber Malkin, Advocate for the Defense, were the lawyers Rudolph von Ihering and Joseph Kohler, the revolutionary Gustav Landauer, the historian Heinrich Graetz, and the poet Heinrich Heine.
7 In Washington, DC, Judge Ginsburg participated in mock trials of characters from *Macbeth* (2017), *Measure for Measure* (2014), *Coriolanus* (2013), *Much Ado about Nothing* (2012), *Henry V* (2010), *Twelfth Night* (2009), *Othello* (2005), *Henry IV 1 & 2* (2004), and *Richard III* (2003).
8 At the reiteration of the trial at the Law Library of Congress, also featuring Judge Ginsburg, Shylock's Counsel Michael Klotz politicised the case, describing the character as a civil rights activist whose threat to Antonio 'was a rebellion against the Venetian law that had treated him so unfairly [and] ... exposed the slave trade and the unfairness that Antonio could profit from selling people'. In his argument, the goal was not primarily monetary justice (as was the case in Venice); rather, restoring Shylock's money to him was a means of clearing his name.

Appendices

A. Some significant twentieth- and twenty-first-century productions of *The Merchant of Venice*

Stage Productions

Year	Director	Location
1901	Frank Benson	Stratford-upon-Avon
1905	Max Reinhardt	Berlin
1907	William Poel	London
1908	Herbert Beerbohm Tree	London
1913	Max Reinhardt	Berlin
1921	Max Reinhardt	Berlin
1922	David Belasco	New York
1928	Winthrop Ames	London
1932	Theodore Komisarjevsky	Stratford-upon-Avon
1934	Max Reinhardt	Venice
1936	Leopold Jessner	Tel Aviv
1938	John Gielgud	London
1938	Hrisan Tsankov	Sofia
1943	Lothar Müthel	Vienna
1940	Bèla Both	Budapest
1944	Alf Söberg	Stockholm
1948	Michael Benthall	Stratford-upon-Avon
1955	Tyrone Guthrie	Stratford, Ontario
1957	Jack Landau	Stratford, Connecticut
1962	Joseph Papp, Gladys Vaughan	New York
1963	Erwin Piscator	Berlin
1967	Michael Kahn	Stratford, Connecticut
1970	Jonathan Miller	London

Appendices 323

1971	Terry Hands	Stratford-upon-Avon
1972	Peter Zadek	Bochum
1973	Ellis Rabb	New York
1978	Georg Tabori	Munich
1978	John Barton	Stratford-upon-Avon
1987	Bill Alexander	Stratford-upon-Avon
1988	Peter Zadek	Vienna
1989	Michael Langham	Stratford, Ontario
1989	Peter Hall	London; New York
1992	Zdravko Mitkov	Sofia
1994	Peter Sellars	Chicago; London; Hamburg; Paris
1998	Róbert Alföldy	Budapest
1999	Trevor Nunn	London
2000	Robert Sturua	Moscow
2001	Andrei Şerban	Paris
2004	Egon Savin	Belgrade
2009	Edward Hall	Liverpool; New York; Tokyo
2010	Daniel Sullivan	New York
2010	László Bocsárdi	Sfântu-Gheorghe; Bucharest; Budapest
2011	Rupert Goold	Stratford-upon-Avon
2015	Nicolas Stemann	Munich
2016	Karin Coonrod	Venice

TV and film

1923	The Jew of Mestri	Peter Paul Felner	Germany
1953	The Merchant of Venice	Pierre Billon	France and Italy
1968	The Merchant of Venice – ORF TV	Otto Schenk	Austria/Germany
1980	The Merchant of Venice – BBC TV	Jack Gold	United Kingdom
1990	Der Kaufmann von Venedig – ZDF/ORF TV	George Moorse, Peter Zadek	Germany/Austria
2001	The Merchant of Venice – DVD	Chris Hunt, Trevor Nunn	United Kingdom
2001	The Maori Merchant of Venice	Don C. Selwyn	New Zealand
2004	William Shakespeare's The Merchant of Venice	Michael Radford	USA

Offshoots and adaptations

Charles Marowitz, *Variations on "The Merchant of Venice"*
1977   Charles Marowitz   London

Arnold Wesker, *The Merchant*
1977   John Dexter   New York

Justus van Oel, *The Arab of Amsterdam*
2008   Aram Adriaanse   Amsterdam

Krzysztof Warlikowski, *African Tales after Shakespeare*
2011   Krzysztof Warlikowski   Liège

János and István Mohácsi, *The Merchant of Venice*
2013   János Mohácsi   Budapest

Aaron Posner, *District Merchants*
2016   Michael John Garcés   Washington, DC

Vanasay Khamphommala, *Business in Venice*
2017   Jacques Vincey   Tours

B. Major actors and creative staff for productions discussed

Lyceum Theatre, London, 1 November 1879

Director: Henry Irving   Designer: Hawes Craven
Music: Hamilton Clarke

Shylock	Henry Irving	*Morocco*	Frank Tyars
Antonio	Henry Forrester	*Tubal*	J. Carter
Portia	Ellen Terry	*Lancelot*	Sam Johnson
Bassanio	J. H. Barnes	*Gobbo*	
Gratiano	Frank Cooper	*Old Gobbo*	Clifford Cooper
Nerissa	Florence Terry	*Salanio*	Arthur Elwood
Jessica	Alma Murray	*Salarino*	Arthur Pinero
Lorenzo	N. Forbes	*Duke*	A. Beaumont

Shakespeare Memorial Theatre, Stratford-upon-Avon, 25 July 1932

Director and designer: Theodore Komisarjevsky

Shylock	Randle Ayrton	*Gratiano*	Gyles Isham
Antonio	Wilfrid Walter	*Nerissa*	Hilda Coxhead
Portia	Fabia Drake	*Jessica*	Dorothy Francis
Bassanio	R. Eric Lee	*Lorenzo*	Ernest Hare

Morocco	Stanley Howlett	*Old Gobbo*	Geoffrey Wilkinson
Arragon	Eric Maxon	*Solanio*	Richard Cuthbert
Tubal	Kenneth Wicksteed	*Salarino*	Roy Byford
Lancelot Gobbo	Bruno Barnabe	*Duke*	Gerald Kay Souper

Campo San Trovaso, Venice, 18 July 1934

Director: Max Reinhardt   Assistant Director: Guido Salvini
Translator: Paola Ojetti   Set designer: Duilio Torres
Costume designer: Titina Rota   Music: Victor de Sabata
Choreographer: Janis Osvald Lehmanis

Shylock	Memo Benassi	*Morocco*	Carlo Ninchi
Antonio	Nerio Bernardi	*Tubal*	Luigi Almirante
Portia	Marta Abba	*Lancelot Gobbo*	Kiki Palmer
Bassanio	Renzo Ricci	*Old Gobbo*	Umberto Giardini
Gratiano	Enzo Bilioti	*Salerio*	Amedeo Nazzari
Nerissa	Laura Adani	*Solanio*	Alfredo Menichelli
Jessica	Andreina Pagnani	*Salarino*	Tino Elrer
Lorenzo	Gino Sabbatini	*Duke*	Guido Riva
Arragon	Carlo Lombardi		

Habima Theatre, Tel Aviv, 14 May 1936

Director: Leopold Jessner   Translator: Simon Halkin
Set designer: Moshe Mokady   Music: Karol Rathaus

Shylock	Aharon Meskin	*Arragon*	Menachem Benjamin
	Shimon Finkel	*Morocco*	Shimon Finkel
Antonio	Zvi Friedland	*Tubal*	Chaim Amitai
Portia	Hanna Rovina	*Lancelot Gobbo*	Avraham Baretz
Bassanio	Jacob Avital	*Old Gobbo*	Baruch Chemerinsky
Gratiano	Raphael Klatchkin	*Salerio*	Zvi Ben-Haim
Nerissa	Hannah Handler	*Solanio*	Shlomo Brock
Portia's maid	Tamima Yudelevich	*Balthazar*	Yehuda Rubinstein
Jessica	Ina Gubinska	*Duke*	Chaim Amitai
Lorenzo	Ari Kutai		

American Shakespeare Festival, Stratford, Connecticut, July 1957

Director: Jack Landau   Set designer: Rouben Ter-Arutunian
Costume designer: Motley   Music: Virgil Thomson

Shylock	Morris Carnovsky	*Bassanio*	Donald Harron
Antonio	Richard Waring	*Nerissa*	Lois Nettleton
Portia	Katherine Hepburn	*Morocco*	Earl Hyman

Städtische Bühne, Ulm, March 1961

Director: Peter Zadek   Assistant Director: Karl Schurr
Translator: A. W. von Schlegel
Set and costume designer: Wilfried Minks
Music: Rudolf Mors, Peter Warlock

Shylock	Norbert Kappen	Jessica	Beate Richard
Antonio	Peeter Bohlke	Lorenzo	Friedhelm Ptok
Portia	Elizabeth Orth	Tubal	Willy Ress
Bassanio	Hermann Schlögl	Lancelot Gobbo	Helmut Erfurth
Gratiano	Peter Striebeck	Old Gobbo	Valentin Jeker
Nerissa	Ursula Siebert		

National Theatre, London, 28 April 1970; adapted for television 1973

Director: Jonathan Miller   Set designer: Julia Trevelyan Oman

Shylock	Laurence Olivier	Morocco	Tom Baker
Antonio	Anthony Nicholls	Arragon	Charles Kay
Portia	Joan Plowright	Tubal	Lewis Jones
Bassanio	Jeremy Brett	Lancelot Gobbo	Jim Dale
Gratiano	Derek Jacobi	Old Gobbo	Harry Lomax
Nerissa	Anna Carteret	Salerio	Richard Kay
Jessica	Jane Lapotaire	Solanio	Michael Barnes
Lorenzo	Malcolm Reid	Duke	Benjamin Whitrow

Royal Shakespeare Theatre, Stratford-upon-Avon, 30 March 1971

Director: Terry Hands   Set designer: Timothy O'Brien
Costume designers: Timothy O'Brien, Tazeena Firth
Music: Guy Woolfenden

Shylock	Emrys James	Arragon	Derek Godfrey
Antonio	Tony Church	Tubal	Jeffery Dench
Portia	Judi Dench	Lancelot Gobbo	Peter Geddis
Bassanio	Michael Williams	Old Gobbo	Sydney Bromley
Gratiano	Geoffrey Hutchings	Salerio	Anthony Pedley
Nerissa	Polly James	Solanio	Alton Kumalo
Jessica	Alison Fiske	Salarino	Miles Anderson
Lorenzo	David Calder	Duke	Peter Woodthorpe
Morocco	Bernard Lloyd		

Appendices

Schaulspielhaus Bochum, Bochum, 30 December 1972

Director: Peter Zadek Translator: Karsten Schälike
Set designer: René Allio Costume designer: Christine Laurent
Music: Peer Raben

Shylock	Hans Mahnke	*Lorenzo*	Friedrich-Karl Praetorius
Antonio	Gunther Lüders	*Arragon*	Karl-Heinz Vosgerau
Portia	Rosel Zech	*Morocco*	Heinrich Giskes
Bassanio	Heinrich Giskes	*Tubal*	Rainer Hauer
Gratiano	Jürgen Prochnow	*Lancelot Gobbo*	Ulrich Wildgruber
Nerissa	Brigitte Janner	*Old Gobbo*	Hermann Lause
Jessica	Elisabeth Stepanek		

Vivian Beaumont Theater, Lincoln Center, New York, 1 March 1973

Director: Ellis Rabb
Set designer: James Tilton Costume designer: Ann Roth

Shylock	Sidney Walker	*Nerissa*	Olivia Cole
Antonio	Josef Sommer	*Jessica*	Roberta Maxwell
Portia	Rosemary Harris	*Lorenzo*	Peter Coffield
Bassanio	Christopher Walken	*Morocco*	Fred Morsell
		Arragon	Alan Mandell
Gratiano	Philip Bosco	*Lancelot Gobbo*	Dan Sullivan

The BBC TV Shakespeare, first broadcast 1980 (UK) and 1981 (USA)

Producer: Jonathan Miller Director: Jack Gold
Set designer: Oliver Bayldon Costume designer: Raymond Hughes

Shylock	Warren Mitchell	*Morocco*	Marc Zuber
Antonio	John Franklyn-Robbins	*Arragon*	Peter Gale
		Tubal	Arnold Diamond
Portia	Gemma Jones	*Lancelot Gobbo*	Enn Reitel
Bassanio	John Nettles	*Old Gobbo*	Joe Gladwin
Gratiano	Kenneth Cranham	*Salerio*	John Rhys-Davies
Nerissa	Susan Jameson	*Solanio*	Alan David
Jessica	Leslee Udwin	*Duke*	Douglas Wilmer
Lorenzo	Richard Morant		

Royal Shakespeare Theatre, Stratford-upon-Avon, 23 April 1987

Director: Bill Alexander   Set designer: Kit Surrey
Costume designer: Andreane Neofitou

Shylock	Antony Sher	Morocco	Hakeem Kae-Kazim
Antonio	John Carlisle	Arragon	Richard Conway
Portia	Deborah Findlay	Tubal	Bill McGuirk
Bassanio	Nicholas Farrell	Lancelot	Phil Daniels
Gratiano	Geoffrey Freshwater	Gobbo	
Nerissa	Pippa Guard	Old Gobbo	Arnold Yarrow
Jessica	Deborah Goodman	Salerio	Michael Cadman
Lorenzo	Paul Spence	Solanio	Gregory Doran
		Duke	Richard Conway

Burgtheater, Vienna, 10 December 1988

Director: Peter Zadek   Translator: Elisabeth Plessen
Set designer: Wilfried Minks   Lighting designer: André Diot
Painting and costume designer: Johannes Grützke
Music: Luciano Berio

Shylock	Gert Voss	Jessica	Julia Stemberger
Antonio	Ignaz Kirchner	Lorenzo	Christian Fries
Portia	Eva Mattes	Arragon	Gert Voss
Bassanio	Paulus Manker/ Friedrich-Karl Praetorius	Morocco	Ignaz Kirchner
		Tubal	Pavel Londovský
Gratiano	Martin Schwab	Lancelot Gobbo	Uwe Bohm
	Stefan Lisewski	Old Gobbo	Urs Hefti
Nerissa	Wiebke Frost	Salerio	Heinz Zuber
	Therese Affolter	Duke	Pavel Londovský

Festival Stage, Stratford, Ontario, 8 May 1989

Director: Michael Langham   Designer: Desmond Heeley

Shylock	Brian Bedford	Morocco	Hubert Baron Kelly
Antonio	Nicholas Pennell	Arragon	Peter Donaldson
Portia	Seana McKenna	Tubal	Brian Tree
Bassanio	Geraint Wyn Davies	Lancelot Gobbo	Eric Coates
Gratiano	Paul Boretski	Old Gobbo	Ian White
Nerissa	Kim Horsman	Salerio	John Innes
Jessica	Susannah Hoffmann	Solanio	Bradley C. Rudy
Lorenzo	Andrew Dolha	Duke	Ian White

Appendices

Cottesloe Theatre, London, 11 June 1999

Director: Trevor Nunn Producer: National Theatre
Set designer: Hildegard Bechtler Lighting designer: Peter Mumford
Music: Steven Edis

Shylock	Henry Goodman	Tubal	John Nolan
Antonio	David Bamber	Lancelot Gobbo	Andrew French
Portia	Derbhle Crotty	Old Gobbo	Oscar James
Bassanio	Alexander Hanon	Salerio	Peter De Jersey
Gratiano	Richard Henders	Solanio	Mark Umbers
Nerissa	Alex Kelly	Balthasar	John Nolan
Jessica	Gabrielle Jourdan		Leigh McDonald
Lorenzo	Daniel Evans/	Leonardo	Mark Springer
	Jack James	Stephano	Michael Wildman
Arragon	Raymond Coulthard	Duke	David Burk
Morocco	Chu Omambala		

Et Cetera Theatre, Moscow, 20 April 2000

Director: Robert Sturua Lighting designer: Andrei Tarasov
Set and costume designer: Georgi Aleksi-Meskhishvili
Music: Ghiya Kancheli

Shylock	Aleksandr Kalyagin	Arragon	Vladimir Skvortsov
Antonio	Victor Verzhbitsky	Morocco	Vladimir Skvortsov
Portia	Anastasiya Kormilitsiina	Shylock's servant	Nikolai Molochkov
Bassanio	Alexei Osipov	Salerio	Sergey Plotnikov
Gratiano	Evgeni Tokarev	Salanio	Vladimir Skvortsov/
Nerissa	Natalya Blagih		Grigory Starostin
Jessica	Maria Skosyreva	Balthazar	Tatyana Vladimirova
Lorenzo	Alexandr Zhogol	Duke	Lyudmila Dmitrieva

Te Tangata Whai Rawa O Weniti [The Maori Merchant of Venice], He Taonga Films, 2001

Director: Don Selwyn Translator: Pei Te Hurinui Jones
Costume designer: Gavin McLean Art direction: Viv Kernick
Music: Clive Cockburn, Hirini Melbourne

Hairoka (Shylock)	Waihoroi Shortland	Morako (Morocco)	Lawrence Makoare
Anatonio (Antonio)	Scott Morrison	Tupara (Tubal)	Andy Sarich
Pohia (Portia)	Ngarimu Daniels	Ranaharoto (Lancelot Gobbo)	Mana Epiha

Patanio (Bassanio)	Te Rangihau Gilbert	*Kaumatua Kobo (Old Gobbo)*	Eru Potaka-Dewes
Karatiano (Gratiano)	Sonny Kirikiri		
Nerita (Nerissa)	Veeshayne Armstrong	*Hararino (Salerio)*	Te Kauhoe Wano
Tiehika (Jessica)	Reikura Morgan	*Haranio (Solanio)*	Wharehoka Wano
Roreneto (Lorenzo)	Te Arepa Kahi	*Parahata (Balthazar)*	Tamati Patuwai
Aragona (Arragon)	Samson Pehi	*Tiuka O Weniti (Duke)*	Joe Naden

William Shakespeare's The Merchant of Venice,
Sony Pictures Classics, 2004

Director: Michael Radford   Screenwriter: Michael Radford
Editor: Lucia Zucchetti   Set designer: Bruno Rubeo
Costume designer: Sammy Sheldon   Music: Jocelyn Pook

Shylock	Al Pacino	*Morocco*	David Harewood
Antonio	Jeremy Irons	*Tubal*	Allan Corduner
Portia	Lynn Collins	*Lancelot Gobbo*	Mackenzie Crook
Bassanio	Joseph Fiennes	*Old Gobbo*	Ron Cook
Gratiano	Kris Marshall	*Salerio*	John Sessions
Nerissa	Heather Goldenhersh	*Solanio*	Gregor Fisher
Jessica	Zuleikha Robinson	*Stephano*	Al Weaver
Lorenzo	Charlie Cox	*Leonardo*	Tony Schiena
Arragon	Antonio Gil-Martinez	*Doctor Bellario*	Norbert Konne
Cush	Marc Maas	*Soldier*	Stephan Koziac
German Count	Jean-Francois Wolff	*Franciscan Friar*	Jules Werner
English Baron	Pieter Riemens	*Clerk*	Julian Next
French Nobleman	Tom Leick	*Duke*	Anton Rodgers

Liverpool Playhouse, Liverpool, 30 January 2009

Director: Edward Hall   Producer: Propeller
Assistant directors: Paul Hart, Gemma Kerr
Set designer: Michael Pavelka
Lighting designer: Ben Ormerod   Music: Jon Trenchard

Shylock	Richard Clothier	*Lorenzo*	Richard Dempsey
Antonio	Bob Barrett	*Arragon*	Thomas Padden

Appendices

Portia	Kelsey Brookfield	*Morocco*	Jonathan Livingstone
Bassanio	Jack Tarlton	*Tubal*	Thomas Padden
Gratiano	Richard Frame	*Lancelot Gobbo*	John Dougall
Nerissa	Chris Myles	*Salerio*	Sam Swainsbury
Jessica	Jon Trenchard	*Duke*	Babou Ceesay

Delacorte Theater, New York, 9 June 2010

Director: Daniel Sullivan   Producer: Public Theater
Set designer: Mark Wendland   Costume designer: Jess Goldstein
Lighting designer: Kenneth Posner   Music: Dan Moses Schreier

Shylock	Al Pacino		
Antonio	Byron Jennings	*Morocco*	Nyambi Nyambi/ Isaiah Johnson
Portia	Lily Rabe		
Bassanio	Hamish Linklater/ David Harbour	*Tubal*	Richard Topol
Gratiano	Jesse L. Martin	*Lancelot Gobbo*	Jesse Tyler Ferguson/ Christopher Fitzgerald
Nerissa	Marianne Jean-Baptiste/ Marsha Stephanie Blake	*Salerio*	Francois Battiste/ Peter Francis James
Jessica	Heather Lind	*Solanio*	Matthew Rauch
Lorenzo	Bill Heck/ Seth Numrich	*Balthasar*	Joe Short
		Stephano	Tyler Caffall
Arragon	Max Wright/ Charles Kimbrough	*Duke*	Gerry Bamman

Royal Shakespeare Theatre, Stratford-upon-Avon, 3 May 2011

Director: Rupert Goold   Producer: Royal Shakespeare Company
Assistant Director: Lisa Blair   Designer: Tom Scutt
Lighting designer: Rick Fisher   Music: Adam Cork

Shylock	Patrick Stewart	*Morocco*	David Ononokpono
Antonio	Scott Handy	*Tubal*	Christopher Wright
Portia	Susannah Fielding	*Lancelot Gobbo*	Jamie Beamish
Bassanio	Richard Riddell	*Old Gobbo*	Des McAleer
Gratiano	Howard Charles	*Salerio*	Steve Toussaint
Nerissa	Emily Plumtree	*Solanio*	Aidan Kelly
Jessica	Caroline Martin	*Balthasar*	Nikesh Patel
Lorenzo	Daniel Percival	*Leonardo*	Daniel Rose
Arragon	Jason Morell	*Duke*	Des McAleer

Campo di Ghetto Nuovo, Venice, 26 July 2016

Director: Karin Coonrod   Producer: Compagnia de' Colombari
Assistant director: Nerina Cocchi   Dramaturg: Walter Valeri
Set and lighting designer: Peter Ksander   Music: Frank London
Costume designer: Stefano Nicolao
Projections and sound: Andrea Santini

Shylock #1	Sorab Wadia	*Lorenzo*	Paul Spera
Shylock #2	Adriano Iurissevich	*Arragon*	Adriano Iurissevich
Shylock #3	Jenni Lea-Jones	*Morocco*	Matthieu Pastore
Shylock #4	Andrea Brugnera	*Tubal*	Ned Eisenberg
Shylock #5	Ned Eisenberg	*Lancilotto*	Francesca Sarah Toich
Antonio	Stefano Scherini	*Old Gobbo*	Andrea Brugnera
Portia	Linda Powell	*Solanio*	Enrico Zagni
Bassanio	Michele Athos Guidi	*Salarino*	Hunter Perske
Gratiano	Sorab Wadia	*Balzarina (Balthasar)*	Monica Garavello
Nerissa	Elena Pelone	*Duke*	Jenni Lea-Jones
Jessica	Michelle Uranowitz		

Bibliography

Ackermann, Zeno, 'Performing oblivion/enacting remembrance: *The Merchant of Venice* in West Germany, 1945 to 1961', *Shakespeare Quarterly* 62:3 (2011), 364–95.
——, and Sabine Schülting, *Precarious Figurations: Shylock on the German Stage, 1920–2010*, Berlin, 2019.
Ahonen, Sirkka, 'Politics of identifying through history curriculum: narratives of the past for social exclusion – or inclusion?', *Journal of Curriculum Studies* 33:2 (2010), 179–94.
Anonymous, *Critical Notes on Shylock as Played by Sir Henry Irving*, British Theatre Museum, London, n.d.
Barber, Ian, 'Archaeology, ethnography, and the record of Maori cannibalism before 1815: a critical review', *Journal of the Polynesian Society* 101:3 (1992), 241–92.
Bartoshevich, Aleksey, 'The Merchant of Venice on the Russian stage', *Toronto Slavic Quarterly* 4 (Spring 2003), http://sites.utoronto.ca/tsq/04/bartoshevich04.shtml (accessed 10 January 2022).
Bassi, Shaul, '*The Merchant in Venice*: re-creating Shakespeare in the Ghetto', *Shakespeare Survey* 70 (2017), 67–78.
——, 'Shylock in the thinking machine: civic Shakespeare and the future of Venice', in *New Places: Shakespeare and Civic Creativity*, ed. Paul Edmondson and Ewan Fernie, London, 2018, pp. 161–78.
——, '"Shylock is dead": Shakespeare in and beyond the Ghetto', in *The Merchant in Venice: Shakespeare in the Ghetto*, ed. Shaul Bassi and Carol Chillington Rutter, Venice, 2021, pp. 25–39.
——, and Carol Chillington Rutter, eds, *The Merchant in Venice: Shakespeare in the Ghetto*, Venice, 2021, https://edizionicafoscari.unive.it/media/pdf/books/978-88-6969-504-9/978-88-6969-504-9_qmZWP0u.pdf

Basso, Ann Mccauley, 'The Portia Project: The Heiress of Belmont on Stage and Screen', PhD dissertation, University of South Florida, 2011.
Bayer, Mark, 'Shylock, Palestine, and the Second World War', in *Shakespeare and the Second World War: Memory, Culture, Identity*, ed. Irena R. Makaryk and Marissa McHugh, Toronto, 2012, pp. 63–82.
Bayerdörfer, Hans-Peter, 'Shylock on the German stage in the post-Shoah era', in *German Shakespeare Studies at the Turn of the Twenty-First Century*, ed. Christa Jansohn, Newark, DE, 2006, pp. 205–23.
Beauman, Sally, *The Royal Shakespeare Company: A History of Ten Decades*, New York, 1982.
Berry, Ralph, 'Komisarjevsky at Stratford-upon-Avon', *Shakespeare Survey* 36 (1983), 73–84.
———, '*The Merchant of Venice*', in *Shakespeare in Performance: A Collection of Essays*, ed. Frank Occhiogrosso, Newark, DE, 2003, pp. 47–57.
Biggs, Murray, 'A neurotic Portia', *Shakespeare Survey* 25 (1972), 153–9.
Billington, Michael, *The Modern Actor*, London, 1973.
Blackadder, Neil, 'Shakespeare on stage in pre-war Germany: from the memoirs of Fritz Kortner', *Upstart Crow* 23 (2003), 63–73.
Boecker, Bettina, 'A tragedy? *Othello* and *The Merchant of Venice* in Germany during the 2015–16 refugee crisis', in *Shakespeare's Others in 21st-Century European Performance*, ed. Boika Sokolova and Janice Valls-Russell, London, 2021, pp. 209–27.
Bonnell, Andrew, *Shylock in Germany: Antisemitism and the German Theatre from the Enlightenment to the Nazis*, London, 2008.
———, 'Shylock and Othello under the Nazis', *German Life and Letters* 63 (2010), 166–78.
Booth, Michael R., 'Pictorial acting and Ellen Terry', in *Shakespeare on the Victorian Stage*, ed. Richard Foulkes, Cambridge, 1986, pp. 78–86.
Bowden, Ross, 'Maori cannibalism: an interpretation', *Oceania* 55:2 (1984), 81–99.
Brereton, Austin, *The Life of Henry Irving*, 2 vols., London, 1908.
Brook, Peter, 'Letter to Trevor Nunn', in *Dramatic Exchanges: The Lives and Letters of the National Theatre*, ed. Daniel Rosenthal, London, 2018, p. 294.
Brooks, Alfred G., 'Foreword', in *Max Reinhardt 1873–1973: A Centennial Festschrift*, ed. G. E. Wellwarth and Alfred G. Brooks, p. 1.
Brown, John Russell, ed., *The Merchant of Venice*, New Arden Series, London, 1955.
———, 'The realization of Shylock', in *Early Shakespeare*, Stratford-upon-Avon Studies 3, London, 1961, pp. 187–209.

Bulman, James C., 'The BBC Shakespeare and "house style"', *Shakespeare Quarterly* 35 (1994), 571–81.

——, 'Shylock, Antonio and the politics of performance', in *Shakespeare in Performance: A Collection of Essays*, ed. Frank Occhiogrosso, Newark, DE, 2003, pp. 27–46.

Burnett, Mark Thornton, *Filming Shakespeare in the Global Marketplace*, London, 2007.

Carlson, Marvin, *The Haunted Stage: The Theatre as Memory Machine*, Ann Arbor, MI, 2001.

——, 'Peter Zadek: the outsider who has come inside', *Theatre Research International* 32:3 (2007), 233–46.

Carnovsky, Morris, 'On playing the role of Shylock', in *The Merchant of Venice*, ed. Francis Fergusson, New York, 1958.

Cartelli, Thomas, 'Redistributing complicities in an age of digital production: Michael Radford's film version of *The Merchant of Venice*', in *A Touch More Rare: Harry Berger, Jr., and the Arts of Interpretation*, ed. Nina Levine and David Lee Miller, New York, 2009, pp. 58–73.

Cartwright, Kent, '*The Merchant "in" Venice* and *The Shylock Project*: fiction, history, and the humanities', in *The Merchant in Venice: Shakespeare in the Ghetto*, ed. Shaul Bassi and Carol Chillington Rutter, Venice, 2021, pp. 141–62.

Cinpoeş, Nicoleta, '"Barbarous temper", "hideous violence", and "mountainish inhumanity": encounters with *The Merchant of Venice* in Romania', in *Shakespeare's Others in 21st-Century Performance: The Merchant of Venice and Othello*, ed. Boika Sokolova and Janice Valls-Russell, London, 2021, pp. 134–54.

Cohen, Derek, *Shakespearean Motives*, New York, 1988.

Cohen, Walter, '"The Merchant of Venice" and the possibilities of historical criticism', *English Literary History* 49 (1982), 765–89.

Cohn, Ruby, 'Shakespeare left', *Theatre Journal* 40:1 (March 1988), 48–60.

Cooper, John R., 'Shylock's humanity', *Shakespeare Quarterly* 21 (1970), 117–24.

Cooper, Roberta Krensky, *The American Shakespeare Theatre: Stratford 1955–1985*, Washington, DC, 1986.

Cottrell, John, *Laurence Olivier*, London, 1975.

Cox, Emma, 'Te Reo Shakespeare: *Te Tangata Whai Rawa O Weniti/The Maori Merchant of Venice*', *Kunapipi* 28:1 (2006), 79–95.

Craig, Edward Gordon, *Henry Irving*, London, 1930.

Crowl, Samuel, 'Looking for Shylock: Stephen Greenblatt, Michael Radford and Al Pacino', in *Screening Shakespeare in the Twenty-First Century*, ed. Mark Thornton Burnett and Ramona Wray, Edinburgh, 2006, pp. 113–26.

Dailey, Alice, rev. of '*The Merchant of Venice* by Edward Hall', *Shakespeare Bulletin* 28:4 (2010), 510–17.
Damerini, Gino, *Il Primo Festival Veneziano del Teatro drammatico*, Venice, 1934.
Danson, Lawrence, *The Harmonies of 'The Merchant of Venice'*, New Haven, CT, 1978.
Dávidházi, Péter, 'Staging Shakespeare's Others and their biblical archetype', in *Shakespeare's Others in 21st-Century European Performance*, ed. Boika Sokolova and Janice Valls-Russell, London, 2021, pp. 269–79.
Delabastita, Dirk, 'More alternative Shakespeares', in *Four Hundred Years of Shakespeare in Europe*, ed. A. Luis Pujante and Ton Hoenselaars, Newark, DE, 2003, pp. 113–33.
Delgado, Maria M., and Dan Rebellato, eds, *Contemporary European Theatre Directors*, London, 2020.
Dessen, Alan C., 'The Elizabethan stage Jew and Christian example: Gerontus, Barabas, and Shylock', *Modern Language Quarterly* 35 (1974), 231–45.
———, 'A 2011 gallimaufry of plays: Shakespeare, Heywood, Marlowe, and Massinger', *Shakespeare Bulletin* 30:1 (2012), 37–47.
'Don Selwyn, actor, director: biography', *New Zealand on Screen*, www.nzonscreen.com/profile/don-selwyn/biography (accessed 26 June 2020).
Drakakis, John, 'Introduction', in *The Merchant of Venice*, ed. John Drakakis, London, 2010, pp. 1–159.
Draper, John W., 'Usury in "The Merchant of Venice"', *Modern Philology* 33 (1935), 37–47.
Drew, Daniel, 'William Shakespeare's *The Merchant of Venice*', *Film Quarterly* 60:1 (2006), 52–6.
Eagleton, Terry, *William Shakespeare*, Oxford, 1986.
Edelman, Charles, ed., *The Merchant of Venice*, Shakespeare in Production, Cambridge, 2002.
Ellis, Ruth, *The Shakespeare Memorial Theatre*, London, 1948.
Elon, Amos, *The Pity of it All: A History of the Jews in Germany, 1743–1933*, New York, 2002.
Feinberg, Anat, 'The Janus-faced Jew: Nathan and Shylock on the postwar German stage', in *Unlikely History: The Changing German-Jewish Symbiosis 1945–2000*, ed. Leslie Morris and Jack Zipes, New York, 2002, pp. 233–50.
———, 'The unknown Leopold Jessner', in *Jews and the Making of Modern German Theatre*, ed. Jeanette R. Malkin and Freddie Rokem, Iowa City, IA, 2010, pp. 232–60.
———, 'The joy of breaking taboos: Jews and post-war German theatre', in *Jews and Theater in an Intercultural Context*, ed. Edna Nahshon, Leiden, 2012, pp. 277–96.

Bibliography

Fenwick, Henry, 'The production', in *The Merchant of Venice*, BBC edition, London, 1980, pp. 17–26.

Fisch, Leon, *The Dual Image: A Study of the Figure of the Jew in English Literature*, London, 1959.

Fischer, Susan L., 'Staging *The Merchant of Venice* in Spain (2015): felicitous "romancing" with money and willful ambiguity?', *Shakespeare Bulletin* 35 (2017), 317–34.

Fischer-Lichte, Erica, 'Theatre as Festive Play: Max Reinhardt's Production of *The Merchant of Venice*', in *Venetian Views, Venetian Blinds: English Fantasies of Venice*, ed. Manfred Pfister and Barbara Schaff, Amsterdam, 1999, pp. 169–80.

Fitzgerald, Percy, *Sir Henry Irving: A Biography*, London, 1906.

Fitzpatrick, Lisa, 'The Staging of *The Merchant of Venice* in Cork: the concretization of a Shakespearean play for a new society', *Modern Drama* 50:2 (2007), 168–83.

Foulkes, Richard, 'Henry Irving and Laurence Olivier as Shylock', *Theatre Notes* 27:1 (1972), 26–35.

———, 'The staging of the trial scene in Irving's "The Merchant of Venice"', *Educational Theatre Journal* 28 (1976), 312–17.

———, 'Helen Faucit and Ellen Terry as Portia', *Theatre Notebook* 31:3 (1977), 27–37.

———, ed., *Shakespeare and the Victorian Stage*, Cambridge, 1986.

Fowler, Benjamin, 'Dangerous border crossings: Nicolas Stemann's *Merchant* in Munich', in *The Merchant of Venice: The State of Play*, ed. M. Lindsay Kaplan, London, 2020, pp. 43–68.

Fraser, William, *Disraeli and his Day*, London, 1891.

Gavrilova, Desislava, 'Interview with Robert Sturua', *Teatar* 7, 8, and 9 (1993), 40–1.

Geary, Keith, 'The nature of Portia's victory: turning to men in "The Merchant of Venice"', *Shakespeare Survey* 37 (1984), 55–68.

Gilbert, Miriam, *The Merchant of Venice*, Shakespeare at Stratford, London, 2002.

———, '"Lend it rather to thy enemy": accentuating difference in *The Merchant of Venice*', in *The Merchant of Venice: The State of Play*, ed. M. Lindsay Kaplan, London, 2020, pp. 17–41.

Girard, Rene, '"To entrap the wisest": a reading of "The Merchant of Venice"', in *Literature and Society: Selected Papers from the English Institute*, ed. Edward Said, Baltimore, MD, 1980, pp. 100–19.

Glassman, Bernard, *Anti-Semitic Stereotypes without Jews: Images of Jews in England, 1290–1700*, Detroit, MI, 1975.

Goldberg, Jonathan, 'Textual properties', *Shakespeare Quarterly* 37:2 (Summer 1986), 213–17.

Granville-Barker, Harley, *Prefaces to Shakespeare*, 2nd series, London, 1930.
Greenberg, Marissa, 'Critically regional Shakespeare', *Shakespeare Bulletin* 37 (2019), 341–63.
Greenblatt, Stephen, 'Marlowe, Marx, and anti-Semitism', *Critical Inquiry* 5 (1978), 291–307.
Gregor, Keith, *Shakespeare in the Spanish Theatre, 1772 to the Present*, London, 2010.
Grochala, Sarah, *The Theatre of Rupert Goold: Radical Approaches to Adaptation and New Writing*, London, 2020.
Gross, John, *Shylock: A Legend and its Legacy*, New York and London, 1992.
Grubb, James S., 'When myths lose power: four decades of Venetian historiography', *Journal of Modern History* 58:1 (1986), 43–94.
Guneratne, Anthony, 'The greatest Shakespeare film never made: textualities, authorship, and archives', *Shakespeare Bulletin* 34:3 (2016), 391–412.
Hamilton, Robert E., 'Post-Soviet wars: part I', Foreign Policy Research Institute, Eurasia Program, 18 December 2017, www.fpri.org/article/2017/12/post-soviet-wars-part-i/ (accessed 19 September 2021).
Hattaway, Michael, *Elizabethan Popular Theatre: Plays in Performance*, London, 1982.
Hatton, Joseph, *Henry Irving's Impressions of America*, vol. 1, London, 1884.
Hawkins, Harriet, *The Devil's Party: Critical Counter-Interpretations of Shakespearian Drama*, Oxford, 1985.
Heijes, Coen, '*The Merchant of Venice*. Dir. Rupert Goold. The Royal Shakespeare Company, The Royal Shakespeare Theatre, Stratford-upon-Avon. A review', *Multicultural Shakespeares: Translation, Appropriation and Performance* 9:24 (2012), 95–100.
———, 'Dutch negotiations with otherness in times of crisis: *Othello* (2006) and *The Arab of Amsterdam* (2008)', in *Shakespeare's Others in 21st-Century European Performance*, ed. Boika Sokolova and Janice Valls-Russell, London, 2021, pp. 171–89.
Henderson, Diane, '*The Merchant in Venice*: Shylock's Unheimlich return', *Multicultural Shakespeare* 15 (2017), 161–76.
Hiatt, Charles, *Henry Irving: A Record and Review*, London, 1899.
Hinely, Jan Lawson, 'Bond priorities in "The Merchant of Venice"', *Studies in English Literature* 20 (1980), 217–39.
Holderness, Graham, 'Radical potentiality and institutional closure: Shakespeare in film and television', in *Political Shakespeare*, ed. Jonathan Dollimore and Alan Sinfield, Manchester, 1985, pp. 182–201; rpt. in *Shakespeare on Television*, ed. J. C. Bulman and H. R. Coursen, Hanover, 1988, pp. 69–75.

Hole, Richard, 'An apology for the character and conduct of Shylock', in *Essays by a Society of Gentlemen at Exeter*, London, 1796, pp. 552–73.
Honigmann, E. A. J., *The Stability of Shakespeare's Text*, London, 1965.
Honneger, Gitta. 'Lost in translation, or "Rather than bury Zadek, I come to praise him!"', *Theater* 40:3 (2010), 116–27.
Hortmann, Wilhelm, *Shakespeare on the German Stage: The Twentieth Century*, Cambridge, 1998.
Hostetter, Anthony, *Max Reinhardt's Grosses Schauspielhaus – Its Artistic Goals, Planning, and Operation, 1910–1933*, Lewiston, NY, 2003.
Houlahan, Mark, 'Hekepia? The mana of the Maori *Merchant*', in *World-Wide Shakespeares: Local Appropriations in Film and Performances*, ed. Sonia Massai, London and New York, 2005, pp. 141–8.
Howard, Jean E., 'The difficulties of closure: an approach to the problematic in Shakespearean comedy', in *Comedy from Shakespeare to Sheridan*, ed. A. R. Braunmuller and J. C. Bulman, Newark, DE, 1986, pp. 113–28.
Hughes, Alun, 'Henry Irving's tragedy of Shylock', *Educational Theatre Journal* 24 (1972), 249–68.
———, *Henry Irving Shakespearean*, Cambridge, 1981.
Irving, Henry, *The Merchant of Venice: As Presented at the Lyceum Theatre under the Management of Mr. Henry Irving*, London, 1879.
———, *Mr. Henry Irving and Miss Ellen Terry in America: Opinions of the Press*, Chicago, 1884.
———, ed., *The Drama: Addresses by Henry Irving*, New York, 1893; rpt. 1969.
Irving, Laurence, *Henry Irving: The Actor and his World*, London, 1951.
Ivanov, Vyacheslav, 'Shakespeare in the productions of Sturua and Chekhidze', *Journal of Arts and Ideas* 12–13 (1987), 27–38.
Jackson, Russell, *Shakespeare in the Theatre: Trevor Nunn*, London, 2019.
James, Henry, *The Scenic Art: Notes on Acting and the Drama, 1872–1901*, New Brunswick, NJ, 1948.
Kahane, Arthur, 'Reinhardt as stage-director', in *Max Reinhardt and his Theatre*, ed. Oliver M. Sayler and Benjamin Blom, New York and London, 1968, pp. 75–88.
Kahn, Coppelia, 'The cuckoo's note: male friendship and cuckoldry in "The Merchant of Venice"', in *Shakespeare's 'Rough Magic': Renaissance Essays in Honor of C. L. Barber*, ed. Peter Erickson and Coppelia Kahn, Newark, DE, 1985, pp. 104–12.
Kemp, T. C., and J. C. Trewin, *The Stratford Festival: A History of the Shakespeare Memorial Theatre*, Birmingham, 1953.
Kennicott, Philip, 'A simplified 'Merchant' still generates interest', *Washington Post*, (28 January 2005), https://www.washingtonpost.

com/archive/lifestyle/2005/01/28/a-simplified-merchant-still-generates-interest/23aaebc5-0213-4dc7-82bd-95f8bd12510b/ (accessed 8 August 2023).

Klimt, Gustav, 'Beethoven Frieze', *Google Arts & Culture*, https://artsandculture.google.com/story/beethoven-frieze/agJyCiwKNIeUIw (accessed 10 February 2021).

Komisarjevsky, Theodore, *The Costume of the Theatre*, London, 1931.

———, and Lee Simonson, *Settings and Costumes of the Modern Stage*, London, 1933.

———, *The Theatre and a Changing Civilisation*, London, 1935.

Kouts, Gideon, 'The Merchant of Venice in the Hebrew press', *European Judaism* 51 (2018), 106–15.

Kvam, Wayne, 'The nazification of Max Reinhardt's Deutsches Theater Berlin', *Theatre Journal* 40 (1988), 357–74.

Lange, Mechthild, *Peter Zadek: Regie im Theater*, Frankfurt, 1989.

Lanier, Douglas, 'New directions: The Merchant of Venice on screen', in *The Merchant of Venice: A Critical Reader*, ed. Sarah Hatchuel and Nathalie Vienne-Guerrin, London, 2020, pp. 171–96.

Lelyveld, Toby, *Shylock on the Stage*, Cleveland, OH, 1960.

Limon, Jerzy, *Gentlemen of a Company: English Players in Central and Eastern Europe 1590–1660*, Cambridge, 1987.

Loepelmann, Götz, interview with, 'The Merchant of Venice by Peter Zadek (Götz Loepelmann), draft notes with a camera', www.youtube.com/watch?v=qmeg-Oe6vNw (accessed 10 March 2022).

MacGowan, Kenneth, *The Theatre of Tomorrow*, New York, 1921.

Mahood, M. M., ed., *The Merchant of Venice*, New Cambridge Shakespeare, Cambridge, 1987.

Malkin, Jeanette, 'Fritz Kortner and other German-Jewish Shylocks before and after the Holocaust', in *Wrestling with Shylock: Jewish Responses to The Merchant of Venice*, ed. Edna Nahshon and Michael Shapiro, Cambridge, 2017, pp. 198–223.

Marek, Georg, 'The Lord of Leopoldskron', in *Max Reinhardt 1873–1973: A Centennial Festschrift*, ed. G. E. Wellwarth and Alfred G. Brooks, Binghamton, NY, 1973, pp. 83–93.

Márkus, Zoltán, 'Der Merchant von Velence: The Merchant of Venice in London, Berlin, and Budapest during World War II', in *Shakespeare and European Politics*, ed. Dirk Delabastita, Jozef de Vos, and Paul Franssen, Newark, DE, 2008, pp. 143–57.

Marshall, F. A., ed., *The Henry Irving Shakespeare*, vol. 3, London, 1892.

Martin, Theodore, *Helen Faucit (Lady Martin)*, Edinburgh and London, 1900.

Marx, Peter W, 'Max Reinhardt', in *The Routledge Companion to Directors' Shakespeare*, ed. John Russell Brown, London, 2008, pp. 636–61.

McDougall, Julie, 'Māori take on Shakespeare: *The Merchant of Venice* in Aotearoa/New Zealand', *Multicultural Shakespeare: Translation, Appropriation and Performance* 8:23 (2011), 93–106.

McGann, Jerome, *The Beauty of Inflection: Historical Method and Theory*, Oxford, 1988.

Mennen, Richard E., 'Theodore Komisarjevsky's production of "The Merchant of Venice"', *Theatre Journal* 31:3 (1979), 386–97.

Mentz, Steven, rev. of *Women Beware Women, The Winter's Tale, The Merchant of Venice*, *Shakespeare Bulletin* 27:4 (2009), 669–81.

Miller, Jonathan, 'Director in interview: Jonathan Miller talks to Peter Ansorge', *Plays and Players* 17:6 (1970), 52–3, 59.

———, Interview by Ann Pasternak Slater, *Quarto: The Literary Review* 10 (September 1980), 9–12.

———, *Subsequent Performances*. Boston, MA, and London, 1986.

Ministry for Culture and Heritage, 'The Treaty in brief', https://nzhistory.govt.nz/politics/treaty/the-treaty-in-brief (accessed 28 June 2020).

Minton, Gretchen E, 'A Polynesian Shakespeare film: *The Maori Merchant of Venice*', *Upstart Crow* 24 (2004), 45–55.

Moisan, Thomas, '"Which is the merchant here? And which the Jew?": subversion and recuperation in "The Merchant of Venice"', in *Shakespeare Reproduced: The Text in History and Ideology*, ed. Jean E. Howard and Marion F. O'Connor, New York, 1987, pp. 188–206.

Moninger, Markus, 'Auschwitz erinnern: Merchant-Inszenierungen im Nachkriegsdeutschland', in *Das Theater der Anderen: Alterität und Theater zwischen Antike und Gegenwart*, ed. Christopher Balme, Tübingen, 2001, pp. 229–48.

Moore, Edward M., 'Henry Irving's Shakespearean productions', *Theatre Survey* 17:2 (1976), 195–216.

Mulryne, J. R., 'History and myth in "The Merchant of Venice"', in *L'Europe de la Renaissance: Cultures et Civilisations*, Paris, 1988, pp. 325–41.

Nahshon, Edna, 'New York City, 1947: a season for Shylocks', in *Wrestling with Shylock: Jewish Responses to The Merchant of Venice*, ed. Edna Nahshon and Michael Shapiro, Cambridge, 2017, pp. 140–67.

———, and Michael Shapiro, eds, *Wrestling with Shylock: Jewish Responses to The Merchant of Venice*, Cambridge, 2017.

Nevo, Ruth, *Comic Transformations in Shakespeare*, London, 1980.

Nikolić, Zorica Bečanović, 'Drags, dyes and death in Venice: *The Merchant of Venice* (2004) and *Othello* (2012) in Belgrade', in *Shakespeare's Others in 21st-Century European Performance,* ed. Boika Sokolova and Janice Valls-Russell, London, 2021, pp. 89–107.

Niziołek, Grzegorz, *Warlikowski: Extra Ecclesiam*, trans. Soren Gauger, Frankfurt, 2015.

Nunn, Trevor, 'An interview with Trevor Nunn', *PBS Masterpiece Theatre: The Merchant of Venice*, 2015.
O'Connor, Kelly Newman, 'RSC's The Merchant of Venice', *The Shakespeare Newsletter*, 62:1 (2012), 27.
Odell, George C. D., *Shakespeare from Betterton to Irving*, 2 vols., New York, 1920.
Olivier, Laurence, *Confessions of an Actor*, London, 1982.
———, *On Acting*, London, 1986.
O'Rourke, James, 'The guilty pleasures of bigotry: ethnic stereotypes in Trevor Nunn's *Merchant of Venice* and Dave Chappelle's pixie sketches', *Shakespeare* 12:3 (2016), 287–99.
Overton, Bill, *Text and Performance: The Merchant of Venice*, London, 1987.
Oz, Avraham, 'Transformations of authenticity: "The Merchant of Venice" in Israel, 1936–1980', *Jahrbuch Deutsche Shakespeare Gesellschaft West*, 1983, pp. 166–77.
———, *The Yoke of Love: Prophetic Riddles in The Merchant of Venice*, Newark, DE, 1995.
Pancheva, Evgenia, 'Nothings, merchants, tempests: trimming Shakespeare for the 1992 Bulgarian stage', in *Shakespeare in the New Europe*, ed. Michael Hattaway, Boika Sokolova, and Derek Roper, Sheffield, 1994, pp. 247–60.
Pavelka, Michael, 'The Merchant of Venice', www.michaelpavelka.com/research/research-excellence-framework/the-merchant-of-venice/ (accessed 4 September 2021).
Perret, Marion D., 'Shakespeare and anti-Semitism: two television versions of "The Merchant of Venice"', *Mosaic* 16:1–2 (1983), 145–63; rpt. in *Shakespeare on Television*, ed. J. C. Bulman and H. R. Coursen, Hanover, 1988, pp. 156–68.
Pettengill, Richard, 'Peter Sellars's *Merchant of Venice*: a retrospective critique of process', *Theatre Research International* 31 (2006), 298–314.
Pikli, Natália, 'Staging *The Merchant of Venice* in Hungary: politics, prejudice and the languages of hatred', in *Shakespeare's Others in 21st-Century European Performance*, ed. Boika Sokolova and Janice Valls-Russell, London, 2021, pp. 152–70.
Piti, Buko, *Bulgarian Society on Racism and Antisemitism*, Sofia, 1937.
Pittman, Monique, 'Locating the bard: adaptation and authority in Michael Radford's *The Merchant of Venice*', *Shakespeare Bulletin* 25:2 (2007), 13–22.
Poltrack, Emma, 'The theatre and working practices of the Propeller Theatre Company (1997–2011)', PhD dissertation, University of Warwick, 2015.

Prescott, Paul, 'Review of Shakespeare's *The Merchant of Venice* (directed by Rupert Goold for the Royal Shakespeare Company) at the Royal Shakespeare Theatre, Stratford-upon-Avon, 19 May, 15 June and 22 September 2011', *Shakespeare* 8:2 (2012), 250–4.

Pullen, Brian, 'The occupations and investments of the Venetian nobility in the middle and late sixteenth century', in *Renaissance Venice*, ed. J. R. Hale, London, 1973, pp. 379–408.

Quadri, Franco, 'Conversazione con Peter Zadek', in *I miei Shakespeare*, ed. Franco Quadri, Milan, 2002, pp. 129–38.

Raab, Michael, 'Peter Zadek', in *The Routledge Companion to Directors' Shakespeare*, ed. John Russell Brown, London, 2008, pp. 858–84.

Richmond, Hugh, *Richard III*, Shakespeare in Performance Series, Manchester, 1989.

Riggio, Milla Cozart, 'Filming Shylock: Radford and Miller', in *Shakespearean Performance: New Studies*, ed. Frank Occhiogrosso, Madison, NJ, 2010, pp. 173–204.

Robertson, W. Graham, *Time Was*, London, 1931.

Rogers, Jami, 'Review of *The Merchant of Venice* performed by Royal Shakespeare Company', *Shakespeare Bulletin* 31:4 (2013), 733–7.

Rothe, Hans, ed., *Max Reinhardt: 25 Jahre Deutsches Theater*, Munich, 1930.

Rowe, Nicholas, *The Works of Mr. William Shakespear*, London, 1709.

Rowell, George, 'A Lyceum sketchbook', *Nineteenth Century Theatre Research* 6:1 (Spring 1978), 1–23.

Royal, Te Ahukaramū Charles, 'First peoples in Māori tradition – ancestors from the natural world', *Te Ara: The Encyclopedia of New Zealand*, https://teara.govt.nz/en/photograph/2411/urewera-in-mist (accessed 26 June 2020).

Rutter, Carol Chillington, 'Shakespeare performances in England, 2009', *Shakespeare Survey* 63 (2010), 338–75.

———, 'Shakespeare's *The Merchant of Venice* in and beyond the Ghetto', *Shakespeare Survey* 70 (2017), 79–88.

———, 'Trying Portia', in *The Merchant in Venice: Shakespeare in the Ghetto*, ed. Shaul Bassi and Carol Chillington Rutter, Venice, 2021, pp. 175–92.

Sakowska, Aleksandra, 'Estranged strangers: Krzysztof Warlikowski's Shylock and Othello in *African Tales After Shakespeare* (2011)', in *Shakespeare's Others in 21st-Century European Performance*, ed. Boika Sokolova and Janice Valls-Russell, London, 2021, pp. 69–88.

Sanders, Wilbur, *The Dramatist and the Received Idea: Studies in the Plays of Marlowe and Shakespeare*, Cambridge, 1968.

Schlueter, June, 'Trivial pursuit: the casket plot in the Miller/Olivier "Merchant"', in *Shakespeare on Television*, ed. J. C. Bulman and H. R. Coursen, Hanover, 1988, pp. 169–74.

Schnapp, Jeffrey T., 'Border Crossings: Italian/German peregrinations of the theater of totality', *Critical Inquiry* 21 (1994), 80–123.

Schülting, Sabine, ' "I am not bound to please thee with my answers": *The Merchant of Venice* on the post-war German stage', in *World-Wide Shakespeares: Local Appropriations in Film and Performance,* ed. Sonia Massai, London, 2005, pp. 65–71.

———, '"Remember Me": Shylock on the postwar German stage', *Shakespeare Survey* 64 (2011), 290–300.

Scott, Clement, *From 'The Bells' to 'King Arthur'*, London, 1897.

Shakespeare, William, *A New Variorum Edition of Shakespeare:* The Merchant of Venice, 7th edition, ed. Horace Howard Furness, Philadelphia, PA, 1888.

'Shakespeare at the National Theatre'. Google Arts & Culture, https://artsandculture.google.com/story/WQVxxgh-hh8A8A (accessed 12 May 2020).

Shapiro, Michael, 'Shylock the Jew onstage: past and present', *Shofar* (Winter 1986), 1–11.

———, 'Literary sources and theatrical interpretations of Shylock', in *Wrestling with Shylock: Jewish Responses to The Merchant of Venice*, ed. Edna Nahshon and Michael Shapiro, Cambridge, 2017, pp. 3–32.

———, 'Boy heroines in male disguise', in manuscript.

Shatirishvili, Zaza, 'The montage of Tbilisi culture', *Film International* 23 (2006), 48–51.

Sher, Antony, 'Shaping up to Shakespeare: Antony Sher in interview with Mark Lawson', *Drama* 4 (1987), 27–30.

Shewring, Margaret, 'A question of balance: Shakespeare's "The Merchant of Venice" on the nineteenth and twentieth century stage', in *L'Image de Venise au Temps de la Renaissance*, ed. M. T. Jones-Davies, Paris, 1989, pp. 87–111.

Silverstone, Catherine, 'Speaking Māori Shakespeare: *The Maori Merchant of Venice* and the legacy of colonisation', in *Screening Shakespeare in the Twenty-First Century*, ed. Mark Thornton Burnett and Ramona Wray, Edinburgh, 2006, pp. 127–45.

Sinfield, Alan, 'Making space: appropriation and confrontation in recent British plays', in *The Shakespeare Myth*, ed. Graham Holderness, Manchester, 1988, pp. 128–44.

Sinsheimer, Hermann, *Shylock: The History of a Character or the Myth of the Jew*, London, 1947.

Slater, Ann Pasternak, *Shakespeare the Director*, Brighton, 1982.

Smallwood, Robert, 'Shakespeare performances in England', *Shakespeare Survey* 53 (2000), 269–70.
Sokol, B. J., 'Review of Shakespeare's *Merchant of Venice* (directed by Edward Hall for the Propeller Company) at the Rose Theatre, Kingston (February 2009)', *Shakespeare* 5:2 (2009), 209–12.
Sokolova, Boika, 'Reading Morocco: four film versions of *The Merchant of Venice*', in *Shakespeare Closely Read: Written and Performance Texts*, ed. Frank Occhiogrosso, Madison, NJ, 2011, pp. 93–116.
———, 'New recruits to the 'maverick' squad: *Othello*, *King Lear*, and *The Merchant of Venice* in London, 2008/09', *Shakespeare Bulletin* 30:2 (2012), 87–97.
———, '"Mingled yarn": *The Merchant of Venice* east of Berlin and the legacy of "Eastern Europe"', *Shakespeare Survey* 71 (2018), 88–102.
———, 'The Bulgarian fortunes of *The Merchant of Venice*', in *Shakespeare in Between*, ed. Jana Wild, Bratislava, 2018, pp. 38–58.
———, and Janice Valls-Russell, eds, *Shakespeare's Others in 21st-Century European Performance: The Merchant of Venice and Othello*, London, 2021.
Sorelius, Gunnar, 'The Stockholm anti-Nazi *Merchant of Venice*: the uncertainty of response', in *Shakespeare and Scandinavia: A Collection of Nordic Studies*, ed. Gunnar Sorelius, Newark, DE, 2002, pp. 193–206.
Spencer, Christopher, ed., *Five Restoration Adaptations of Shakespeare*, Urbana, IL, 1965.
Stern, Ernst, *My Life, My Stage*, trans. Edward Fitzgerald, London, 1951.
———, *Bühnenbildner bei Max Reinhardt: Mit 80 Zeichnungen des Verfassers*, Berlin, 1955.
Stewart, Patrick, 'Playing Shylock', in *Players of Shakespeare: Essays in Shakespearean Performance by Twelve Players with the Royal Shakespeare Company*, ed. Philip Brockbank, Cambridge, 1985, pp. 11–28.
Stoker, Bram, *Personal Reminiscences of Henry Irving*, 2 vols., London, 1906.
Stone, Maria, 'Challenging cultural categories: the transformation of the Venice Biennale under fascism', *Journal of Modern Italian Studies* 4:2 (1999), 184–208.
Stříbrný, Zdeněk, *Shakespeare and Eastern Europe*, Oxford and New York, 2000.
Styan, J. L., *The Shakespeare Revolution: Criticism and Performance in the Twentieth Century*, Cambridge, 1977.
———, *Max Reinhardt*, Cambridge, 1982.
Sullivan, Patrick J., 'Strumpet wind: the National Theatre's "Merchant of Venice"', *Educational Theatre Journal* 26 (1974), 31–44.

Symington, Rodney, *The Nazi Appropriation of Shakespeare: Cultural Politics in the Third Reich*, Lewiston, NY, 2005.
Szucs, Aniko, 'The relativization of victim and perpetrator in the Hungarian productions of *The Merchant of Venice* and *Mein Kampf*', in *Jews and Theater in an Intercultural Context*, ed. Edna Nahson, Leiden, 2012, pp. 297–317.
Tennenhouse, Leonard, 'The counterfeit order of "The Merchant of Venice"', in *Representing Shakespeare: New Psychoanalytic Essays*, ed. Murray Schwartz and Coppelia Kahn, Baltimore, 1980, pp. 54–69.
Terry, Ellen, *Ellen Terry's Memoirs*, ed. and with additional material by Edith Craig and Christopher St John, New York, 1932.
———, *Four Lectures on Shakespeare*, ed. Christopher St John, London, 1932.
Thomson, Peter, *Shakespeare's Theatre*, London, 1983.
Thompson, Ayanna, *Shakespeare in the Theatre: Peter Sellars*, London, 2018.
Tollini, Frederick, *The Shakespeare Productions of Max Reinhardt*, Lewiston, NY, 2004.
Trewin, J. C., *Shakespeare and the English Stage, 1900–1964*, London, 1964.
Ugenti, Elio, 'Filming Shylock', in *Shylock e il suo mercante*, ed. Vittorio Pavoncello, Ariccia, 2016, pp. 127–52.
Valls-Russell, Janice, '*Le Marchand de Venise* (Business in Venice)' (review), *Shakespeare Bulletin* 36 (2018), 319–23.
———, '*The Merchant of Venice* in France (2001 and 2017): deconstructing a malaise', in *Shakespeare's Others in 21st-Century European Performance*, ed. Boika Sokolova and Janice Valls-Russell, London, 2021, pp. 108–26.
Verch, Maria, '"The Merchant of Venice" on the German stage since 1945', *Theatre History Studies* 5 (1985), 84–94.
Volbach, Walther, 'Memoirs of Max Reinhardt's theatres 1920–1922', *Theatre Survey* 13 (1972), 1–92.
Wayne, Valerie, '*Te Tangata Whai Rawa O Weniti, The Maori Merchant of Venice* by Don C. Selwyn and Ruth Kaupua-Panapa (review)', *The Contemporary Pacific* 16:2 (2004), 425–9.
Wells, Stanley, 'Television Shakespeare', *Shakespeare Quarterly* 33 (Fall 1982), 261–77; rpt. in *Shakespeare on Television*, ed. J. C. Bulman and H. R. Coursen, Hanover, 1988, pp. 41–9.
Wesker, Arnold, *Plays*, vol. 4. *The Journalists, The Wedding Feast, The Merchant*, Harmondsworth, 1980.
Williams, Raymond, *Drama in a Dramatised Society*, Cambridge, 1975.
Williams, Simon, 'The director in the German theater: harmony, spectacle and ensemble', *New German Critique* 29 (1983), 107–31.

Winter, William, *Henry Irving*, New York, 1885.
Wulf, Josef, *Theater und Film im Dritten Reich*, Berlin and Vienna, 1966; rpt. 1983.
Zadek, Peter, *My Way: Eine Autobiographie, 1926–1969*, Cologne, 1998.
——, and James Leverett, 'Radical stagings of Shakespeare', *Performing Arts Journal* 4:3 (1980), 106–21.
Zer-Zion, Shelly, 'The Anti-Nazi plays of Habimah during the 1930s and the making of Eretz-Israel Bildung', *The German-Jewish Experience Revisited*, ed. Steven E. Aschheim and Vivian Liska, Berlin, 2015, pp. 247–64.
——, '*The Merchant of Venice* in Mandatory Palestine and the State of Israel', in *Wrestling with Shylock: Jewish Responses to The Merchant of Venice*, ed. Edna Nahshon and Michael Shapiro, Cambridge, 2017, pp. 168–97.
——, 'Shylock on the shores of Mandatory Palestine: Shakespeare's *The Merchant of Venice* directed by Leopold Jessner, Tel Aviv, 1936', *Forum Modernes Theater* 19 (2004), 163–79.
Zimbardo, Rose, 'Understanding Shakespeare in the seventeenth and eighteenth centuries', in *Comedy from Shakespeare to Sheridan*, ed. A. R. Braunmuller and J. C. Bulman, Newark, DE, 1986, pp. 215–28.
Zitner, Sheldon, 'Wooden O's in plastic boxes', *University of Toronto Quarterly* 51 (Fall 1981), 1–12; rpt. in *Shakespeare on Television*, ed. J. C. Bulman and H. R. Coursen, Hanover, 1988, pp. 31–41.

Index

Abraham, F. Murray 260n.1
Adenauer, Konrad 176, 212
Adriaanse, Aram 188–9
Albee, Edward 161
Aleksi-Meskhishvili,
    Georgi 266
Alexander, Bill 129–31, *135*,
    136–45, 147–50, 152–56,
    232, 253
Alföldy, Róbert 180–1
Allio, René 219
Almeida Theatre, London 177,
    243, 254, *255*
Als, Hilton 245, 248
American Repertory
    Theater, Cambridge,
    Massachusetts 194n.3
American Shakespeare
    Theater, Stratford,
    Connecticut 158
Ames, Winthrop 58
Andrews, Nigel 298
Angelov, Yuri 180
Ansorge, Peter 86, 92
anti-Semitism
    in the 1930–40s 75–6, 174–6
    contribution of *The Merchant of
        Venice* to 165–7
    history of in England 20–5
    in the late nineteenth
        century 35–7
    in North America 157–9, 244
    origins of modern 76–7
    and other forms of othering
        132–3, 137–8, 179–84,
        187–93, 236–7, 269–70
    and race 184–7, 235
    in the Third Reich 100, 146,
        166, 172–4, 208–9, 212,
        214–15, 261n.9
Appia, Adolphe 197
Arendt, Hannah 84
Aristotle 23
Arliss, George 58, 88, 160
Assmann, Aleida 212
Ayrton, Randle 75–7, 81

Bab, Julius 206
Bakhtin, Mikhail 264
Bamber, David 236
Bancroft family 30, 45–6
Barber, John 5
Barnabe, Bruno 66–8
Barnes, Clive 161
Barrett, Bob 280, 333
Barton, John 230, 243, 253
Baruch, Bernard 161
Bassermann, Albert 205–6

Bassett, Kate 178, 253
Bassi, Shaul 306–7, 309, 315, 320n.1
Batashov, Andrei 180
Bateman family 33
Bayldon, Oliver 119, *122*
BBC Television 111–28, 158
Beamish, Jamie 255
Bechtler, Hildegard 233
Beckett, Samuel
  Waiting for Godot 114, 274
Beethoven, Ludwig van 234–5
Bellini, Giovanni 200
Benassi, Memo 207
Benson, Frank 59–60, 62, 75
Berliner Ensemble 86, 212
  and Brechtian techniques 161
Betterton, Thomas 26
Billington, Michael 90, 99, 101, 104, 232–3, 237, 252
Billon, Pierre 288, 296, 299, 300, 302
Black Lives Matter 178, 185
Blair, Tony 231
  and New Labour 230–1
Blanch, Lesley *63*
B'nai B'rith, Anti-Defamation League of 158
Bocsárdi, László 181
Bolgar, Nadya 174
Booth, Edwin 30
Booth, Michael 47
Bordone, [Paris] 85
Boston, Matthew 187
Both, Béla 175
Botticelli, [Sandro] 120, 303
Bozso, Péter 180
Bradshaw, Peter 298
Brahm, Otto 196, 198
Braithwaite, Lilian 59
Brandes, Georg 49, 200
Brantley, Ben 244, 247

Brecht, Bertolt 161, 264, 306
  and epic theatre 264
Brett, Jeremy 87
Bridges-Adams, William 59–60, 76
British Theatre Museum 39, 43
Broadhurst Theatre 243
Brookfield, Kelsey *278*, 279–80
Brooklyn Academy of Music, New York 277
Brown, Ivor 60, 64
Brown, Michael 185
Brugnera, Andrea 315, *316*
Bryden, Ronald 109
Burbage, Richard 10
Burdett-Coutts, Baroness 33
Burgtheater, Vienna 173, 177, 197, 212, 220–3, *224*, 225, *226*
Burt, David 240
Bush, Maren *186*
Butler, Paul 178–9, 260n.1
Byrne, Christopher 244

Ca' Foscari University, Venice 317–18, 320n.1
Calder, David 177
Calimani, Dario 317
Campo del Ghetto Nuovo, Venice 307
Campo San Trovaso, Venice 198, 200, *201*
Canadian Shakespeare Festival, Stratford, Ontario 158
Canaletto 119–20
Carlisle, John *135*, 139, 142
Carnovsky, Morris 160
Carpaccio, [Vittore] 200
Casa di Reclusione, Padua 307
Castiglione, Baldassare
  Courtier, The 18
Cavendish, Dominic 275
Ceesay, Babou 277

Centro Dramático Nacional,
    Madrid 177
Chaucer, Geoffrey
    Prioress's Tale, The 21
Chekhov, Anton 60
Chichester Festival Theatre
    261n.6, 8
Church of the Holy Sepulchre,
    Auckland 295
Clapp, Susannah 233, 239
Clive, Kitty 29, 73
Close, Del 178
Clothier, Richard 277, 281
Cockburn, Clive 291
Cohen, Derek 130
Coleridge, Samuel Taylor 29
Collins, Lynn 303
Comédie Française, Paris 187–8
Commedia dell'arte tradition 65–6,
    75–7, 116, 173, 315
Compagnia de' Colombari 171,
    307–8, 315, *316*
Coonrod, Karin 307–8, 315,
    316
Corduner, Allan 302
Cork, Adam 253
Cote, David 245
Coveney, Michael 235, 279
Cox, Charlie 304
Craig, Edward Gordon 197
Craven, Hawes 35
Christiansen, Richard 178
Coetzee, J. M. 182
Cromwell, Oliver, and Jews 21
Crotty, Derbhle *234*, 239, 241

Dachau 166
Danailov, Stefan 180
Daniels, Ngarimu 291
Davis, Akeem 186
Dawison, Bogumil 61
De Jersey, Peter 236

de Jong, Nicholas 236
de Primoli, Count 85, 118
de Sabata, Victor 202
*Death of Usury, or, The Disgrace
    of Usurers, The* 23
Debar, Andrée 289
Delhomme, Benoît 299
Dench, Judi 6, 242n.5
Deneslow, Anthony 144
Deutsch, Ernst 159, 214, 288
Deutsches Theater, Berlin 196–8,
    207–9, 214
    Kammerspiele 166, 192,
        193, 198
Dexter, John 162
Diaghilev, Serge 62
Diary of Anne Frank, The 214
Dickson, Andrew 230, 253
Discourse upon Usury, A 23
Disraeli, Benjamin 35, 58, 84,
    88, 132
D'Jazzy 188
Dmitrieva, Lyudmila 273
Doggett, Thomas 27
Dolzhansky, Roman 265
Donat, Robert 59
Donnellan, Declan 233
Drake, Fabia 65, 71, 74, 76
Drews, Wolfgang 197
Drury Lane Theatre, London 28
Dyer, Anson 285
Dziemianowicz, Joe 244, 250

East European productions 174–5,
    179–84, 263–75
Ebert, Roger 298
Edinburgh International Festival
    212, 222
Edward I and Jews 21
Egri, Kati 181
Eichmann, Adolf 215
Eisenberg, Ned 315, *316*

Index

El Hamus, Sabri Saad 189
Elizabethan stage conventions 9–16
Epstein, Alvin 165
Et Cetera Theatre, Moscow 263–72, *273*, 274–5
Evans, Daniel 240
Eyre, Richard 230

Fagin, as Jewish type 88
Faktor, Emil 208
Fallada, Hans
  Little Man, What Now? 216
Farrell, Nicholas *155*
Faucit, Helen 49–50, 54–5
Feldman, Adam 277
Fellini, [Federico]
  La Dolce Vita 160
Felner, Peter Paul 286–7, *295*, 299–303
Fichman, Jacob 313
Fielding, Susannah *254*, 255, *256*, 257
Fiennes, Joseph 300
Findlay, Deborah 149, *155*
Finkel, Shimon 310, *312*
Fiorentino, Giovanni
  Il Pecorone (The Simpleton) 286
Fisher, Gregor 300
Fisher, Rick 254
Folger Theatre, Washington, DC 158, 185, *186*, 187
Fondazione Giorgio Cini, Venice 320n.1
Forrester, Henry 38
Fortuyn, Pim 189
Frank, Otto 214
Freedland, Jonathan 297
French, Andrew 235
Freud, Sigmund 100
Fuchs, Georg 62
Furst, Joshua 247

Garcés, Michael John 185, *186*
Gardner, Lyn 276
Gáspár, Sándor 183
Genet, Jean
  The Maids 276
Gielgud, John 216, 227n.1
Gil, Antonio 301
Gilbert, Te Rangihau 293
Ginsburg, Ruth Bader 308, 318, 321n.7, 321n.8
Giorgione 47, 85
Godard, Colette 215, 217–18, 221
Gold, Jack 112–13, 115–18, 120, 122, 122–5, 127–8
Gonzalez, Thomas 191
Goodman, Henry 229, 231–3, 235, 237–8, 240–1, 242n.2, 245
Goodman Theatre, Chicago 177–9
Goold, Rupert 171, 177, 243, 252–54, *254*, 255, *257*, 260, 261n.6, 261n.8
Graetz, Heinrich 321n.6
Grant, Steve 141
Granville, George (Lord Lansdowne)
  Jew of Venice, The 25–8, 30, 162
Greenblatt, Stephen 245, 248
Greer, Germaine 140
Gross, John 232–3
Grosses Schauspielhaus, Berlin 198, 207–8
Grützke, Johannes 222
Guthrie, Tyrone 230

Haagensen, Erik 245
Habima Theatre, Tel Aviv 306–10, *311*, *312*, *313*, 314–15
Haider, Jörg 221
Haimi, Ilan 190
Hajewska-Krysztofik, Małgorzata 184

Halevi, Moshe 310
Hall, Edward 171, 263, 275–7, 278, 279–84
Hall, Peter 136
Hands, Terry 5–6, 8, 242n.5
Handy, Scott 254
Hanson, Alexander 234, 237
Harbour, David 261n.2
Hardwicke, Cedric 59
Harewood, David 301
Harlan, Veit
  Jud Süß 218, 288
Harron, Mary 140
Hart, Heinrich 204
Hazlitt, William 29
Headlong (Theatre Company) 253
Hedges, Ann 232
Heine, Heinrich 30, 321n.6
Henders, Richard 236
Hepburn, Katharine 160, 244
Higgons, Bevil 25
Himes, Geoffrey 185
Hobson, Harold 102
Hoffman, Dustin 136
Hoffman, Philip Seymour 178
Holbrook, Hal 260n.1
Holt, Thelma 230
homophobia 141, 181–2, 183, 236, 247
Horn, Richard Hengist
  'Dramatic Reverie' 220
Houseman, John 158
Hoyle, Martin 140
Hugh of Lincoln 21
Hughes, Raymond 120
Humperdinck, Engelbert 202
Hungarian Theatre [of Cluj], Romania 181
Hunt, Chris 231
Hunt, William Holman 131
Huttner, Jan Lisa 297

Ibsen, Henrik 163–4
Ihering, Herbert 173, 207
Irons, Jeremy 300–1, *302*
Irving, Henry 9, 32–41, 43–61, 68, 74, 76, 78, 83–5, 88, 91–3, 97, 104, 110, 124, 156–7, 159–60, 167, 196, 205, 214, 231, 253
  anonymous account of Irving as Shylock 38
Iurissevich, Adriano 315, *316*

Jacobsohn, Siegfried 198
James, Emrys 5
James, Henry 49, 287
James, Oscar 235
Jennings, Byron 244–5
Jessner, Leopold 157, 171, 306–7, 309–10, *311*, *312*, *313*, 314–15, 317, 321n.5
  Jessnertreppe 321n.5
  topical theatre / *Zeittheater* 306
Jones, Celeste *186*
Jones, Gemma *126*
Jones, Pei Te (Pete) Hurinui 289, 304n.1
Jordan, Thomas
  'The Forfeiture' 22
Jourdan, Gabrielle 239

Kahane, Rein Arthur 197
Kahn, Michael 260n.1
Kākahi, Tohu 293
Kalyagin, Aleksandr 271–2, *273*
Kaminskaya, Natalia 265, 267
Kancheli, Ghiya 267
Kappen, Norbert 215
Karasek, Hellmuth 215
Kariv, Avraham 314
Kean, Charles 30, 32, 42, 44, 50
Kean, Edmund 29–30, 32, 51, 132
Kelly, Aidan 258

Index

Kempe, Will 10
Kerr, Alfred 207
Kerrigan, John 123, 128
Khamphommala, Vanasay
  Business in Venice 190
Khodosh, Ilya 275
Kind, Heather 249
King, Rodney 177–8
King's Men 16
Kingston, Jeremy 131
Kirchner, Ignaz 222–3
Kirnarskaya, Dina 265, 275
Klajn, Hugo 174
Klimt, Gustav 234, 239
Klotz, Michael 321n.8
Koch, Georg August 173
Kohler, Joseph 321n.6
Kokoschka, Oskar 62
Komisarjevskaya, Vera 59
Komisarjevsky, Theodore 63, 59–82, 93, 159, 167
Kormilitsina, Anastasiya 268
Korngold, E. W. 199
Kortner, Fritz 205, 207, 217
Krauss, Werner 173, 205, 207–8, 220, 286–7
Kraut, Werner 214

Lambert, J. W. 92
Landauer, Gustav 321n.6
Landovský, Pavel 226
Langham, Michael 158–9
Lea-Jones, Jenni 315, *316*
Lessing, Gotthold Ephraim
  Nathan the Wise 159, 214–15
Letts, Quentin 252
Levick, H.
  Golem, The 310
Lewis, Leopold
  Bells, The 33
Ligazhevska, Natalia 270
Lincoln Center Theater, New York 160, 260n.1

Linklater, Hamish 244, 261n.2
Literary Trial of *The Merchant of Venice* 189, 307, 313–14
Liverpool Playhouse, Liverpool 278
Locker, Malka
  Chronicle of 1936 314
Loepelmann, Götz 216, 218
Logan, John 253
Lopez, Ruy, physician to Elizabeth I 21
Lord Chamberlain's Men 16
Löwenadler, Holger 175
Lüders, Günther 219–20
Lyceum Theatre, London 31–3, 59, 84, 195
Lyly, John 3

Macaulay, Alistair 232
Macklin, Charles 28, 32, 52, 73–4, 77, 132
Macready, William 30
Magritte, René 266
Mahnke, Hans 218–20
Malkin, Dov Ber 321
Mantegna, Andrea 219
McDiarmid, Ian 243
Major, Tamás 175
Mamalev, Georgi 180
Manker, Paulus 227
Marks, Peter 185
Marlowe, Christopher
  Jew of Malta, The 22, 82, 116
  Tamburlaine 19
Marrella, Fabrizio 38
Marshall, Kris 300
Marta, Guido 204
Martin, Theodore 49–50
Mattes, Eva 222
medieval dramatic tradition 6, 7, 10, 19, 22–3, 165
Melbourne, Hirini 291
Méliès, Georges 285

Mellish, Fuller 40, 42, 48, 52, 57, 58
The Merchant in Venice 307–9, 315, *316*, 320n.1
The Merchant of Venice, animated film, dir. Anson Dyer 285
The Merchant of Venice, feature films
  Der Kaufmann von Venedig (The Jew of Mestri), dir. Peter Paul Felner 286, 295, 299–303
  Dil Farosh, dir. D. N. Madhok 287
  Dil Farosh, dir. M. Udvadia 287
  Le Marchand de Venise, dir. Pierre Billon 288, 296, 299–300, 302
  Merchant of Venice, The, silent film 285–7, 301
  Merchant of Venice, The, dir. Lois Webber and Phillips Smalley 285
  Un miroir de Venise (Une mésaventure de Shylock), dir. Georges Méliès 286
  Te Tangata Whai Rawa O Weniti, or The Maori Merchant of Venice, dir. Don Selwyn 285, 289–93, 294, 295–6, 304n.1, 304n.2, 305n.3, 5, 6
  William Shakespeare's The Merchant of Venice, dir. Michael Radford 243, 249–50, 261n.5, 297–301, 302, 303–4
  Zalim Saudagar, dir. J. J. Madan 287
Meskin, Aharon 310, *311*, 320n.4
Meyerhold, V. E. 59, 62
Mićanović, Dragan 182
Miguel-Stearns, Teresa 319

Miller, Jonathan 8, 83–7, 90–9, 101–2, *103*, 104–13, 116–20, 124–5, 127, 129, 148, 157, 160–4, 167, 221, 231–3, 242n.1, 242n.4, 253, 261n.9
Milton, John
  Paradise Lost 304
Minks, Wilfried 222
Mitchell, Warren 112–14, 116, *126*
Mitkov, Zdravko 179–80
'Mock Appeal in the Matter of Shylock v. Antonio' 308, 317–19
Mohácsi brothers, János, István, András 183
Moissi, Alexander 205–7
Monet, [Claude] 119
Morgan, Reikura 296
Morley, Sheridan 232, 240
Morrison, Scott 293
Moscow Art Theatre 62, 309
  Imperial Theatre and State Theatre 59
Moshinsky, Elijah 120
Mossovet Theatre, Moscow 261n.7
Mostel, Zero 162
Mozas, Océane 191
Munby, Jonathan 261n.3
Munich Kammerspiele 166, 192, *193*, 198
Mundruczó, Kornél 181
Muru, Selwyn 292–3, *294*, 305n.4
Mussolini, Benito 79, 196, 198, 209
Müthel, Lothar 173, 220

Nathan, David 144, 232, 241
Nathan, John 252, 258, 260
National Theatre, Belgrade 174, 182
National Theatre, Budapest 175, 183

National Theatre, London 8,
  83–102, *103*, 104–110, 111,
  124, 127, 160, 171, 221,
  229–33, *234*, 235–42
  Cottesloe Theatre 233
  Olivier Theatre 233–4
National Theatre, Sofia 174–5,
  179–80
National Theatre / Royal Dramatic
  Theatre, Stockholm 175–6
Nettles, John 122
De Nieuwe Theatre,
  Amsterdam 189–90
Nightingale, Benedict 89, 92,
  100, 109
Nolan, John 238–9
Norman, Neil 253
Nowy Theatre, Warsaw 184
Nunn, Trevor 171, 229–33,
  234, 235–42

Ojetti, Paola 195
Old Vic, London 85, 111, 287
Olivier, Laurence 83–102, *103*,
  104–10, 112, 113, 132, 156,
  160, 231, 242n.1, 245, 269n.9
Omambala, Chu 235
Oman, Julia Trevelyan 85–6, 118
Orlik, Emil 200
Ormerod, Ben 277
Ortolani, Olivier 225
Osipov, Alexei 268
Otway, Thomas
  Venice Preserved 33

Pacino, Al 243–9, 298, 301, *302*
Palestine 157, 306, 308–15
Palitzsch, Peter 221
Papp, Joseph 244
Parihaka 293
Paton, Maureen 153
Pavelka, Michael 276–7

Penn, Alexander 314
Peter, John 151, 234, 235, 240
Petrarch 96, 118
Phillips, Michael 235
philo-Semitism 174–6,
  212–15, 227
Picasso, [Pablo] 62, 69
Piper 119
Pirandello, Luigi 166
Pirchan, Emil 321n.5
Piscator, Erwin 159–60, 306
Playfair, Nigel 59
Plaza, Carlos 177
Plowright, Joan 92, 95–6, *103*
Plumtree, Emily 255, 257
Podet, Rabbi Allen 130
Poel, William 58, 159
Ponto, Erich 214, 288
Pook, Jocelyn 304
Porten, Henny 287
Posner, Aaron
  District Merchants 184–5,
  186, 187
Power, Ben 253
Presley, Elvis 254–5, 260
Propeller 263, 275–7, *278*, 279–84
  Pocket Merchant 284n.4
Pryce, Jonathan 261n.3
Public Theater, New York 177, 243
  Delacorte Theater 243, 244–51
Puccini, [Giacomo]
  Turandot 255
Purves, Libby 252

Queen's Theatre, London 216

Raban, Jonathan 6
Rabb, Ellis 160–2, 260n.1
Rabe, Lily 244, 249–51
racism 236, 238, 250, 269, 300–1
Radford, Michael 243, 297–301,
  302, 303–4

Radin, Victoria 146–7
Rátóti, Zoltán 181
Reagan, Ronald 115, 153,
    178, 221
Regisseur 59, 75, 79
Reinhardt, Max 176, 195–200,
    201, 202, *203*, 204–10,
    211, 214
    Drehbühne (stage revolve)
        199–200
    Manifesto 197–8
    Massenregie 202–3, 206
    Midsummer Night's Dream, A
        195, 199, 209
    Oedipus Rex 198
    Shakespeare Cycle 199, 206
Rembrandt 120
Rich, Frank 139
Richards, David 178
Riddel, Richard 258
Rio degli Ognissanti, Venice
    200, *201*
Roberts, David 131
Robinson, Zuleikha 303
Rorrison, Hugh 213
Rose, Charlie 246
Rose, Paul 173
Rose Theater, Berlin 173
Rosenbaum, Ron 298
Rota, Titina 200
Rothschild family 35, 37, 84, 88,
    132, 221
Rovina, Hanna 314
Royal Shakespeare Company (RSC),
    Stratford-upon-Avon 5–6, 86,
    129–56, 177, 229, 242n.3,
    230, 232, 242n.5, 243, 252–4,
    257–61, 261n.8
    The Other Place 243
    Royal Shakespeare Theatre 146
    Shakespeare Memorial Theatre
        59, 65–79

Rue, Seth *186*
Ruskin, John 49

Sartre, Jean-Paul
    Huis Clos 276
Savin, Egon 182
Schälike, Karsten 219
Schappes, Morris 158
Schauspielhaus Bochum 216, 219
Schenk, Otto 217
Schildkraut, Rudolph 205–6
Schlegel, August 219
Schüller, Hans 215
Scott, A. O. 298
Scott, George C. 244
Scutt, Tom 254, *255*
Sellars, Peter 177–9, 181, 190,
    232, 252, 260n.1
Selwyn, Don C. 289–93,
    294, 295–7
Şerban, Andrei 187–8
Sessions, John 300
Seweryn, Andrzej 187
Shakespeare, William
    All's Well that Ends Well 120
    Antony and Cleopatra 119
    As You Like It 119
    Coriolanus 321n.7
    Hamlet 10, 30, 33, 84,
        211, 261n.6
    Henry IV 1&2 321n.7
    Henry V 321n.7
    King Lear 75, 99, 182,
        211, 261n.6
    Macbeth 252, 261n.6,
        261n.8, 321n.7
    Measure for Measure
        211, 321n.7
    Midsummer Night's Dream, A
        120, 195, 199, 209, 215, 319
    *Much Ado about
        Nothing* 321n.7

Othello 33, 83, 99, 100, 101,
  182, 211, 261n.6, 321n.7
Richard III 83, 132, 321n.7
Romeo and Juliet 252, 261n.6
Taming of the Shrew, A 68
Tempest, A 252, 261n.8, 292
Twelfth Night 321n.7
Shakespeare's Globe,
  London 261n.3
Shakespeare In and Beyond the
  Ghetto 308, 320n.1
Shakespeare Theater, Washington,
  DC 260n.1
Shaw, Glen Byam 216
Shaw, Sebastian 75
Sher, Antony 129–34, 135,
  136–56
Simon, Michel 288
Shortland, Waihoroi 292, 294
Shota Rustaveli Dramatic Theatre,
  Tbilisi 264
Shylock 265, 284n.2
  see also Sturua, Robert
Siddons, Sarah 29
Silva, Geno 178
Siragusa, Mario 318
Skosyreva, Maria 273
Skvortsov, Vladimir 269–70
Smalley, Phillips 286
Söberg, Alf 175–6
Spencer, Charles 252, 257
Spiegelman, Art
  Maus 184
Spielberg, Steven
  Schindler's List 299
Städtische Bühne, Ulm (Germany)
  212
Stanislavsky, Konstantin 309–10
Stemann, Nicolas 192, 193
Stern, Ernst 200
Stewart, Patrick 243, 253,
  257–9, 261n.8

Stockbridge Playhouse,
  Massachusetts 165
Stoker, Bram 33–4, 53
Stone, Oliver, Wall Street 221
Stroux, Karl Heinz 214
Sturua, Robert 263–72,
  273, 274–5
  see also Shylock
Sucher, C. B. 225
Sullivan, Daniel 171, 177–251
Surrey, Kit 145–6, 148–9
Svevo, Italo 86
Swainsbury, Sam 280

Tabori, George 165–7
Taylor, Paul 140, 232, 252
Tchaikowsky, André 261n.4
te reo kohatu 289–90
Teachout, Terry 245
Telbin, William 42
Terry, Ellen 33, 42, 47–57,
  71, 74, 96
Thacker, David 177, 252
Thatcher, Margaret 153, 221
Theater in der Josefstadt,
  Vienna 207
Theatre Biennale, Venice 195,
  198, 200, 201, 202, 203, 204,
  207, 209
Théâtre de la Place, Liège 184
Theatre Festival of Bassano del
  Grappa 307
Theatre for a New Audience, New
  York 260n.1
Théâtre Olympia, Tours 189–91
Thomson, Desson 298
Tilton, James 160
Tintoretto 119, 308, 317
Titian 35, 119
Tivoli Theatre, Budapest 180
Tolkien, J. R. R.
  The Hobbit 216, 228n.1

Torres, Duilio 200, *201*
Tree, H. Beerbohm 57, 61
Trenchard, Jon 279
Tresnjak, Darko 260n.1
Trueman, Matt 253
Tsankov, Hrisan 174–5
Turia, Tariana 295
Turner, J. M. W. 119
Tynan, Kenneth 83

Udwin, Leslee 117
Umbers, Mark 236
usury, history of in England 23–5

van Oel, Justus
  The Arab of Amsterdam 189–90
Vasco, Eduardo 177
vaudeville 113, 211, 243, 246–7, 249–50
Velázquez, [Diego] 301
Veneto, as analogue for Belmont 18
Venice, and trade 17–19
Verdi, [Giuseppe]
  Rigoletto 44
Vermeer, [Johannes] 120
Veronese, Paolo 35, 64, 85, 119, 200
Verzhbitsky, Viktor 267
Victorian staging 30–1, 32–58, 69, 78
Vincey, Jacques 189, 190–1
Volbach, Walther 207
von Ihering, Rudolph 321n.6
Voss, Gert 222–5, *224*, *226*

Wadia, Sorab 315, *316*
Wagner, [Richard]
  Parsifal 255
Wallace, Craig 186

Walker, Sydney 261n.1
Walter, Bruno 202
Wardle, Irving 89
Warlikowski, Krzsystof
  African Tales after Shakespeare 182, 183–4
Webber, Lois 285
Wegener, Paul 207
Weimar Republic 196, 231
Weiss, Peter
  Marat / Sade 165
Welles, Orson 286
Wells, Roseanne 279, 280
Wendland, Mark 251
Wesker, Arnold 232
  Merchant, The 162–5
Whiti-o-Rongomai, Te 293
Wiener, Robert 207
Wigger, Stefan 221
Wilde, Oscar 87
Wilders, John 119
Wildgruber, Ulrich 219–20
Wills, W. G., *Iolanthe* 57
Winer, Linda 251
Winter, William 33, 41
Woffington, Peg 29
Wolf, Matt 232, 237

Young, B. A. 6

Zadek, Peter 171, 177, 211–23, 224, 225, 226, 227, 230, 232, 245, 252, 281
  Volkstheater 217, 219, 228n.2
Zaslavsky, Grigory 265, 267
Zech, Rosel 220
Zhitinkin, Andrey 261n.7, 265
Zintsov, Oleg 265
Zitner, Sheldon 118
Zolotovich, Lubomir 174–5

EU authorised representative for GPSR:
Easy Access System Europe, Mustamäe tee 50,
10621 Tallinn, Estonia
gpsr.requests@easproject.com

www.ingramcontent.com/pod-product-compliance
Lightning Source LLC
Chambersburg PA
CBHW071202240426
43668CB00032B/1867